FamilyCircle

CHRISTMAS TREASURY
1 · 9 · 8 · 8

Other Books by Family Circle

EDITORIAL STAFF

Editor, Book Development — *Carol A. Guasti*
Editorial Production Coordinator — *Kim E. Gayton*

PROJECT STAFF

Project Editor — *Ceri Hadda*
Book Design — *Bessen Tully & Lee, Inc.*
Silhouette Art — *Maggie Zander*
Typesetting — *Gary Borden, Alison Chandler, Carlos Torres*
Special Assistant — *Kristen J. Keller*

MARKETING STAFF

Manager, Marketing & Development — *Margaret Chan-Yip*
Promotion/Fulfillment Manager — *Pauline MacLean Treitler*
Special Assistant — *Donna Sebring*

Cover Photo — *Ralph Bogertman*
Photography — *Robert Ander; Tom Berry; David Bishop;*
Ralph Bogertman; Jon Bonjour; David Glomb; Dennis Gottlieb;
Ronald G. Harris; James Kozyra; Taylor Lewis; Mort Mace; Maris/Semel;
Bill McGinn; Rudy Muller; Jeff Niki; Leonard Nones; Bradley Olman;
Ron Schwerin; Gordon E. Smith; Michael Soluri; Bob Stoller;
Theo; René Velez; Eugenia Wilson

Published by The Family Circle, Inc.
110 Fifth Avenue, New York, NY 10011

Copyright© 1988 by The Family Circle, Inc.

Manufactured in the United States of America

10 9 8 7 6 5 4 3 2 1

Library of Congress Cataloging in Publication Data
Main entry under title:

The Family circle christmas treasury.
Includes index.
1. Christmas decorations   2. Christmas cookery.
I. Family Circle, Inc.   II. Title: Christmas treasury.
TT900. C4F36   1986   745.594'1   86-11598

ISBN 0-933585-08-X
ISSN 0892-3604

Family Circle

CHRISTMAS TREASURY

1 · 9 · 8 · 8

TABLE OF CONTENTS

INTRODUCTION 1

Chapter I: *THANKSGIVING AND HOLIDAY MAKE-AHEADS* 2

A Celebration Of Thanks:

    Traditional Thanksgiving Dinner 4

    Talking Turkey 12

    Thanksgiving Dinner With A Twist 16

    The Right Stuffing 24

    Leftover But Not Forgotten 27

Thanksgiving Decorations to Use All Through the Season 30

Food Gifts to Make Right Now 36

Crafts to Start Right Now 46

Chapter II: *IT'S BEGINNING TO LOOK A LOT LIKE CHRISTMAS* 56

Outdoor Scenes 58

Remarkable Ribbon 60

Wrap It Up 63

Timing is Everything When You Send a Gift By Mail 64

Holiday Hints 66

A Holiday Guide to "Sticky Situations" 68

It's a Snap to Capture the Fun 69

Christmas Card Quiz 70

Chapter III: *CHRISTMAS COUNTRY CLASSICS.* 74

Tartan Time 76

White Christmas 82

Folk Art Favorites 92

Country Accents Throughout the House 98

The Country Hearth:

    A Regal Roast Beef Dinner 102

    Holiday Cookies 110

Chapter IV: *A CENT-SATIONAL CHRISTMAS* 118

     Cent-sational Decorations 120

     Cent-sational Gifts 132

     Gourmet Gifts to Make 138

     Cent-sational Entertaining:

         Provençal Cocktail Party 144

         Old Vienna Dessert Buffet 151

     Ways to Entertain Without Going Broke 157

Chapter V: *CHRISTMAS THROUGH A CHILD'S EYES* 158

     A Gingerbread Christmas 160

     A Rootin' Tootin' Christmas 166

     Gifts For Children 172

     The Right Toy At The Right Time 192

     Gifts Children Can Make 194

     Edible Gifts From Young Chefs 198

Chapter VI: *CHRISTMAS IN A FLASH* 204

     Presto! Yuletide Magic 206

     Time-Smart & Tempting Finger Foods 218

     Quick Fix Desserts:

         No-Bake Frozen Pies 224

         No-Bake Treats 228

     Muffins & Quick Breads 230

Chapter VII: *RING IN THE NEW!* 234

     New Year's Sparkle 236

     Party Perfect 240

     Puttin' on the Glitz:

         New Year's Eve Cocktail Party 242

         Punches with Panache 251

     New Year's Day Open House 254

Introduction

Maybe it's the child in us that never grows up. Maybe it's the anticipation, the excitement, the wish that it could be "Christmas all year long." Somewhere in this holiday season we reach for the magic that seems to otherwise elude us all year. This is the time when we most cherish family, food and joyful gatherings. And that's what this 1988 Christmas Treasury is all about. From the first chapter where we celebrate Thanksgiving to the last section on ringing in the New Year, we share with you the spirit of the holidays—the giving, the warmth, the generosity. Try our many craft projects to beautify your home or to delight a loved one—or, if cooking is your art, our gourmet feasts are a wonderful way to make family get-togethers memorable. There are practical considerations too: tips on photography (to capture precious moments!), gracious solutions to sticky situations, mailing information and more. Look for the special "gift-wrapped" tip boxes for important advice, and for the holiday trivia boxes that contain little-known facts and lore about the season. Throughout the 1988 Treasury, there are symbols above some projects and recipes which help identify skill level and preferences. They are:

💲 *Low-Cost*   ◀◀ *Make-Ahead*   ➘ *Quick and Easy*   *Low-Calorie*   ◥ *Bazaar*

But perhaps the best part of this book is the memories it might inspire. New traditions started, gifts crafted by hand and treasured, feasts that bring together family and friends. There is no season as special as this one, and we at Family Circle wish you and yours a very merry Christmas and the happiest of New Years.

CHAPTER 1

Tis the season . . .
. . . to loosen belt buckles
and gather 'round the
groaning board. Anyone
for seconds . . . or thirds?

A traditional Thanksgiving dinner: Roast Holiday Turkey with Savory Stuffing and Giblet Gravy; Acorn Squash Rings and Green Beans; Cranberry Orange Relish; Autumn Squash Bisque; Cranberry Bread; Marinated Vegetables; Candied Yams; Creamed Onions.

Season Première:
Thanksgiving And Holiday Make-Aheads

Thanksgiving heralds the beginning of the holiday season, so that's where we begin this book—with two delicious Thanksgiving feasts. The first is a traditional turkey dinner, complete with savory stuffing, candied yams and scrumptious holiday pies. The second is an out-of-the-ordinary brace of roasted capons dinner, with curried pumpkin soup and cranberry ice. (There are also terrific recipes for leftovers!) After the day of feasting, it's time to start those Christmas crafts and projects that require a little more time. There are beautiful decorations for your home, creative gifts, even gourmet treats to inspire you. Now that Santa has made his debut in the Macy's Thanksgiving Day Parade, the holiday season is officially here!

A Celebration Of Thanks

A Traditional Thanksgiving Dinner

(for 6)

Autumn Squash Bisque*
Roast Holiday Turkey with Giblet Gravy and
Savory Stuffing*
Acorn Squash Rings and Green Beans*
Creamed Onions*
Candied Yams*
Marinated Vegetables*
Mixed Greens with Russian Dressing*
Cranberry Orange Relish*
Cranberry Bread*
Pumpkin Nut Muffins*
Traditional Holiday Pies
(recipes start on page 14)

*Recipes follow

Note: *To serve 12, double all of the recipes*
for the vegetables and the soup.

Southern Pecan Pie; Mincemeat Pie; Pilgrim Pumpkin Pie

Work Plan

Up to 1 Month Ahead:
• Prepare and freeze Traditional Holiday Pies, Pumpkin Nut Muffins (if you have a microwave) and Cranberry Bread (or prepare bread and pies the day before and refrigerate pies; make muffins just before serving time).

Up to 3 Days Before:
• Prepare Russian Dressing.
• Prepare Cranberry Orange Relish.

The Day Before:
• Prepare Marinated Vegetables; refrigerate.
• Thaw turkey, if necessary.
• Prepare Savory Stuffing, but do not stuff turkey; refrigerate stuffing and turkey separately.
• Cook, peel and refrigerate onions; make bread crumbs for Creamed Onions.
• Prepare Autumn Squash Bisque through Step 2; refrigerate.
• Bake and slice squash rings for Acorn Squash Rings and Green Beans; refrigerate.
• Bake, peel and slice yams for Candied Yams; refrigerate.
• If you are not using a microwave to thaw and bake Pumpkin Nut Muffins, sift together dry ingredients, combine and refrigerate liquid ingredients (do not combine dry and liquid ingredients until baking time).

Early in the Day:
• Wash and drain greens for salad; pack in plastic bags and refrigerate.
• Trim green beans for Acorn Squash Rings and Green Beans; refrigerate.

5 Hours Before:
• Stuff and begin roasting turkey.
• Prepare Giblet Gravy.

1½ Hours Before:
• Continue preparing Acorn Squash Rings and Green Beans, Candied Yams, Creamed Onions.
• Slowly reheat Autumn Squash Bisque.

1 Hour Before:
• Bake Pumpkin Nut Muffins, or thaw and bake in the microwave.

At Serving Time:
• Add cream and eggs to Autumn Squash Bisque.
• Reheat Giblet Gravy.
• Slice turkey.

During Dinner:
• Reheat Traditional Holiday Pies.
• Whip cream for pies.

Autumn Squash Bisque

Makes 6 servings (6 cups).

1 **pound butternut squash, pared, halved, seeded and cubed**
2 **tart apples, pared, cored and cubed**
1 **medium-size onion, chopped (½ cup)**
2 **slices white bread, trimmed and cubed**
4 **cups chicken broth**
1½ **teaspoons salt**
¼ **teaspoon pepper**
¼ **teaspoon ground rosemary**
¼ **teaspoon ground marjoram**
2 **egg yolks, slightly beaten**
¼ **cup heavy cream**
Apple slices and fresh rosemary sprig for garnish (optional)

1. Combine the squash, apples, onion, bread, chicken broth, salt, pepper, rosemary and marjoram in a large saucepan. Bring to boiling. Lower the heat and simmer, uncovered, for 35 minutes, or until the squash and apples are tender. Remove the pan from the heat. Cool to lukewarm.
2. Working in batches, spoon the soup into the container of an electric blender or food processor. Cover; whirl until puréed. Return the soup to the saucepan. Reheat the soup gently over very low heat.
3. Mix together the egg yolks and the cream in a small bowl. Beat in a little of the hot soup. Add the yolk mixture to the soup in the saucepan, stirring. Heat gently to serve; do not boil or the eggs will curdle. Transfer to a soup tureen. Garnish with thin apple slices with the skin left on and a fresh rosemary sprig, if you wish.

Roast Holiday Turkey

Roast at 325° for 4½ to 6 hours.
Makes 12 servings.

1 **turkey, 12 to 16 pounds, giblets removed and reserved for Giblet Gravy**
Savory Stuffing (recipe, page 8)
Melted butter
Giblet Gravy (recipe, page 8)

1. Preheat the oven to slow (325°).
2. Stuff the turkey body and neck cavity with the Savory Stuffing. Sew the cavities closed. Place the turkey, breast side up, on a rack in a shallow roasting pan. Brush the turkey all over with the melted butter.
3. Roast in the preheated slow oven (325°) for 4½ to 6 hours, depending on the size of the bird, or until the drumstick joint moves easily or a meat thermometer registers 180° to 185° with the bulb in the thickest part of the thigh, not touching the bone. Remove the turkey from the oven. Let stand for at least 20 minutes before carving. Serve with the Giblet Gravy.
4. To store any leftovers, remove the stuffing from the turkey and refrigerate separately from the turkey.

WHAT TO DO WITH THE TURKEY LEFTOVERS

- After the Thanksgiving feast, remove the stuffing from the turkey cavity and refrigerate separately. Wrap slices, cubes and shreds of turkey in freezer wrap, bags, foil, etc. in recipe or meal-size portions, label carefully and freeze. Use within three to six weeks. Freeze extra stuffing and gravy in separate containers and use within two to three weeks.
- Break up the carcass and use to make Turkey Broth *(recipe, page 28)*. Plan to make the broth within 2 days. Broth can be frozen in containers if not used within three days.

GOOD GRAVY!!

Our quick fix-it tips can make even less-than-perfect gravy turn out just right.

LUMPY GRAVY: Force the gravy through a sieve with a rubber spatula, or whirl in a blender until smooth. Transfer the gravy to a saucepan and gently simmer until heated through.
TOO-THICK GRAVY: Transfer the gravy to a saucepan. Whisk in, 1 tablespoon at a time, the liquid used to make the gravy until the gravy reaches the desired consistency.
TOO-THIN GRAVY: Transfer the gravy to a saucepan. Gently boil until reduced to the desired consistency.

💲

Giblet Gravy

Makes about 3 cups.

	Turkey giblets
2	**cups water**
1	**bay leaf**
1/2	**teaspoon salt**
1/4	**teaspoon pepper**
2	**tablespoons butter or margarine**
2	**tablespoons all-purpose flour**
1	**cup milk**

1. Combine the turkey giblets, except the liver, the water, bay leaf, salt and pepper in a medium-size saucepan. Bring to boiling. Lower the heat, cover and simmer for 1 hour, or until tender. Add the liver and simmer for 15 minutes longer. Drain the mixture, reserving 1 cup of the broth. Discard the bay leaf. Finely chop the giblets and reserve to add to the gravy in Step 2, if you wish.
2. Melt the butter or margarine in a medium-size saucepan; stir in the flour until smooth. Add the reserved 1 cup of turkey broth. Cook over medium heat, stirring constantly, until the mixture thickens and boils. Stir in the milk and the chopped giblets, if you wish. Gently heat to serving temperature. Season to taste with salt and pepper.

💲 🎜

Savory Stuffing

Use to stuff the turkey, or bake at 350° for 35 minutes.
Makes 14 cups (enough for a 12- to 14-pound turkey).

2	**large onions, diced**
2	**cups celery, diced**
2	**cloves garlic, finely chopped**
6	**tablespoons butter or margarine**
15	**cups cubed day-old French bread (two 7-ounce loaves)**
1/3	**cup chopped parsley**
2	**teaspoons ground sage**
1	**teaspoon poultry seasoning**
1/2	**teaspoon pepper**
3	**cups chicken broth**

1. Sauté the onion, celery and garlic in 4 tablespoons of the butter in a large skillet over medium heat for 3 minutes, or until the onion softens.
2. Combine the sautéed vegetables, the bread cubes, parsley, sage, poultry seasoning and pepper in a large bowl. Mix well.
3. Melt the remaining 2 tablespoons of butter in a saucepan. Add the melted butter and the chicken broth to the stuffing; toss to mix. Stuff the turkey and roast. Or spoon into a 13 x 9 x 2-inch baking pan or other shallow, greased baking dish. Bake, uncovered, in a preheated moderate oven (350°) for 35 minutes, or until heated through.

ROUX—THE DO'S AND DON'TS

When making roux, the flour-and-fat thickening agent for gravies, remember:
- Do mix the melted fat (pan drippings or butter) and flour together thoroughly over medium heat until smooth.
- Do cook the roux long enough to dispel the uncooked flour taste, for 1 to 2 minutes.
- Do stir constantly while cooking to distribute the heat evenly and allow the starch granules in the flour to swell evenly; the starch is what absorbs the liquid and causes the thickening.
- Don't use too high heat or the flour will burn, causing a bitter taste, and the starch will shrink, causing the gravy not to thicken.

Acorn Squash Rings and Green Beans

Bake at 350° for 60 to 65 minutes.
Makes 6 servings.

2   acorn squash (1 pound each), trimmed
4   tablespoons (½ stick) butter
1½ pounds green beans, trimmed
1   tablespoon Worcestershire sauce
¼   teaspoon pepper

1. Preheat the oven to moderate (350°).
2. Bake the squash in the preheated moderate oven (350°) for 30 minutes. Remove the squash from the oven; leave the oven on. Slice each squash into 3 equal rings about 1 inch thick. Discard the seeds and pulp.
3. Melt 1 tablespoon of the butter in a small saucepan. Brush the squash slices with the butter. Arrange in a 13 x 9 x 2-inch baking dish.
4. Return to the moderate oven (350°) and bake for 30 to 35 minutes, or until tender.
5. Meanwhile, cook the green beans in boiling salted water to cover in a large saucepan for 5 to 10 minutes, or until crisp-tender. Drain and transfer to a large bowl.
6. Melt the remaining 3 tablespoons of butter in the small saucepan. Stir in the Worcestershire sauce and the pepper. Pour over the beans. Toss to coat well. Divide the beans into 6 equal bunches. Stuff 1 bunch into the center of each squash ring. Arrange around the Roast Holiday Turkey.

Creamed Onions

Makes 6 servings.

40 small white onions
⅓   cup butter or margarine
⅓   cup all-purpose flour
1   teaspoon salt
¼   teaspoon white pepper
¼   teaspoon ground nutmeg
3   cups milk
½   cup heavy cream
**   Buttered Crumbs (recipe follows)**
**   Parsley sprig for garnish**

1. Cook the onions, covered, in boiling salted water in a large saucepan until tender, for about 15 minutes. Drain, reserving the cooking liquid. Peel the onions when they are cool enough to handle.
2. Melt the butter or margarine in a large saucepan over low heat. Stir in the flour, salt, pepper and nutmeg; cook for 2 minutes. Remove the pan from the heat. Stir in the milk and the cream until the mixture is smooth.
3. Bring the mixture to boiling over medium heat; lower the heat. Simmer for about 5 minutes, stirring constantly with a wooden spoon, until the sauce is thick and smooth.
4. Add the onions and cook until the onions are heated through. If the sauce is too thick, thin it with some of the reserved cooking liquid.
5. Spoon the onions and the cream sauce into a heated serving bowl. Top with the Buttered Crumbs and garnish with the parsley sprig.

Buttered Crumbs: Remove the crusts from 2 slices of bread. Pulverize the bread into crumbs using a food processor or electric blender. Melt 3 tablespoons of butter or margarine in a skillet over medium heat. Add the crumbs. Cook, stirring constantly, until the crumbs turn golden. Remove from the heat at once to prevent burning. *Makes about 1 cup.*

Did You Know . . .

That the dance, turkey trot, is named after our Thanksgiving bird!

Candied Yams

Bake at 375° for 30 minutes.
Makes 6 servings.

2   large yams or sweet potatoes (about 1¼ pounds), scrubbed
⅓   cup light corn syrup
2   tablespoons light brown sugar
2   tablespoons bourbon
2   tablespoons butter
**   Chopped pecans (optional)**

1. Preheat the oven to moderate (375°). Grease a shallow 1-quart baking dish.
2. Cook the yams in boiling salted water to cover in a large saucepan for 30 minutes, or just until tender. Drain. When cool enough to handle, peel. Slice crosswise into ¼-inch-thick slices.
3. Arrange the yams in the prepared baking dish. Stir together the corn syrup, sugar and bourbon in a small bowl. Pour evenly over the yams. Dot with the butter.
4. Bake in the preheated moderate oven (375°), basting several times, for 30 minutes, or until glazed and heated through. Sprinkle with the chopped pecans, if you wish.

Marinated Vegetables

Makes 6 servings.

- ⅓ cup vegetable or olive oil
- ¼ cup red wine vinegar
- ¼ cup chopped parsley
- ¼ cup chopped sweet red pepper
- 1 tablespoon chopped sweet pickle
- 2 teaspoons Dijon-style mustard
- ½ teaspoon salt
- ¼ teaspoon pepper
- 3 medium-size carrots, decoratively sliced crosswise
- 1 cup cauliflower flowerets
- 1 cup zucchini sticks (1 medium-size zucchini)
- 1 cup red onion rings
- ½ pound small or button mushrooms

1. Combine the oil, vinegar, parsley, red pepper, sweet pickle, mustard, salt and pepper in a jar with a screw-top lid. Cover; shake until well blended. Reserve.
2. Cook the carrots and the cauliflower in boiling water to cover in a saucepan for 3 minutes, or just until the carrots brighten in color. Drain; run under cold water to stop the cooking.
3. Combine the carrots, cauliflower, zucchini, onion and mushrooms in a medium-size bowl. Shake the dressing and pour over the vegetables. Toss well to coat. Marinate, covered, in the refrigerator overnight.

Russian Dressing

Makes 3½ cups.

- 1 small onion, coarsely chopped (¼ cup)
- 1 small sweet green pepper, halved, seeded and diced
- 2 hard-cooked eggs, coarsely chopped
- 4 sweet pickles, coarsely chopped
- 1 clove garlic
- 2 cups mayonnaise
- ¼ cup bottled chili sauce
- 1 teaspoon cayenne pepper
- ½ teaspoon Worcestershire sauce
- ½ teaspoon liquid red-pepper seasoning
- ½ teaspoon salt
- ¼ teaspoon pepper

Combine the onion, sweet green pepper, eggs, pickles and garlic in the container of an electric blender or food processor. Cover; whirl until chopped. Add the mayonnaise, chili sauce, cayenne pepper, Worcestershire sauce, liquid red-pepper seasoning, salt and pepper. Whirl until very smooth. Transfer to a cruet. Refrigerate until ready to serve.

Cranberry Orange Relish

Makes 3 cups.

- 2 cups fresh or frozen whole cranberries, thawed if frozen
- 1 orange, unpeeled, quartered and seeded
- ½ lemon, unpeeled, quartered and seeded
- 1 cup sugar
- ¼ to ½ cup Cointreau OR: orange-flavored liqueur
  Orange slices for garnish

1. Combine the cranberries, orange and lemon in the container of a food processor. Cover; whirl until finely chopped. Transfer to a medium-size bowl.
2. Stir in the sugar and the Cointreau or orange-flavored liqueur. Let the mixture stand at room temperature, covered, for 12 hours. Refrigerate until ready to serve. Garnish with the orange slices or use to fill hollowed-out oranges.

Cranberry Bread

Bake at 350° for 1 hour and 5 minutes.
Makes 12 servings.

    1   tablespoon all-purpose flour
    1½ cups fresh or frozen cranberries,
            thawed if frozen, coarsely chopped
    ½   cup chopped walnuts
    2   cups sifted all-purpose flour
    1½ teaspoons baking powder
    ½   teaspoon salt
    1   cup sugar
    ¼   cup vegetable shortening
    1   egg, slightly beaten
    ¾   cup orange juice
    1   tablespoon grated orange rind

1. Preheat the oven to moderate (350°). Grease an 8½ x 4½ x 2⅝-inch loaf pan.
2. Sprinkle the 1 tablespoon of flour over the cranberries and the chopped walnuts on wax paper; toss to coat. Reserve.
3. Sift together the 2 cups of flour, the baking powder and salt into a large bowl; stir in the sugar.
4. Cut the shortening into the flour mixture with a pastry blender until crumbly. Beat the egg with the orange juice in a small bowl. Stir into the flour mixture just until the dry ingredients are moistened. Stir in the cranberry walnut mixture and the orange rind. Spoon into the prepared loaf pan.
5. Bake in the preheated moderate oven (350°) for 1 hour and 5 minutes, or until a wooden toothpick inserted in the center comes out clean. Turn out onto a wire rack to cool. This bread is easier to slice a day after baking.

Keep cranberries autumn-fresh all year long: Freeze in unopened packages and use as you need them. (They can even be chopped while still frozen!)

Pumpkin Nut Muffins

Bake at 350° for 20 minutes.
Makes 2 dozen muffins.

    2   cups sifted all-purpose flour
    1   teaspoon baking soda
    ½   teaspoon baking powder
    ½   teaspoon ground cinnamon
    ½   teaspoon ground nutmeg
    ¼   teaspoon ground ginger
    2   eggs, slightly beaten
    ⅓   cup buttermilk
    ⅓   cup butter, melted
    1   tablespoon molasses
    ½   teaspoon vanilla
    1   cup sugar
    1   cup canned pumpkin
    ½   cup chopped pecans
    ½   cup raisins

1. Preheat the oven to moderate (350°). Grease 24 muffin-pan cups, 2¼ inches in diameter.
2. Sift together the flour, baking soda, baking powder, cinnamon, nutmeg and ginger onto wax paper.
3. Beat together the eggs, buttermilk, melted butter, molasses, vanilla, sugar and pumpkin in a large bowl. Stir in the dry ingredients, all at once, just until moistened. Fold in the chopped pecans and the raisins. Spoon into the prepared muffin-pan cups, filling almost to the top.
4. Bake in the preheated moderate oven (350°) for 20 to 25 minutes, or until a wooden toothpick inserted in the centers comes out clean. Remove the muffins from the cups and cool on wire racks. Serve warm.

Microwave Directions *(for a 650-watt variable power microwave oven):* Place two 2½-inch paper cupcake liners into each of 18 microwave-safe muffin cups. Prepare the muffin batter as above. Divide the batter equally among the lined cups. Microwave 6 at a time at full power for 4½ minutes. Remove the muffins from the pans, peel off the outer paper liners and cool on wire racks. *Makes 1½ dozen large muffins.*

Note: *Uncooked-batter-filled paper cupcake liners can be frozen. To bake, place 6 frozen filled paper liners in microwave-safe muffin cups. Microwave at full power for 6 minutes.*

Talking Turkey

*Here are some holiday-tested hints to make your Thanksgiving
meal a gobbling success!*

BUYING AND PREPARING THE BIRD

• When buying a turkey, allow one pound per serving if the bird weighs 12 pounds or less, ½ pound per serving for birds over 12 pounds.
• Remember, a bigger bird is a better buy and it will provide you with leftovers.
• For just two people, consider buying a frozen boneless turkey or roll. A small family with a preference for white meat would be pleased with a roasted turkey breast.

STORING

Fresh turkeys: Refrigerate at all times. Cook within 1 to 2 days of purchase.
Frozen whole turkeys: Store in the original wrapper for up to 12 months at 0° F or lower.

THAWING

The National Turkey Federation recommends these two methods.
Conventional (long) Method:
Thawing time — 3 to 4 days, about 24 hours for each 5 pounds of whole frozen turkey.
• Leave the turkey in the original wrapper.
• Place the frozen turkey on a tray in the refrigerator.
Cold Water (short) Method:
Thawing time — about 30 minutes per pound of whole frozen turkey.
• Leave the turkey in the original wrapper.
• Place the turkey in a sink or large pan.
• Completely cover with cold water.
• Change the water every 30 minutes.
• Keep the turkey immersed in the cold water at all times.
Note: *Never thaw a turkey at room temperature. Once thawed, cook or refrigerate immediately.*

STUFFING

When? Just before you roast the turkey is the time to stuff it. You run the risk of food poisoning if you do this earlier.

How much? Allow ¾ cup stuffing per pound of bird for turkeys weighing more than 10 pounds, ½ cup stuffing per pound for smaller birds.
Note: *Never freeze stuffing that is in a cooked or raw bird. Also, remove all of the stuffing from the cooked bird, wrap separately and refrigerate.*

TIMETABLE FOR ROASTING TURKEY (325°)

BIRD WEIGHT (pounds)	STUFFED (hours)	UNSTUFFED (hours)
6 to 8	3 to 3½	2½ to 3½
8 to 12	3½ to 4½	3 to 4
12 to 16	4 to 5	3½ to 4½
16 to 20	4½ to 5½	4 to 5
20 to 24	5 to 6½	4½ to 5½

• Do not roast turkey at a very low temperature overnight.

TESTING FOR DONENESS

• A meat thermometer inserted in the meatiest part of the thigh reads 180°F to 185°F.
• Turkey juices run clear.
• Drumsticks move up and down easily.

RESTING PERIOD

Let the turkey stand at room temperature for 20 minutes. This allows the juices to settle and the meat to firm up for easier carving.

GOT A QUESTION?

• The U.S.D.A. Meat and Poultry Hotline at 1-800-535-4555 will answer questions about your holiday bird from 10 A.M. to 4 P.M. (EST), Monday-Friday, no weekends or holidays.
• The Butterball Turkey Talk-line at 1-800-323-4848 will answer any questions about preparing the holiday turkey and trimmings. The toll-free Talk-line will operate from November 2 through

December 24, Monday-Friday, 8 A.M. to 8 P.M. (CST), Thanksgiving Day, 6 A.M. to 7 P.M. (CST) and Christmas Eve Day, 8 A.M. TO 6 P.M. (CST).

MICROWAVE COOKING DIRECTIONS FOR TURKEY
(625- to 700-watt microwave oven)

If frozen, thaw the turkey as directed in the general directions. Thawing a turkey in the microwave is not recommended.

First Steps:

1. Free the legs from the tucked position. Do not cut the band of skin.

2. Remove the neck meat and giblets from the neck and body cavities. To microwave, place 3 cups water, ½ teaspoon salt, the neck, gizzard and heart in a 2-quart microwave-safe casserole; cover. Microwave at half power for 35 minutes. Add the liver, cover and microwave for 10 minutes more. The cooked neck, giblets and stock may be used in making the turkey gravy or mixed with the stuffing.

3. Rinse the turkey and drain well.

4. If desired, stuff the neck and body cavities loosely. Cover any exposed stuffing with plastic wrap.

5. Turn the wings back to hold the neck skin in place. Return the legs to the tucked position. No trussing is necessary.

6. Make a Browning Sauce: Microwave ½ stick butter in a microwave-safe bowl at full power for 30 to 40 seconds, or until melted. Blend in ¼ teaspoon paprika and ⅛ teaspoon browning and seasoning sauce. Stir well before using.

To Cook:

1. Place the turkey, breast side down, in a microwave-safe dish. If the turkey tips, level it with a microwave-safe item so it will cook evenly.

2. Brush the back of the turkey with 1 tablespoon of the Browning Sauce.

3. See the Microwave Oven Cooking Schedule for the cooking time. Use the schedule closest to the weight of the turkey. Follow Part I and Part II Cooking Times without any delaying interruptions.

4. Microwave at full power for Time 1. Rotate the turkey one half-turn. Microwave for Time 2. Remove and discard the drippings.

5. Turn the turkey, breast side up. If stuffed, remove the plastic wrap. Brush with the Browning Sauce. Level if the turkey tips.

6. Microwave at half power for Times 3, 4 and 5. At the end of each Time, rotate the turkey one quarter-turn; discard the drippings and brush the turkey with the Browning Sauce. If overbrowning occurs, shield with small pieces of aluminum foil. After Time 5, check for doneness. A meat thermometer inserted in the thickest part of the thigh (not touching the bone) should register 180° to 185°F; in thickest part of the breast, 170°F; in the center of the stuffing, 160° to 165°F. If any of these temperatures have not been reached, cook for Time 6. Recheck the temperature; cook longer if necessary.

7. Cover the turkey with aluminum foil. Let stand for 15 to 20 minutes before carving.

MICROWAVE OVEN COOKING SCHEDULE
for Stuffed or Unstuffed Turkey
Approximate cooking time in 625- to 700-watt microwave ovens

Weight		4lb.	5lb.	6lb.	7lb.	8lb.	9lb.	10lb.	11lb.	12lb.
Times		**Part I—Breast down at full power**								
	1	8 min.	10 min.	12 min.	14 min.	16 min.	18 min.	20 min.	22 min.	24 min.
	2	8 min.	10 min.	12 min.	14 min.	16 min.	18 min.	20 min.	22 min.	24 min.
		Part II—Breast up at half power								
	3	8 min.	10 min.	12 min.	14 min.	16 min.	18 min.	20 min.	22 min.	24 min.
	4	8 min.	10 min.	12 min.	14 min.	16 min.	18 min.	20 min.	22 min.	24 min.
	5*	8 min.	10 min.	12 min.	14 min.	16 min.	18 min.	20 min.	22 min.	24 min.
	6	8 min.	10 min.	12 min.	14 min.	16 min.	18 min.	20 min.	22 min.	24 min.
Total cooking time:		48 min.	60 min.	72 min.	84 min.	96 min.	108 min.	120 min.	132 min.	144 min.

*Check for doneness after Time 5.

💲 ⦉⦉⦉
Mincemeat Pie

Pie like grandma used to make is simplified with ready-made mincemeat.

Bake at 425° for 40 minutes.
Makes one 9-inch pie.

1 **jar (28 ounces) ready-to-use mincemeat**
1 **large apple, cored and diced**
1 **cup coarsely chopped walnuts**
½ **cup firmly packed brown sugar**
¼ **cup brandy or rum (optional)**
1 **tablespoon lemon juice**
   Homemade Pastry (recipe, page 23)
   OR: piecrust mix for a double-crust 9-inch pie

1. Preheat the oven to hot (425°).
2. Stir together the mincemeat, apple, chopped walnuts, brown sugar, brandy or rum if you wish, and lemon juice in a medium-size bowl until well mixed.
3. Prepare the Homemade Pastry or piecrust mix. Center dough in a 9-inch pie plate; fold up and press together the dough overhang. Make a rope edge: Using a wooden skewer, press diagonally, twisting slightly, into the dough all around the edge to make even, widely-spaced ridges.
4. Spoon the mincemeat mixture into the piecrust.
5. Bake in the preheated hot oven (425°) for 40 minutes, or until golden brown. Cool the pie on a wire rack for 1½ hours.

💲 ⦉⦉⦉
Pilgrim Pumpkin Pie

This old-fashioned pie will bring back many Thanksgiving memories.

Bake at 400° for 40 minutes.
Makes one 9-inch pie.

   Piecrust mix for a double-crust pie
1 **can (16 ounces) pumpkin**
1 **can (12 ounces) evaporated milk**
2 **eggs**
¾ **cup firmly packed brown sugar**
2 **teaspoons pumpkin pie spice**
½ **teaspoon salt**
½ **cup heavy cream, whipped**

1. Prepare the piecrust mix. Roll out half of the dough and line a 9-inch pie plate. Roll out the remaining dough. Make a button design *(see Pastry Crust Designs, page 15)*: Using a sewing thimble, cut out pastry rounds, moisten them, place them just touching around the rim of the pie plate and poke holes in them with a skewer.
2. Preheat the oven to hot (400°).
3. Place the pumpkin, evaporated milk, eggs, brown sugar, pie spice and salt in a large bowl. Beat with an electric mixer at medium speed until well mixed.
4. Place the pastry-lined pie plate on the middle oven rack. Spoon in the pumpkin mixture.
5. Bake in the preheated hot oven (400°) for 40 minutes, or until a knife inserted in the center comes out clean. Cool the pie on a wire rack for 1½ hours. Pipe out a whipped cream garnish.

⦉⦉⦉
Southern Pecan Pie

A delightful chocolate variation follows.

Bake at 375° for 45 minutes.
Makes one 9-inch pie.

½ **package piecrust mix**
4 **eggs, slightly beaten**
1 **cup sugar**
½ **teaspoon salt**
1½ **cups dark corn syrup**
1 **teaspoon vanilla**
1 **cup chopped pecans**
¼ **cup all-purpose flour**
1 **cup halved pecans**

1. Preheat the oven to moderate (375°).
2. Prepare the piecrust for a 9-inch single crust pie. Fit into a pie plate, following the directions for a sunburst design *(see Pastry Crust Designs, page 15)*, if you wish.
3. Blend the beaten eggs, sugar, salt, corn syrup, vanilla and chopped pecans in a medium-size bowl; stir in the flour. Pour the mixture into the pie plate. Arrange the pecan halves in a design on the filling. If making a sunburst design, fold the edge in over the filling, toward the center.
4. Bake in the preheated moderate oven (375°) for 45 minutes, or until the center is almost set but still soft. (The filling will set as it cools.) Cool the pie on a wire rack.

Variation: Add 2 ounces of melted bittersweet chocolate to the filling. Bake as directed.

$ ⟪

Pumpkin Mince Pie

Two favorite flavors packed into one delicious pie.

Bake at 425° for 15 minutes, then at 350° for 35 minutes.
Makes 8 servings.

1⅓ **cups ready-to-use mincemeat**
2 **teaspoons grated orange rind**
1 **nine-inch unbaked pastry shell with a high fluted edge**
2 **eggs**
1 **can (14 ounces) sweetened condensed milk**
1 **teaspoon ground cinnamon**
½ **teaspoon ground nutmeg**
½ **teaspoon ground ginger**
¼ **teaspoon salt**
1 **can (16 ounces) pumpkin**
½ **cup heavy cream, whipped**
    Slivers of orange rind for garnish

1. Preheat the oven to hot (425°).
2. Combine the mincemeat and the grated orange rind in a 2-cup measure. Spoon the mixture into the pastry shell, spreading evenly.
3. Beat the eggs in a large bowl until frothy. Stir in the milk, cinnamon, nutmeg, ginger, salt and pumpkin. Mix well until smooth. Pour over the mincemeat layer in the pastry shell.
4. Bake the pie in the preheated hot oven (425°) for 15 minutes. Lower the heat to moderate (350°) and continue baking for 35 minutes, or until the tip of a knife inserted into the filling 1 inch from the edge comes out clean. Cool the pie on a wire rack. Garnish with the whipped cream and the orange rind slivers just before serving.

Did You Know . . .

That the Hebrew word for "big bird" is tukki.

PASTRY CRUST DESIGNS

For a special look, add one of the following designs to your pie's pastry rim:

Button: Use a sewing thimble to cut dainty pastry rounds, place them, just

touching, around the rim (moisten it first) and poke holes with a skewer.

Ruffle: Place your left thumb and forefinger about ½ inch apart on the inside rim of the

pastry; with your right forefinger on the outside, gently pull the pastry in, as shown.

Sunburst Design: Fit the bottom crust into the pie plate, leaving a 1½-inch overhang.

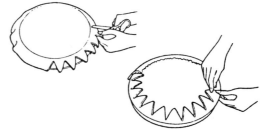

With scissors, snip even, sawtooth cuts all around and fold the edge in over the filling, toward the center.

Thanksgiving Dinner With A Twist

(for 8)

Curried Pumpkin Soup*
*Brace of Roasted Capons with Oyster
and Rice Stuffing**
Green Beans with Lemon Vodka Butter*
Candied Carrots*
Mashed Potato Soufflé*
Stuffed Onions*
Southern Corn Sticks*
Mulled Cider with Apple Brandy*
Cranberry Ice*
Orange-Glazed Cherry Pie*
Sugar-Dusted Apple Pie*

*Recipes follow

***Brace of Roasted Capons with Oyster and Rice Stuffing; Curried Pumpkin Soup;
Green Beans With Lemon Vodka Butter; Candied Carrots; Stuffed Onions;
Mashed Potato Soufflé; Southern Corn Sticks; Mulled Cider with Apple Brandy***

Work Plan

Up to 1 Month Ahead:
• Prepare and freeze Orange-Glazed Cherry Pie and Sugar-Dusted Apple Pie (or prepare pies the day before and refrigerate).

Up to 2 Weeks Ahead:
• Prepare and freeze Cranberry Ice.

The Day Before:
• Prepare Curried Pumpkin Soup; refrigerate.
• Prepare Stuffed Onions but do not dot with butter or add liquid to pan; refrigerate.
• Prepare mashed potato base for Mashed Potato Soufflé; refrigerate.
• Make Oyster and Rice Stuffing, but do not stuff capons; refrigerate Stuffing and capons separately.

Early in the Day:
• Prepare spiced cider base for Mulled Cider with Apple Brandy.
• Trim beans for Green Beans with Lemon Vodka Butter.
• Pare carrots for Candied Carrots.

3 Hours Before:
• Stuff and roast capons.
• Make Gravy.

1½ Hours Before:
• Complete and bake Stuffed Onions.
• Complete and bake Mashed Potato Soufflé.

1 Hour Before:
• Prepare Southern Cornsticks.

At Serving Time:
• Finish Mulled Cider with Apple Brandy.
• Reheat Curried Pumpkin Soup.
• Cook Candied Carrots and Green Beans with Lemon Vodka Butter.
• Reheat Gravy.

During Dinner:
• Reheat Orange-Glazed Cherry Pie and Sugar-Dusted Apple Pie.
• Whip cream for pies.
• Beat Cranberry Ice, if desired.

Curried Pumpkin Soup

Makes 8 servings (7 cups).

1   **medium-size onion, coarsely chopped (½ cup)**
1   **clove garlic, finely chopped**
¼   **cup (½ stick) butter or margarine**
1   **can (16 ounces) solid-pack pumpkin purée OR: 2 cups homemade pumpkin purée**
4   **teaspoons curry powder**
¼   **teaspoon salt**
¼   **teaspoon pepper**
⅛   **teaspoon sugar**
⅛   **teaspoon ground nutmeg**
1   **bay leaf**
4   **cups chicken broth or stock**
2   **cups milk**
½   **cup toasted coconut for garnish**

1. Sauté the onion and the garlic in the butter or margarine in a large saucepan over medium heat until very soft, for about 5 minutes.
2. Stir in the pumpkin purée, curry powder, salt, pepper, sugar, nutmeg and bay leaf. Pour in the broth or stock. Bring to boiling over medium heat. Lower the heat and simmer for 30 minutes. Remove from the heat. Discard the bay leaf.
3. Stir in the milk. Reheat gently; do not boil. Garnish with the toasted coconut.

Note: *This soup may be made the day before. Refrigerate and reheat very gently.*

Did You Know . . .

That turkey probably wasn't served at the first Thanksgiving! Instead, historians believe that venison, duck, goose, seafood and eels were the fare.

Brace of Roasted Capons with Oyster and Rice Stuffing

Roast at 375° for 2 hours.
Makes 8 servings plus leftovers.

Oyster and Rice Stuffing:
- 2 cups finely chopped onion
- 1 cup finely chopped celery
- 1½ cups (3 sticks) butter or margarine
- 6 cups cooked white rice
- ½ cup finely chopped parsley
- 1 teaspoon salt
- ½ teaspoon pepper
- 1½ pints shucked oysters in their own liquor
- 1 egg, slightly beaten

- 2 capons (about 6 pounds each)
  Half of a lemon
- ¼ cup currant jelly
- 2 tablespoons water
  Gravy (recipe follows)

1. Prepare the Oyster and Rice Stuffing: Sauté the onion and the celery in 1 cup of the butter or margarine in a large saucepan over medium heat until the onion is softened, for about 3 minutes.
2. Remove from the heat. Stir in the rice, parsley, salt and pepper. Reserve.
3. Drain the liquor from the oysters into a small saucepan; reserve the oysters. Bring the liquor just to boiling. Halve the oysters, if large, and add to the hot liquid. Cook for about 1 minute, or until the edges of the oysters just begin to curl. Drain. Stir the oysters into the rice mixture. Cool the mixture slightly. Stir in the egg.
4. Melt the remaining ½ cup butter or margarine in a small saucepan; reserve.
5. Preheat the oven to moderate (375°).
6. Rinse the capons. Pat dry inside and out with paper toweling. Rub the interior with the lemon half. Cut off the wing tips, if you wish, and set aside with the necks, gizzards, hearts and livers to make stock for the Gravy.
7. Stuff the neck and body cavities with the Stuffing. Close the cavities with string and skewers or by sewing with heavy white thread. Prick the legs and backs of the capons. Place on a rack in a shallow roasting pan.
8. Roast in the preheated moderate oven (375°) for 2 hours, or until the leg joints move easily and the juices run clear. Baste with the pan juices and the melted butter or margarine every 30 minutes.
9. Heat the currant jelly and the water in a small saucepan until the jelly melts. Brush the capons with the glaze and return to the oven for 5 minutes longer. Serve with the Gravy.

Did You Know . . .

That approximately 40 million Thanksgiving Day cards are exchanged every year.

Gravy

Makes 8 servings (about 1½ cups).

- Necks, gizzards, hearts and livers from 2 capons (wing tips, optional)
- 1 medium-size carrot, pared and cut into 1-inch pieces
- 1 medium-size onion, quartered
- 4 sprigs parsley
- 1 bay leaf
- 4 cups water
- 2 tablespoons pan drippings from roasted capons
- 3 tablespoons all-purpose flour

1. Prepare the stock: Combine the necks, gizzards, hearts, wing tips if you wish, carrot, onion, parsley, bay leaf and water in a medium-size saucepan. Set aside the livers.
2. Bring to boiling over medium heat. Lower the heat and simmer for 45 minutes. Add the livers and simmer for 15 minutes longer, or until the stock is reduced to about 2 cups. Discard the capon pieces, except the livers, the vegetables, parsley and bay leaf. Remove the livers and coarsely chop. Reserve the chopped livers and the stock for the Gravy.
3. Prepare the Gravy: Transfer the capons to a platter. Remove all but about 2 tablespoons of the fat from the roasting pan. Stir the flour into the drippings. Cook on the stove-top over medium heat for 2 minutes, scraping up any browned bits from the bottom of the pan.
4. Pour in the reserved stock. Bring to boiling over medium heat, stirring constantly, until the Gravy thickens and is smooth. Lower the heat; simmer for 5 minutes. Strain the Gravy into a warmed gravy boat. Stir in the reserved chopped livers. Serve with the capons.

⑂ ⑃ ⑄

Green Beans with Lemon Vodka Butter

Makes 8 servings.

12 ounces fresh green beans, trimmed
1   tablespoon vodka
1   tablespoon butter or margarine,
     softened
2   teaspoons lemon juice
⅛   teaspoon salt

1. Cook the beans in boiling water to cover in a medium-size saucepan over medium heat for 5 minutes, or until crisp-tender. Drain.
2. Return the beans to the saucepan. Add vodka, butter, lemon juice and salt. Stir well to coat.
3. Arrange the beans, in separate bundles if you wish, on the platter around the capons.

⑂ ⑄

Stuffed Onions

Bake at 350° for 45 minutes.
Makes 8 servings.

8   medium-size onions (2½ pounds),
     outer skin removed
¼   cup (¼ stick) butter or margarine
½   pound bulk sausage
2   cups soft white bread crumbs (4 slices)
¼   cup milk
¼   cup chopped parsley
¼   teaspoon leaf thyme, crumbled
⅛   teaspoon salt
⅛   teaspoon pepper
     Additional butter or margarine
     (optional)
½   cup beef broth or stock
½   cup dry white wine
     Chopped parsley (optional)

1. Cut off the top quarter of the onions and reserve for another use. Scoop out the center of each onion, using a sharp paring knife, leaving a shell about ¼ inch thick on the sides and a 1-inch deep cavity. Chop the onion centers, measure 2 cups and reserve.
2. Preheat the oven to moderate (350°). Grease a shallow, flameproof baking dish large enough to hold the onions.
3. Cook the onion shells in boiling salted water in

a large saucepan for 5 minutes. Remove with a slotted spoon. Drain upside down on paper toweling.
4. Sauté the reserved chopped onion in the butter or margarine in a large skillet over medium heat. Crumble the sausage into the skillet; sauté until no longer pink.
5. Meanwhile, soak the bread crumbs in the milk in a small bowl. Squeeze dry and add to the sausage. Cook, stirring, for 5 minutes. Season with the parsley, thyme, salt and pepper.
6. Arrange the onions close together in the prepared dish. Slice a thin layer off the bottoms, if necessary, so they stand upright.
7. Fill the onion shells with the stuffing, mounding high. (The recipe may be prepared ahead up to this point. Refrigerate the onions.) Dot the tops with butter or margarine, if you wish. Pour the broth and the wine into the dish. Bring the liquid in the pan to boiling on top of the stove.
8. Bake in the preheated moderate oven (350°) for 10 minutes, basting occasionally. Cover and bake for 35 minutes longer.
9. Transfer the onions to a serving dish. Boil the liquid to reduce by half, for about 5 minutes. Pour over the onions. Sprinkle with parsley.

⑂ ⑄

Mashed Potato Soufflé

Bake at 325° for 50 to 55 minutes.
Makes 8 servings.

4   pounds Idaho potatoes, pared and
     boiled until fork-tender
½   cup (1 stick) butter or margarine, at
     room temperature
½   cup milk
1   cup grated onion (3 to 4 medium-size
     onions)
2   egg yolks
1   teaspoon salt
½   teaspoon white pepper
4   egg whites
⅛   teaspoon cream of tartar
1   small onion, thinly sliced
1   teaspoon softened butter or margarine

1. Preheat the oven to slow (325°).
2. Mash the warm potatoes with the ½ cup butter or margarine and the milk in a large bowl until smooth. Stir in the grated onion, egg yolks, salt and pepper. (The recipe may be prepared ahead

up to this point. Refrigerate.)

3. Beat the egg whites with the cream of tartar in a medium-size bowl until soft peaks form. Fold into the potato mixture.

4. Spoon the mixture into a 1½- to 2-quart soufflé dish or 2-quart casserole dish. (If using a soufflé dish, mound the mixture high; run a spatula around the outer edge of the mixture to give a rounded look.) Press the thin onion slices evenly on top of the potato mixture. Brush with the 1 teaspoon softened butter or margarine.

5. Bake on the lowest oven rack, if using a soufflé dish, or middle oven rack, if using a casserole dish, in the preheated slow oven (325°) for 50 to 55 minutes, or until the top is golden.

Candied Carrots

Makes 8 servings.

2   pounds baby carrots, pared
¼   cup (½ stick) butter or margarine
¼   cup light brown sugar
     Dash ground nutmeg

1. Cook the carrots in boiling water to cover in a large saucepan until crisp-tender, for about 10 minutes. Drain.

2. Melt the butter or margarine in the same saucepan. Add the carrots. Sprinkle with the sugar and nutmeg. Cook, stirring occasionally, for 5 minutes, or until the carrots are glazed. Arrange the carrots around the capons.

Southern Corn Sticks

These old-fashioned corn sticks have a distinctive, cornmeal texture.

Bake at 450° for 15 to 20 minutes.
Makes 28 sticks.

2   eggs
2   cups buttermilk
2   cups white or yellow cornmeal (not
     stone-ground)
1   teaspoon baking soda
1½   teaspoons salt

1. Preheat the oven to very hot (450°). Generously grease corn stick pans.

2. Beat the eggs in a small bowl until frothy. Add the buttermilk.

3. Stir together the cornmeal, baking soda and salt in a large bowl. Pour in the buttermilk mixture. Beat until the batter is smooth.

4. Fill the corn stick pans three-quarters full.

5. Bake in the preheated very hot oven (450°) for 15 to 20 minutes, or until corn sticks begin to pull away from sides of the pans and a wooden pick tests clean. Unmold the sticks. Repeat with remaining batter. Serve warm with butter.

Did You Know . . .

That the first Macy's Thanksgiving Day Parade was in 1924—and that the average life of a parade float is 2 to 3 years!

Mulled Cider with Apple Brandy

Makes 8 servings.

6   cardamom pods, crushed
12   whole allspice, crushed
3   slices (½ inch thick) fresh gingerroot
6   thin orange slices, halved (1 small
     orange)
24   cloves
12   two-inch cinnamon sticks
8   cups apple cider
¼   cup firmly packed dark brown sugar
1   teaspoon ground nutmeg
1   cup apple brandy (Calvados OR:
     apple jack)

1. Tie together the cardamom, allspice and gingerroot in a small piece of cheesecloth. Put a cinnamon stick in the center of each orange half-slice and stud each rind with 2 cloves.

2. Combine the cider, sugar, nutmeg, spices in cheesecloth and orange slices in a large stainless steel or enameled saucepan. Bring to boiling. (The recipe may be prepared ahead up to this point. Let stand.) Lower the heat and simmer for 10 minutes over medium heat. Add the apple brandy. Heat for 3 minutes longer. Discard the cheesecloth. Transfer the cider to a silver punch bowl. If serving the hot cider in fine glassware, ladle down the side of a teaspoon into each glass.

Sugar-Dusted Apple Pie

Bake at 425° for 15 minutes, then at 375° for 40 minutes.
Makes 6 servings.

1 **recipe Homemade Pastry (recipe, page 23) OR: 1 package (11 ounces) piecrust mix**
6 **cups thinly sliced, pared tart apples (2¼ pounds)**
½ **to 1 cup sugar**
2 **tablespoons quick-cooking tapioca**
1 **teaspoon grated lemon rind**
1 **teaspoon lemon juice**
½ **teaspoon ground cinnamon**
¼ **teaspoon salt**
2 **tablespoons butter, softened**
1 **tablespoon milk or heavy cream (optional)**
1 **tablespoon sugar**

1. Prepare the Homemade Pastry or the piecrust mix. Divide the dough in half and refrigerate one half. Roll out the other half on a lightly floured surface into an 11-inch circle. Fit into a 9-inch pie plate.
2. Place the apple slices in a large bowl. Sprinkle the sugar, tapioca, lemon rind, lemon juice, cinnamon and salt over the apples; toss gently to mix. Let stand for 15 minutes.
3. Preheat the oven to hot (425°).
4. Arrange a row of the apple slices around the outer edge of the bottom crust. Arrange other rows in concentric circles towards the center. Pile the remaining slices over the circles, building the center higher than the sides. Dot the top evenly with the butter.
5. Roll out the second half of the dough on a lightly floured surface into an 11-inch circle. Cut an X in the center for a steam vent. Fit over the filling. Turn back the corners of the X. Trim the overhang to 1 inch. Fold under flush with the rim. Pinch to make a stand-up edge and flute.
6. Bake in the preheated hot oven (425°) for 15 minutes. Lower the heat to moderate (375°) and continue baking for 40 minutes, or until the pastry is golden. Brush the top with the milk or heavy cream, if you wish. Sprinkle with the sugar. Bake for 5 minutes longer. Transfer the pie to a wire rack. Serve warm or at room temperature.

Cranberry Ice

A refreshingly tart ice that becomes deliciously smooth when whipped.

Makes 8 servings (5½ cups ice, 7 cups when whipped).

1 **pound (about one and one-third 12-ounce bags) fresh or frozen cranberries (4 cups), thawed if frozen**
4 **cups water**
2½ **cups sugar**
¼ **cup fresh lemon juice**

1. Combine the cranberries and the water in a medium-size saucepan. Cook over medium-high heat until the berries soften and pop. Press through a fine strainer placed over a bowl. Reserve the liquid and discard the solids.
2. Add the sugar and the lemon juice to the cranberry juice; stir well. Pour into freezer trays or an 8 x 8-inch square metal tray. Freeze for 3 hours, or until completely frozen.
3. Serve as an ice. Or break into pieces and beat in a chilled bowl until smooth; serve immediately.

Orange-Glazed Cherry Pie

Bake at 400° for 15 minutes, then at 350° for 40 to 45 minutes.
Makes 6 servings.

1 **recipe Homemade Pastry (recipe, page 23) OR: 1½ packages (11-ounce package) piecrust mix**
2½ **teaspoons finely grated orange rind**
2 **cans (16 ounces each) tart, pitted cherries, drained and syrup reserved**
¼ **cup cornstarch**
1 **cup sugar**
1 **teaspoon lemon juice**
¼ **teaspoon ground cinnamon**
1 **tablespoon butter, softened**
¼ **cup 10X (confectioners' powdered) sugar**
1½ **teaspoons orange juice**

1. Prepare the Homemade Pastry or the piecrust mix, adding 1½ teaspoons of the orange rind. Divide the pastry in half. Cover and refrigerate

one half. Roll out the other half on a lightly floured surface into an 11-inch circle. Fit into a 9-inch pie plate.

2. Combine ¾ cup of the reserved cherry syrup with the cornstarch in a small saucepan; stir until smooth. Add the sugar, lemon juice and cinnamon. Cook over medium-high heat, stirring constantly, until the mixture thickens slightly and bubbles. Cook for 1 minute. Remove from the heat. Transfer to a small bowl. Stir in the cherries. Let cool slightly.

3. Preheat the oven to hot (400°).

4. Spoon the filling into the prepared crust. Dot the filling with the butter.

5. Roll out the remaining dough on a lightly floured surface into a 13 x 9-inch rectangle, about ⅛ inch thick. Cut lengthwise into eight or nine ½-inch-wide strips, using a pastry cutter. Weave the strips over the filling to form a lattice. Moisten the underside edges of the lattice with water; press to the bottom crust. Pinch to make a stand-up edge and flute.

6. Bake on a cookie sheet in the preheated hot oven (400°) for 15 minutes. Lower the heat to moderate (350°). Continue to bake for 40 to 45 minutes, or until the filling begins to bubble. Cover the crust with aluminum foil if the edges begin to brown too quickly.

7. Meanwhile, stir together the 10X (confectioners' powdered) sugar, orange juice and remaining 1 teaspoon of orange rind in a small bowl until smooth. Brush the crust and lattice with the glaze. Return the pie to the oven for 2 minutes, or until the glaze sets. Cool the pie on a wire rack.

Homemade Pastry: Combine 2 cups *un*sifted all-purpose flour and 1 teaspoon salt in a medium-size bowl. Cut in ¾ cup chilled vegetable shortening with a pastry blender until the mixture is crumbly. Gradually add 6 to 8 tablespoons ice water. Work until the dough is soft enough to gather into a ball, but is not sticky. Refrigerate, covered, until well chilled. *Makes enough for a double-crust 9-inch pie.*

Orange-Glazed Cherry Pie; Sugar-Dusted Apple Pie; Cranberry Ice

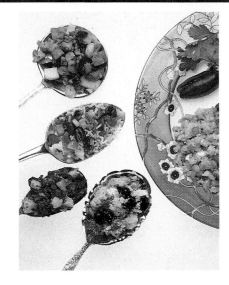

$ ‹‹‹
Tex-Mex Stuffing

Makes 10 cups (enough for a 12-pound turkey or 5 whole chicken breasts).

2 *medium-size onions,*
   finely chopped
¼ *cup (½ stick) butter*
1 *large sweet green pepper,*
   halved, seeded and
   finely chopped (1 cup)
3 *medium-size celery*
   stalks, finely chopped
   (1 cup)
   Turkey giblets, finely
   chopped (optional)
   Turkey liver, finely
   chopped (optional)
2 *canned hot jalapeño*
   peppers, seeded and
   finely chopped
1 *clove garlic, finely*
   chopped
8 *cups crumbled cornbread*
2 *hard-cooked eggs,*
   coarsely chopped
2 *cans (8 ounces each) corn*
   niblets, drained
1 *cup turkey or chicken*
   broth
2 *teaspoons chili powder*
½ *teaspoon salt*
¼ *teaspoon pepper*

1. Sauté the onion in the butter in a large skillet until softened, for about 3 minutes. Stir in the sweet green pepper and the celery; sauté for 3 minutes. Stir in the turkey giblets and liver if

THE RIGHT STUFF–ING

For many holiday diners, turkey is an excuse to eat stuffing. Here are a few of our favorite turkey fillers. (Of course, you can use them to stuff chicken, game hens and other birds, too.)

you wish, jalapeño peppers and garlic; sauté for 5 minutes.
2. Combine the cornbread, hard-cooked eggs and corn in a large bowl. Pour in the turkey or chicken broth; toss to moisten. Add the sautéed vegetables, chili powder, salt and pepper.
3. Stuff the turkey and roast according to your favorite recipe. Or spoon the dressing into a greased, shallow 3-quart baking dish. Bake, covered, in a preheated moderate oven (350°) for 45 minutes. Uncover during the last 10 minutes for a crusty top.

$ ‹‹‹
Apricot Pecan Rice Stuffing

Makes 12 cups (enough for a 12- to 14-pound turkey).

2 *cups coarsely broken*
   pecans
6 *tablespoons butter or*
   margarine
2 *medium-size onions,*
   chopped (1 cup)
2 *large celery stalks, diced*
   (1 cup)
   Turkey giblets, finely
   chopped (optional)
   Turkey liver, finely
   chopped (optional)
6 *cups cooked white rice*
2 *cups coarsely chopped*
   dried apricots
¼ *cup chopped parsley*
2 *teaspoons leaf thyme,*
   crumbled
1 *teaspoon leaf sage,*
   crumbled
½ *teaspoon salt*
¼ *teaspoon pepper*
1 *can (13¾ ounces) chicken*
   broth

1. Sauté the pecans in 2 tablespoons of the butter or margarine in a large skillet over medium heat until golden, for 3 minutes. Transfer the pecans with a slotted spoon to a large bowl.
2. Sauté the onions and the celery in the remaining 4 tablespoons of butter or margarine in the

same skillet until the onion softens, for about 3 minutes; do not let the onion brown. Add the turkey giblets and liver, if you wish, and sauté for 5 minutes longer. Combine with the pecans in the bowl.

3. Add the rice, apricots, parsley, thyme, sage, salt and pepper to the pecan-vegetable mixture; toss gently to mix. Pour in the chicken broth; stir well to moisten.

4. Stuff the turkey and roast according to your favorite recipe. Or spoon the stuffing into a greased, shallow 3-quart baking dish. Bake, covered, in a preheated moderate oven (350°) for 35 minutes, or until heated through.

💲 📻
Cranberry Cornbread Stuffing

Makes 16 cups (enough for a 14- to 16-pound turkey).

- 2 **cups cranberries, fresh or frozen, thawed if frozen**
- 1 **cup water**
- ½ **cup sugar**
- 1 **pound sausage meat**
- 8 **cups crumbled cornbread (homemade or store-bought)**
- 2 **large red Delicious apples, pared, cored and diced (about 3 cups)**
- 2 **medium-size celery stalks, diced (½ cup)**
- 1 **medium-size onion, finely chopped (½ cup)**
- ¼ **cup chopped parsley**
- 2 **teaspoons leaf thyme, crumbled**
- 2 **teaspoons leaf marjoram, crumbled**
- ½ **teaspoon salt**
- ¼ **teaspoon pepper**

1. Combine the cranberries, water and sugar in a medium-size saucepan. Bring to boiling over medium heat. Lower the heat and simmer for 10 minutes. Drain well. Transfer to a large bowl.

2. Sauté the sausage in a medium-size skillet, breaking up into small pieces with a wooden spoon, until lightly browned and no longer pink, for about 5 minutes. Drain the excess fat. Combine with the cranberries in the bowl.

3. Add the cornbread, apples, celery, onion, parsley, thyme, marjoram, salt and pepper to the cranberry-sausage mixture; toss gently to mix.

4. Stuff the turkey and roast according to your favorite recipe. Or spoon the stuffing into a greased, shallow 4½-quart baking dish. Bake, covered, in a preheated moderate oven (350°) for 45 minutes, or until heated through. Uncover during the last 10 minutes for a crusty top.

💲 📻
Apple Pecan Stuffing

Makes 14 cups (enough for a 14-pound turkey).

- 2 **cups coarsely broken pecans**
- 6 **tablespoons butter or margarine**
- 2 **medium-size onions, chopped (1 cup)**
- 2 **medium-size celery stalks with leaves, diced**
- 6 **cups packaged plain croutons OR: 6 cups toasted bread cubes (12 slices)**
- 4 **large tart apples, pared, cored and cut into ½-inch cubes**
- 5½ **ounces cooked ham, cut into ¼-inch cubes (1 cup)**
- 3 **eggs, slightly beaten**
- ¼ **cup chopped parsley**
- 2 **teaspoons leaf thyme, crumbled**
- ½ **teaspoon pepper**

1. Sauté the pecans in 2 tablespoons of the butter or margarine in a large skillet until golden, for 3 minutes. Transfer the pecans with a slotted spoon to a large bowl.

2. Sauté the onion and the celery in the remaining 4 tablespoons of butter or margarine in the same skillet until the onion softens, for 3 minutes. Do not brown. Combine with the pecans in the bowl.

3. Add the packaged croutons or toasted bread cubes, apples, ham, eggs, parsley, thyme and pepper to the pecan-vegetable mixture; toss gently to mix.

4. Stuff the turkey and roast according to your favorite recipe. Or spoon the stuffing into a greased, shallow 4½-quart baking dish. Bake, covered, in a preheated moderate oven (350°) for 40 minutes, or until heated through. Uncover during the last 5 minutes for a crusty top.

Microwave Directions
(for a 650-watt variable power microwave oven):
Combine the butter or margarine, onions and celery in a 3-quart microwave-safe baking dish or casserole with a cover. Cover tightly. Microwave at full power for 8 minutes. Stir in the remaining ingredients. Cover tightly. Microwave at full power for 8 more minutes. Serve immediately or cover the dish with aluminum foil and set aside for up to 20 minutes before serving.

💲 🎁 Pork and Spinach Stuffing

Makes 8 cups (enough for a 10- to 12-pound turkey).

1   **large onion, finely chopped (1 cup)**
2   **cloves garlic, finely chopped**
6   **tablespoons butter or margarine**
    Turkey giblets, finely chopped (optional)
1   **pound ground pork**
    Turkey liver, finely chopped (optional)
2   **packages (10 ounces each) frozen chopped spinach, thawed and drained**
3   **cups day-old white bread cubes (6 slices)**
3   **eggs, slightly beaten**
½   **cup chopped parsley**
1   **teaspoon leaf thyme, crumbled**
1   **teaspoon leaf marjoram, crumbled**
½   **teaspoon pepper**
¼   **teaspoon salt**

1. Sauté the onion and the garlic in 3 tablespoons of the butter or margarine in a large skillet until the onion softens, for about 3 minutes. Transfer to a large bowl.
2. Melt the remaining 3 tablespoons of butter or margarine in the skillet. Sauté the turkey giblets, if you wish, for 10 minutes, or until tender. Add the pork, breaking up with a wooden spoon. Continue to cook until the pork is no longer pink, for about 7 minutes. Stir in the turkey liver, if you wish; cook for 2 minutes. Combine the pork mixture with the onion in the bowl.
3. Combine the spinach, bread cubes, eggs, parsley, thyme, marjoram, pepper and salt with the pork-vegetable mixture in the bowl.
4. Stuff the turkey and roast according to your favorite recipe. Or spoon the stuffing into a greased, shallow 2-quart baking dish. Bake, covered, in a preheated moderate oven (350°) for 35 minutes, or until heated through. Uncover during the last 5 minutes for a crusty top.

💲 🎁 Brandied Chestnut Stuffing

Makes 8 cups (enough for a 10- to 12-pound turkey).

2   **cups finely chopped mushrooms (about 5½ ounces)**
5   **tablespoons butter**
1   **large onion, finely chopped**
2   **medium-size celery stalks, finely chopped (1 cup)**
1   **pound sausage meat**
4   **cups crumbled day-old white bread (8 slices)**
1   **cup turkey or chicken broth**
1   **can (15½ or 16 ounces) chestnuts, rinsed, drained and coarsely chopped OR: 2 cups coarsely chopped, peeled, cooked fresh chestnuts**
¼   **cup brandy**
¼   **cup chopped parsley**
2   **teaspoons leaf thyme, crumbled**
1   **bay leaf, crumbled**
½   **teaspoon salt**
¼   **teaspoon pepper**

1. Sauté the mushrooms in 2 tablespoons of the butter in a large 12-inch skillet until golden, for about 5 minutes. Transfer with a slotted spoon to a small bowl.
2. Sauté the onion and the celery in the remaining 3 tablespoons of butter for 3 minutes. Add the sausage, breaking up into small pieces with a wooden spoon. Sauté until the sausage is lightly browned and no longer pink, for about 5 minutes. Remove from the heat. Drain the excess fat.
3. Add the bread and the turkey or chicken broth to the skillet; stir to moisten. Stir in the chestnuts, brandy, parsley, thyme, bay leaf, salt and pepper. Return to the heat; stir to mix thoroughly for 2 minutes. Remove from the heat and stir in the mushrooms.
4. Stuff the turkey and roast according to your favorite recipe. Or spoon the stuffing into a greased, shallow 2-quart baking dish. Bake, covered, in a preheated moderate oven (350°) for 45 minutes, or until heated through. Uncover during the last 10 minutes for a crusty top.

Leftover, But Not Forgotten

Some innovative—and delicious—ways to make the most of your Thanksgiving bird.

💲

Grilled Turkey, Cheese and Tomato Sandwiches

Makes 4 servings.

8	**slices bread**
	Butter or margarine
4	**slices cooked turkey**
2	**slices Swiss cheese (1 ounce each)**
8	**thin tomato slices**
	Salt and pepper
2	**eggs**
½	**cup milk**
¼	**teaspoon salt**
	Dash cayenne
2	**tablespoons butter or margarine**

1. Spread the bread on one side with butter or margarine. Arrange 1 slice of turkey, ½ slice of cheese and 2 tomato slices on 4 of the buttered sides. Sprinkle with the salt and pepper. Top with the remaining 4 slices of bread, buttered sides in.
2. Beat the eggs with the milk, salt and cayenne in a shallow dish. Melt the 2 tablespoons butter or margarine in a large skillet or griddle. Dip the sandwiches in the egg mixture to coat both sides, using a flat spatula.
3. Brown the sandwiches in the butter or margarine, turning to brown both sides and melt the cheese.

💲 〈〈〈

Turkey in Cheddar Cheese Sauce

Bake at 425° for 4 minutes.
Makes 4 servings.

4	**slices buttered toast, cut in half**
8	**slices cooked turkey**
2	**tablespoons butter or margarine**
2	**tablespoons all-purpose flour**
¼	**teaspoon salt**
⅛	**teaspoon pepper**
1½	**cups milk**
4	**ounces Cheddar cheese, shredded (1 cup)**
4	**slices cooked bacon, halved**

1. Preheat the oven to hot (425°).
2. Put 1 slice of toast in each of 4 au gratin dishes. Arrange 2 turkey slices on the toast.
3. Melt the butter or margarine in a medium-size saucepan; stir in the flour, salt and pepper. Heat for 1 minute. Pour in the milk. Cook, stirring constantly, until the sauce thickens and bubbles; cook for 3 minutes longer. Add the cheese and stir until the cheese melts. Remove from the heat. Spoon ½ cup of the sauce over each of the dishes.
4. Bake in the preheated hot oven (425°) just until the sauce starts to bubble around the edges, for about 4 minutes. Top with the bacon.

Did You Know . . .

That about 71 million turkeys are consumed each year, mostly for Thanksgiving dinner.

🄢 🄚

Turkey and Broccoli with Curry Sauce

This elegant turkey recipe is a good choice for a holiday buffet.

Bake at 350° for 20 minutes.
Makes 6 servings.

- 3 **tablespoons butter or margarine**
- 1 **small onion, chopped (¼ cup)**
- 3 **tablespoons all-purpose flour**
- ½ **teaspoon salt**
- ⅛ **teaspoon pepper**
- 2 **teaspoons curry powder**
- 1 **cup Turkey Broth (recipe at right) OR: canned chicken broth**
- 1 **cup light cream**
- 1 **teaspoon tomato paste**
- 2 **packages (10 ounces each) frozen broccoli spears, thawed**
- 12 **slices cooked turkey (1 pound)**
- ¼ **cup sliced unblanched almonds**
  Chutney

1. Preheat the oven to moderate (350°).
2. Melt the butter or margarine in a medium-size saucepan. Sauté the onion just until softened. Stir in the flour, salt, pepper and curry powder. Heat for 1 minute. Stir in the turkey or chicken broth and the cream. Cook, stirring constantly, until the sauce thickens and bubbles, for about 5 minutes. Add the tomato paste and cook for 3 minutes longer.
3. Pour half the sauce into an 8-cup shallow baking dish. Arrange the broccoli along the sides; overlap the turkey slices in the middle. Pour the remaining sauce over the turkey. Sprinkle with the almonds.
4. Bake in the preheated moderate oven (350°) for 20 minutes, or until the sauce is bubbly. Serve with the chutney and additional almonds.

Turkey Broth

Makes 8 cups.

- **Carcass of 12- to 14-pound turkey**
- 2 **quarts water**
- 2 **stalks celery, broken in half**
- 1 **carrot, pared and quartered**
- 1 **onion, quartered**
- 6 **peppercorns**
- 1 **large bay leaf**
- 1 **tablespoon salt**

1. Combine all the ingredients in a large kettle. Bring to boiling over medium heat; lower the heat to simmer. Cook, uncovered, for 2 to 3 hours. Pour through a strainer.
2. When the bones are cool enough to handle, remove the meat and use in recipes. Chill the broth in the refrigerator. Remove all fat. Freeze the broth if not used within three days.

🄢 🄚

Turkey Soup with Egg Dumplings

Makes 6 servings.

- ½ **cup sifted all-purpose flour**
- ¼ **teaspoon salt**
- 2 **tablespoons butter or margarine, softened**
- 2 **eggs, beaten**
- 6 **cups Turkey Broth (recipe above) OR: canned chicken broth**
- 1 **teaspoon salt**
- ⅛ **teaspoon pepper**
- ½ **teaspoon leaf thyme, crumbled**
- ⅛ **teaspoon turmeric (optional)**
- 1 **medium-size onion, chopped (½ cup)**
- 1 **package (10 ounces) frozen corn**
- 1 **package (10 ounces) frozen baby limas**
- 1 **cup chopped cooked turkey**
  Chopped parsley (optional)

1. Sift the flour with the ¼ teaspoon salt. Stir into the butter or margarine in a medium-size mixing bowl. Add the eggs, beating until well blended.
2. Bring the turkey or chicken broth to boiling in a large saucepan or kettle with the 1 teaspoon salt,

the pepper, thyme and, if you wish, turmeric. Add the onion, corn, limas and turkey. Return the soup to boiling.

3. Drop the dumpling batter by teaspoonfuls into the boiling soup to make 12 dumplings. Lower the heat to keep the soup simmering. Cover and cook for 20 minutes, or until the dumplings are cooked through.

4. Serve in warm soup plates or bowls. Sprinkle with the chopped parsley, if you wish.

$ **◀◀◀**

Cream of Turkey Soup

Makes 6 servings.

1   teaspoon salt
⅛   teaspoon pepper
5   cups Turkey Broth (recipe, page 28)
       OR: canned chicken broth
1   large carrot, pared and chopped
       (½ cup)
½   cup chopped celery
2   medium-size leeks, washed well and
       chopped (1 cup)
1   small parsnip, pared and chopped
       (½ cup)
1   tablespoon dry sherry (optional)
½   cup light cream
1   cup chopped cooked turkey
2   tablespoons chopped parsley or
       watercress

1. Add the salt and the pepper to the turkey or chicken broth in a large saucepan; heat to boiling. Add the carrot, celery, leeks and parsnip. Lower the heat and simmer until the vegetables are barely tender, for about 20 minutes. Remove from the heat.

2. Pour the soup through a strainer into a bowl. Purée the vegetables in an electric blender. Return the purée and the broth to the pan. Add the sherry, if you wish, cream and turkey to the soup.

3. Heat just to simmering over medium heat. Do not boil. Add the parsley or watercress and serve.

$ **▒**

Turkey with Mushrooms and Snow Peas

Makes 4 servings.

2   tablespoons vegetable oil
1   medium-size onion, cut into 8 wedges
½   pound medium-size mushrooms,
       quartered
½   cup sliced water chestnuts
1   teaspoon salt
       Pinch pepper
¼   cup dry sherry
½   cup Turkey Broth (recipe, page 28) OR:
       canned chicken broth
2   teaspoons cornstarch
2   tablespoons soy sauce
1½ cups cooked turkey, cut into 2-inch
       strips
1   package (6 ounces) frozen snow peas,
       thawed and drained
       Hot cooked rice

1. Heat the oil in a large skillet over medium-high heat. Add the onion and stir-fry for about 2 minutes. Add the mushrooms, water chestnuts, salt, pepper and sherry; stir-fry for 1½ minutes.

2. Pour the turkey or chicken broth over the vegetables and bring to simmering. Combine the cornstarch and the soy sauce in a small cup; stir into the broth. Cook for 30 seconds, or until the sauce thickens and clears. Add the turkey and the snow peas. Stir gently for 1 minute, or until heated through. Serve over the hot cooked rice.

Did You Know . . .

That turkey was eaten by American astronauts at the first Thanksgiving dinner on the moon, in 1969.

Thanksgiving Decorations To Use All Through The Season

SUNSHINE POTPOURRI

Easy: Achievable by anyone.
Materials: 2 cups dried thyme leaves; ½ cup each dried white flower petals (rose, daisy, cosmos, clematis, statice) and dried yellow flower petals (rose, marigold, acacia, freesia, goldenrod, poppy, nasturtium); ⅓ cup tiny flower heads or florets (Queen Anne's lace, yarrow, baby's breath); ¼ cup chamomile flower heads; ¼ cup each dried lemon verbena leaves and dried mint leaves; ⅛ cup orris root chips or 1 teaspoon orris root powder.

Directions:
Mix all ingredients together and display in a container with a tight-fitting lid. To layer for display, don't mix the ingredients; place the ingredients in separate layers in a glass jar or bowl.

SPICE NUGGETS

Easy: Achievable by anyone.
Materials: 1″ and 1½″ Styrofoam® balls; craft glue; nonaerosol hair spray; powdered spices of your choice (spices that work well include ginger, cinnamon, allspice, nutmeg, cloves, *fines herbes,* orris root, sandalwood, frankincense, dried diced orange peel; for a kitchen theme use ground thyme, sage, oregano, basil, parsley).

Directions:
1. Coat each ball in a mixture of equal parts craft glue and water. Allow the excess to drain for one minute.
2. Sprinkle each ball with powdered spice to coat evenly. Dry for two hours and spray with nonaerosol hair spray to prevent flaking.
Optional: Decorate each spice ball with a sprig of artificial greenery or berries. Or attach tiny bows, cones or shiny beads as colorful accents.

POMANDERS

Easy: Achievable by anyone.
Materials: Oranges; lemons; limes; whole cloves; skewer; light tack hammer; orris root powder.

Directions:
1. Outline any design you like on the rind with a pencil.
Optional: Use a rind peeler to remove rind, following the design. You can also cover the entire fruit with cloves instead of removing the rind.
2. With a skewer, poke pilot holes along the design. Insert one clove into each hole using a light tack hammer.
3. Roll the finished fruit in orris root powder to help preserve it. The fruit will darken and shrink a bit as it dries.
Optional: When the pomanders have dried, display them in baskets, or tie them individually with ribbon, leave a ribbon loop at the top and hang them on your tree or from the edge of a shelf or mantel.

CINNAMON STICK CENTERPIECE & PLACE CARDS

Easy: Achievable by anyone.
Materials: Approximately twenty-seven 16″-long cinnamon sticks for centerpiece; twelve 4″-long cinnamon sticks for each place card; floral tape; tacky glue; assortment of dried flowers (larkspur, statice, lavender, rosebuds or blooms) and small pinecones; pale green (or your favorite color) 2″-wide and ¼″-wide velvet and 1″-wide and ¾″-wide grosgrain ribbon.

Directions:
1. Wrap 4 cinnamon sticks together with floral tape; don't cut the tape.
2. Add the rest of the sticks by holding a few sticks at a time against the original sticks and winding tape around the whole bundle. Try to keep a rather flat bottom so the centerpiece won't roll when it's placed on the table.
3. Insert flowers by dipping their ends in glue before placing them among the cinnamon sticks. Glue pinecones among the flowers.
4. Wrap velvet ribbon around the bundle and tie it in a bow. Add a

Sunshine Potpourri; Spice Nuggets; Pomanders; Cinnamon Stick Centerpiece and Place Cards

bow of grosgrain ribbon on top. Glue a few small flowers and cones to the knot portion of the bow.

5. Make place cards in same way, using the smaller cinnamon sticks and ¼"- and ¾"-wide ribbons.

FRESH ROSE WREATH

Easy: Achievable by anyone.

Materials: 20"-diameter grapevine wreath; branches of eucalyptus, rosemary and sage; 1 to 1½ dozen roses; floral wire; floral water picks.

Directions:

1. Insert the ends of eucalyptus branches to cover the grapevine wreath. Use floral wire to "tame" any errant stems by tying them to the grapevine.

2. Insert (add floral wire if necessary) small bunches of rosemary and sage branches, with more at the bottom of the wreath than at the top.

3. Fill each water pick with water, replace the rubber cap, place a short rose stem in it and poke the pick through the wreath.

Optional: Considering the cost of roses, you may want to substitute carnations for all or some of the roses. For eucalyptus, you can use any variety your florist has, although the familiar "silver dollar" eucalyptus *(Eucalyptus cinerea)* will give the wreath a more formal look.

Pine Cone & Dried Flower Wreath

PINE CONE & DRIED FLOWER WREATH

Easy: Achievable by anyone.
Materials: 18″- to 20″-diameter wire wreath base; 65 pine cones; 1 bunch white immortals; 6 to 7 flat protea; 6 to 8 curly protea; 1 bunch decorum; 1¾ yds 2″-wide brown velvet ribbon; white glue.

Directions:
Beginning with the pine cones, wire on everything except the dried flowers. See the photo for the general arrangement, or arrange as you please. Glue or wire on the dried flowers, if you wish. Tie a bow with the ribbon and wire it on. Attach a wire loop for hanging.

HYDRANGEA WREATH

Easy: Achievable by anyone.
Materials: 10″-diameter Styrofoam® ring; 10 fresh or dried hydrangea heads; 3 doz 3″ wooden picks; floral wire; floral tape; 5 yds ¼″-wide gold tinsel ribbon; 9″ beige pillar candle; 12″ hurricane globe.

Directions:
1. Insert the hydrangea heads into the Styrofoam® ring using wooden picks and short pieces of wire covered with floral tape.
2. Attach a gold bow with streamers and scatter small gold tinsel bows on picks.
3. Use as a wreath to hang, or as a centerpiece with the candle in the hurricane globe placed in the middle of the ring.

Hydrangea Wreath

USING NATURAL MATERIALS

EVERGREENS: Spray with acrylic floor wax to trap moisture inside the greens. *Note: Do not get wax on furniture or other wood surfaces.*

LEAFY GREENS: To add a glossy finish, spray or rub on "Green Glow," "Plant Shine" or "Leaf Polish."

FRUITS: Purchase as green and firm as possible, and refrigerate immediately. To prepare for use:
• **Whole Fruit** (except citrus)— Dip in a bowl of "Klear" and dry the fruit. Push a wire through the fruit (*see* FIG. I, 1, *page 35*) and suspend from a hanger or broom handle.
• **Half Fruit**—Dip the cut side into melted paraffin; let dry. Repeat the dipping process and dry.

NUTS AND CONES: Dip the nuts in "Klear" and let dry. Drill a small hole approximately ½ inch into the ends of the nuts or backs of the cones. Insert heavy floral wire, approximately the same diameter as the hole, and apply a drop of glue with a hot glue gun at the opening. Let dry thoroughly. Attach the wire end to a wreath or decoration.

Note: Nuts, cones and dried fruits can be reused if you keep them in airtight plastic bags containing moth flakes. Store in a cool, dry place.

Punch Bowl Centerpiece

PUNCH BOWL CENTERPIECE

Easy: Achievable by anyone.

Directions:

Surround an old porcelain or crystal punch bowl (ours is Chinese) with a variety of greens, fruits and pine cones all set on large, glossy leaves.

The bowl can be used for punch, salad, soup, mousse or anything else you want to serve at an open house.

Apples 'N Berries Centerpiece

APPLES 'N BERRIES CENTERPIECE

Easy: Achievable by anyone.
Materials: Lady apples; cranberries; boxwood; "popcorn tree" berries; No. 22 or 24 gauge floral wire; floral picks; silver basket.

Directions:
1. To prepare fruit for decorations, medium-size fruit (about the size of an apple) should be wired to a floral pick. Cut two 5"-long pieces of No. 22 or 24 gauge wire. Insert one wire through the apple near the bottom end (*see* FIG. I, 1). At the same level, insert the second wire at right angles to the first. Twist the wires around a floral pick; don't puncture the fruit with the pick.
2. Smaller fruit (such as a crab apples) need to be attached to a floral pick with only one wire.
3. Very small fruit (such as cranberries) need a wire stem. At one end of a piece of green floral wire, bend a U-shaped "shepherd's crook." Push its straight end through a cranberry so the "crook" goes into the berry top.

4. To make a string of berries, wire the first berry (*see Step 3*), push the wire through the rest of the berries and twist the wire against the last berry to serve as a knot.

FIG. I, 1
TO WIRE FRUIT

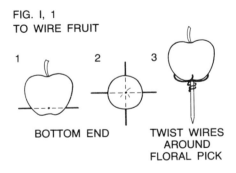

Food Gifts To Make Right Now

If you get a head start on those preserves, liqueurs and fruitcakes, you'll be doing double duty. They all improve with a bit of "aging," and you'll have more time for all the other Christmas preparations that loom ahead.

Cranberry Orange Liqueur

Start this delicious ruby-red cordial a few weeks before you plan to give it as a gift.

Makes about 1¼ quarts.

    1   package (12 ounces) cranberries
    1   orange
    1   bottle (750 ml) vodka
    1½ cups sugar
    ¾   cup water

1. Chop the cranberries coarsely. Pare the orange with a vegetable parer, using only the thin orange part, no white.
2. Combine the cranberries, orange parings and vodka in a glass or plastic 1-gallon container. Cover and let steep at room temperature for 3 to 4 weeks.
3. Strain into a clean container. Filter or siphon off the clear liquid if the mixture is cloudy.
4. Combine the sugar and the water in a medium-size saucepan. Bring to boiling over medium heat and boil for 1 minute; cool.
5. Stir the sugar syrup into the cranberry-orange liquid; taste. If you want a sweeter liqueur, prepare additional sugar syrup.

Plum Conserve

The luscious flavor of tree-ripe plums lasts all winter long in this rich preserve.

Makes four ½-pint jars.

    2   pounds fresh plums, halved, pitted and
          sliced (about 5 cups)
    2   cups sugar
    2   eating oranges, finely chopped with
          peel
    2   lemons, finely chopped with peel
    1   cup raisins
    ½   cup slivered almonds

1. Combine the plums and the sugar in a heavy Dutch oven. Mix in the chopped oranges and lemons and the raisins.
2. Simmer over medium-high heat. Cook, stirring often, for 15 minutes, or until the mixture thickens and becomes like jam. Remove from the heat. Stir in the almonds.
3. Fill four hot sterilized ½-pint jars to within ¼ inch of the top, following the General Directions for Canning and Hot Water Bath Process *(see page 39)*, and seal.
4. Process for 10 minutes in a hot water bath, following the General Directions.

Cranberry Orange Liqueur

Apricot Orange Chutney

Made from dried apricots, a whole orange, candied ginger and golden raisins, this chutney is delicious both in sandwiches and as a condiment.

Makes 3 pints.

1   **pound dried apricots**
1   **large onion (about ½ pound), peeled and cut into eighths**
1   **navel orange, washed, cut into eighths and trimmed**
2   **cloves garlic, peeled**
5   **slices candied ginger**
1½ **to 1¾ cups firmly packed light brown sugar**
2½ **cups cider vinegar**
½   **cup golden raisins**
1   **tablespoon salt**
1   **teaspoon crushed red pepper flakes**
1   **three-inch cinnamon stick**

1. Place the dried apricots in the container of a food processor fitted with the metal blade. Cover and process with on and off bursts until the apricots are minced. Transfer the apricots to a large, heavy saucepan.
2. Process the onion, orange, garlic and candied ginger until minced; add to the apricots in the pan. Stir in the brown sugar, vinegar, raisins, salt, pepper and cinnamon stick.
3. Bring the mixture to boiling over medium heat. Lower the heat and simmer, stirring often to prevent burning, for 45 minutes to 1 hour, or until the mixture is thickened and clear. Towards the end of the cooking time the chutney must be stirred almost constantly to prevent burning.
4. Remove the cinnamon stick. Transfer the mixture to three hot, sterilized 1-pint jars. Seal immediately and store in the refrigerator. Or process, following the General Directions for Canning and Hot Water Bath Process *(see page 39)*.

Oriental Barbecue Sauce

A delicious marinade and basting sauce for grilled or broiled beef, chicken or fish. Marinate beef overnight, chicken about 1 hour and baste fish just before broiling.

Makes 2½ cups.

1   **cup soy sauce**
1   **cup water**
6   **tablespoons brown sugar**
¼   **cup grated, pared, fresh gingerroot**
4   **teaspoons Oriental sesame oil***
2   **teaspoons rice vinegar**
2   **teaspoons finely chopped garlic**
¼   **teaspoon crushed red pepper flakes**

Mix together all the ingredients in a large bowl. The sauce can be stored in the refrigerator in ½-pint jars for up to 6 weeks.

***Note:** Oriental sesame oil has more flavor than regular sesame oil. It can be found in the Oriental food section of your supermarket or in a specialty food store.*

Vanilla Pear Butter

Try this fresh-tasting sauce spooned over biscuits, muffins, pancakes or ice cream.

Makes 4 cups.

3½ **pounds firm, ripe Bartlett pears, peeled, cored and quartered**
½   **cup sugar**
¼   **cup lemon juice (2 lemons)**
½   **cup (1 stick) butter, cut into 8 pieces**
2½ **teaspoons vanilla**

1. Combine the pears, sugar and lemon juice in a large, heavy Dutch oven or casserole. Bring to boiling over medium heat. Cook, covered, for 15 minutes, or until the pears are very tender and mushy.
2. Drain the pears well over a small, heavy-bottomed saucepan, reserving the juices. Bring the juices to boiling. Cook over medium heat, stirring frequently, until reduced to ¼ cup. Be careful not to let the mixture burn.

3. Place the pears in the work bowl of a food processor or, working in batches, in the container of an electric blender. Process until well blended. Pour into a large bowl. Add the hot reduced liquid. Add the butter and stir until melted. Stir in the vanilla. The pear butter can be stored in jars in the refrigerator for up to 4 weeks.

Tarragon Pears

The perfect accompaniment to roast pork.

Makes six 1-pint jars.

1½ **cups granulated sugar**
1½ **cups firmly packed brown sugar**
1½ **cups cider vinegar**
1½ **cups water**
1½ **tablespoons leaf tarragon OR: 6 four-inch sprigs fresh tarragon**
8 **pounds firm, ripe pears**
8 **cups water**
1 **tablespoon salt**
1 **tablespoon cider vinegar**
6 **sprigs fresh tarragon (optional)**

1. Combine the granulated and brown sugars, the 1½ cups vinegar and water in a large kettle. Add the leaf or fresh tarragon, wrapped in several thicknesses of cheesecloth. Heat to boiling over medium heat, stirring until the sugar dissolves. Cover and simmer for 5 minutes. Turn off the heat and let stand while preparing the pears.
2. Cut the pears in half; pare, core and cut into thin slices. Place in a large bowl with the 8 cups water, the salt and the 1 tablespoon vinegar.
3. Sterilize six 1-pint jars and prepare a large, deep kettle for a water bath, following the General Directions for Canning and Hot Water Bath Process *(see right)*.
4. Reheat the syrup to boiling. Drain and add ⅓ of the pears; simmer for 5 minutes. Spoon the pears into two prepared jars. Add a sprig of fresh tarragon to each jar, if you wish. Repeat with the remaining pears, cooking in two parts to prevent overcooking. Add enough of the pear syrup to each jar to fill to within ½ inch of the top; seal the jars. Process in a hot water bath for 15 minutes, following the General Directions.

GENERAL DIRECTIONS FOR CANNING AND HOT WATER BATH PROCESS

Follow all the directions carefully and do not take any shortcuts.

1. Place the hot water bath canner on a surface burner. Add water to half-fill the canner (a tea kettle does this job easily), cover the canner and bring the water to boiling while preparing the jars and food.
2. Wash the jars in hot sudsy water. Rinse well and leave in hot water until ready to use.
3. Place new domed lids in a bowl and cover with boiling water. Keep in water until ready to use.
4. Follow individual recipe directions.
5. Remove the jars from the water, one at a time; place on paper toweling or a clean cloth. Pack and/or ladle the food into the jars, leaving the headroom specified in the individual recipe.
6. Wipe the tops and outside rims of the jars with a clean cloth. Place the domed lids on top and screw the metal rings on tightly, but do not use force.
7. Place the jars in the canner rack and lower into rapidly boiling water, adding additional boiling water to the kettle if the level of water is not 2 inches above the jars. Cover the kettle and return to a full boil.
8. Process, following the time given in the individual recipe and calculating from the time that the water comes to a second boil. ***Note:*** *For those who live at altitudes above sea level, when the recipe directions call for processing for 20 minutes or less, add 1 minute for each 1,000 feet; when processing for more than 20 minutes, add 2 minutes for each 1,000 feet.*
9. Remove the jars from the canner with tongs and place, at least 3 inches apart, on a wire rack or cloth-lined surface until cool, for about 12 hours.
10. Test all the jars, to be sure they are sealed, by tapping with a spoon. A clear ringing sound means a good seal. If the jars are not properly sealed, store in the refrigerator and plan to use within a month, or pour the contents of the jar into a bowl and process again from Step 5.
11. Remove the metal rings. Wipe the jars with a clean dampened cloth. Label, date and store the jars in a cool, dark, dry place.

Brandied Golden Fruitcakes

🔳 🔲
Brandied Golden Fruitcakes

A versatile recipe that gives you the choice of making the fruitcake into loaves, one-bite miniature cakes or a selection of each.

Bake at 300°: miniatures for 30 minutes, loaves for 55 minutes.
Makes 6 small loaves or 4 dozen miniature cakes.

1   **container (4 ounces) candied red cherries, halved**
1   **container (4 ounces) candied citron**
1   **cup golden raisins**
1   **package (8 ounces) pitted dates, chopped**
½   **cup brandy**
3   **cups sifted all-purpose flour**
2   **teaspoons baking powder**
1   **teaspoon ground allspice**
½   **teaspoon salt**
1   **cup (2 sticks) butter, softened**
1½ **cups firmly packed dark brown sugar**
3   **tablespoons molasses**
1   **teaspoon grated orange rind**
6   **eggs**
1   **cup coarsely chopped pecans**
    Brandy Glaze (recipe follows)
    Cherry halves and pecans for garnish

1. Combine the cherries, citron, raisins, chopped dates and brandy in a medium-size bowl. Let macerate for about 30 minutes.
2. Grease six 5 11/16 x 3¼ x 2-inch aluminum foil loaf pans, dust with flour and tap out the excess. Or, for the miniature cakes, arrange 48 (1 package) 2-inch midget aluminum foil baking cups on cookie sheets.
3. Preheat the oven to slow (300°). Sift together the flour, baking powder, allspice and salt onto wax paper.
4. Beat the butter and the sugar in a large bowl with an electric mixer at medium speed until well blended. Beat in the molasses and the orange rind. Beat in the eggs, one at a time, until the batter is light and fluffy.
5. Stir in the flour mixture gradually until smooth. Stir in the fruit mixture and the chopped pecans. Divide the batter equally among the loaf pans, or spoon the batter into the foil baking cups, filling ⅔ full.
6. Bake the cakes in the preheated slow oven (300°), 55 minutes for the loaves, 30 minutes for the miniatures, or until the centers spring back

when lightly pressed with a fingertip. Cool the loaves on wire racks for 10 minutes, remove from the pans and cool completely. For the miniatures, cool completely in the foil cups on wire racks.

7. Spoon the Brandy Glaze over the tops of the cakes; garnish with the cherry halves and pecans.

Brandy Glaze: Combine 2 cups sifted 10X (confectioners' powdered) sugar, 2 tablespoons orange juice and 2 teaspoons brandy in a small bowl; blend well. *Makes about ½ cup.*

🔳
Light Fruitcake Batter

Makes 8½ cups batter.

1½ **cups (3 sticks) butter or margarine, softened**
3   **cups sugar**
6   **eggs**
1½ **cups dairy sour cream**
¼   **cup lemon juice**
5½ **cups unsifted all-purpose flour**
1½ **teaspoons baking soda**
1   **teaspoon salt**
    Chopped candied or dried fruits or nuts (see individual recipes)
    Nonstick vegetable spray
    Spirits (see individual recipes)
    Honey Glaze (recipe, page 42)

1. Preheat the oven to slow (300°).
2. Beat the butter and sugar in a large bowl with an electric mixer at high speed until fluffy. Beat in the eggs, one at a time, until well blended.
3. Combine the dairy sour cream and the lemon juice in a small bowl until well blended. Sift the flour, baking soda and salt onto wax paper.
4. Turn mixer to low and add the dry ingredients alternately with the sour cream mixture, starting and ending with the dry ingredients.
5. Measure batter into medium-size bowls, following individual recipes. Stir in the spice and add candied and/or dried fruits and/or nuts, according to individual recipes. Spray molds liberally with nonstick vegetable spray. Spoon batter into molds that hold twice the volume of the batter. (For example, 2 cups batter in a 4-cup mold.) Continue until all the batter is used.
6. Arrange the molds on one shelf of the oven, separating as much as possible.

7. Bake in the preheated slow oven (300°) for 1 hour, 15 minutes, or until a wooden skewer inserted near the center comes out clean. Cool in the molds on wire racks for 15 minutes. Loosen the cakes around the edges of the molds and invert onto the wire racks. Cool completely.
8. Drizzle with spirits and brush with the Honey Glaze. Wrap each cake tightly in a plastic bag. Allow to mellow for at least 2 weeks at room temperature, or freeze for up to 1 year.

Honey Glaze: Combine 2 cups honey, ½ cup lemon juice and 2 teaspoons lemon rind in a small saucepan. Heat to boiling. Lower the temperature and simmer for 5 minutes. Brush on the fruitcakes while still warm. *Makes enough to coat up to 6 cakes.*

Dark Fruitcake Batter

Makes 9 cups batter.

1½ **cups (3 sticks) butter or margarine**
3 **cups firmly packed light brown sugar**
6 **eggs**
6 **cups unsifted all-purpose flour**
1 **tablespoon baking powder**
1 **teaspoon salt**
1 **cup dry sherry, apple juice or orange juice**
  Chopped candied or dried fruits or nuts (see individual recipes)
  Nonstick vegetable spray
  Spirits (see individual recipes)
  Dark Fruitcake Glaze (recipe follows)

1. Preheat the oven to slow (275°).
2. Beat the butter or margarine and the brown sugar at high speed in a large bowl with an electric mixer until light and fluffy. Beat in the eggs, one at a time, until well blended.
3. Sift together the flour, baking powder and salt onto wax paper.
4. Turn the mixer speed to low and add the sifted dry ingredients alternately with the sherry, apple juice or orange juice, beginning and ending with the dry ingredients.
5. Measure the batter into medium-size bowls, following the individual recipes. Stir in the spice and add the candied and/or dried fruits and/or nuts, according to the individual recipes. Spray molds liberally with nonstick vegetable spray.

Spoon the batter into molds that hold twice the volume of the batter. (For example, 2 cups batter in a 4-cup mold.) Continue until all the batter is used.
6. Arrange the molds on one shelf of the oven, separating as much as possible.
7. Bake in the preheated slow oven (275°) for 1½ hours, or until a wooden skewer inserted near the center comes out clean. Cool in the molds on wire racks for 15 minutes. Loosen the cakes around the edges of the molds and invert onto the wire racks. Cool completely.
8. Drizzle with spirits and brush with the Dark Fruitcake Glaze. Decorate as desired. Wrap each cake tightly in a plastic bag. Allow to mellow for at least 2 weeks at room temperature, or freeze for up to 1 year.

Dark Fruitcake Glaze: Combine 1 jar (2 pounds) strawberry jam and ½ cup brandy, sherry or apple juice in a small saucepan. Heat to boiling. Lower the temperature and simmer for 5 minutes. Brush on the fruitcakes while still warm. *Makes enough to coat up to 6 cakes.*

California Fruitcake

Bake at 300° for 1 hour, 15 minutes.
Makes one 6-cup cake.

3 **cups Light Fruitcake Batter (recipe, page 41)**
¾ **teaspoon ground nutmeg**
1½ **cups chopped dried apricots**
1½ **cups cashews**
¼ **cup apricot brandy**
  Honey Glaze (recipe, above left)

1. Preheat the oven to slow (300°).
2. Prepare the Light Fruitcake Batter with the nutmeg. Add the chopped apricots and the cashews.
3. Spray a 6-cup mold with nonstick vegetable spray; allow to dry completely. Spoon in the fruitcake batter.
4. Bake in the preheated slow oven (300°) for 1 hour, 15 minutes, or until a wooden skewer inserted near the center comes out clean. Cool completely.
5. Drizzle with the apricot brandy. Brush with the Honey Glaze and garnish as desired.

Old World Fruitcake

Bake at 275° for 1½ hours.
Makes one 7-cup cake.

3½ cups Dark Fruitcake Batter (recipe, page 42)
1 teaspoon ground cinnamon
2 cups chopped walnuts
1 cup dried currants
½ cup chopped pineapple
¼ cup Canadian whiskey
Dark Fruitcake Glaze (recipe, page 42)

1. Preheat the oven to slow (275°).
2. Prepare the Dark Fruitcake Batter with the cinnamon. Fold in the chopped walnuts, dried currants and chopped pineapple.
3. Spray a 7-cup mold with nonstick vegetable spray; allow to dry completely. Spoon in the fruitcake batter.
4. Bake in the preheated slow oven (275°) for 1½ hours, or until a wooden skewer inserted near the center comes out clean. Cool completely. Drizzle with the Canadian whiskey.
5. Brush with the Dark Fruitcake Glaze and garnish as desired.

Hawaiian Ring

Bake at 300° for 1 hour, 15 minutes.
Makes one 4-cup cake.

2 cups Light Fruitcake Batter (recipe, page 41)
½ teaspoon ground nutmeg
1 cup chopped candied pineapple
½ cup chopped walnuts
½ cup golden raisins
¼ cup brandy
Honey Glaze (recipe, page 42)

1. Preheat the oven to slow (300°).
2. Prepare the Light Fruitcake Batter with the ground nutmeg. Fold in the chopped pineapple and walnuts and the raisins.
3. Spray a 4-cup ring mold with nonstick vegetable spray; allow to dry completely. Spoon in the fruitcake batter.
4. Bake in the preheated slow oven (300°) for 1 hour, 15 minutes, or until a wooden skewer

inserted near the center comes out clean. Cool completely.
5. Drizzle with the brandy. Brush with the Honey Glaze and garnish as desired.

Southern Fruitcake

Bake at 275° for 1½ hours.
Makes one 4-cup cake.

2 cups Dark Fruitcake Batter (recipe, page 42)
¾ teaspoon ground cloves
¾ cup chopped dried apricots
¾ cup raisins
½ cup sliced almonds
¼ cup bourbon
Dark Fruitcake Glaze (recipe, page 42)

1. Preheat the oven to slow (275°).
2. Prepare the Dark Fruitcake Batter with the cloves. Fold in the chopped apricots and the raisins and sliced almonds.
3. Spray a 4-cup mold with nonstick vegetable spray; allow to dry completely. Spoon in the fruitcake batter.
4. Bake in the preheated slow oven (275°) for 1½ hours, or until a wooden skewer inserted near the center comes out clean. Cool completely.
5. Drizzle with the bourbon. Brush with the Dark Fruitcake Glaze and garnish with fruits and nuts as desired.

TO FREEZE FRUITCAKES

- Do not brush the cakes with glaze.
- Wrap the cakes in cheesecloth soaked in sherry or brandy.
- Then wrap the cakes in heavy-duty aluminum foil, freezer-weight plastic wrap or large freezer bags.
- Seal the wrap around the cakes.
- Label, date and freeze for up to 1 year. Thaw before glazing and decorating.

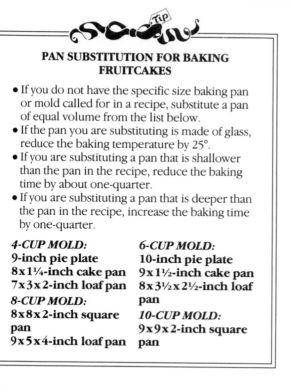

PAN SUBSTITUTION FOR BAKING FRUITCAKES

- If you do not have the specific size baking pan or mold called for in a recipe, substitute a pan of equal volume from the list below.
- If the pan you are substituting is made of glass, reduce the baking temperature by 25°.
- If you are substituting a pan that is shallower than the pan in the recipe, reduce the baking time by about one-quarter.
- If you are substituting a pan that is deeper than the pan in the recipe, increase the baking time by one-quarter.

4-CUP MOLD:
9-inch pie plate
8 x 1¼-inch cake pan
7 x 3 x 2-inch loaf pan

8-CUP MOLD:
8 x 8 x 2-inch square pan
9 x 5 x 4-inch loaf pan

6-CUP MOLD:
10-inch pie plate
9 x 1½-inch cake pan
8 x 3½ x 2½-inch loaf pan

10-CUP MOLD:
9 x 9 x 2-inch square pan

Yankee Fruitcake

Bake at 275° for 1½ hours.
Makes one 4-cup cake.

2   **cups Dark Fruitcake Batter (recipe, page 42)**
¾ **teaspoon ground allspice**
¾ **cup chopped candied mixed fruits**
¾ **cup chopped pecans**
½ **cup dried currants**
¼ **cup brandy**
    Dark Fruitcake Glaze (recipe, page 42)

1. Preheat the oven to slow (275°).
2. Prepare the Dark Fruitcake Batter with the allspice. Fold in the chopped candied mixed fruits and pecans and the currants.
3. Spray a 4-cup mold with nonstick vegetable spray; allow to dry completely. Spoon in the fruitcake batter.
4. Bake in the preheated slow oven (275°) for 1½ hours, or until a wooden skewer inserted near the center comes out clean. Cool completely.
5. Drizzle with the brandy. Brush with the Dark Fruitcake Glaze and garnish with fruits and nuts as desired.

Cherry Ring

Bake at 300° for 1 hour, 15 minutes.
Makes one 4-cup cake.

2   **cups Light Fruitcake Batter (recipe, page 41)**
½ **teaspoon ground ginger**
1   **cup chopped candied cherries**
1   **cup chopped cashew nuts**
¼ **cup cream sherry**
    Honey Glaze (recipe, page 42)

1. Preheat the oven to slow (300°).
2. Prepare the Light Fruitcake Batter with the ginger. Fold in the chopped candied cherries and cashew nuts.
3. Spray a 4-cup ring mold with nonstick vegetable spray; allow to dry completely. Spoon in the fruitcake batter.
4. Bake in the preheated slow oven (300°) for 1 hour, 15 minutes, or until a wooden skewer inserted near the center comes out clean. Cool completely.
5. Drizzle with the cream sherry. Brush with the Honey Glaze and garnish with fruits and nuts as desired.

Sunshine Fruitcake

Bake at 275° for 1½ hours.
Makes one 3-cup cake.

1½ **cups Dark Fruitcake Batter (recipe, page 42)**
½ **teaspoon ground cinnamon**
½ **cup chopped candied orange peel**
½ **cup dried currants**
½ **cup sliced almonds**
¼ **cup brandy**
    Dark Fruitcake Glaze (recipe, page 42)

1. Preheat the oven to slow (275°).
2. Prepare the Dark Fruitcake Batter with the cinnamon. Fold in the chopped orange peel and the currants and sliced almonds.
3. Spray a 3-cup mold with nonstick vegetable spray; allow to dry completely. Spoon in the fruitcake batter.
4. Bake in the preheated slow oven (275°) for 1½

hours, or until a wooden skewer inserted near the center comes out clean. Cool completely.

5. Drizzle with the brandy. Brush with the Dark Fruitcake Glaze and garnish as desired.

Irish Fruitcake

This classic dark fruitcake uses stout or dark ale for a richer, more mellow flavor.

Bake at 325° for 1½ hours.
Makes one 10-inch tube cake.

1 **jar (1 pound) candied mixed fruits**
1 **package (11 ounces) currants**
1½ **cups chopped walnuts**
2 **tablespoons grated orange rind**
4 **cups all-purpose flour**
2 **teaspoons pumpkin pie spice**
1 **teaspoon baking soda**
1 **teaspoon salt**
1 **cup (2 sticks) butter or margarine**
1⅓ **cups firmly packed brown sugar**
3 **eggs**
1 **cup stout or dark ale**
Brandy or sherry
Royal Rum Frosting (recipe follows)
Candied red and green cherries for garnish
Decorating gels (optional)

1. Combine the candied fruits, currants, chopped walnuts and orange rind in a very large bowl.
2. Sift together the flour, pumpkin pie spice, baking soda and salt onto wax paper. Sprinkle 1 cup of the flour mixture over the fruits and nuts and toss with a wooden spoon to coat evenly.
3. Preheat the oven to slow (325°).
4. Beat the butter or margarine, brown sugar and eggs in a large bowl with an electric mixer at high speed for 3 minutes, or until the mixture is fluffy.
5. Turn the mixer speed to low. Stir in the remaining flour mixture alternately with the stout or ale, beating after each addition just until the batter is smooth.
6. Pour the batter over the prepared fruits and nuts; fold together just until well blended. Spoon the batter into a greased and floured 10-inch angel food tube pan.
7. Bake in the preheated slow oven (325°) for 1½ hours, or until a long wooden skewer inserted near the center of the cake comes out clean.

Cool in the pan on a wire rack for 15 minutes. Loosen the cake around the edge and tube of the pan with a knife. Turn out onto the wire rack and cool completely. Sprinkle with brandy or sherry. Wrap in cheesecloth and store in a metal box with a tight-fitting lid for at least 2 weeks, so the cake can mellow.

8. Frost the top of the cake with the Royal Rum Frosting and garnish the top with the candied red and green cherries. Make designs in the center with decorating gels in tubes, if you wish.

Royal Rum Frosting: Beat ¼ cup (½ stick) butter or margarine and 2 cups 10X (confectioners' powdered) sugar until well blended in a small bowl with an electric mixer at medium speed. Beat in 2 tablespoons rum and 1 teaspoon vanilla until smooth and spreadable. *Makes enough to frost the top of a 10-inch tube cake.*

Note: This recipe can be baked in smaller containers and given as gifts. Spoon into four 4-cup molds and bake at 300° for 40 minutes, or until done.

Georgia Fruitcake

Bake at 300° for 1 hour, 15 minutes.
Makes one 3-cup cake.

1½ **cups Light Fruitcake Batter (recipe, page 41)**
½ **teaspoon pumpkin pie spice**
½ **cup chopped dried peaches**
½ **cup chopped candied citron**
½ **cup sliced almonds**
¼ **cup peach brandy**
Honey Glaze (recipe, page 42)

1. Preheat the oven to slow (300°).
2. Prepare the Light Fruitcake Batter with the pumpkin pie spice. Fold in the chopped peaches and citron and the sliced almonds.
3. Spray a 3-cup mold with nonstick vegetable spray; allow to dry completely. Spoon in the fruitcake batter.
4. Bake in the preheated slow oven (300°) for 1 hour, 15 minutes, or until a wooden skewer inserted near the center comes out clean. Cool completely.
5. Drizzle with the peach brandy. Brush with the Honey Glaze and garnish as desired.

Crafts To Start Right Now

Whether they're quick "boutique" items or more elaborate gifts, you'll be glad you planned ahead.

CROCHETED EDGING

Average: For those with some experience in crocheting.

Materials: J. & P. Coats Knit-Cro-Sheen Cotton Thread (175-yd ball): 11 yds will make 5″ of edging; steel crochet hook No. 7, OR ANY SIZE HOOK TO OBTAIN STITCH GAUGE BELOW; tapestry needle.

Gauge: Edging = 1½″ wide; one scallop = 2″.

Directions:

1. Square Edging *(for items with square corners):* Measure longest edge of item to be trimmed and multiply this number by 4. Using normal tension, work a chain 2″ longer than total measurements.

2. Foundation Chain: Note: *All rnds are worked from right side.*
First Side—Rnd 1: Dc in 8th ch from hook (beg ch-7 counts as 1 dc and ch-2 sp), * ch 2, sk next 2 ch, dc in next ch *; rep from * to * 3 times, with safety pin mark last dc made; rep from * to * in multiples of 6 dc, counting marked st as first dc of first multiple. Continue working as above until measurement is equal to length of First Side of item you are edging, or slightly shorter by less than one multiple of 6 dc (will stretch); *ch 5, dc in same ch as last dc—corner made; do not fasten off.* ***Second Side-Fourth Side:*** Continue to work remaining sides as follows: * Ch 2, sk next 2 ch, dc in next ch; rep from * until there are the same number of ch-2 sps as there are on First Side, and make ch 5, dc in same ch as last dc for each corner. On Fourth Side, work until there is *one ch-2 sp less* than on First Side, ch 2. Being careful not to twist work, dc in 3rd ch of beg ch-7—*joining dc made;* ch 5 for corner, sk next ch from joining—dc, sl st in next ch. Cut foundation chain 1½″ from last dc, undo extra ch sts to within 2 ch of last dc; pull thread to tighten last ch, then fasten thread-end in same ch where joining-dc was worked. ***Rnd 2:*** Ch 1 sc in same ch as joining, ** (ch 3, sc in next dc) 4 times, [* ch 1, in next dc work: dc, ch 4, dc; ch 1 sc in next dc, (ch 3, sc in next dc) 4 times]; rep from * to within next corner-sp, ch 2, in corner-sp work: dc, ch 5, dc; ch 2, sc in next dc **; rep from ** to ** around. Join last ch-2 with sl st to first sc. ***Rnd 3:*** Sl st in each of first 2 ch of next lp, sc over same lp, ** (ch 3, sc over next ch-3 lp) 3 times, [* ch 1, *over next ch-4 lp work: (dc, ch 1) 5 times and dc—scallop made;* ch 1, sc over next ch-3 lp, (ch 3, sc over next ch-3 lp) 3 times]; rep from * to within next corner-lp, ch 2, *over next ch-5 lp work: (dc, ch 1) 7 times and dc—corner scallop made;* ch 2, sc over next ch-3 lp **; rep from ** to ** around. Join last ch-2 with sl st to first sc. ***Rnd 4:*** Sl st in each of first 2 ch of next lp, sc over same lp, (ch 1, sc over next ch-3 lp) twice, [* ch 1, dc in first dc of scallop, (ch 2, dc in next dc) 5 times, (ch 1, sc over next ch-3 lp) 3 times]; rep from * across side, ch 1, dc in first dc of corner scallop, (ch 2, dc in next dc) 7 times, (ch 1, sc over next ch-3 lp) 3 times **; rep from * to ** around, end with dc in last dc of last corner scallop, ch 1. Join with sl st to first sc. ***Rnd 5: Note:*** *To work shell, ch 2, dc in same st as last sl st.* Sl st in each of next ch and next sc, [* work shell, sk next sc, sl st in first dc of scallop, (work shell, sl st in next dc) 5 times, work shell, sk next sc, sl st in next sc]; rep from * across side, work shell, sk next sc, sl st in first dc of corner scallop, (work shell, sl st in next dc) 7 times, work shell, sk next sc, sl st in next sc **; rep from * to ** around, work shell. Join last shell with sl st to first sl st. Fasten off.

3. Shell Border On Foundation Chain Edge: With right side facing you, attach thread with sl st to any corner-ch and working in single lp of each ch as follows: [* work shell, sk next 2 ch, sl st in next ch at base of dc; rep from *] around. Join last shell with sl st to starting ch. Fasten off.

4. Straight Edging *(for items without corners):* Measure edge of item to be trimmed. Using normal tension, work a chain 2″ longer than measurement.

5. Foundation Chain—Row 1 *(right side):* Dc in 8th ch from hook, with safety pin, mark dc just made, * ch 2, sk next 2 ch, dc in next ch; rep from * across in multiples of 6 dc, counting marked st as first dc of first multiple. Continue working as above, until measurement is equal to length of edge of item or is slightly

46

Crocheted Edging

shorter by less than one multiple of 6 dc (will stretch). Cut foundation chain 1½" from last dc; undo extra ch sts to within 2 ch of last dc; pull thread-end to tighten last ch. **Row 2:** Ch 1, turn, sc in first dc, (ch 3, sc in next dc) twice; rep from [bracket to bracket] of Rnd 2 Square Edging across, end with second dc from end, ch 3, sc in next dc, ch 3, sk next 2 ch, sc in next ch. **Row 3:** Ch 3, turn, sc over first ch-3 lp, ch 3, sc over next ch-3 lp; rep from [to] of Rnd 3 Square Edging across, end with sc over last ch-3 lp, ch 1, hdc in last sc. **Row 4:** Ch 1, turn, sc in first hdc, ch 1 sc over next ch-3 lp; rep from [to] of Rnd 4 Square Edging across, end with sc over last ch-3 lp, ch 1, sc in 2nd ch at end. **Row 5:** Turn, sl st in first sc; rep from [to] of Rnd 5 Square Edging across, ch 1. Fasten off.

6. Shell Border On Foundation Chain Edge: With right side of work facing you, attach thread with sl st in first ch and working in single lp of each ch rep from [to] of Shell Border Square Edging across, end with ch 1. Fasten off.

7. Attaching Edging: Steam press on wrong side, stretching edge if necessary. Hand-baste or machine-sew to purchased items.
Optional: Weave ribbon through ch-3 sps of Row (Rnd) 2.

LOG CABIN AFGHAN
(about 60" x 80")

Average: For those with some experience in crocheting.
Materials: Any 4-ply worsted weight yarn: 14 oz Dark Gold (A), 21 oz Brown (B), 18 oz Red (C), 25 oz Light Blue (D), 7 oz each Rust (E) and Green (F); 11 oz each Avocado Green (G) and Peach (H); crochet hook size H, OR ANY SIZE HOOK TO OBTAIN STITCH GAUGE BELOW; yarn needle.
Gauge: Each square should be about 9¾" square.

Directions:
1. Make 48 motifs all exactly the same. Each motif has 7 sections (*see* FIG. I, 2A): 1 is worked in rnds, 2 through 7 are worked in rows. The finishing border on each motif is worked completely around the square. Follow FIG. I, 2A when working each section for proper placement. Crochet over ends of yarn wherever possible to conceal ends and save weaving in these ends later.
2. Motif — Section 1 (Center Square): With color A, ch 2. **Rnd 1** *(right side):* Make 8 sc in 2nd ch from hook, join with sl st in first sc, ch 1, turn. **Rnd 2:** Sc in first sc; ** *yo hook, insert hook in next sc, yo and draw up a lp, yo and draw through one lp on hook, (yo and draw through 2 lps on hook) twice — long-dc made;* keeping long-dc to back of work, sc in *same* sc where the long-dc was made to form a bobble on reverse side; make a long-dc in *same* place where sc was just made; keeping long-dc in back of work, sc in *next* sc to form next bobble; rep from ** 2 times more; work a long-dc, sc and long-dc all in last sc, join with sl st in first sc — 8 bobbles formed; ch 1, *turn.* **Rnd 3:** Sc in first long-dc; *make 3 hdc in next sc — corner made;* (sc in next 3 sts, make corner in next st) 3 times; sc in next 2 sts, join with sl st in first sc. Fasten off, leaving a 2" end which will be covered over by next row (first row of section 2). **Note:** *Hereafter, always*

leave a 2" end when fastening off.
3. Section 2 — Row 1: With right side of section 1 facing, attach B by making a lp on hook and inserting hook in center hdc of last corner made, yarn over and draw up a lp, yarn over and draw through both lps on hook to complete the first sc. **Note:** *Whenever a new color is attached, always work in same way and complete the first sc.* Sc in each of next 5 sts, 3 sc in center hdc of next corner, sc in next 6 sts (last sc is in center hdc of a corner group). Fasten off. *Turn.* (After the work is turned, the last stitch made is in upper right corner.) **Row 2:** Attach C to first sc as before, sc in each of next 6 sc (7 sc on first side), 3 sc in corner sc, 1 sc in each of next 7 sc. Fasten off. *Turn.* (Last stitch is again in upper right corner.) **Row 3:** Attach B to first sc as before, work as for last row having 8 sc on each side and 3 sc in the corner. Fasten off. *Turn.* **Row 4:** Attach C to first sc and work as for Row 2 having 9 sc on each side and 3 sc in the corner. Fasten off. *Turn.* **Row 5:** Attach B to first sc and work as for Row 2 having 10 sc on each side and 3 sc in the corner. Fasten off. Section 2 is now completed.
4. Section 3 — Row 1: With right side of square facing and holding work so that last st made on section 2 is at upper right corner, attach D to *end* of row just made and complete first sc as before, sc in end of next 4 rows, sk worked corner st of center square, sc in next 5 sts, make 3 sc in corner st, sc in next 5 sts, sk worked corner st on center square, sc in *end* of next 5 rows. There are 10 sc on each side edge and 3 sc in the corner. Fasten off. *Turn.* (Last st made is now at upper right corner.) **Row 2:** Attach E to first sc, sc in next 10 sc, make 3 sc in corner, sc in next 11 sc. Fasten off. *Turn* as before. **Row 3:** Attach D and work as for Row 2 of this section having 12 sc on each side and 3 sc in the corner. Fasten off. *Turn.* **Row 4:** Attach E to first sc. Work as for Row 2 of this section having 13 sc on each side and 3 sc in the corner. Fasten off. *Turn.* **Row 5:**

Log Cabin Afghan

Attach D to first sc. Work as for Row 2 of this section having 14 sc on each side and 3 sc in corner. Fasten off. Section 3 is completed.

5. Section 4—Row 1 *(right side):* Attach F to *end* of row just completed as before, sc in *end* of next 4 rows, sc in next 11 sc (there are 16 sc on this side), 3 sc in corner st, sc in next 11 sc, sc in *end* of next 5 rows. Fasten off. *Turn* as before. **Row 2** *(wrong side):* Attach G to first sc, * long-dc in next sc to make a bobble on right side of work, sc in next sc; rep from * to corner st; in corner st make long-dc, sc and long-dc, sc in next sc, ** long-dc in next sc, sc in next sc; rep from ** to end of row. Fasten off. *Turn.* There are 8 bobbles on first and second side with a bobble, sc and bobble in corner st *or* a

total of 9 bobbles with sc in between on each side. **Row 3** *(right side):* Attach F to first sc and complete sc as before; sc in each long-dc and sc until there are 18 sc on first side, make 3 sc in corner st, work 18 scs in sts on next side. Fasten off. *Turn.* **Row 4** *(wrong side):* Rep row 2 of this section. Fasten off. *Turn.* There are 9 bobbles on first and second side with bobble, sc and bobble in corner st *or* a total of 10 bobbles with sc in between on each side. **Row 5** *(right side):* Attach F to first sc, work as for Row 3 of this section, having 20 sc on first side, 3 sc in corner st and 20 sc on second side. Fasten off. Section 4 is completed.

6. Section 5: Work as for Rows 1-5 of section 4 repeating color sequence as follows: **Row 1** *(right side):* With H

having 20 sc on first side, 3 sc in corner st and 20 sc on second side. **Row 2** *(wrong side):* With A having 11 bobbles on each side of square. **Row 3** *(right side):* With H having 22 sc on each side and 3 sc in corner sc. **Row 4** *(wrong side):* With A having 12 bobbles on each side of square. **Row 5** *(right side):* With H having 24 sc on each side and 3 sc in corner st. Fasten off. Mark first st of Row 5. Section 5 is completed.

7. Section 6—Row 1: With wrong side of motif facing, hold work so that marked st is at upper right corner. Attach C in end of marked st, remove marker, sc in end of next 4 rows, sc in next 21 sc (26 sc on first side), make 3 sc in corner st, sc in next 21 sc, sc in end of next 5 rows (26 sc on second side), ch 1, *turn.*

FIG. I, 2A LOG CABIN AFGHAN MOTIF SECTIONS

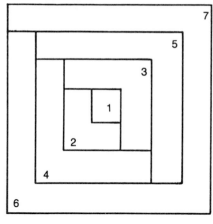

FIG. I, 2B LOG CABIN AFGHAN UPPER EDGE STRIP

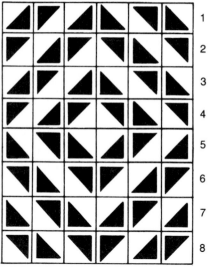

Row 2 *(right side):* Sc in first sc and in each sc across to next corner sc (27 sc on first side); make 3 sc in corner st, make 27 sc on second side. Fasten off. *Turn.* **Row 3** *(wrong side):* Attach B in first sc, * ch 1, sk next sc, sc in next sc; rep from * to within one st of corner st, ch 1, sk next st, make 3 sc in corner st; ** ch 1, sk next sc, sc in next sc; rep from ** across row (14 sc with ch-1 between on each side and 3 sc in corner st). Fasten off. *Turn.* **Row 4** *(right side):* Attach C in first sc; * *yo hook, insert hook from front to back in sc on row below ch-1 and draw up a lp to height of row in work, yo and draw through 3 lps on hook— long-hdc made;* sc in next sc. Rep from * to corner sc, 3 sc in corner sc, sc in next sc, ** make long-hdc in sc below ch-1, sc in next sc; rep from ** to end of row, ch 1, *turn.* **Row 5** *(wrong side):* Sc in first st and in each st across to corner st (30 sc on first side); make 3 sc in corner st, work 30 sc on second side. Fasten off. Section 6 is completed.

8. Section 7—Row 1: With wrong side facing, attach D to end of row just completed as before, sc in end of next 4 rows, sc in each of next 25 sts (30 sc on first side), make 3 sc in corner st, sc in each of next 25 sc, sc in end of next 5 rows (30 sc on second side), ch 1, *turn.* **Row 2** *(right side):* Work as for row 2 of section 6 having 31 sc on each side and 3 sc in corner st. Fasten off. *Turn.* **Row 3** *(wrong side):* With E, work as for Row 3 of section 6 having 16 sc on each side with ch-1 between and 3 sc in corner st. Fasten off. *Turn.* **Row 4** *(right side):* With D, work as for Row 4 of section 6 having 33 sts on each side and 3 sc in corner st, ch 1, *turn.* **Row 5** *(wrong side):* Work as for row 5 of section 6 having 34 sc on each side with 3 sc in corner st. Fasten off. Section 7 is completed.

9. Border: With right side of motif facing, attach B in the corner *(C st)* of section 6, thus making first sc, make

hdc and sc in same place, sc in next 31 sc, make 1 sc in end of next 4 rows; work sc, hdc and sc in end of next row for second corner; make 1 sc in each of next 35 sc (make sure not to sk first st); make sc, hdc and sc in next st for 3rd corner; make 1 sc in each of next 35 sc; sc, hdc and sc in end of row for 4th corner; make sc and sc in end of next 4 rows, 1 sc in each of next 31 sc. Join with sl st in first sc. Fasten off. There are 35 sc on all 4 sides with sc, hdc and sc in each corner.

10. Blocking: Pin each motif to measurement; dampen and leave to dry. Do not press.

11. Assembling Motifs: Following FIG. I, 2B for joining, pin motifs together to form 8 strips of 6 motifs per strip. Identify each strip with a numbered tag, marking upper edge of each strip. With color B and yarn needle, sew strips of motifs together from right side by sewing through *back* loops only of each corresponding sc along side edges of motifs, keeping seams as flexible as crocheted motifs. Be sure corners of motifs are matched. After all strips are joined, pin strips together in numerical sequence, keeping upper edge of each strip in same direction; sew strips together as before.

12. Outer Border—Rnd 1: With right side of afghan facing, attach B to center sc of any outer corner, this counts as first sc, make 2 more sc in same corner st, * sc in each sc to within 1 sc of the seam joining the next square; *insert hook in the sc, yo and draw lp through, insert hook in seam, yo and draw lp through, there are 3 lps on hook, yo and draw through all 3 lps on hook—dec made;* rep from * across side, ending with 3 sc in next outer corner. Work in same manner around outer edge of the other 3 sides of afghan as established. Join with sl st in first sc. Ch 1, *do not turn.* **Rnd 2:** Sc in joining and in each sc around, being sure to make 3 sc in each corner st, join with sl st in first sc. Fasten off.

PRETTY 'N PINK PATCHWORK THROW
(about 60" square)

Average: For those with some experience in quilting.

Materials: 2 yds each pink floral print and pink solid 45"-wide preshrunk cotton or blend fabric; 1⅞ yd preshrunk muslin or other fabric for backing; 62" square cotton/poly batting; beige and pink thread; 1 skein light blue embroidery floss; embroidery needle; yardstick; fabric marking pencil; basting thread; pins; sewing machine.

Directions *(¼" seams allowed):*
1. Double the fabric lengthwise, pin carefully and mark. This lets you mark and cut double the amount instead of cutting each piece individually. On the doubled solid fabric and just inside the selvage, mark one border strip 2½" x 60½" and one border strip 2½" x 55½". On the remaining doubled fabric, mark a grid of 4½" squares. Mark one more square at the end of the border strips. You will need 49 solid pink squares. On the doubled floral fabric just inside the selvage, mark one binding strip 1½" x 61½" and one binding strip 1½" x 60½". Mark and cut 4½" squares as you did the solid squares. You will need 49 floral pink squares.
2. Seam the 4½" squares into rows of 14. Alternate solid and floral squares in each row. Start the first row with a solid square and end the row with a floral square. Start the second row with a floral square. Continue alternating for each row. Then sew the 14 rows together to form the checkerboard patchwork top. Sew the short solid borders to opposite sides and then the long solid borders to the top and bottom.
3. Cut the 1⅞" yardage for backing into two 65" sections and seam two selvage edges together with a ½" seam. Press the seam open and spread the backing on the floor wrong side up. Center the cotton/poly batting on the backing. Then cen-

Pretty 'N Pink Patchwork Throw;
Double Wedding Ring Pillow (page 52)

ter the checkerboard, right side up, on the batting and smooth all three layers flat. Secure with basting stitches using white thread. Stitch by hand or machine through all thicknesses diagonally across the squares forming the checkerboard. Use pink thread across the solid pink squares and beige thread across the floral pink squares. Trim the edges even with the quilt top.
4. Fold the floral binding strips in half lengthwise and press. Pin the short binding strips to opposite sides of the quilt, right sides together and raw edges even. Sew in place with a ⅜" seam.
5. Turn the binding to the wrong side of the quilt, turn under a ⅜" hem and slipstitch in place. Repeat at the top and bottom, turning in ½" at each end.
6. Split the embroidery floss into two strands and do the feather stitch *(see Stitch Guide, page 270)* ¼" from the edge of the squares on the border.

DOUBLE WEDDING RING PILLOW
(about 18″ square)

Average: For those with some experience in quilting.

Materials: ½ yd pink floral print and 1 yd pink solid 45″-wide preshrunk cotton or blend fabric; 1 skein light blue embroidery floss; embroidery needle; 20″ square muslin; 20″ square cotton/poly batt; thread to blend with fabrics; about 4 oz polyester fiberfill for stuffing; cardboard for pattern; pencil; scissors; pins; sewing machine.

Directions:

1. Enlarge the pattern pieces in FIG. I, 3A, following the directions on page 271. Add a ¼″ seam allowance to the patterns and cut from cardboard. Double the solid fabric and cut four half rings (A) and four end pieces (B). From the floral fabric cut one D, then double the remaining floral fabric and cut two C's. You should have 8 A's, 8 B's, 4 C's and 1 D.
2. Sew the C's to the inside curve of the A's and a B to each end of the A's. This will make the four side sections. Now sew the completed side sections to D (center). *(See FIG. I, 3B.)*
3. Lay the square of muslin on a flat surface. Cover with the cotton/poly batting and center the pieced ring on top. Secure the layers with long sewing pins and machine quilt ¼″ from the seam edge on the floral pink sections C and D. Then form an "X" across the D section from corner to corner.
4. Separate the embroidery floss into two strands and do the feather stitch *(see Stitch Guide, page 270)* on solid pink ¼″ from the seam edges.
5. Machine stitch around the raw edges through all layers and cut away the excess batting and muslin. Center the completed ring right side down on a 20″ solid pink square and use the quilted ring as a pattern to cut out the back. Pin around the outside edges and machine stitch a ¼″ seam. Leave a 6″ opening to turn and stuff the pillow.
6. Clip the curves, turn, stuff and close the opening with a blind stitch.

FIG. I, 3A

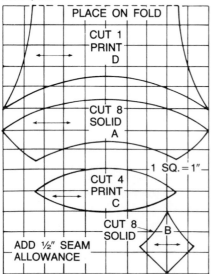

FIG. I, 3B
PIECING/SEWING

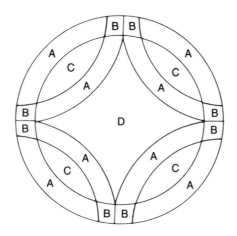

LOOK OF LACE TABLECLOTH
(about 45″ in diameter)

Challenging: Requires more experience in crocheting.

Materials: Clark's Big Ball No. 30 (350-yd ball): 10 balls Ecru; steel crochet hook No. 13, OR ANY SIZE HOOK TO OBTAIN STITCH GAUGE BELOW.

Gauge: Rnds 1 through 10 = 3¼″; motif = 3″.

Directions:

1. Motif Circle 1: Make 1. **Motif 1:** Make 1. Ch 10, join with sl st to form a ring. **Rnd 1:** Ch 3 for first dc, work 25 dc in ring, join with sl st to top of starting ch—26 dc counting starting ch. **Rnd 2:** * Ch 5, skip 1 dc, sl st in next dc. Repeat from * around, join—13 loops. **Rnd 3:** Sl st to center of next ch-loop, * ch 3, 3 dc in same loop, sl st in center ch of next loop. Repeat from * around, join to bottom of first ch-3. **Rnd 4:** Sl st to top of ch-3 of last rnd, ch 3 for first dc, 3 dc in same space, * ch 2, 4 dc in top of ch-3 of next group. Repeat from * around, end ch 2, join. **Rnd 5:** Ch 3 for first dc, dc in each of next 3 dc, 3 dc in ch-2 space, * dc in each of next 4 dc, 2 dc in next ch-2 space. Repeat from * to last ch-2 space, work 3 dc in last ch-space, join—80 dc. **Rnd 6:** Ch 3 for first dc, retaining last loop of each dc on hook, dc in each of next 3 sts, yo and through all loops on hook, * ch 5, retaining last loop of each dc on hook, work dc in each of next 4 sts, yo and through all loops on hook (dc cluster made). Repeat from * around, end ch 5, join to top of first cluster—20 clusters. **Rnd 7:** Sl st in next ch-loop, * in ch-loop work (sc, hdc, 2 dc, ch 4, sl st in 4th ch from hook, 2 dc, hdc, sc) *; repeat from * to * 3 times more (mark these 4 loops as inner joining loops where motif will be joined to center of tablecloth); ** in next loop work (sc, hdc, 2 dc, ch 16, sl st in 16th ch from hook, 2 dc, hdc, sc) **;

Look of Lace Tablecloth

*** [in next loop work (sc, hdc, 2 dc, ch 4, sl st in 4th ch from hook, 2 dc, hdc, sc)] 3 times (mark these 3 loops for side joinings; at these loops motifs will be joined together) ***; repeat from ** to ** once; **** in next loop work (sc, hdc, dc, ch 18, sl st in 18th ch from hook, 3 dc, hdc, sc) ****; repeat from * to * until there are 4 loops (mark these loops for outer joining loops); repeat from **** to **** once; repeat ** to ** once; repeat from *** to *** once; repeat ** to ** once—20 filled loops. Join to first sc and fasten off. **Motif 2:** Make 15. Make same as Motif 1 through Rnd 6. **Rnd 7 (Joining Rnd):** Work same as Motif 1 to **, in next loop work•(sc, hdc, 2 dc, ch 8, sl st in corresponding loop on adjoining motif, ch 8, sl st in first ch of group, 2 dc, hdc, sc)•; work side joinings by working (sc, hdc, 2 dc, ch 2, sl st in corresponding loop on adjoining motif, ch 2, 2 dc, hdc, sc) in each of next 3 sts; repeat from•to•to join next loop; join last loop by working sc, hdc, dc, ch 9, sl st in corresponding loop on adjoining motif, ch 9, 3 dc, hdc, sc; complete same as Motif 1. At end of last motif there will be 16 joined motifs. **Motif 3:** Make 1. Work same as Motif 2 working joinings on both sides—17 motifs joined into a circle.

2. Motif Circle 2: Make 1. Make same as Motif Circle 1 for a total of 33 motifs. Set both motif circles aside.

3. Tablecloth: Beginning at center, ch 10, join with sl st to form a ring. **Rnd 1:** Ch 3 for first dc, work 22 dc in ring. Join with sl st to top of starting ch—23 dc counting starting ch. **Rnd 2:** Ch 3 for first dc, dc in same st as starting ch, 2 dc in each dc around, join with sl st to top of starting ch—46 dc. **Rnd 3:** Ch 3 for first dc, dc in next dc, work 67 dc evenly spaced around—68 dc counting starting ch. Join. **Rnd 4:** * Ch 5, skip 3 dc, sl st in next dc. Repeat from * around, join to first sl st—17 loops. **Rnd 5:** Sl st to center of next loop, * ch 3, work 3 dc in same loop, sl st in center ch of next loop. Repeat from * around, end by joining with sl st to base of first ch-3. **Rnd 6:** Sl st to top of starting ch of previous rnd, ch 3 for first dc, work 3 dc in same space, * ch 2, 4 dc in top of ch-3 of next group. Repeat from * around, end ch 2, join. **Rnd 7:** Ch 3 for first dc, dc in each of next 3 dc, 4 dc in ch-2 space, * dc in each of next 4 dc, 3 dc in ch-2 space. Repeat from * around, join—120 dc. **Rnd 8:** Ch 4 for first trc, retaining last loop of each trc on hook, work trc in each of next 4 sts, yo and through all loops on hook, * ch 6, retaining last loop of each trc on hook, trc in each of next 5 sts, yo and through all loops on hook (trc

cluster made). Repeat from * around, end ch 6, join to top of first cluster—24 trc clusters. **Rnd 9:** * In next ch-6 loop work sc, hdc, 3 dc, hdc, sc. Repeat from * around, join to first sc—24 groups. **Rnd 10:** Sl st to first hdc of next group, sc in first hdc, ch 5, skip 3 dc, sc in next hdc, * ch 5, sc in center dc of next group, ch 5, sc in first hdc of next group, ch 5, skip 3 dc, sc in next hdc. Repeat from * around as established, end ch 5, join to first sc—36 ch-loops. **Rnd 11:** Sl st in 2 ch, ch 3 for first dc, work 2 dc in same loop, * ch 3, 3 dc in next loop. Repeat from * around, end ch 3, join—36 3-dc groups with ch-3 between each. **Rnd 12:** Sl st to next ch-3 loop, ch 3 for first dc, 2 dc in same space, * ch 3, 3 dc in next ch-loop. Repeat from * around, end ch 3, join. **Rnd 13:** Repeat Rnd 12. **Rnd 14:** Sl st to center of ch-3 loop, ch 4 for first dc and ch 1, * (dc in first dc of next group, ch 1, skip 1 dc, dc in next dc, ch 1, dc in ch-loop, ch 1) 2 times, dc in center dc of next 3-dc group, ch 1, dc in ch-loop, ch 1. Repeat from * around as established, join to 3rd ch of starting ch—96 ch-1 spaces. **Rnd 15:** Sl st in ch-1 space, ch 4 for first dc and ch 1, * dc in next ch-1 space, ch 1. Repeat from * around, join to 3rd ch of starting ch. **Rnd 16:** Sl st in ch-space, ch 5 for first dc and ch 2, * dc in next ch-space, ch 2. Repeat from * around, join to 3rd ch of starting ch. **Rnd 17:** Repeat Rnd 16. **Rnd 18:** Work same as Rnd 16 with ch-3 between dc. **Rnd 19:** Sl st in ch-space, ch 7 for first dc and ch 4, dc in same ch-space, * in next ch-space work dc, ch

4 and dc. Repeat from * around, join to 3rd ch of starting ch. **Rnd 20:** Sl st to center of next ch-space, * ch 5, sl st in next ch-space. Repeat from * around, end ch 5, join—96 ch-loops. **Rnd 21:** Repeat Rnd 5. **Rnd 22:** Sl st to top of starting ch of previous rnd, sc in top of ch-3, * ch 5, sc in top of next ch-3. Repeat from * around, join. **Rnd 23:** Sl st in ch-loop, ch 3 for first dc, 2 dc in same space, * (ch 5, sc in next ch-loop) 11 times, ch 5, 3 dc in next ch-loop. Repeat from * around, eliminate 3 dc on last repeat, join to top of starting ch—8 3-dc groups around. **Rnd 24:** Sl st in 3 dc and into next ch-loop, ch 3 for first dc, 2 dc in same loop, * (ch 5, sc in next ch-loop) 10 times, (ch 5, 3 dc in next ch-loop) 2 times. Repeat from * around, eliminate 3 dc at end of last repeat, join to top of starting ch—3-dc group on each side of 3-dc group of Rnd 23. **Rnd 25:** Sl st in 3 dc and into next ch-loop, ch 3 for first dc, 2 dc in same space, * (ch 5, sc in next ch-loop) 9 times, (ch 5, 3 dc in next ch-loop) 3 times. Repeat from * around, eliminate 3 dc at end of last repeat, join. **Rnd 26:** Ch 8 for first dc and ch 5, * (sc in next ch-loop, ch 5) 10 times, (3 dc in next ch-loop, ch 5) 2 times. Repeat from * around, end with 2 dc in same loop as starting ch, join to 3rd ch of starting ch. **Rnd 27:** Sl st to next ch-loop, * (sc in ch-loop, ch 6) 11 times, 3 dc in next loop, ch 6. Repeat from * around, join. **Rnd 28:** Sl st to center of next ch-loop, * sc in ch-loop, ch 6. Repeat from * around, join. **Rnd 29:** Repeat Rnd 28. **Rnd 30:** Repeat Rnd 5. **Rnd 31:** Sl st to top of starting ch of previous rnd, ch 5 for first dc and ch 2, dc in next dc of same group, * ch 2, dc in top of ch-3 of next group, ch 2, dc in next dc of same group. Repeat from * around as established, join to 3rd ch of starting ch. **Rnd 32:** Sl st in next ch-loop, ch 5 for first dc and ch 2, * dc in next ch-2 space, ch 2. Repeat from * around, join to 3rd ch of starting ch. **Rnds 33 through 35:** Repeat Rnd 32. **Rnds 36 and 37:** Repeat Rnd 32 with ch-3 between dc.

Joining Rnd: When joining Motif Circle 1 to Rnd 37, work along side marked for inner joinings. Join crochet thread to first ch-4 of any motif, * [ch 4, retaining last loop of each dc on hook, work dc in each of next 2 ch-loops on Rnd 37, yo and through all loops on hook (joint dc made), ch 4, sl st in next ch-4 loop of motif] 3 times, ch 4, joint dc over next 2 ch-loops of Rnd 37, ch 4 **, sl st at center of ch-16 joining (single joining), ch 4, joint dc over 2 spaces on Rnd 37, ch 4, sl st in first ch-4 loop of next motif; repeat from * to ** once, sl st at center of first ch-16, ch 4, joint dc in 2 spaces on Rnd 37, ch 4, sl st at center of next ch-16 (double joining), ch 4, joint dc in 2 spaces on Rnd 37, ch 4, sl st in first ch-4 loop on next motif. Continue joining Motif Circle 1 to Rnd 37; when working, use a total of 12 double joinings and 5 single joinings evenly spaced around. **Note:** *All ch-loops of Rnd 37 should have a portion of a joint dc worked in them. At all times there is a ch-4 between joint dc and sl st to motif. On each motif of the Circle, four ch-4 and two ch-16 loops are worked as part of the joining to Rnd 37. If you have miscounted the loops on Rnd 37, one more or less double joinings will make no difference in the pattern so long as all ch-loops of Rnd 37 have been worked and the work lies flat.* **Rnd 38: Note:** *Work around outer joining loops of Motif Circle 1. Joint ch-16/ch-18 trc: At the point where these 2 chs meet at sides of each motif, work trc at center and over all chs.* Join thread with sl st in ch-4 loop of any motif, * (ch 6, sl st in next ch-4 loop) 3 times, ch 6, in same group as ch-18 work trc in center dc of group, ch 6, trc over both loops of ch-18, ch 6, joint ch-16/ch-18 trc at center, ch 6, trc over both loops of ch-18 trc at center, ch 6, in same group as ch-18 work trc in center dc of group, ch 6, sl st in ch-4 loop of next motif. Repeat from * around, join—153 spaces around; 9 spaces between each joint ch-16/ch-18 trc. Cut thread. **Rnd 39:** Join thread at trc over joint ch-16/ch-18 trc, * sc in trc, (ch 4, sc in next ch-loop) 2 times, ch 4, sc in next trc, (ch 4, sc in next ch-loop) 2 times, (ch 4, sc in sl st, ch 4, sc in ch-loop) 2 times, ch 4, sc in next ch-loop, ch 4, sc in next trc, (ch 4, sc in next ch-loop) 2 times, ch 4. Repeat from * around, join to first sc—14 loops between each joining ch-16/ch-18 trc; 238 loops around. **Rnd 40:** Sl st to center of next ch-space, sc in ch-space, * ch 5, sc in next ch-space. Repeat from * around, end ch 5, join. **Rnds 41 through 43:** Repeat Rnd 40. At end of last rnd, cut thread. **Rnd 44:** Join thread in loop directly over joint ch-16/ch-18 trc of Rnd 38, ch 3 for first dc, 2 dc in same space, * (ch 6, sc in next loop) 17 times, ch 6, 3 dc in next loop. Repeat from * around, eliminate 3 dc at end of last repeat, join. **Rnd 45:** Work around in ch-loop pattern as established, work 3 dc in loops on both sides of 3 dc of Rnd 44. **Rnds 46 through 48:** Work ch-loop pattern as established, continue diamond shape same as on Rnds 25 through 27. **Rnd 49:** Continue in ch-loop pattern, at each 3 dc work as follows: sc in loop before 3 dc, ch 6, sc in center dc of group, ch 6, sc in next loop. **Rnds 50 through 52:** Work in ch-loop pattern with ch-7 instead of ch-6 between sc. At end of last rnd, cut thread. **Rnd 53:** On all sides, mark loop at exact center between diamond motifs of Rnds 44 through 48. Join thread in one marked loop, ch 3 for first dc, 2 dc in same loop, * work in pattern as established to next marked loop, 3 dc in marked loop. Repeat from * around as established, join. **Rnds 54 through 57:** Work in pattern as established, continue working diamond motifs as before. **Rnds 58 through 62:** Work in pattern as established. **Joining Rnd:** When joining Motif Circle 2 to Rnd 62, work along side of motifs marked for inner joinings. Sl st to center of next loop, ch 3, sl st in first ch-4 loop on motif, 4 dc in same loop as ch 3; * ch 2, sc in next loop, ch 3, sl st in next

ch-4 loop on motif, 4 dc in same loop as ch-3; repeat from * until all ch-4 loops of motif have been worked and there are 4 dc below each ch-4 loop of motif; ch 2, sc in next ch-loop, ch 3, sl st at center of ch-16 groups, 4 dc in same loop, ch 2, sc in next loop, beginning with first ch-4 loop on next motif. Join as before. Continue around as established, join. Cut thread. **Rnd 63:** Working at outer edge of Motif Circle 2, work same as Rnd 38. **Rnd 64:** Repeat Rnd 39. **Rnd 65:** Sl st to center * in next ch-space, ch 3, 3 dc in same space, sl st in next ch-space. Repeat from * around, join. **Rnd 66:** Sl st to top of ch-3 of previous rnd, ch 5 for first dc and ch 2, dc in next dc of same group, * ch 2, dc in top of ch-3 of next group, ch 2, dc in top of next group, ch 2, dc in next dc. Repeat from * around, join. **Rnd 67:** Sl st to center of next ch-space, ch 5 for first dc and ch 2, * dc in next ch-space, ch 2. Repeat from * around, join. **Rnds 68 and 69:** Repeat Rnd 67. **Rnd 70:** Sl st in 2 chs, ch 3 for first dc and complete st as a joint dc in next ch-space, * ch 6, joint dc in next 2 spaces. Repeat from * around, join. **Rnd 71:** * Ch 6, sc in next ch-space. Repeat from * around, join. **Rnd 72:** Sl st to center of next ch-space, * ch 3, 3 dc in same space, sl st in next ch-space. Repeat from * around, join to bottom of first ch-3. **Rnd 73:** Sl st to top of ch-3 of previous rnd, ch 3 for first dc, 2 dc in same space, * ch 2, 3 dc in top of ch-3 of next group. Repeat from * around, join. **Rnd 74:** Sl st to next ch-space, ch 3 for first dc, 2 dc in same space, * ch 3, 3 dc in next ch-space. Repeat from * around, join. **Rnds 75 and 76:** Repeat Rnd 74. **Rnd 77:** * Ch 6, sc in next ch-space. Repeat from * around, join. **Rnd 78:** Repeat Rnd 72. **Rnd 79:** Repeat Rnd 66. **Rnds 80 through 83:** Repeat Rnd 67. **Rnd 84:** Repeat Rnd 70. **Rnd 85:** Sl st to center of next ch-space, * sc in next ch-space, ch 8. Repeat from * around, join.

4. Finishing—Scallop Edge:

Note: The scallops are worked one at a time. Work the first scallop as given, then divide the remainder of the cloth into even sections and work approximately 37 more scallops around. **Row 1:** Sl st to next ch-space, ch 3 for first dc, work 11 dc in same space, sl st in next ch-space. Turn. **Row 2:** * Ch 5, skip 1 dc, sc in next dc. Repeat from * across—6 ch-loops. Join in corresponding ch-space. Turn. **Row 3:** Sl st to center of ch-space, * ch 3, 2 dc in same space, sl st in next ch-space. Repeat from * across, join to next ch-space. Turn. **Row 4:** Ch 4, sc in next ch-space, ch 2, * 3 dc in top of ch-3 of group of last row, ch 2. Repeat from * across, join to corresponding space. Turn. **Row 5:** Ch 3, sl st in same space as last sl st, * ch 2, dc in ch-2 space, ch 2, dc at center of 3-dc group. Repeat from * across, join to corresponding space. Turn. **Row 6:** Sl st in next ch-loop, 3 dc in each ch-space across, join to corresponding loop. Turn. **Row 7:** Sl st in next ch-space, ch 4, skip 1 dc, * working over next 3 dc work 3-dc cluster, ch 4, skip 1 dc. Repeat from * across, join in corresponding space. Turn. **Row 8:** In each ch-space work sc, hdc, 4 dc, hdc, sc.

For great children's presents that you can make ahead, see Christmas Through A Child's Eyes, Chapter V.

CHAPTER 2

T is the season...
... for peace on earth.
Beautiful wreaths are
displayed everywhere,
symbols of hospitality
and friendship.

In this chapter: decorations to make, ways to wrap gifts, when to mail packages!

It's Beginning To Look A Lot Like Christmas

Christmas is coming—and now's the time to deck your halls, indoors and out. We show you how to create a dazzling display of lights for your windows, or make elegant centerpieces for your holiday table. There's a gift mailing schedule to help you avoid delivery delays and a guide to help you cope with those "sticky situations" that always seem to arise during the holidays. You can even discover your "Christmas Card personality" with our fun quiz—it'll make the whole family smile!

Outdoor Scenes

The twinkling lights of Christmas herald the holiday season.

BEAUTIFUL BAY WINDOW

Easy: Achievable by anyone.
Materials: Strings of multicolor miniature lights.

Directions:
Outline the trim of a bay window with strings of lights. Place your decorated Christmas tree in front of the window for a spectacular view from outdoors.

Beautiful Bay Window

ICICLE MAGIC

Easy: Achievable by anyone.
Materials: Icicle lights; evergreen boughs.

Directions:
Create a magical wintry effect by outlining a window with evergreen boughs, and stringing icicle lights on the top and bottom.

TREES THAT KEEP LIVING AND GIVING

Celebrate the holiday spirit both indoors and out. Plant one tree; adorn the other.

It's always a bit sad to have to throw out your tree after Christmas, so this year why not choose one with roots? The smaller ones come in pots and the larger ones have rootballs wrapped in burlap. This way you can have your Christmas tree indoors, and continue to enjoy it outdoors for years to come. • Before the ground freezes, dig a hole in the yard 2 feet across and at least 1½ feet deep; you can always refill it to the correct depth if you choose a smaller tree. To prevent the soil dug out of the hole from freezing, store it in the garage or basement. • Plan to keep the tree indoors no more than 10 days. • Set it in the coolest part of the room and keep the rootball moist. • When you plant the tree, adjust the hole you dug so it's twice the size of the rootball and slightly deeper. • Remove the tree from its container (with a burlapped tree, loosen the ties and plant as is; the burlap will eventually disintegrate). • Put back enough soil so the top of the tree's rootball will sit just slightly exposed. Hold the tree straight while you fill in, packing soil around the ball. Cover the area with 3 inches of mulch (hay or evergreen boughs).

Another way to make festive use of a living tree is to decorate one of the evergreens in your yard with a Christmas feast for the birds. • Scoop peanut butter into the scales of pinecones. • Fill orange cups with sunflower seeds: Slice 1 inch off the top of an orange and scoop out the pulp; poke four holes around the rim and tie ribbons through for hanging. • Cover a piece of suet with netting and tie it to the tree trunk. • Mix raisins and nuts in an empty coconut shell; drill holes in the shell near the top for hanging. • String garlands of cranberries and popcorn on heavy thread. • Dress up the tree with colorful red bows and shiny red apples.

Icicle Magic

Remarkable Ribbon

Dress up decorations, transform gift boxes, create dazzling bows!

💲 RIBBON PINE CONES

Easy: Achievable by anyone.
Materials: 3 yds #5 Glimmer ribbon, cut into 52 2″-long pieces *(see Materials Shopping Guide, page 272)*; 1 yd ⅛″-wide Picette ribbon or braid; 104 flat head pins; 1 bead head pin; 3″ Styrofoam® egg; white craft glue.

Directions:
Fold and glue the Glimmer strips into triangles. At the narrow end of the egg, pin two triangles, seam side down, opposite each other so that the tips meet ¼″ beyond the end of the egg, using a pin in each corner. Pin two more triangles opposite each other in the spaces between the first two, with tips meeting. Place two triangles opposite each other ¼″ down, with their tips resting on the seams of the triangles in the first row. Pin two more triangles opposite each other in the remaining spaces. Place four more triangles with their tips in line with the tips of the first row. Continue to alternate rows in this manner until the egg is completely covered. With 12″ of Picette ribbon, make a hanger. Make an 8-loop florist bow with the remaining ribbon and attach both the hanger and florist bow to the large end of the egg with a bead head pin and glue.

Ribbon Pine Cones

SWANS A-SWIMMING

Easy: Achievable by anyone.
Materials: 4 to 6 glass swans (size is optional, ours are 7″ long and 7″ tall); greens, real or artificial; glass ornaments, 3 per swan; 6 to 8 yds (1 yd each per swan) 3 different color-coordinated ribbons approximately ⅞″ wide, ⅝″ wide and ⁷⁄₁₆″ wide; 2¾″-wide ribbon long enough to make a table runner; 4 to 6 small candle holders and 12″ candles.

Directions:
Fill each swan with 3 ornaments interspersed with small pieces of greenery. Tuck in a bow made of 3 ribbons of varying width; each ribbon should be 1 yd long. Layer narrow widths over wider widths. Alternate swans and candles on the ribbon runner, set to glide down the center of the table or buffet.

Swans A-Swimming

Ribbon Fans

TAKE A BOW!

Easy: Achievable by anyone.
Materials: Three spools ¾"- or 1¼"-wide self-sticking ribbon in red, green and white; scissors; curling ribbon or string.

Directions:
Cut 13 to 15 strips of ribbon 12" long (use all three colors). Fold each strip in half; unfold. Moisten the ends and fold them in to the center crease

without overlapping the ends; press to form a double bow. Dry for 10 minutes. Cut a small triangle on one side in the center of the ribbon. Do

the same on the other side, leaving ¼" in the center. Cut a 54" piece of curling ribbon or string and lay it on a flat surface. Alternating the colors, place all the ribbon pieces on top of the curling ribbon alongside of each other, close together but not touching. Bring up both ends of the curling ribbon, crossing one in front of the other and pulling quickly and tightly. Now knot the curling ribbon and cut off the excess.

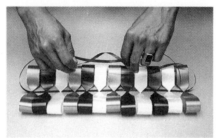

RIBBON FANS

Easy: Achievable by anyone.
Materials: 2¾"-wide or wider ribbon, using 10" to 12" per fan; stapler; needle and thread, or wire.

Directions:
Using a 10" to 12" piece of ribbon, fold it in ½" accordion pleat folds, folding first one way, then the other. Staple, stitch or wrap a piece of wire around the bottom.

RIBBONS AND FLOURISHES

• Try placing ribbons slightly off center. Split a ribbon to varying widths for a decreasing stripe effect. Two colors or shades of ribbon can easily be woven into a nostalgic basket-weave pattern.
• Use paper for trimming as well as wrapping. Make a bow by stapling strips of paper together like the spokes of a wheel. Draw the paper over a dull edge to create curls.
• Ordinary items, such as small toys, candy and old greeting cards, make eye-catching trims and may be used to hint at the contents of the package.
• If you run low on a favored wrapping paper, wrap the gift in a matching solid and use the scraps as trim.
• Dress up the obvious. If the gift is a tie or a giveaway shape, use trims and bows to give the package a little extra pizzazz.
• Coordinate the wrapping of different gifts for a dazzling foot-of-the-tree array.

Wrap It Up!

*Be sure to wrap your gifts in style and
mail them off well protected.*

ORGANIZE YOURSELF

• Begin to buy wrapping paper, ribbons, transparent tape, parcel wrapping paper and labels in November. (Or better yet, buy these just after Christmas the year before.)
• Clear a space on a table or counter that is large enough to accommodate the largest package.
• Assemble all the packages to be wrapped, dividing them by sizes.

LINING THE BOX

Materials: Tissue paper; adhesive seal; gift box.

Directions:
1. Pleat two or three thicknesses of paper as wide as the width of the box.
2. Do the same for the length.
3. Cross the tissue papers to line the box.
4. Place the gift in the tissue papers and fold the lining over the gift. Use an adhesive seal to close the layers of tissue and "dress up" the package.

WRAPPING BASICS

• To estimate how much wrapping paper you will need to cover a boxed gift, use enough to go around three of the box's sides one time and one of the narrow sides two times.
• To wrap a square or rectangular box, center the wrapping paper beneath the box. The paper should extend over both ends a little more than half the box's depth. Fasten the ends by folding the top flap down, the sides in and the bottom flap up. Secure with tape. Turn the package over and decorate with ribbon and bow.
• For a round or tubular package, there are three options. The first is to wrap the package leaving extra wrapping paper at both ends, gather the ends and tie them with ribbon or yarn (this leaves a crinkle of gift wrap at each end). Or cut a large circle of wrapping paper and gather the wrap at the top for a perfect ruffle of paper. For a larger item, such as a basketball, lay out two rectangles of wrapping paper on an "X." Gather the ends and tie.
• Label each box as soon as it has been wrapped.
• Save the small pieces of wrapping paper for the smaller packages.

THE RIGHT IMPRESSION

Select the gift wrap you use with as much care as you do the gift itself. And be adventurous!

• Want to make a first class impression? Forget brown paper or the Sunday comics. Most people believe that the fancier the wrapping, the more exciting the present.
• If you want to add to the element of surprise, disguise packages to look like something they're not. A big box can conceal a small present. Large, hard-to-wrap gifts, such as tricycles, giant stuffed animals and wagons, fit neatly into jumbo plastic gift bags. Stuff tissue in the bags to help disguise the shapes.
• Vary package shapes by wrapping some gifts in cylindrical containers, others in handle bags or cube-shaped boxes. Posters and prints can be rolled up and wrapped inside gift wrap cardboard tubes. Smaller items can be wrapped inside the cardboard tubes on which paper toweling comes.

Timing Is Everything When You Send a Gift By Mail

Select the proper container

Fiberboard containers (commonly found in supermarkets or hardware stores) are generally strong enough to mail things of average weight and size—up to 10 lbs. Paperboard cartons (similar to suit boxes) can also be used for items of up to 10 lbs. Some boxes have what is known as a "test board" rating, which indicates how strong they are. For example, a corrugated fiberboard box (125-lb test board) is good for mailing weights up to 20 lbs. High-density items, such as tools, require a stronger container (strength is indicated by a round imprint on a bottom corner of the box).

Package gifts with care

• *Soft goods,* such as clothing, pillows or blankets, should be placed in a self-supporting box or tear-resistant bag, the box closed with reinforced tape, the bag sealed properly.
• *Perishables,* such as cheese, fruit, vegetables, meat or anything with an odor, must be placed in an impermeable container filled with absorbent cushioning and sealed with filament tape.
• *Fragile items,* such as glasses, dishes or photography equipment, are safest packaged in fiberboard containers (minimum 175-lb test board) and cushioned with foamed plastic or padding. Seal the package and reinforce with filament tape.
• *Shifting contents,* including books, tools or nails, should be packaged in fiberboard containers (minimum 175-lb test board). Make sure that you use interior fiberboard separators or tape to prevent the contents

of the parcel from shifting in transit. Seal the package and reinforce it with filament tape.
• *Awkward loads,* such as gloves, pipes or odd-shaped tools or instruments, require special packaging. Use fiberboard tubes or boxes with length not more than 10 times their girth. Cushioning must be of preformed fiberboard or foamed plastic shapes and the closure should be as strong as the tube itself.

Use adequate cushioning

If you are mailing several gift items in one package, wrap them individually and protect each one from the other with padding or foamed plastic. To prevent one item from damaging another, make sure you fill the box completely with cushioning material, leaving no empty space. Polystyrene, shredded, rolled or crumpled newspaper, "bubble" plastic and fiberboard are all good cushioning materials. So are plastic foam chips, plastic egg cartons cut into pieces and packing straw. Commercially available foam shells or airpocket padding can also be used, as well as padded mailing bags (good for small items).

Seal your carton properly

Use one of three recommended types of tape to secure your parcel: pressure-sensitive filament tape, nylon-reinforced Kraft paper tape or plain Kraft paper tape. All three types are available in stationery stores or five-and-dime stores. There's no need to wrap the container with brown paper—paper sometimes rips in handling. *Do not tie your*

package with string or twine! This can become entangled in the mail-processing equipment.

Request special markings

Certain phrases printed on the outside of your parcel will alert Postal Service employees to the nature of its contents. Mark breakable objects FRAGILE in three places: above the address, below the postage and on the reverse side. Packages of food or other items which can decay should be marked PERISHABLE in the same locations. The words DO NOT BEND on your package will signal a fragile item, but the sender must have first protected these and similar articles with stiffening material. Ask the clerk at your post office to stamp your packages appropriately.

Insure your packages

Any gift sent by mail should be insured. You can insure your package in varying amounts for up to $400. The cost is minimal and you have the added security of knowing that, in case anything does happen to the package, you will be reimbursed. If you are mailing something that is worth more than $400 or if you are sending cash or an irreplaceable item through the mail, send it by registered mail.

Use ZIP codes

The easiest way to delay delivery of mail is to forget the ZIP Code, or to use the wrong one. So, when addressing a package, be sure to include the ZIP code in both the recipient's and your return address.

Follow these other pointers on mailing gifts so they arrive in perfect condition:

- **USE A HEAVY GIFT WRAP.** Thicker, heavier paper has a better chance of arriving without being torn.
- **CONSIDER A DESIGNED GIFT BOX.** Many boxes come decorated with holiday motifs.
- **BOWS DON'T TRAVEL WELL.** Instead, decorate packages with flat trims, stickers, yarn or tinsel tie.
- **ALWAYS MAIL A WRAPPED PRESENT INSIDE ANOTHER BOX.** Many gift boxes just aren't meant for shipping, so be sure to choose a box that is sturdy enough to support its contents and withstand the wear and tear of delivery.

Time it right

The Postal Service offers a wide range of delivery options for mailing packages, depending on the amount of money you want to spend and the time you've allowed for delivery. A good general rule to follow is to mail early in the day and early in the month. First-class letters and cards sent coast-to-coast should arrive within 3 to 4 days, those sent within a state should arrive within 2 to 3 days and those mailed to an address within a city should reach their destination in 2 days. However, as we all know, the Christmas season is the busiest time of the year for mail carriers, so it's best to allow at least two weeks for domestic delivery of holiday cards and gifts, just to be on the safe side.

See page 141 for pointers on sending food gifts.

DOMESTIC MAIL SERVICES

You can choose any one of three services to send packages up to 70 lbs and 108 inches (length plus girth) by mail.

SERVICE	DESCRIPTION	COST	TIME
PRIORITY MAIL	Packages receive the same attention as first-class letters. Shipped by air, these parcels can be sent from any post office station or branch to any address in the U.S.	Determined by weight and distance traveled. A 2-lb package from New York to Chicago: $2.40; a 5-lb package: $4.86. A 2-lb package from New York to Los Angeles: $2.40; a 5-lb package: $6.37.	3-4 days
PARCEL POST	Takes longer than priority mail, but costs less. Packages can be mailed from any post office station or branch and are delivered directly to the addressee.	Determined by weight and distance traveled. A 2-lb package from New York to Chicago: $2.24; a 5-lb package: $3.29. A 2-lb package from New York to Los Angeles: $2.35; a 5-lb package: $6.25.	8 days
EXPRESS MAIL	Guaranteed to be delivered on time to the addressee by 3 P.M. the next business day. Packages are automatically insured for up to $500. If mail is late, you can obtain a full postage refund by applying to originating post office.	For direct delivery anywhere in the U.S., a 2-lb package: $12.00; a 5-lb package: $15.25. For recipient pick-up at post office, a 2-lb package: $9.85; a 5-lb package: $13.10.	Overnight

Note: *Prices are accurate at time of press.*

INTERNATIONAL MAIL

Destination	Air Parcels	Airmail Letter/Card
North and Northwest Africa	24 Nov	1 Dec
Australia	24 Nov	24 Nov
Caribbean/West Indies	12 Dec	12 Dec
Central and South America	5 Dec	5 Dec
Europe	1 Dec	5 Dec
Far East	1 Dec	5 Dec
Mid-East	24 Nov	28 Nov
Southeast Asia	24 Nov	24 Nov
Southeast Africa	24 Nov	1 Dec
West Africa	24 Nov	1 Dec

Note: *These dates are for mailing from the continental U.S. only. Check with your local post office on September 1 to confirm mailing dates if you wish to ship your packages.*

Holiday Hints

Smart ideas for the season!

Ribbon Holder

The cardboard tube that's inside a roll of wrapping paper makes a neat holder for ribbon rolls. Slit the tube lengthwise, squeeze the sides together and slip on the rolls of ribbon. When you release the tube, it will expand and hold the ribbon spools securely. A 36-inch-long tube will hold as many as 32 spools of 1-inch ribbon. Stand the holder on one end or hang it in a closet for easy accessibility.

Wax Catchers

Because candle wax is difficult to remove from a tablecloth, make your own drip catchers from white plastic meat trays or colored plastic coffeecan lids. Cut a circle about 3 inches in diameter from a tray or lid; use pinking shears to make the edge decorative. Then cut a hole in the center large enough to slip the candle through. After each use, discard the drip catcher.

Kid Power

Save on wrapping time next year. After Christmas, sit the kids down with scissors, glue, this year's holiday cards and gift boxes. They can decorate the boxes with cutouts or whole cards.

Returning The Thought

When Christmas is over, instead of putting the cards you received in a box in the attic, put them in a bowl on the kitchen table. Once a week, pull out one card and think of something nice to do for the person or family who sent it. You might write a short note, pay a visit, send a small bouquet of flowers, bake a cake or simply make a phone call— each one a gesture greatly enjoyed not only by the person on the receiving end, but also by you. It's a wonderful way to make the spirit of Christmas last through the year.

Photo Opportunity

Christmas trees and other holiday decorations have sprung up all over the shopping malls by the time Thanksgiving arrives. Why not take advantage of such beautiful backgrounds? Photograph your children in their "Sunday best" and you will have up-to-the-minute pictures to enclose with your holiday greeting cards to relatives and friends. You may even find a shot that's suitable for a photo greeting card.

Gifts From Afar

If you have many relatives living halfway across the country, here's an idea to make gift buying easier. Starting a month or two in advance, write to the chamber of commerce in the city nearest to each relative and ask for the names of local restaurants and shopping centers. Then request information from selected places about gift certificates. In most cases, certificates are available in whatever amount you wish to spend. Send a gift certificate for a restaurant to grandparents, for a bookstore to young adults or for a music store to teenagers.

Easy Hang-Ups

Want to hang holiday decorations on your metal front and back doors without attaching a permanent hook? Put large magnets on the backs of decorative items to hold them in place. You can make wreaths of lightweight cardboard, cover them with colorful fabric, stuff them lightly with quilt batting, trim them with lace, ribbon and silk flowers and glue magnets to their backs. The large magnets hold the wreaths securely on the doors and the wreaths can be displayed on the inside or on the outside of the doors. At other times of the year, you can make and hang valentine hearts, Easter rabbits, etc. in the same way.

Video Visit

If you live far from loved ones, before Christmas make a videotape of a typical day showing you at home and at work. Include local scenes and places of interest. Then send a copy to relatives who can't join you for the holidays.

Wrapping Wagon

To make the hectic time of wrapping packages easier for you and your family, turn a toy wagon into a "Christmas carriage." Fill it with seasonal paper, ribbons, tape, scissors, stickers and cards and attach a bright red bow to the handle. Each child and adult can pull the wagon into the privacy of a bedroom to do up wonderful "secret" packages, and wheel it back to the family area so that it's ready for the next person.

Seasonal Storage

When putting out your holiday decorations, place the everyday items you are temporarily replacing in the box in which the seasonal decorations were stored. This way they're not stuffed haphazardly in cabinets and drawers, and are as neatly organized as the items replacing them were.

Decoration Source

To keep costs down yet have a supply of party decorations for clubs and children's groups, check with local grocery stores at the end of a holiday season. They use a variety of seasonal and theme decorations, from tissue-paper streamers to large stage-size props. Most stores will be more than willing to donate used items to add to your "supply closet."

The Perfect Present

If you are looking for a gift for someone who is difficult to please, find a pretty bottle and insert the amount of money you had planned to spend on him or her. (At a secondhand shop, look for a spice rack filled with small bottles—they'll work perfectly for this purpose!) Attach a label, such as IN CASE OF EMERGENCY, BREAK GLASS or NO GOOD IF SEAL IS BROKEN, seal the bottle with colorful tape, wrap—and relax.

HOLIDAY PLANT CARE

Five tips to help keep your festive plants in colorful bloom for weeks.

During the holidays many of you will receive seasonal flowering plants as gifts. They can be just the right touch for table centerpieces, entry hallways and mantel decorations. Given proper care, plants such as poinsettia, ornamental pepper, Christmas cactus, cyclamen and Jerusalem cherry can last all through the holidays. Here are tips that will help you keep your gift plants healthy, fresh and blooming.

- **PROVIDE BRIGHT, INDIRECT LIGHT.** Plants need light to bloom, but direct sun may wilt flowers. Give plants a quarter turn each week to keep them from leaning toward the source of light.
- **GIVE THE PLANTS COOL TEMPERATURES.** To prolong bright colors, keep flowering plants in cool places. Most plants will do well in temperatures of 65° to 75° F during the day and 50° to 60° F at night. Don't put them near a heater, radiator or stove—or next to a fireplace.
- **KEEP THE PLANTS OUT OF DRAFTS.** Although flowering plants prefer cooler temperatures, cold drafts from an open window can harm them. Don't place them up against a windowpane either; moisture can condense on the cold glass and freeze leaves to the pane.

- **KEEP SOIL MOIST BUT NOT SOGGY.** Flowering plants and those with lots of foliage generally require more frequent watering. When the soil feels dry to a depth of ½ inch to 1 inch, water. Overwatering can cause roots to rot, but drought for long periods can be equally damaging. Always water until the water runs out the drainage holes in the side or bottom of the pot; empty the excess from the pot saucer. If the plant is wrapped in decorative foil, remove it or check to make sure the pot can drain.
- **REMOVE FADED BLOOMS.** As soon as a flower loses color and vibrancy, pinch or cut it off. This not only keeps the plant attractive, but prevents the plant from setting seed. A plant that sets seed will not be encouraged to continue blooming.

Keep in mind that holiday and gift plants are grown in greenhouses under the most favorable conditions, conditions that are hard to duplicate at home. With a little extra attention, however, you should be able to enjoy your blooming plants for weeks.

A HOLIDAY GUIDE TO "STICKY SITUATIONS"

Knowing the right thing to do can help you handle holiday bloopers smoothly.

By Letitia Baldrige

Q. Holiday party time also seems to be spill time. If a guest knocks something over, what's the polite thing to do?
A. It depends on the spill—and the guest. If it's a drop of gravy, a string bean or a spot of chocolate sauce, tell your guest not to worry. Make a quick swipe with a damp towel or whatever is needed.

If it's a serious spill, and your guest seems quite upset, don't be bashful—run to the kitchen, all the while assuring the guest that, "I have just the thing to fix it in a jiffy. Don't worry." Then do what you can but be quick. When you've made the save, conclude briskly, "Ah, *that* should do it."

If, in fact, that doesn't do it, even though your heart may be breaking, smile and get on with being a gracious host. Even if it's all just an act, launch your guests into a new and provocative subject of conversation and smile a lot. *All* your guests—present and future spillers—will love you for it.

Q. Many people aren't aware of how much liquor they consume in delicious holiday concoctions such as spiked punch or eggnog. Whose responsibility is it to see that the guest who has had too much to drink doesn't try to drive home?
A. It is the host's role to attend to this responsibility, and every guest's to support him or her in preventing any person under the influence of alcohol from getting behind the wheel of a car. There are three steps a host must take:

1. Take away the drinker's car keys, and do not give them back even if he/she gets angry or threatening.
2. Arrange alternate transportation. Ask another guest to do the driving, or call a taxi service.
3. If these options are not available, prepare to bed down the guest somewhere—in a child's bed, on a sofa or even in a makeshift bed on the floor—until the effects of the alcohol have worn off.

Q. I don't like drug use at my parties. If a guest who doesn't know this should arrive with a supply of cocaine or marijuana, what can I do about it?
A. Remember that it is *your* home and you don't want illegal substances used there. Don't make a sermon out of it. Draw the guest aside. Ask him to stop and not pass it around. Be pleasant, but firm.

Despite the looks some guests might give you, I promise you will be respected for your decisiveness.

Q. What should I do when someone shows up at my door with a Christmas present, and I haven't anything to give in return? Also, there are people who have been on my gift list for years that I'd like to remove because I really don't see them any more. How can I do this without creating hurt feelings?
A. If you receive a gift graciously, and don't fly into a flurry of embarrassment, you allow friends to enjoy having done something special and unexpected for you. One way to be prepared for gift-bearing guests is to whip up some food gifts to keep on hand and give those as your guests are departing.

If someone sends you a gift, don't run out and buy one in return. A prompt, gracious thank-you note enclosed in a Christmas card is an appropriate response.

Cutting back a large gift list is proper and economical, but there are ways to make your decision not seem like a rejection. Make your card more personal to show you still care and want to keep in touch.

Q. Like most hostesses, I am often asked by my invited guests, "Is there anything we can do or bring?" I have always answered, "No, just bring yourselves." Recently I heard that it was perfectly good form to say, "Yes." Can you clarify this?
A. You are correct that many guests ask this as a rhetorical question. Some of your friends, however, may appreciate the time and effort you put into your parties; then accepting the offer of help is paying a compliment to your friends' sensitivity.

Be specific in your response. If the offer is made as they arrive, suggest they help light the candles, pass around hors d'oeuvres, refill drinks or uncork a bottle. If they ask in advance, suggest picking up a near-by guest, bringing chocolates or a bottle of wine or soda.

It's A Snap To Capture The Fun

Remember all your holiday good times with photos.

It's often tricky to get good photographs at parties: things happen so quickly, faces and situations are constantly changing, and you're trying to capture that most ephemeral element—spontaneous fun. So at your next party, take time out to be a little more camera-conscious. Follow these tips from the pros for picture-perfect results!

LEARN TO SEE WHAT THE CAMERA SEES

The photographer's most difficult task is learning to see his or her subject matter.
- Pay attention to what's in the viewfinder. That's the key. Many people try to imagine the people they're photographing as lifesize. So they keep backing up—trying to get more and more of the surrounding scenery in. Later, after the photograph is developed, they're surprised and disappointed to see that the people in the photographs are tiny and unrecognizable. Learning to really see what the camera sees is the critical difference between being a good photographer and someone who simply takes ordinary pictures.
- Another big mistake in photographing people is not getting close enough. If you cram too much into the picture, faces get lost, people are out of focus and somebody is bound to have his eyes closed. The nicest photographs are often those that just include head and shoulders. Be aware of just how close you can get. Ordinary cameras with regular lenses can get within about four feet of the subject, but there are many cameras now available with a close-up lens that allows you to move in to as little as 18 inches.

- To take really effective pictures of people at parties, you must also learn to wait—for the right light, the right subject, that moment when everything's working within the frame of the viewfinder. That's when you've got the perfect shot.

BE SPONTANEOUS

Many people who photograph parties will try to control what's going on. This can be a mistake, because spontaneity is what parties are all about. People talking, eating and laughing are great subjects, so you shouldn't try to orchestrate or arrange them. Instead, capture the fun with candid shots.
- Try to avoid the obvious poses—when people notice you or look directly into the camera. It's the interaction between people that makes a dynamic and interesting photograph. A good technique is to stand unobtrusively at the fringe of the party and wait, camera ready. Nothing may be happening and then, for an instant, someone says something funny, a subtle shift takes place and you've got that rare human element that makes a terrific photograph.
- Try using a slightly longer lens—about 85 millimeters—to get candids. It's an effective way to get excellent shots because you're the observer, not the intruder. The longer lens allows you to stand back and watch. People are relaxed, not rigidly paying attention to you.
- Some photographers suggest using even longer lenses (90-135 millimeters) at parties so you can stay far away but still get good close-ups without making people self-conscious, awkward or embarrassed.

Christmas Card Quiz

What do your Christmas cards say about you?
Take this fun Hallmark holiday quiz and find out!

Choose one letter for each of the following questions:

1. When you select Christmas cards, you:

   a. *Spend a great deal of time looking at designs and reading verses, sometimes more than once.*

   b. *Read quite a few verses before you select, concentrating on a particular kind of card.*

   c. *Approach card selection as another item on your to-do list and get it done rather quickly.*

   d. *Think card selection is fun—not as serious as many things in life.*

2. You are selecting a card for that special person in your life. Which card would you choose?

   a. *(Card shows a rural, wildlife snow scene)*

   Darling, I love you and need you so much,
   I love your warm smile,
   Your soft, gentle touch . . .
   No treasure on earth could ever compare
   With the joy we have known
   And the love that we share . . .

   b. *(A puppy and a kitten together in a chair by a Christmas tree)*

   Being with you at Christmastime . . . is the very best present of all.

   c. *(A red card with a red foil heart and green foil letters)*

   I love you . . . at Christmastime and always.

   d. *(Cute critter by a decorated tree in the snow)*

   All I want for Christmas . . . is all your love.

3. You are selecting a card to give to your boss. Which card would you choose?

   a. *(Christmas bells with ribbons and holly)*

   This special card is coming
   To wish you Christmas cheer
   And then a world of happiness
   Throughout the coming year—
   And then it's meant especially
   To tell you one thing more—
   "You're the kind of boss
   That it's a pleasure working for."

   b. *(A cat, dressed for winter, leaning against the North Pole)*

   Santa thinks you're just about the nicest person . . . south of the North Pole! (And so do I!)

   c. *(Christmas tree decorated in golden tones)*

   Just want you to know that working for you gives a special pleasure to my days.

   d. *(Long note pad with green lettering)*

   Boss, there are two things about this Christmas card you're sure to like: 1. It says you're one terrific boss—2. It wasn't bought on company time! Merry Christmas!

4. You are selecting a card for a very good friend. Which card do you choose?

a. *(Poinsettias, note paper and pen on red background)*

I'm thinking of you at the holidays . . .
remembering happy times we've shared,
quiet talks we've had,
funny things we've laughed about,
moments spent
in simply sharing friendship.
I'm thinking of you at the holidays
and wishing you all the joy
your friendship has brought to me.

b. *(Young children on a snowy walk)*

For my friend—
You don't just brighten up my holidays . . .
You brighten up my life.

c. *(A pine branch with snow and red bird)*

. . . There are families and jobs and errands
and a million other reasons
to be too busy for friendship.
That's why it seems so extra special
to have found you—
because you've become
a very good friend . . .

d. *(Pup on toppling decorated Christmas tree branch)*

You're the kind of friend I'd go out on a limb for . . . Especially if there were candy canes on it.

5. Which card would you choose for a friend that you have fun with?

a. *(Living room with decorated tree that the cat is toppling; the dog is racing through, destroying packages)*

" . . . all is calm, all is bright."

b. *(Cartoon figure out in the snow)*

Christmas is that wonderful time of the year—
Joy is in the air, love is in the heart . . .
Fudge is in the fridge.

c. *(Glossy card with decorated "Twilight Zone" door)*

Get ready to enter a new dimension. A dimension not only of sight and sound, but of mind. A journey into a land
whose only boundaries are those of your
own imagination. Your next stop . . . The Mall!

d. *(Santa's elf checking a list)*

The *bad* news is you were too naughty this year to get any gifts . . . the *good* news is they wanna make a 4-part mini-series based on why!

6. You are selecting a card to buy in quantity to send to friends, relatives, neighbors, etc. Which card do you choose?

a. *(An interior with a lighted Christmas tree and stockings hung from the mantle)*

Those warm times shared in past Decembers—
The mind still sees, the heart remembers.
Especially at Christmas—it's so nice
To remember you.

b. *(Small animal in moon-shaped boat decorated for Christmas floating in starry sea)*

May the magic of Christmas fill your heart the whole year through.

c. *(A teddy bear framed by a filigree wreath design created by using a high-tech laser beam)*

Warmest wishes for a very Merry Christmas.

d. *(Santa's reindeer are doing aerobics led by a deer on TV)*

Here's hoping your holidays are shaping up great!

7. You want to send a card to reflect your interest in peace. Which card do you select?

a. *(The outline of a dove with olive branch embossed on pale blue)*
The inside is blank for a personal note.

b. *(Misty painting of child among evergreens with white doves)*
May Christmas surround you with wonder and fill you with peace.

c. *(Script on color wash with star image)*
Christmas . . . A message of peace,
as the light of winter stars reflects
On the new-fallen snow . . .
A message of hope, as the world
prepares to renew itself in beauty . . .
A message of love, as the gifts
of joy and caring are shared by every
heart . . . in every home.

d. *(Cartoon drawing of dog and cat curled up together in front of the fire)*
Peace to you at Christmas.

8. Which card would you choose for a friend who has a birthday close to Christmas?

a. *(Gift wrapped package on holiday table)*
May your December birthday
bring much happiness to you—
All life's best and brightest things
and special dreams come true,
a wealth of cherished memories
too special to forget—
May this December birthday
be your very best yet!

b. *(Little white mouse laden with gifts)*
May your holidays be happy
And your birthday happy, too,
And may this special time of year
Bring lots of joy to you.

c. *(A regal-looking "doorman" presenting a beautifully wrapped gift)*
The inside is blank for a personal note.

d. *(Lettering on front and Santa inside)*
For your Christmas birthday, Santa is
going to make a special
appearance . . . in his birthday suit!

9. You want a card to add a note of humor for the man in your life at Christmas. Which card would you choose?

a. *(A humorously ornery Santa)*
He knows when you've been snacking,
He knows when you're pigging out,
He knows if you've been eating right . . .
Santa's using new standards this year.

b. *(Bundled-up animal on a sled)*
"C'mon it's lovely weather
for a sleigh ride together
with you." You pull.

c. *(A savvy-looking woman)*
You don't have to give me expensive
gifts for Christmas . . . but if you don't,
life won't be easy from here on in.

d. *(Cartoon character seen first in mountain-climbing gear, then in diving suit)*
For you I would climb the highest
mountain . . .
Swim the deepest sea—
But don't make me spend Christmas
With your family.

10. Which card would you choose to send to your list of business associates?

a. *(Gold foil card with embossed "Season's Greetings")*
With wishes for a happy holiday
season
And all good wishes for the year
ahead.

b. *(Deer bounding through snowy hills)*
To wish you all the joys of the season.

c. *(A glossy, stylized Christmas lily on gold)*
Remembering you is one of the special
joys of the season.

d. *(Black card with gold saxophone tied with ribbon)*
Happy holidays and all that jazz.

SCORING: Count the total number of each letter you selected.

INTERPRETATION: You probably scored higher on one letter, but you may have chosen several of another letter. The following interpretations describe the way you communicate through your personality, your home and the messages you send.

If you chose mostly:

a's—You like the traditional way of thinking and enjoy being proper when the occasion calls for it, warm and comfortable in other situations. You may sometimes say you wish Christmas were a little more like it used to be. Your home probably reflects your love of tradition and is a refuge for family and friends. You love sending Christmas cards, possibly keep organized records and you look forward to receiving cards. Displaying favorite cards in your home is a tradition you enjoy.

b's—You love whimsey and fantasy and have a light-hearted view of life, always looking for the silver lining. You may have collected lots of favorite ornaments and Christmas decorations and enjoy getting them out for the holidays. There's a good chance you have some gingham and floral prints in your home and like to decorate with interesting knick-knacks. People probably find your home cheerful and happy. You think it's fun to send cards and enjoy opening the ones you receive.

c's—You are probably a people person who enjoys open communication. You may tend to be practical in your approach to things and insist upon quality. Your home is likely to be somewhat tailored with emphasis on the functional. You like to sit down with a mug of hot tea and discuss the important things in life with a friend. You very likely use Christmas cards as a way to communicate with family and friends about events in your life.

d's—You like to have a good time, and people count on your humor to lift their spirits or add life to a party. Even when things don't go your way, you're likely to see the humor in the situation. Your home probably contains some real conversation pieces, perhaps items that friends bring you from trips or give you on special occasions. You are probably quick to serve a new recipe and take it in stride if it isn't a hit. You like to make people smile—a day without laughter is like a day without sunshine for you.

CREATE A TRADITION — SAVE THE CHRISTMAS CARDS THAT TELL YOUR STORY

That first Christmas card in the mail often marks the beginning of the holiday season for many Americans. In fact, each year Americans exchange 2.2 billion Christmas cards. The average American household receives 26 holiday cards a year.

Here are some tips to help you decide which cards to save and to increase the likelihood that posterity will find your collected cards both valuable and informative. Keep the Christmas cards that reflect:

- Social milieu — fashions, cars, computers, slang, TV shows, celebrities and sports.
- Crazes and fads — breakdancing, hula-hoops, skateboards, nerds, "Valley" talk, hair styles, popular songs — that are around only for a short time. Santa might be shown in a hot tub or playing a TV game show.
- Current events and interests — the Statue of Liberty, Halley's Comet, the Bicentennial and space exploration.
- Lifestyle changes — male/female roles, dating, divorce, step-families, women's humor, dieting.
- Controversial social issues, past or present — war, prohibition, the atomic bomb, politics, chauvinism and current events.
- Your collections and special interests — match books, license plates, cars, needlework, movie stars, aerobics, etc. are often shown on cards. A connoisseur of cats might save cards that feature felines.
- Special materials and processes — musical cards, laser-cut cards, movable cards, pop-ups, fold-outs, cloth cards, plastic cards, cards with add-ons and cards in unusual sizes and shapes.
- Firsts — for example, cards with coupons for ice cream, cards with redeemable food coupons, or the first brass ornament Christmas card.
- Post cards — a collection craze at the turn of the century, they are back reflecting signs of the times.
- Most importantly, save the cards you love. They reflect what was important to you during stages of your life and someday will show what it was like "in the good old days."

CHAPTER 3

T is the season . . .
. . . to unwrap family ornaments, brimming with memories — of a special person, a far-away place, a Christmas long ago.

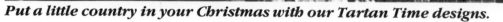

Put a little country in your Christmas with our Tartan Time designs.

Country Classics

Christmas is a time to celebrate traditions—either those passed down through generations or those you create yourself. In this chapter, we show you three charming country themes to help create the mood of your choice: Bask in the warm welcome of Tartan Time, *enjoy the elegance of a lacy* White Christmas *or revel in the simple beauty of* Folk Art Favorites. *And don't forget to fill your cookie jar with* Kris Kringle Cookies, French Jelly Hearts *and* Pecan Bourbon Balls— *from our hearth to yours.*

Tartan Time

The stuff that memories are made of:
Cheery plaids in red, green and gold that welcome family and friends.

RUFFLED RIBBON WREATH

Average: For those with some experience in sewing.

Materials: 12½ yds 2¾"-wide tartan cotton ribbon in a desired pattern; Styrofoam® wreath form 18" in diameter, 1" thick and 2¾" wide; white craft glue; straight pins; stapler; 1 chenille stem.

Optional: 2 bunches wheat; 2 fern pins or 2 pieces No. 18 wire bent into hairpins 2" long.

Directions:

1. Cut a 20½-foot length of ribbon. Following the diagram in FIG. III, 1, pleat the entire length, which will be enough for two ruffles. Cut the ruffle in half. Glue and pin the first ruffle onto the wreath so that the unstapled edge falls about ¼" from the outside edge. Attach the second ruffle, placing the stapled edge 1" from the inside edge.

2. Cut a 5-foot length of ribbon and cut it into thirds lengthwise. Braid these 3 lengths together. Glue and pin the braid around the center of the wreath.

3. If desired, crisscross the bunches of wheat and fasten them to the wreath with fern pins. Trim the stems of wheat evenly.

4. Use the last 4 yds of ribbon to tie a bow. Twist the chenille stem around the knot of the bow and cut off the ends, leaving 2". Push the stem into the wreath between the braid and the ruffle.

FIG. III, 1 RUFFLED RIBBON WREATH

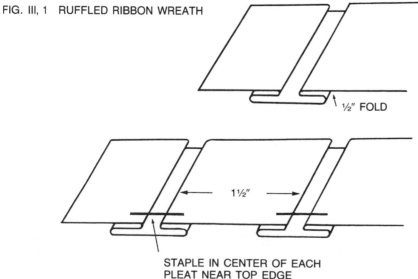

½" FOLD

1½"

STAPLE IN CENTER OF EACH
PLEAT NEAR TOP EDGE

TARTAN ORNAMENTS

Easy: Achievable by anyone.

Materials: Plaid fabric; gold stretch cord; medium and large Styrofoam® balls (about 9½" and 12½" in circumference); small and medium bells *(see Materials Shopping Guide, page 272 for items listed above)*; spool wire; small safety pin.

Directions:

1. For the medium Styrofoam® balls, cut the fabric 5¾" x 18"; for the large balls, 7¼" x 25".

2. Press under ½" on each long edge and stitch ¼" from the fold to make a casing. Attach plain gold stretch cord to a safety pin and pull it through one casing. Gather the fabric up tightly and tie the cord ends into a knot. Cut the cord ends. Repeat at the other casing, but do not tie the cord together. Insert the Styrofoam® ball, knot and cut the cord.

3. Arrange the gathers evenly around the ball.

4. Wrap the stretch cord around the ball three or four times equally spaced and knot the ends. Make a 2-loop bow and wrap the center with spool wire.

5. Cut two 7" pieces of stretch cord and secure a bell at each end. Center the pieces over the bow and wrap the wire ends around the center. Attach to the knot on the top of the ball, pulling the wire ends under all cords and twisting the wire around itself on the top, leaving the ends to attach to the tree.

Ruffled Ribbon Wreath

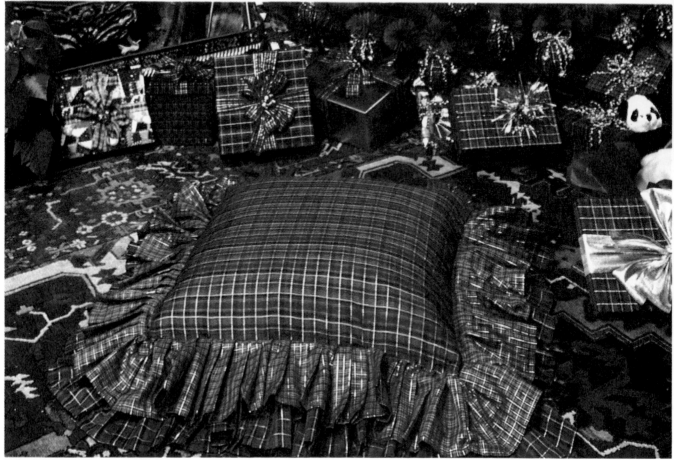

Plaid Pillow

PLAID PILLOW
(26″ square, plus ruffles)

Average: For those with some experience in sewing.

Materials: 46″-wide coordinating fabrics: ¾ yd for pillow top, same for pillow bottom, 1⅞ yds for 8″ ruffle, 2¼ yds for 10″ ruffle *(see Materials Shopping Guide, page 272)*; synthetic stuffing.

Directions:

1. Cut two 27″ squares, for the pillow top and bottom.

2. Cut 9¾ yds of 8″-wide ruffle strips. With right sides together, stitch the ends together into one long strip. Press. Turn under and press ¼″, then ½″ along one long edge; edgestitch, for the hem.

3. With the right side up, turn 1½″ under at the right end of the strip and press. Working toward the left, and measuring from the fold, mark off 1″, 2″, 1″, 2″, etc. across the strip at the top and bottom edges.

4. Bring the 2″ marks to the 1″ marks, pin and press. Machine baste across the pleats ½″ from the top edge, leaving the last two pleats at the end free. Flip the ruffle over (wrong side up). Bring the left end over the right to the 1″ mark (forming a loop) and make the last pleat. Pin on the wrong side and cut away any excess fabric.

5. Repeat Steps 2 through 4 for the 10″ ruffle.

6. With the right side up and the top edges matching, place and pin the 10″ ruffle inside the loop of the 8″ ruffle. Stitch over the previous stitching at the top edges.

78

7. Divide and pin-mark the ruffle into quarters. With right sides together, edges matching and quarter marks at the corners, pin the ruffle to the pillow top, easing in excess fabric around the corners. Machine baste. Pin the bottom square over the ruffle, matching all edges. Stitch just inside the previous stitching, leaving an opening for turning. Turn right side out. Stuff. Edgestitch the opening.

TARTAN PRESENTS

Easy: Achievable by anyone.
Materials: Gift box; plaid fabric (enough to cover box and top); ribbon or stretch cords; spray glue; white glue; bells *(see Materials Shopping Guide, page 272 for items listed above)*; picture wire.

Directions:

1. Measure the width and two sides of the box, and add 3″ for turning. Repeat across the length and ends. Cut a rectangle of these measurements from the fabric. (To reduce fraying, you may use pinking shears to cut the edges.)
2. Centered on the wrong side of the fabric, draw an outline of the box bottom. Extend the four lines to the fabric edges, adding ¼″ outside the drawn lines at each corner for the turn under. Cut out the excess wedge on the cutting (outside) lines at each corner.
3. Spray the wrong side of the fabric with glue and place the box at the center. Turn up each end section, pressing the fabric to the box, around the corners and over the top edge to the inside. On the side panels, fold and glue the ¼″ turn under to the wrong side of the fabric. Apply a line of glue to the folded edges and press the sides up and over the box to the inside.
4. Follow Step 1 to measure the box top, adding the depth of each inside rim plus ½″. Cut the fabric rectangle and cover the box top, following Steps 2 and 3, pressing the fabric over the rim to the inside box top. Cut a rectangle to the measurements of the inside box top. Spray and adhere the wrong side of the fabric to the inside of the box top.
5. To trim the box, cut two pieces of ribbon the same lengths as the lengthwise and crosswise measurements of the box top fabric. Spray glue the ends of the crosswise piece of ribbon and center it across the box top, gluing the ends to the inside rim. Repeat, gluing the lengthwise ribbon to the box top. Glue ribbon to the box bottom in the same way.
6. Thread a 10″ piece of wire through four bells. Make a 4-loop bow from the ribbon. With the bells at the center, wrap the bell wire around the bow, then around the center of the ribbons on the box top.

POINSETTIAS: EASY CARE YEAR-ROUND PLANTS

Poinsettias, native to Mexico, are a natural addition to any holiday home.

Caring for a poinsettia is easy. As long as the plant is in bloom, keep it in a well-lighted spot (direct sun isn't necessary once it is past blooming), with evenly moist (not soggy) soil. Feed the poinsettia every two weeks, *year-round*, with a complete fertilizer, such as 10-15-10.

Follow this "holiday" schedule for poinsettia care:

- Cut back the bracts (the large, brightly colored modified leaves that are often mistakenly called flowers) on **Saint Patrick's Day.**
- Repot the plant into a larger container on **Memorial Day,** and put the plant outdoors for the summer.
- Cut the stems back by six inches on **Independence Day.**
- Move the plant back indoors to a sunny window on **Labor Day.**
- On **Columbus Day,** start giving the plant 14 hours of darkness daily. It is a photoperiodic plant, setting colorful bracts and blooms (the small yellow berries in the center of the bracts) in response to shorter daylight periods. Cover it with a large cardboard box if you don't have a light-tight closet—it must have *absolute* darkness. Continue the darkness treatment for 8-10 weeks, putting the plant during the day in a window where it will receive four to six hours of direct sun. Water and feed as usual. As soon as the poinsettia comes into bloom, discontinue the closet procedure.

With this care—and a bit of luck—you'll have a colorful plant again for **Christmas.**

Highland Ribbon Ornament

HIGHLAND RIBBON ORNAMENT

Easy: Achievable by anyone.
Materials: 3″-diameter Styrofoam® ball; ¼ yd red plaid with gold accent taffeta fabric (will make more than 1 ornament); ¾ yd each ¼″-wide red and green satin ribbons; gold wrapping paper; white glue; red thumbtack; straight pins; 1 bell-shaped gold filigree end cap; scissors; paper for pattern; pencil; ruler; eyepin.

Directions:
1. To cover the ball with the plaid fabric, first make a paper pattern. Draw a 5″ x 2″ rectangle on paper. Mark the midpoints of both the long and short edges. Draw a curved line from the midpoint on the short edge to the midpoint on the long edge. Repeat until a petal shape is obtained. This is the guide for the fabric. Cut 6 of these shapes, placing the pattern on the bias. Cover the ball with these petals, pinning one end of each petal to the same point on the ball and pinning each free end to the same opposite point. Stretch and trim the excess. Evenly space the petals around the ball and pin to secure them.
2. Cover the seams with ribbon glued and pinned over them. Cut ⅛″-wide strips of gold paper. Glue them

centered over the ribbon. Glue additional ribbons at angles to the seams. Center a gold strip on each.
3. Insert a red thumbtack into the bottom center of the ball. Make a small hole in the top of the ornament to insert an eyepin. Slip an eyepin through the endcap. Dip the end of the eyepin in glue. Insert the eyepin into the ornament.

BONNIE SCOTLAND STOCKING

Average: For those with some experience in sewing.
Materials: ½ yd tartan wool; ½ yd iron-on interfacing; 20″ ½″-wide plaid-covered welting cord; ⅔ yd 1½″-wide red plaid ribbon.

Directions:
1. Enlarge the stocking pattern in Fig. III, 2 on brown paper, following the directions on page 271. (The pattern includes a ½″ seam allowance all around.)

2. Press the interfacing to the wrong side of the fabric. Use the pattern to cut out the front and back, cutting on the bias grain of the fabric.
3. With right sides together, seam (½″) the front to the back, leaving an opening at the top. Clip the toe curve. Turn rightside out. Turn the top edge ½″ to the inside and slipstitch *(see Stitch Guide, page 270).*
4. Measure the stocking around the top edge. Cut the cuff this length, plus 1″, on the fabric straight grain. With right sides together, seam (½″) together the short ends. Fold the cuff in half. With wrong sides facing and raw edges even, seam (½″) the cuff to the top of the stocking.
5. Slipstitch the plaid welting to the folded edge of the cuff, ending with a knot at the center back. Turn the cuff down over the top of the stocking.
6. Rosette: Finger-pleat the plaid ribbon, sew a gathering row at the pleated edge and pull up the thread to create a rosette. Stitch the rosette to the cuff *(see photo).*

FIG. III, 2 BONNIE SCOTLAND STOCKING

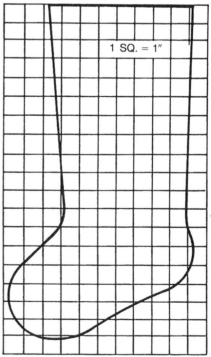

1 SQ. = 1″

Tartan Tree Skirt

TARTAN TREE SKIRT
(34″ in diameter)

Average: For those with some experience in sewing.

Materials: 1½ yds 60″-wide plaid and 1 yd 45″-wide green polyester taffeta.

Directions *(½″ seams allowed):*
1. Cut a 36″-diameter circle of plaid. From its center, cut a 5″-diameter circle. Cut a straight line between the two circles *across one half only* of the skirt *(see photo)*. Cut the lining the same as the skirt. Cut about 6 yds (pieced as needed) of 7″-wide plaid for the ruffle. Cut two 24″ x 1½″ plaid ties.

2. Ruffle: Fold the ruffle strip in half (3½″ wide), lengthwise, right side out; turn in each end and press. Gather the raw edges. Stitch the ruffle to the skirt edge, right sides together and raw edges even, pulling up the gathers to fit.

3. Ties: At each long edge, turn ⅜″ to the wrong side and press. Fold each in half lengthwise, turn in one raw end, press and edgestitch. With right sides together and raw edges even, stitch a tie at the top of each straight edge of the skirt ½″ below the inner circle.

4. With right sides together, ruffles and ties toward the center, pin the lining to the skirt. Stitch all edges, leaving one straight edge open. Turn right side out and stitch closed.

White Christmas

Snowy lace and frothy flourishes recall a romantic era of seasonal charm.

WHITE LACE ORNAMENTS

Easy: Achievable by anyone.

General Materials: 4″ x 6″ purchased white lace doilies (from crafts shops); ½″-wide "daisy" lace by the yard; fabric stiffener; paper toweling; stiff paper; scissors; 1⅝″-long cardboard tube; plastic wrap; transparent tape; gold-edge white ribbon; glue gun and glue sticks; thick craft glue *(see Materials Shopping Guide, page 272)*.

General Directions:

The lace and doilies are dipped into fabric stiffener, draped and allowed to dry. They are covered with plastic wrap to prevent sticking. When the shapes are dry, they are combined with white ribbons to create the ornaments.

NOSEGAY CONES

1. For each cone, you will need General Materials plus one 4″ doily, ⅓ yd of ⅛″-wide ribbon and fancy candy or silk flowers to fill the cone. Form a 4″-diameter circle of stiff paper into a cone shape; tape. Trim the bottom edge so the cone will sit upright.
2. Make a solution of 3 parts fabric stiffener to 1 part water. Saturate the doily with stiffener, wring out the excess and pat between two layers of paper toweling. Gently smooth out the doily to its original circle shape.
3. Form the lace doily around the tip of the paper cone, arranging the lace so that it will have a neat point and overlap slightly to form an asymmetrical cone. Allow the doily to dry overnight covered with plastic wrap.
4. Gently remove the plastic wrap from the doily. Cut an 8″ piece of ribbon and tie a small bow. Glue the bow to the front of the cone. Cut a 4″ piece of ribbon, form a loop and glue it to the top back of the cone for hanging. Fill the cone with wrapped candies or silk flowers.

LACE FAN

1. For two fans, you will need one 6″ doily and ⅔ yd ribbon, plus General Materials. Spread out a piece of plastic wrap. Carefully cut the doily in half. Dip the doily halves in the fabric stiffener solution, squeeze out the excess and blot between paper toweling. Fold the raw edge ⅛″ to the back of each doily and press down. Pinch each doily into pleats at each curve along its outer edge. Let the doilies dry overnight.
2. Cut the ribbon into two 8″ and two 4″ pieces. Tie the 8″ pieces into small bows and glue one to the base of each fan. Form loops with the 4″ strips and glue one at the top of each fan for hanging.

LACE CHAINS

One yd of lace will make ¼ yd of finished chain. Cut the lace into 6½″ lengths. Dip the lengths into the fabric stiffener solution and squeeze out the excess. Blot between paper toweling. *Form one piece into a circle, overlapping the ends. Repeat, slipping the next length through the first circle, overlapping the ends.* Repeat from * to * until the desired length is reached. Dry on plastic wrap.

White Christmas

Detail of White Lace Ornaments

LACE ROSETTES

1. For each rosette, you will need General Materials plus one 4″ doily and 4″ of ribbon. Spread out a piece of plastic wrap. Dip the doily in the fabric stiffener solution, squeeze out the excess and blot between paper toweling.
2. To form a rosette, smooth out the doily. Gently pleat each curve in the doily design, pinching the center of the doily into a point. Keep the doily round as you work. Dry overnight. Glue a ribbon loop to the back of the doily for hanging.

PATCHWORK LACE STOCKING

Average: For those with some experience in sewing.
Materials: 15″ strip beading lace; assorted lace scraps; ⅔ yd ⅜″-wide brown ribbon; 1 yd muslin; ½ yd dark brown fabric; ½ yd polyester fiberfill; thread; scissors; sewing machine.

Directions:
1. Enlarge the pattern for the stocking in FIG. III, 3, following the directions on page 271. Cut 2 muslin, 1 brown and 1 fiberfill stocking, allowing ½″ seams.
2. Baste together 1 muslin, the fiberfill and the dark brown stockings.
3. Stitch the lace down side by side in horizontal rows starting with one row of beading lace at the top. Beginning at the curve, stitch lace pieces down vertically, ending with a row of beading lace at the toe. Thread the ribbon through the beading lace.
4. Place the remaining muslin stocking against the right side of the lace stocking; sew around the edges, leaving the top open. Clip the curves, turn and press.

FIG. III,3 PATCHWORK LACE STOCKING

1 SQ. = 2″

5. Fold down the top edge, turn the edge under and slipstitch. Stitch a ribbon loop to the top back of the stocking to hang.

SWEET HEARTS

Easy to Average: Tatting requires some experience in crocheting.
Materials: Medium-weight unbleached linen or muslin; fiberfill or potpourri; sewing thread; needle; scissors; paper for pattern; tracing paper; pencil; carbon paper (optional); fine point black pen; acrylic paint; small stiff paint brush; lace for edging.
Note: To make your own tatted edging, you need heavy crochet cotton; tatting shuttle; size 6 steel crochet hook (for joining ring). Instructions for tatting are on page 86.

Directions:
1. Draw freehand on scrap or pattern paper a large heart 6½″ or 7½″ high and wide. Using the pattern, draw two hearts on the fabric. Decorate before cutting out the hearts.
2. To decorate, choose a picture you like (perhaps a child's drawing), trace it and transfer it to a fabric heart using carbon, or draw it directly onto the fabric if the drawing shows through the cloth. Using the black pen, outline the design with a broken line to simulate stitches. Paint colors on with a thin wash of acrylic paint so the black outlines will show through. Apply with an almost dry brush to prevent the paint from spreading beyond the outlines. (Practice drawing and painting on scrap pieces of your chosen fabric to perfect the technique.)
3. When dry, cut out the heart pieces and sew the right sides together, making a ¼″ seam and leaving a 2″ opening for stuffing. Turn, stuff with fiberfill or potpourri and blindstitch (see Stitch Guide, page 270) to close. Blindstitch lace edging all around the heart to finish.

Patchwork Lace Stocking; Home Sweet Home Sampler; Sweet Hearts; Beary Christmas

Simple Tatted Ring Edging: Abbreviations: ds—double stitch, p—picot, j—join. Picots in this edging are ½" spacing. Make a ring of 5 ds, p, 5 ds, p, 5 ds, p, 5 ds, close ring. * Leaving ½" of thread between rings, make another ring of 5 ds, j to last picot of previous ring, 5 ds, p, 5 ds, p, 5 ds, close ring. Repeat from * until you have the number of rings desired. Cut the thread and whipstitch *(see Stitch Guide, page 270)* the end to the back of the last ring.

BEARY CHRISTMAS

Average: For those with some experience in sewing.

Materials: ⅛ yd dark brown or camel-colored print or solid, or unbleached muslin or linen; matching thread; scrap of light brown or camel-colored fabric for foot pad; polyester stuffing; black and brown embroidery floss; ribbon; scissors; needle; pencil.

Directions:

1. Enlarge the pattern pieces in FIG. III, 4, following the directions on page 271. Cut out all pieces as indicated on the pattern, adding a seam allowance.

2. To sew an ear, put the right sides together. Sew, leaving it open at one end. Clip the curve. Turn and press. Repeat for the other ear. Turn the open edges to the inside of each ear and slipstitch *(see Stitch Guide, page 270)* in place.

3. Sew the body, right sides together, leaving it open at the top. Clip the curves and turn. Stuff with polyester stuffing until very tight and hard, up to the head opening. Make a running stitch *(see Stitch Guide, page 270)* ¼" around the top of the body. Draw up tight until the opening is closed. Slipstitch closed.

4. Sew a leg right sides together. Leave it open at the foot, clip the curves and turn. Stuff it tight and hard up to the foot opening. Turn the edges of the foot pad under and slipstitch in place on the bottom of the leg. Repeat for the other leg.

5. For an arm, sew 2 pieces with right sides together, leaving an opening on the back side of the arm. Clip the curves and turn. Stuff it until tight and hard and slipstitch closed. Repeat for the other arm.

6. Matching the points on the pattern with right sides together, sew the gusset to the head on both sides, base of head point A to point B. Clip the curves. Then sew from the front of the head, point C, all the way up through point B and the gusset, which is now folded in half. This forms the point of the nose. Clip the curves, turn and stuff tight. Run a double thread ¼" below the open edge all around. Pull up tight and slipstitch closed.

7. Mark the eyes, mouth and ears on the head. Run a thread with a large knot through the center of the right eye and out through the right ear line. Pull tight. Repeat until you have a dimple for the eye and ear. Sew the ear in place. Repeat for the left eye and ear. With black embroidery floss, embroider the eyes and mouth. Then position the head onto the body and sew in place. Embroider the front and back sides of each paw. Then attach the arms and legs to the body as indicated by *. Slipstitch in place.

8. Tie a ribbon around the bear's neck.

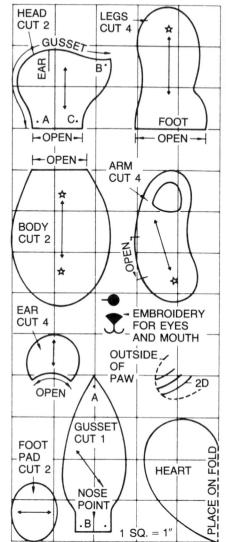

FIG. III, 4 BEARY CHRISTMAS

HOME SWEET HOME SAMPLER

Challenging: Requires more experience in embroidery.

Materials: ½ yd white broadcloth for background and backing; ⅛ yd navy cotton fabric; ⅜"-wide ribbon or border fabric; fusible webbing; solid color scraps in red, green, brown, black and white; calico scraps with the basic color: purple in a 6"-diameter circle, green 3" x 5", blue 2¾" x 5" and light brown 1" x 2¾"; machine with zigzag attachment. *For frame:* ¼ yd navy print; ½ yd polyester batting; four 14" stretcher bars; adhesive tape; staple gun and staples. *For embroidery,* the following embroidery floss:

1. red	**10.** med. brown
2. dk. red	**11.** black
3. dk. green	**12.** orange
4. med. green	**13.** blue grey
5. med. blue	**14.** lt. gold
6. purple	
7. dk. pink	A—French knot
8. curry	B—Chain stitch
9. aqua	C—Satin stitch

Directions:

1. Enlarge the embroidery pattern in FIG. III, 5 and transfer it to a 16" square of white broadcloth, following the directions on page 271.

2. Following the diagram, embroider the pattern around the center. Cut the calico pieces for the center circle, sky, sun and ground cover. Secure with fusible webbing, following the diagram. Zigzag stitch in place.

3. Cut the solid color pieces for the house, barn, tree and wheelbarrow and zigzag stitch in place. Embroider the windows, doors, flowers, etc. according to the diagram.

4. Cut a 4" x 44" strip of navy fabric, fold under one edge ¼" and sew the folded edge to the picture, mitering the corners. Center ⅜"-wide ribbon or border fabric over the edge of the navy border around the white broadcloth square and stitch down, mitering the corners.

5. Lay the picture over the same size batting and backing and baste the three layers together. Quilt around the border strip and around the inside and outside of the calico circle in the center.

6. Make a frame from the four stretcher bars. Cut polyester batting wide enough to encircle each side of the frame and hold it in place on the back with tape. Cut navy print the same width. Starting with one inside corner, staple the fabric to the back, pull the fabric over the front and staple the fabric to the back outside edge. Fold the fabric at a right angle for the corners. Continue stapling to the inside edge, then the outside edge, ending with a folded corner.

7. Center the picture in the frame, turn over carefully and staple the picture to the back of the frame, stretching it tightly. Trim the edges of the picture close to the staples.

FIG. III, 5   HOME SWEET HOME SAMPLER   1 SQ. = 1"

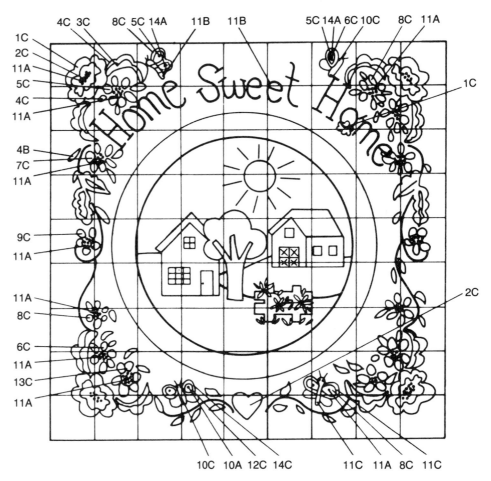

FIG. III, 6 "ANTIQUE" LACE DOLLS
HALF PATTERN

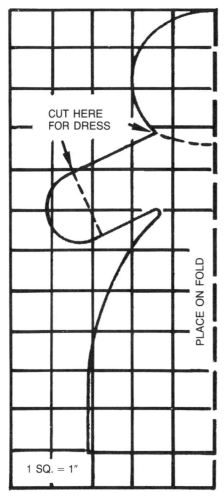

CUT HERE
FOR DRESS

PLACE ON FOLD

1 SQ. = 1"

"ANTIQUE" LACE DOLLS

Average: For those with some experience in sewing.

Materials: Old or purchased lace, crocheted doilies and trims in various shapes and sizes; unbleached muslin for doll bodies; red and green fabrics for dolls' dresses; ribbons; cords for hangers; fine-tipped indelible brown and pink markers.

Directions (¼" seams allowed):
1. Enlarge and mark the pattern in FIG. III, 6, following the directions on page 271.
2. Cut two body sections from the muslin and one dress front from a colored fabric.
3. Place a muslin body over FIG. III, 6A and trace the face in place with a brown marker. Color the cheeks pink.
4. Trim about ¾" from the dress sleeves. With right sides up, place the dress over the body front. Over the dress baste a lace apron, with the finished edge toward the bottom and cut edges in the seams. Other cut edges, such as sleeve edges, can be covered with a narrow lace trim (see photo). Baste a lace bonnet over the head, with cut edges in the seam. Over the dress front place the body back, right side down. Fold a 4" piece of cord in half and slip it between the body pieces at the top of the head, matching raw edges. Stitch around the doll, leaving an opening at the bottom for turning. Clip the corners and curves. Turn right side out and stuff. Slipstitch (see Stitch

FIG. III, 6A
ACTUAL SIZE

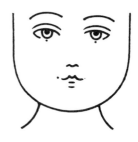

Guide, page 270) the opening closed.
5. Slipstitch bits of lace or trim, as desired, to the dress or bonnet. For the "cape collar" on the green dress, cut a circle a little larger than the doll's neck out of the center of a doily. Slash from the doily edge to the cutout. Turn under the cut edges and drape the collar around the doll. Turn under and slipstitch one back edge over the other.

Create a "Wall Christmas Tree" with Victorian flair. Attach a wire loop to an artificial tree wreath so it can be hung on a door or wall. Drape tiny gold bead roping on the "tree" as garland; intersperse with three gold-trimmed white fans. Use green spool wire to fasten the fans and garland to the tree form. Wire a 2-inch-wide red satin ribbon to the base of the tree in a bow.

"Antique" Lace Dolls

Lace And Taffeta Stocking; Victorian Brocade Stocking

LACE AND TAFFETA STOCKING

Average: For those with some experience in sewing.

Materials: ½ yd white nylon lace; ½ yd old gold taffeta (or moire); ½ yd polyester fleece interlining; ½ yd white lining fabric; medium-size pearl beads (amount varies with lace design); 1½ yds white/gold lace trimming *(see Materials Shopping Guide, page 272)*; 1½ yds 1½"-wide moss velvet ribbon; ¼ yd gold cord; thread to match all materials; paper for pattern; pins; scissors; ruler.

Directions:

1. Enlarge the pattern in FIG. III, 7, following the directions on page 271. Make a full-size paper pattern.

2. Using the pattern, cut the lace, taffeta, fleece and lining. Place one lace piece, right side up, on the right side of a taffeta piece. Place both on a fleece piece. Baste all together along all edges. Repeat for the second set.

3. Sew the pearl beads to accent the lace. Do not sew any within the seam allowance.

4. Place the stocking pieces with right sides together and all edges even. Sew together along all but the top edge. Slash the seam at the curves. Turn the stocking to the right side.

5. Sew the lining pieces together. Insert the lining in the stocking. Sew the top edges of the stocking and lining together.

6. For the ruffle, cut one 28" x 5¾" piece of taffeta with the short end parallel to the grain. On one long edge, turn up 1" to the right side of the fabric. Baste near the cut edge.

7. Sew white/gold lace over the cut edge with the scalloped edge of the lace ¼" above the folded edge of the taffeta. Pleat the unhemmed long edge to fit the top edge of the stocking.

8. Sew the pleated cuff to the stocking near the cut edges. Turn under the short end at the back and sew, overlapping slightly, to the opposite short end.

9. Sew velvet ribbon to the top edge of the stocking as binding. Sew white/gold lace over the ribbon, turning the top lace edge under the gold before sewing.

10. Cut streamers of ribbon. Sew to the stocking.

11. Make a bow of separate loops sewn over the streamers. Sew a "knot" of ribbon to the center of the bow.

12. Make a hanger loop of gold cord and sew it to the inside top of the stocking.

VICTORIAN BROCADE STOCKING

Average: For those with some experience in sewing.

Materials: ½ yd red metallic brocade; ½ yd polyester fleece interlining; ½ yd white lining fabric; 4½ yds ⅜"-wide green satin ribbon; 2 yds 1"-wide white cotton lace; 3½ yds ¼"-wide gold picot edge braid; 1 yd 1½"-wide red velvet ribbon; thread to match all materials; paper for pattern; pins; scissors; ruler; pencil.

Directions:

1. Enlarge the pattern pieces in FIG. III, 7, to full size following the directions on page 271.

2. Using the pattern, cut the brocade, lining and fleece. Place one brocade piece, right side up, on a fleece piece. Baste together along all edges. Repeat for the second brocade piece. Mark the heel and toe on the right side of the brocade. Sew a straight edge of lace to the marking, gathering the lace as necessary to allow it to lie flat. Invisibly stitch the scalloped edge of the lace to the stocking. Sew one long edge of green ribbon slightly overlapping the straight edge of the lace. Sew the free edge of the ribbon to the stocking, gathering the edge slightly as necessary. Sew gold picot edge braid over each edge of ribbon.

3. Place the stocking pieces with right sides together. Sew together along all but the top edge. Slash the seam at the curves. Turn the stocking to the right side.

4. Sew the lining pieces together. Insert the lining into the stocking. Sew the lining to the stocking along the top edge.

5. For the cuff, cut two 18" pieces of red velvet ribbon and one 18" piece of green satin ribbon. Sew one long edge of each piece of velvet ribbon to each edge of satin ribbon. Sew gold braid over each stitching line. Cut a 26" piece of lace. Gather it to fit one edge of the velvet ribbon. Sew it to the ribbon. Sew gold braid over the stitching line. Sew green satin ribbon to the opposite long edge of the velvet ribbon cuff. Pin the cuff to the stocking with the green ribbon inside the stocking at the binding. Sew to the stocking on the lining side, stitching along the free edge of ribbon. Overlap and invisibly sew the back edges of the cuff.

6. Make a half-rosette bow of 2" loops of green ribbon. Cut 5 streamers of varying lengths and sew them to the back of the bow. Sew the bow to the cuff.

7. Make a flat disc of picot braid and sew it to the center of the bow. Make a hanger loop of green ribbon. Sew it to the inside of the stocking.

FIG. III, 7 LACE AND TAFFETA STOCKING

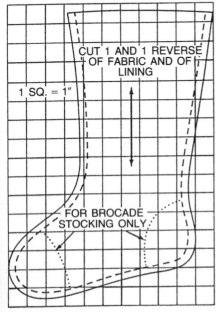

1 SQ. = 1"

CUT 1 AND 1 REVERSE OF FABRIC AND OF LINING

FOR BROCADE STOCKING ONLY

Folk Art Favorites

*Celebrate the season with festive hearts and flowers in
eye-catching colors and hand-crafted designs.*

💲🔧

FOLK ART ORNAMENTS

Average: For those with some experience in sewing and embroidery.
Materials *(for one ornament):* 1 each red and white 5" felt squares; small felt pieces in Kelly green, dark orange, red and fuchsia; fusible webbing; Persian yarn, about 2 yds for each ornament: yellow-orange, fuchsia, red, orange, light and dark greens; ⅛ yd ⅜"-wide red satin ribbon; polyester fiberfill; white and red thread; hot-glue gun; pinking shears.

Directions:
1. Enlarge the half-patterns in Fig. III, 8 on folded paper, following the directions on page 271. Cut out the layers of appliqué shapes separately. Unfold them to make the full patterns. Trace the various layers of shapes on the fusible webbing. Cut out the shapes. Cut out the background shapes from the white felt. Following the package directions on the fusible webbing, fuse the appliqués to the felt squares and hearts.
2. Make embroidered lines and dots over the appliqués, using long, straight and French knot stitches *(see Stitch Guide, page 270)*. All greens are worked using two of the three strands of yarn. All reds, oranges and fuchsias are worked using the full three strands of yarn.

3. Pin each ornament top to a red back. Stitch around three sides and four corners, leaving an opening for stuffing. Stuff with a small amount of polyester fiberfill and finish stitching. Trim the red back to ¼", using pinking shears. Heat the glue gun; fold the ribbon into a loop and glue it to the top back of the ornament.

FIG. III, 8   FOLK ART ORNAMENTS

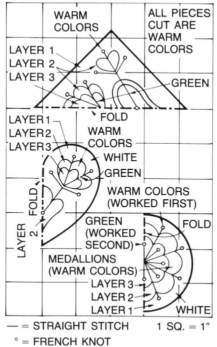

— = STRAIGHT STITCH   1 SQ. = 1"
° = FRENCH KNOT

💲

TREE SKIRT

Average: For those with some experience in sewing and embroidery.
Materials: 15 felt ornaments without ribbon loops; 1 yd white felt; 1¾" x 72" red felt edge strip.

Directions:
1. From the white felt, cut out a 36" circle. Cut a 4"-diameter hole in the center of the circle. Slash once from the circle to the outside edge. With white thread, staystitch both sides of the slash and around the center circle. Cut two 1½" x 72" strips of red felt. Place a red strip under the outside edge of the skirt with ½" showing. Stitch close to the circle edge. Repeat with a second row of stitching ¼" inside the first row. Trim the edge of red felt ¼" from the white with pinking shears, if desired.
2. Make 15 felt tree ornaments up through Step 2, above. Trim the edges with pinking shears and fuse each to a red back. Arrange the ornaments around the outside edge of the skirt and stitch in place around the outside edge of the white shapes.

Folk Art Tree

Dove Of Peace

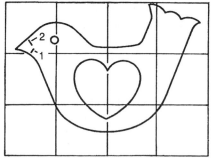

DOVE OF PEACE

Easy: Achievable by anyone.
Materials *(for four doves):* 9" x 12" sheet of white felt (makes 4 doves and 8 heart-shaped wings); blue embroidery thread or 6-strand embroidery floss, divided; embroidery needles; eight 5mm blue sequins for eyes; four ½" green leaf sequins; polyester fiberfill or cotton balls; vanishing fabric marker; white glue; 28" ⅜"-wide woven ribbon for tie at neck *(optional)*; tracing paper.

FIG. III, 9   DOVE OF PEACE

1 SQ. = 1"

Directions:
1. Enlarge the dove pattern in FIG. III, 9 onto tracing paper, following the directions on page 271. Separately trace the heart shape in the center. Cut out both shapes.
2. Trace 8 doves and 16 hearts on the felt, using a vanishing marker. Cut them out with small scissors. Allow 2 to 3 days for the ink to evaporate completely, then proceed.
3. Pin together the matching pieces of the doves.
4. Use two strands of floss (1⅓ yds long) in the needle. Separate the felt layers at the beak and run the thread through the bottom layer, ⅜" from the tip of the beak; *leave a 3" end hanging.* Rejoin the layers and work a long overcast stitch *(see line 1 in* FIG. III, 9*).* Then continue around the bird body using ⅛" overcast stitches *(see Stitch Guide, page 270)* evenly spaced ⅛" apart. When you reach the back of the head, stuff the dove firmly, then continue overcasting, ending with a long stitch *(see line 2 in* FIG. III, 9*).* Cut the thread, leaving another 3". Tie the thread-ends together inside the beak layers and cut off the excess.
5. Glue a peace leaf between the beak layers. Glue on the sequin eyes.
6. Overcast (20" thread) and stuff 8 pairs of hearts, with the starting 3" thread-end extending ¼" below the center on the back piece. Bring the last stitch through the back below the other thread-end and tie so the knot will be hidden when the heart is glued to the dove *(see position in photo).*
7. Add a ribbon tie around the neck, if desired.
8. Sew a hanger cord at the top edge of the neck/back, making sure the dove is balanced; tie the ends to make a loop.

COUNTRY VILLAGE

Average: For those with some experience in woodworking.

Directions:
Cut wood as shown. Paint as per photo, or as you like. We chose dark paint for the doors and windows, and varied the roofs, hip, gable and flat.

FIG. III, 10   COUNTRY VILLAGE

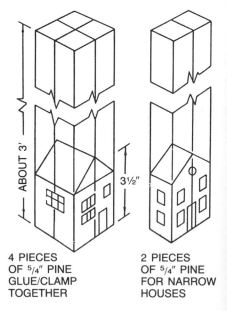

4 PIECES
OF ⁵/₄" PINE
GLUE/CLAMP
TOGETHER

2 PIECES
OF ⁵/₄" PINE
FOR NARROW
HOUSES

ABOUT 3'

3½"

Country Village; Village Doorstop

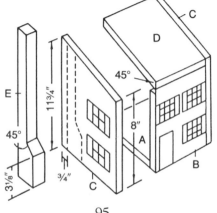

💲 🔨

VILLAGE DOORSTOP

Average: For those with some experience in woodworking.

Directions:
Glue and nail as shown. Sand the wood, fill as needed. Paint as shown, or as you like.

FIG. III, 11 VILLAGE DOORSTOP
(6½"W. x 5½"D. x 12"H.)

A (½ x 6) PINE (1) ½" x 5½" x 5" BOTTOM
B (½ x 6) PINE (1) ½" x 5½" x 7½" FRONT
C (½ x 6) PINE (2) ½" x 5½" x 11¾" SIDES
D (½ x 6) PINE (1) ½" x 5½" x 7" ROOF
E (5/4) PINE (1) 5/4" x 1⅝" x 14" CHIMNEY

95

Folk Art Frames

FOLK ART FRAMES
*(about 7¼" x 9¼" and
10½" x 12¼")*

Average: For those with some experience in woodworking.

Materials *(for one frame for a
5" x 7" picture):* ¾" x 1½" x 36" piece pine; ½" brads; 1½" brads; wood glue; ¼" pine scrap for hearts; miter box; hammer; saw; router; black and red acrylic paints; antiquing stain; sponge and cloths; 5" x 6⅞" piece glass; 5" x 6⅞" piece cardboard; photograph; screw eyes; wire.

Directions:
1. Use a router to cut a 5/16" x ¼" deep groove along one edge of ¾" pine.
2. Using a miter box, cut 2 pieces with an outside edge of 7⅜" and 2 pieces with an outside edge of 9¼". (The grooved edge is the inside edge. The angle is 45°.) Glue the frame together and secure with nails.
3. Cut hearts from ¼" pine. Round their edges with sandpaper and paint them red. Paint the frame black. Glue the hearts in place.
4. For painted corners, use a sponge for a soft effect. Stain the front and sides of the frame with antiquing stain and wipe it off to "antique."
5. Place the glass in the frame, then the photograph and cardboard backing; fasten with ½" brads.
6. Hang the frame using screw eyes and wire.
Note: *For larger frames, increase all dimensions proportionately, and follow directions above.*

HEART SHELF

Average: For those with some experience in staining and decorative painting.

Materials: Unstained wood shelf with heart cut-out on backboard (available at country craft stores); oil paints: leaf green light, leaf green medium, leaf green dark, cadmium red light, burnt alizarin, burnt umber and black; white acrylic paint; palette and palette knife; odorless turpentine; wide mouth container for turpentine; soft rags; clear oil base antiquing glaze; varnish; wood sealer; clear acrylic spray; brushes: PH Red Sable small 6 or 8, PH Red Sable medium 10 or 12, PH Red Sable large 14 or 16, sponge brush and #1 liner or scroll brush; tracing paper; graphite paper; stylus or ballpoint pen that does not write; masking tape; medium fine sandpaper.

FIG. III, 12 HEART SHELF

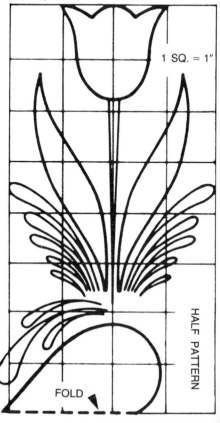

Directions:

1. Stain the shelf using burnt umber mixed in turpentine. Spread it on with a rag and wipe it off with a clean rag. Repeat to make the stain darker, if desired. Allow the shelf to dry and apply a coat of wood sealer. When the sealer is dry, sand lightly.

2. Using the sponge brush and white acrylic paint, paint the background for the design as shown in the photo. Let it dry. Seal the acrylic background by misting on several light coats of clear acrylic spray.

3. Enlarge the pattern in Fig. III, 12, following the directions on page 271. Trace the design onto tracing paper and transfer the pattern to the project: Center the design on the project, tape it in place and slip a sheet of graphite paper between the traced design and the prepared surface. Be sure the right side of the graphite is down. Neatly and *lightly* go over the lines on the tracing paper with a stylus or ballpoint pen that does not write to transfer the pattern.

4. Squeeze the oil colors onto the palette and use the turpentine to thin the reds to the consistency of soft butter. Thin the greens to the consistency of heavy cream. Using the large brush, paint the tulips cadmium red light. Wipe the brush and apply a little burnt alizarin to the left side of each tulip, blending the two colors together where they meet each other. (This shading is optional.)

5. The large green strokes are painted in thinned leaf green dark, the medium strokes in leaf green medium and the smaller strokes in leaf green light. The edges of the heart-shaped cutout are painted red. Use the liner or scroll brush and the black paint to outline the edges of the white acrylic areas and use the black paint to cover the bottom edge of the shelf.

6. When the design is completely finished, allow the paint to dry thoroughly. This will take several days depending upon the temperature, humidity and air circulation. When the paint is completely dry, apply a coat of oil base varnish.

Heart Shelf

THE CHRISTMAS BOOK

To preserve your fondest Christmas memories, keep a "Christmas Book." Cover a loose-leaf binder with Christmas fabric. In it, put the children's letters to Santa (so graciously returned on Christmas Eve), a brief description of what you did to celebrate, and ideas for future Christmases. It's a delight to see how your family changes over the years — and a real treat for your children to read their letters to Santa from years ago.

7. To antique, mix a little burnt umber oil paint into a tablespoon of oil base antiquing glaze. Brush this over the painted design. Use a soft rag to wipe off as much of the antiquing glaze as you desire. Let the glaze dry well and apply a final coat of varnish.

KISSING BALL

Materials: A block of oasis (available at florist shops); chicken wire; No. 18 wire for hanger; boxwood or other clippings; cranberry strings and lady apples *(optional)*; red ribbon; floral picks.

Directions:

1. To make the core, wrap a block of oasis with chicken wire, bending it to cover every side. Twist small pieces of heavy-gauge wire through the chicken wire to hold the edges in place. Soak the oasis in water and hang it on a coat hanger until the excess water drips off.

KISSING BALL

WIRE →

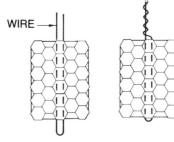

OASIS BLOCK COVERED IN CHICKEN WIRE

2. Cut a 4-foot-long wire and bend it in half. Push the wire through the bottom of the oasis *(see illustration above)* so its U-shaped end will rest against the oasis bottom. At the oasis top, twist the wire again. Then twist the wire ends at a length to reach a ceiling hook.
3. From a coat hanger, hang the core at eye level in your work

COUNTRY ACCENTS THROUGHOUT THE HOUSE

Nothing says "welcome" like a little touch of country!

space. Cut boxwood or other clippings and push them into the oasis. Trim them, if needed, to form a round ball. Add cranberry strings and clusters of lady apples *(see Directions, page 35 and tip box, page 34)*, if you wish.
4. Fold a 12"-long ribbon in half and cut fishtail ends. At the folded end, twist a wire that is attached to a floral pick and push the pick into the bottom of the ball. Attach a loop of ribbon to cover the hanger.
5. Spray the ball (avoiding the ribbons) with wax, if you wish.

COUNTRY CHARMERS:

• Buy pine- or spice-scented candles, potpourri and sprays to add a holiday air throughout the house.
• Tuck boughs of pine and holly around picture frames, on window sills and along the mantel.
• Hang ornaments from ribbons in the window or from mirrors.
• Use old quilts as tablecloths and sofa throws.
• Place candles in windows, always on fireproof plates or trays. Remember to tie back curtains to keep them out of the way.
• Hang mistletoe in strategic places!
• Make the most of pine cones. Use them as placecard holders, centerpieces or shelf objects. You can give pine cones holiday pizzazz by spray-painting them gold or silver, or spraying them with glue and rolling them in glitter. Or leave them plain and trim with holiday-bright ribbons.
• Hang garlands and swags in doorways and through stair bannisters, as well as on the tree.
• Frame doorways and windows with wide tartan craft ribbon; add bows in corners or directly above the doorway for a "gift box" effect.
• Baskets give any room country flair. Fill them with ornaments, pine cones, nuts, fruit, greenery or other Christmas-y items and place them in every room of the house.

Christmas-In-The-Country Quilt

"CHRISTMAS-IN-THE-COUNTRY" QUILT

(wallhanging, about 55" x 65"; full-size quilt, about 76" x 86")

Challenging: For those with more experience in quilting.

Note: *Measurements are given first for the wallhanging; the full-size quilt appears in parenthesis.*

Materials: 8 yds small cream print (11 yds); 1½ yds small red print (A) (2½ yds); 1½ yds small red print (B) (2½ yds); 3 yds small green print (6 yds); ½ yd small yellow print (1 yd); embroidery floss: 1 skn black, 2 skn gold (1 black, 3 gold); 1 pre-shrunk full-size poly/cotton batting (full-size); 3 water soluble pens (5); three 4-oz balls cream yarn (6); tapestry needle; 53" dowel (for wallhanging).

Directions:

Note: *All seams are pressed open. All seams are ¼"; due to shrinkage, add ¼" to all seams of the flower pieces, A through J. (See page 100.)*

1. Pre-shrink all fabrics and press. Enlarge the patterns for the pieced square in FIG. III, 13A, following the directions on page 271. Cut out the following: A—10 (21), B—10 (21), C—20 (42), D—20 (42), E—10 (21), F—20 (42), G—30 (63), H—80 (168), using 2 different red prints, I—60 (126), J—30 (63), and 130" (275") ⅝"-wide bias green print for the stem.

2. To begin the pieced square, follow the diagram for the colors and position of each pattern piece. Sew four H's together, alternating red colors, at the side seams so that the points meet in the center. Press. Sew J to the top two center H's and the two I's to the side H's. Press. To complete the bud, sew G across the bottom of the four H's. Press. Repeat for the other two buds. To form the center, sew D to C, press, sew to the left side of E. Press. Repeat again for the right side. Press the edges under on the bias strip and appliqué in place for the stems, using a slipstitch. Leave open at the top of the center stem at the X's. Fold that piece back against the sewn stem and pin in place. This will keep the stem free for sewing the center bud in place later. Sew A to B, press. Sew the other side of B to the completed stem section. This completes the center section.

3. To complete the square, sew one F to the right side of the left bud, press. Sew the left side of the center bud to the other side of F, leave open below the O so the stem can be slipped in later. Press. Set aside. Take the remaining bud and sew the other F to the left side. Press. Attach those 2 pieces to the right side of the center section. Press. Sew the other 2 bud sections all the way across the left side of the center section and left side of the F section, leaving open at this time between the T and the O.

CHRISTMAS-IN-THE-COUNTRY QUILT

FIG. III, 13A PIECED SQUARE

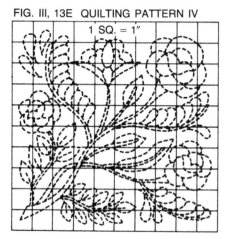

FIG. III, 13B QUILTING PATTERN I

1 SQ. = 1"

FIG. III, 13C QUILTING PATTERN II

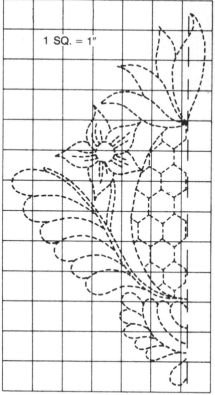

1 SQ. = 1"

FIG. III, 13D QUILTING PATTERN III

1 SQ. = 1"

FIG. III, 13E QUILTING PATTERN IV

1 SQ. = 1"

FIG. III, 13F BORDER

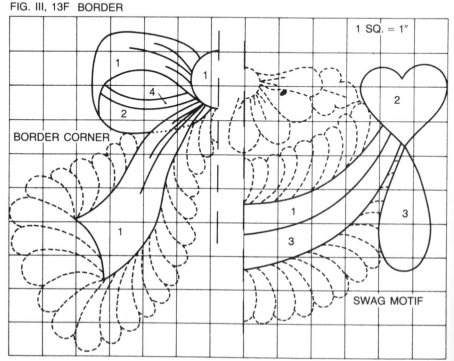

1 SQ. = 1"

BORDER CORNER

SWAG MOTIF

Press. Slip the unsewn portion of the stem under the tip of the center bud. Slipstitch in place. Press. It should measure 10″. Repeat the square 10 (21) times.

4. Cut 10 (21) 10″ squares of the cream print fabric and sew to the sides of the pieced squares, alternating the squares so the flowers appear to run diagonally. Press.

5. From the cream print, cut 2 border strips 10″ x 58″ (11″ x 79″). Center and sew them to the top and bottom of the quilt center. Leave open ¼″ from each edge. Cut 2 side borders 10″ x 67½″ (11″ x 88½″). Center and sew them to the quilt sides, ending the seam at the corners. Miter all four corners, sew and press.

6. For the border, enlarge the pattern in FIG. III, 13F, following the directions on page 271; cut out 20 (26) green and 20 (26) red swags, 14 (22) hearts, 14 (22) green teardrops and 4 (4) red bows. Appliqué in place using the freezer paper method. *(See box, at right.)* Wash the quilt top, remove the freezer paper, dry and press.

7. To embroider, use three strands of floss and chain stitch *(see Stitch Guide, page 270)* in gold around the outside of the red hearts and between the green and red swag. Embroider the bow in black and gold, following the lines on the pattern. Enlarge the quilting patterns in FIGS. III, 13B, C, D and E, following the directions on page 271, and transfer the quilting patterns to borders, pieced squares and plain squares, using a water soluble pen. Half patterns are indicated by large lines. After completing Pattern II (FIG. III, 13C), place the design on the diagonal. Complete Pattern III (FIG. III, 13D) by continuing the flower along the arrows. Broken lines indicate quilting stitches. The four square designs are repeated as needed. A light table works best for transferring.

8. Fill in the background of each of the four square designs, using a ruler, by making diagonal lines ⅛″ apart. This causes the background to be very flat and the design to become raised. Do the same for the border background, except run the lines perpendicular to the border.

9. To make the quilt back, cut two pieces 45″ x 70″ (45″ x 91″) and sew them together along the long edge. Press. Trim down one long side to be 60″ wide for the wallhanging only. Save the extra fabric for casings to use for hanging the quilt.

10. Cut the batting the same size and put it on the wrong side of the backing. Attach the quilt top to both layers using long basting stitches.

11. Starting in the center of the quilt, quilt all traced design lines, as well as within ¼″ of each individual piece of pieced square and each appliquéd piece.

12. The final process is called stuff work. Using a tapestry needle and yarn doubled, run the needle *only* between the quilt top and batting. Begin each area to be stuffed by running the needle down at one edge and through to the other side, just within the quilting lines. Pull the yarn carefully until it just slips inside between the top layer and batting. Clip the other end of the yarn right next to the fabric. Taking the needle and poking down through the top layer, the yarn can be pushed or pulled to adjust if necessary. Continue the process until the leaf or berry is fat and full. Holes made by the large needle can be easily pushed back together with the needle, once an area is finished. With a final washing, the fibers all settle back into place.

13. To finish the quilt, cut bias binding 2½″ x 270″ (340″) out of the green fabric. Cut the quilt back and batting to the edges of the quilt. Sew on the binding, using a ½″ seam. Miter the corners. Before finishing the top edge of the quilt, sew a 3″ casing into the seam line at the back side of the quilt, the whole length. Turn under ½″ along the other side of the casing. Slipstitch to the backing, allowing room for a dowel rod (for the wallhanging only). To remove the quilting design lines, wash the entire quilt, dry and hang.

FREEZER PAPER METHOD OF APPLIQUÉ

Place the freezer paper so the dull side faces up. Trace all patterns to the exact finished size (no seam allowance). Cut out the patterns and place, shiny side down, on the wrong side of the fabric. Leave room for a generous ⅛-inch seam allowance around each piece. Iron the freezer paper with a hot iron. The wax side will stick to the fabric (until washed out later). Cut around each bonded piece leaving a seam allowance. Apply a glue stick to the seam allowance and roll the glued edges over the freezer paper to make perfect curves and edges. Arrange the appliqué pieces on the background fabric and attach in place by using the glue stick on the back side of each piece. When dry, sew in place, using a single thread in a matching color, around each piece. To remove the freezer paper, soak the project in cold water for 10 to 15 minutes to dissolve the glue and release the wax. Blot with a towel to remove moisture. Make a slit on the back side underneath each appliquéd piece. Cut away the underside of all appliquéd pieces to ¼ inch to ⅛ inch of seam line (this makes it easier for quilting later). Using a seam ripper, carefully pull out the freezer paper. When all the paper is removed, soak in cold water again to remove any remaining glue. When almost dry, press with steam iron. Trim all excess fabric, including seams (this makes fewer layers to quilt and allows for smaller, closer stitches). Do not trim too closely and handle the pieces gently to prevent the seams from pulling out.

The Country Hearth

Regal Roast Beef Dinner

(for 12)

Warm Shrimp Appetizer Salad*
Regal Roast Beef*, Rich Pan Gravy*
Roasted Potatoes*
Savory Winter Squash*
Baked Baby Tomatoes*
Buttered Asparagus*
Fluted Mushrooms*
Cranberry Wine Mold*
Yorkshire Popovers*
Cranberry Pear Tart*
(regular and low-calorie
versions included)
Apple Cream Cheese Pie*

*Recipes follow

*Regal Roast Beef; Buttered Asparagus; Baked Baby Tomatoes; Roasted Potatoes;
Fluted Mushrooms; Cranberry Wine Mold; Savory Winter Squash; Yorkshire Popovers*

Work Plan

Up to 1 Month Ahead:
• Bake and freeze Apple Cream Cheese Pie (or prepare up to several days ahead and refrigerate).

Up to Several Days Ahead:
• Prepare and refrigerate filling, and bake shell for Cranberry Pear Tart.

The Day Before:
• Prepare ingredients for Warm Shrimp Appetizer Salad; refrigerate.
• Prepare Cranberry Wine Mold; refrigerate.
• Prepare Savory Winter Squash.

Early in the Day:
• Unmold Cranberry Wine Mold; refrigerate.
• Finish Cranberry Pear Tart by filling shell, covering with meringue and baking.
• Make Fluted Mushrooms.
• Hollow out tomatoes for Baked Baby Tomatoes.
• Make batter for Yorkshire Popovers.

3½ to 4½ Hours Before:
• Let beef for Regal Roast Beef come to room temperature, then roast.

2½ Hours Before:
• Boil potatoes for Roasted Potatoes; add to oven.

1 Hour Before:
• Prepare Warm Shrimp Appetizer Salad.
• Make Rich Pan Gravy.
• Bake Yorkshire Popovers.
• Prepare and heat Baked Baby Tomatoes.
• Reheat Savory Winter Squash.

Warm Shrimp Appetizer Salad

Most of the ingredients can be prepared a day ahead; the shrimp topping is quickly cooked just before serving.

Makes 12 servings.

2 **heads Belgian endive**
1 **medium-size head romaine lettuce**
1 **small head chicory**
2 **zucchini (about 8 ounces each)**
1 **bag (6 ounces) red radishes**
2 **small red onions**
½ **cup extra-virgin olive oil**
⅓ **cup fresh lemon juice (2 to 3 lemons)**
1 **tablespoon Worcestershire sauce**
1 **teaspoon dry mustard**
½ **teaspoon salt**
¼ **teaspoon white pepper**
¼ **cup vegetable oil**
1½ **pounds uncooked medium-size shrimp in the shell (1¼ pounds peeled and cleaned)**
2 **cloves garlic, finely chopped**

1. Trim the stem end of the Belgian endives. Cut the endives lengthwise into quarters. Separate into individual leaves. Wrap in paper toweling, place in a plastic bag and store in the refrigerator.
2. Separate the romaine and the chicory into leaves. Wash and dry. Tear into bite-size pieces. Wrap the greens in paper toweling, place in a plastic bag and refrigerate.
3. Cut the zucchini into 2½ x ½-inch strips. Cut each radish into 4 or 6 wedges. Halve the red onions and slice crosswise. Wrap each vegetable separately in a plastic bag and refrigerate.
4. Combine the olive oil, lemon juice, Worcestershire sauce, mustard, salt and pepper in a jar with a tight-fitting lid. Shake well to blend; set aside.
5. Just before serving, heat the vegetable oil in a large skillet. Add the shrimp and the garlic; sauté over medium-high heat just until the shrimp are pink and tender, for about 3 minutes. Remove with a slotted spoon to a bowl. Add the zucchini strips to the skillet; sauté until crisp-tender, for about 4 minutes. Remove the skillet from the heat. Stir in the red onion slices and the radishes. Return the shrimp and their juices to the skillet. Shake the dressing and add to the

shrimp mixture. Stir to mix well. Place the greens in a large, shallow salad bowl. Spoon the shrimp mixture over, toss and serve.

Regal Roast Beef

Since the days of King Henry VIII, beef has been a British favorite and today it's still America's favorite celebration meat.

Roast at 325° for 2 hours.
Makes 12 servings, plus leftovers.

1   **eye round roast (about 6 pounds)**
    Seasoned salt and pepper
    All-purpose flour
3   **large carrots, chopped**
3   **stalks celery, cut into sticks**
1   **large onion, chopped (1 cup)**
1   **large onion, cut into wedges**
    Rich Pan Gravy (recipe follows)
    Parsley sprigs for garnish

1. Allow the meat to stand at room temperature for at least 1 hour before roasting. Sprinkle the beef with the seasoned salt and pepper and rub with the flour to coat well.
2. Preheat the oven to slow (325°).
3. Sprinkle the chopped carrots, celery sticks and chopped onions in the bottom of a shallow roasting pan. Place the roast on top and arrange the onion wedges on top of the roast. Insert a meat thermometer near the center of the roast, if you wish.
4. Roast in the preheated slow oven (325°) for 2 hours for rare (130° on a meat thermometer), 2 hours, 20 minutes for medium (145° on a meat thermometer) or 2 hours, 40 minutes for well done (160° on a meat thermometer).
5. Remove the roast from the roasting pan to a heated serving platter. Cover lightly with aluminum foil and allow to rest for at least 30 minutes in a warm place.
6. Prepare the Rich Pan Gravy. Preheat the oven to very hot (450°) to make the Yorkshire Popovers.
7. At serving time, arrange the trimmings *(recipes follow)* and the parsley sprigs on the platter around the roast beef and serve with the Rich Pan Gravy.

Rich Pan Gravy: Remove the vegetables from the roasting pan with a slotted spoon and discard. Tip the pan and ladle off ¼ cup of the fat for making the Yorkshire Popovers. Bring the pan drippings to bubbling over medium heat; stir in ½ cup all-purpose flour with a wire whisk until very smooth. Cook, stirring constantly, for 2 minutes. Add the 4 cups reserved vegetable cooking liquid and cook, stirring constantly, until the mixture thickens and bubbles, for 3 minutes. Taste and season with bottled gravy coloring, if you wish, and salt and pepper. Serve bubbling hot with the sliced Regal Roast Beef. *Makes 4 cups.*

Roasted Potatoes

Roast at 325° for 2 hours.
Makes 12 servings.

12   **medium boiling potatoes**
½   **cup vegetable oil**
     Salt and freshly ground pepper

1. Preheat the oven to slow (325°).
2. Pare the potatoes and place in a kettle. Add 3 cups water and bring to boiling over medium heat. Lower the heat, cover the kettle and cook for 10 minutes.
3. Remove the potatoes from the kettle to a large shallow pan with a slotted spoon. Remove and reserve the cooking water for the Rich Pan Gravy.
4. Drizzle the oil over the potatoes to coat evenly; sprinkle with the salt and pepper.
5. Bake in the preheated slow oven (325°), turning and brushing with the oil several times, for 2 hours, or until the potatoes are richly golden. Serve on the platter with the Regal Roast Beef.

💲 �️

Savory Winter Squash

Hubbard squash, named for Mrs. Hubbard of Marblehead, Massachusetts, is the traditional squash served in New England. You can also use butternut, Turk's head or acorn squash.

Bake at 300° for 1½ hours, then at 325° for 45 minutes.
Makes 12 servings.

- **1 small Hubbard squash OR: 2 butternut squash OR: 4 large acorn squash**
- **¼ cup (½ stick) butter or margarine, sliced**
- **2 teaspoons salt**
- **½ teaspoon freshly ground pepper**
- **1 small onion, grated**

1. Preheat the oven to slow (300°).
2. Scrub the whole squash and place on either a jelly-roll or baking pan.
3. Bake in the preheated slow oven (300°), turning several times, for 1½ hours for acorn squash, 2 hours for butternut squash and 2½ hours for Hubbard squash, or until the squash begins to sink and is tender when a 2-tined fork is inserted.
4. Allow to cool until easy to handle. Cut the squash in half and scoop out the seeds. Scoop the squash from the skin with a large spoon and place in a large bowl. Mash with a potato masher until smooth. (If you have baked a Hubbard squash, use 8 cups of the mashed squash in the recipe and pack the remaining squash in serving-size portions in freezer containers. Label, date and freeze.)
5. Beat the butter or margarine, salt, pepper and grated onion into the mashed squash until smooth. Spoon into a 10-cup casserole and cover with aluminum foil. (The recipe may be prepared up to this point. Refrigerate.) Allow to stand at room temperature before heating.
6. At serving time, preheat the oven to slow (325°).
7. Bake in the preheated slow oven (325°) for 45 minutes, or until heated through. Keep warm.

🔥

Baked Baby Tomatoes

Bake at 325° for 20 minutes.
Makes 12 servings.

- **12 small ripe tomatoes**
- **¼ cup (½ stick) butter or margarine**
- **1 teaspoon leaf basil, crumbled**
  Salt and pepper

1. Preheat the oven to slow (325°).
2. Wipe the tomatoes with a damp cloth. Remove the cores with a sharp paring knife. Arrange the prepared tomatoes, core-side down, in a 13 x 9 x 2-inch baking dish.
3. Heat the butter or margarine, basil and salt and pepper in a small saucepan until the butter or margarine melts. Spoon over the tomatoes to coat evenly.
4. Bake in the preheated slow oven (325°) for 20 minutes, or just until tender. Serve on the platter with the Regal Roast Beef.

Note: *Baked Baby Tomatoes can be varied to make containers for other vegetables on the holiday table. In Step 2, remove a little of the tomato along with the core to make a cup; arrange the tomatoes, core-side up, in the baking dish. If they wobble, cut off a sliver from the bottom of each. After baking, fill with lightly steamed peas and/or cauliflower for an especially festive combination.*

🔥

Buttered Asparagus

Makes 12 servings.

- **3 pounds fresh asparagus, trimmed OR: 3 packages (10 ounces each) frozen asparagus spears**
- **¼ cup (½ stick) butter or margarine, sliced**
  Salt and freshly ground pepper
  Chopped parsley

1. Soak the fresh asparagus in salted warm water for 5 minutes; remove from the water to a large skillet. OR: Place the frozen asparagus directly into a large skillet. Add 1 cup water to the skillet.
2. Bring to boiling over medium heat. Lower the heat, cover and cook for 7 minutes, or until the

fresh spears are crisply tender. OR: Cook the frozen asparagus for 3 minutes. Separate the spears with 2 forks and steam for 3 minutes longer, or just until tender.

3. Drain the cooking liquid from the skillet and add to the reserved potato cooking water.

4. Add the butter or margarine to the skillet. Toss gently until the butter or margarine melts and coats the asparagus. Season with the salt, freshly ground pepper and chopped parsley. Serve on the platter with the Regal Roast Beef.

Note: To trim asparagus, cut off the very bottom of the spears with a sharp knife. Use a swivel-bladed peeler to remove the tough outer skin of the spear bottoms.

Fluted Mushrooms

Makes 12 servings.

1 **pound medium-size mushrooms**
  Butter or margarine

1. Cut off the stems close to the caps. (Set them aside for another dish.)

2. With a sharp-tipped, thin-bladed knife, mark the center of a cap. Starting there, make a curved cut, about ⅛ inch deep, to the edge. Repeat around the cap to make 8 evenly spaced cuts.

3. Make a second curved cut just behind each line, slanting the knife so you can lift out the narrow strip.

4. Brown the caps in butter or margarine. Serve on the platter with the Regal Roast Beef.

Yorkshire Popovers

Baked with a little of the fat from the roast, these sky-high hot-breads add glamour, not work, to the menu.

Bake at 450° for 40 minutes.
Makes 12 very large popovers.

¼ **cup fat from roast**
3 **cups all-purpose flour**
1 **teaspoon salt**
6 **eggs**
3 **cups milk**

1. Measure 1 teaspoon fat from the roast into each of twelve 6-ounce custard cups. (Or you can add 1 teaspoon vegetable oil to each.)

2. Preheat the oven to very hot (450°). Place the cups on a 15 x 10 x 1-inch jelly-roll pan and place in the oven while it preheats.

3. Combine the flour and the salt in a large bowl; add the eggs and the milk. Beat with an electric mixer on high speed for 2 minutes, or until smooth. Ladle the batter into the hot custard cups, dividing evenly.

4. Bake in the preheated very hot oven (450°) for 30 minutes. Cut a small slit in the side of each popover with the tip of a paring knife for the steam to escape. Bake for 10 minutes longer, or until crisp and dark brown. Serve hot with the Regal Roast Beef and the Rich Pan Gravy.

Cranberry Wine Mold

Although cranberries grow in many parts of the country, New Englanders like to claim this holiday berry as their own.

Makes one 8-cup mold.

1 **package (12 ounces) fresh cranberries**
1½ **cups sugar**
¾ **cup red wine**
¾ **cup water**
1 **package (6 ounces) raspberry-flavored gelatin**
1 **cup chopped walnuts**

1. Rinse the cranberries in a strainer and remove any stems. Place the berries in a large saucepan. Add the sugar, wine and water to the saucepan and stir to blend.

2. Bring to boiling over medium heat. Lower the heat and cook for 5 minutes, or until the berries burst. Remove the saucepan from the heat and stir in the raspberry-flavored gelatin until the gelatin dissolves.

3. Place the saucepan in the freezer and chill, stirring several times, for 30 minutes, or until the gelatin becomes syrupy.

4. Fold the chopped walnuts into the gelatin mixture until well blended. Pour into an 8-cup mold or deep bowl. Refrigerate for 4 hours, or overnight.

5. To unmold, run a thin-bladed knife around the

edge of the mold. Dip the mold into a pan of hot water for 30 seconds. Invert the mold onto a serving plate. Return the gelatin mold to the refrigerator until serving time.

Always chill gelatin until it is syrupy before folding in any solid ingredients. This way, they'll remain suspended in the gelatin rather than falling to the bottom.

Cranberry Pear Tart

A pear adds just a touch of sweetness to the cranberry filling.

Bake tart shell at 375° for 12 to 15 minutes; bake meringue at 400° for 3 to 6 minutes.
Makes 8 servings.

Cranberry Filling:
- ¼ **cup water**
- ¾ **cup sugar**
- ½ **cup red currant jelly**
- 3 **cups fresh or frozen cranberries (12-ounce package), thawed if frozen**
- 1 **firm, ripe pear, pared, cored and chopped (1 cup)**

Tart Shell:
- ½ **cup (1 stick) butter**
- 1¼ **cups all-purpose flour**
- ¼ **cup sugar**
- ⅔ **cup finely chopped or ground walnuts**
- ½ **teaspoon ground cinnamon**
- 2 **egg yolks**

Meringue:
- 4 **egg whites**
- ⅛ **teaspoon cream of tartar**
- ½ **cup sugar**

1. Combine the water, the ¾ cup sugar and the jelly in a medium-size saucepan. Place over medium heat until the jelly melts and the sugar dissolves.
2. Bring to boiling; add the cranberries and the pear. Cook, uncovered, over medium heat until the cranberries pop and the mixture thickens slightly, for 10 to 15 minutes. Cool completely.
3. Preheat the oven to moderate (375°).
4. Cut the butter into the flour in a medium-size bowl with a pastry blender until crumbly. Mix in the ¼ cup sugar, the walnuts and cinnamon. Add the egg yolks; mix lightly with a fork just until the pastry holds together and cleans the side of the bowl. Press the dough over the bottom and up the side of a 9-inch tart pan with a removable bottom. Prick the bottom with a fork. Refrigerate for 30 minutes.
5. Bake the shell in the preheated moderate oven (375°) for 12 to 15 minutes, or until golden. Cool completely.
6. Spoon the cooled Cranberry Filling into the cooled pastry shell.
7. Reset the oven to hot (400°).
8. Beat the egg whites with the cream of tartar in a medium-size bowl until soft peaks form. Gradually beat in the ½ cup sugar until stiff, but not dry, peaks form. Spread half the meringue over the top of the tart. Pipe the remaining meringue in a lattice pattern.
9. Bake in the preheated hot oven (400°) for 3 to 6 minutes, or until the meringue is golden brown. Decorate with additional cranberries, if you wish.

Reduced-Calorie Cranberry Pear Tart

Here is a low calorie version of the Cranberry Pear Tart. By using more of the sweeter tasting pears, we've been able to use less sugar and even eliminate the currant jelly, for a lower calorie filling. We've also used a packaged piecrust mix rather than the homemade recipe, which is packed with fattening nuts. We've halved the amount of meringue, but there is still a generous amount for the topping.

Bake tart shell at 375° for 12 to 15 minutes; bake meringue at 400° for 3 to 5 minutes.
Makes 8 servings.

Cranberry Filling:
- ⅓ **cup sugar**
- ¼ **cup water**
- 1 **pound firm, ripe pears, pared, cored and chopped (3 cups)**
- 1½ **cups fresh or frozen cranberries, thawed if frozen**

Tart Shell:
- ½ **of 11-ounce package piecrust mix**

Meringue:
- 2 **egg whites**
- ⅛ **teaspoon cream of tartar**
- ¼ **cup sugar**

1. Combine the ⅓ cup sugar, the water, pears and cranberries in a medium-size saucepan. Bring to boiling over medium-high heat. Lower the heat; cook, uncovered, over medium heat until the cranberries pop and the mixture thickens slightly, for 10 to 15 minutes. Remove from the heat and cool completely.
2. Make the piecrust mix following the label directions for a 9-inch single-crust pie. Press the dough evenly over the bottom and up the side of a 9-inch tart pan with a removable bottom. Prick the bottom with a fork. Refrigerate for 30 minutes.
3. Meanwhile, preheat the oven to moderate (375°).
4. Bake the crust in the preheated moderate oven (375°) for 12 to 15 minutes, or until golden. Cool completely. Increase the oven temperature to hot (400°).
5. Spoon the Cranberry Filling into the cooled pastry shell.
6. Beat the egg whites with the cream of tartar in a medium-size bowl until soft peaks form. Gradually beat in the ¼ cup sugar until stiff, but not dry, peaks form. Pipe the meringue in a lattice pattern over the top of the tart.
7. Bake in the preheated, hot oven (400°) for 3 to 5 minutes, or until the meringue is golden brown.

TIPS ON APPLE CREAM CHEESE PIE (right)

- Peel apples and slice them just before using, so they won't turn brown.
- Always soften cream cheese before using it in a dessert; you'll avoid getting lumps and excess air bubbles.

Apple Cream Cheese Pie

Bake at 400° for 5 minutes, then at 450° for 10 minutes, then at 400° for 30 minutes.
Makes 8 servings.

Crust:
- ½ **cup (1 stick) butter or margarine**
- ⅓ **cup sugar**
- ¼ **teaspoon vanilla**
- 1 **cup all-purpose flour**

Filling:
- 2 **packages (8 ounces each) cream cheese, softened**
- ⅔ **cup sugar**
- 2 **eggs**
- 1 **teaspoon vanilla**
- 4 **cups thinly sliced peeled apple (see tip, below left)**
- ½ **teaspoon ground cinnamon**
- ½ **teaspoon ground nutmeg**
- ¼ **cup chopped walnuts**

- 2 **cups heavy cream**
   Additional apple slices for garnish

1. Preheat the oven to hot (400°).
2. Cream the butter or margarine and the ⅓ cup sugar in the large bowl of an electric mixer at high speed until fluffy. Blend in the ¼ teaspoon vanilla; add the flour, mixing well. Spread onto the bottom of an 8-inch springform pan.
3. Bake in the hot oven (400°) for 5 minutes, or until lightly browned. Cool slightly. Increase the oven temperature to very hot (450°).
4. Combine the cream cheese and ⅓ cup of the sugar in the large bowl of an electric mixer at high speed until fluffy. Blend in the eggs and the 1 teaspoon vanilla. Pour into the pastry-lined pan. Toss the apples with the remaining sugar, the cinnamon and nutmeg. Spoon over the cream cheese mixture. Sprinkle with the chopped walnuts.
5. Bake in the preheated very hot oven (450°) for 10 minutes. Lower the temperature to hot (400°) and continue baking for 30 minutes. Using a spatula, loosen the cake from the side of the pan. Cool in the pan on a wire rack. When completely cooled (4 to 5 hours), remove the side of the pan. Garnish with the additional apple slices and the cream, whipped and piped into rosettes.

Holiday Cookies

*It just wouldn't be Christmas without a batch
of goodies fresh from the oven.*

Chocolate Thumbprints

*A chocolate version of the classic recipe. Fill the center
with frosting and a cherry or jelly and nuts.*

Bake at 350° for 20 minutes.
Makes about 2½ dozen.

- 2 **cups all-purpose flour**
- ⅓ **cup unsweetened cocoa powder (not a mix)**
- ½ **teaspoon salt**
- 1 **cup (2 sticks) butter or margarine**
- ¾ **cup sugar**
- 2 **eggs, separated**
- ½ **teaspoon vanilla**
- 2 **cups finely chopped pecans**
- 1 **can (16 ounces) vanilla-flavored frosting**
  Candied red and green cherries

1. Preheat the oven to moderate (350°).
2. Sift together the flour, cocoa and salt onto wax paper.
3. Beat the butter or margarine and the sugar until light in the large bowl of an electric mixer at high speed. Beat in the egg yolks and the vanilla until well blended.
4. Lower the mixer speed to slow; add the flour mixture, mixing just until blended.
5. Lightly beat the egg whites in a small bowl. Place the chopped pecans in a shallow dish.
6. Shape the dough, 1 tablespoon at a time, into balls between very lightly moistened palms. Drop the balls into the egg whites, a few at a time, then roll in the chopped pecans with two forks. Place, 1 inch apart, on lightly greased cookie sheets. Press a hollow into the center of each ball, using a cork or your thumb.
7. Bake in the preheated moderate oven (350°) for 15 minutes. Press down the centers again. Bake for 5 minutes longer, or until the pecans are golden and the cookies are firm. Remove to a wire rack with a spatula; cool completely.
8. Fill a pastry bag or tube fitted with a medium star tip with the frosting. Pipe a rosette of frosting in the center of each cookie. Decorate with the cherries.

From top, left: Chocolate Thumbprints; Kris Kringle Cookies; Nutty Brownie Cookies; Molasses Jacks; Almond Crescents; Fruit and Nut Lebkuchen; French Jelly Hearts; Pecan Bourbon Balls; Jelly Diagonals; Fruitcake Fingers; Buttery Crisps

Molasses Jacks

Chewy cookies are studded with multicolored candies.

Bake at 350° for 12 minutes.
Makes 7 dozen.

- ¾ **cup (1½ sticks) butter or margarine**
- 2½ **cups firmly packed brown sugar**
- 1 **cup molasses**
- 3 **cups all-purpose flour**
- 1½ **teaspoons baking soda**
- ¼ **teaspoon salt**
- ½ **cup flaked coconut**
- ½ **cup chopped walnuts**
  Multicolored milk chocolate candies
  OR: Semisweet chocolate pieces

1. Beat the butter or margarine and the sugar in a large bowl with an electric mixer at high speed until light and fluffy. Beat in the molasses until well blended.
2. Sift together the flour, baking soda and salt onto wax paper; slowly beat into the creamed mixture just until blended. Stir in the coconut and the chopped walnuts. Cover with plastic wrap and refrigerate overnight.
3. Preheat the oven to moderate (350°).
4. Drop the dough by teaspoonfuls, 2 inches apart, on greased cookie sheets. Press 4 or 5 candies into each mound of dough.
5. Bake in the preheated moderate oven (350°) for 12 minutes. Cool for 1 minute on the cookie sheets on wire racks. Remove the cookies with a spatula and cool on the wire racks.

Buttery Crisps

Pretty pink sugar, nuts and candied fruit top these rich cookies.

Bake at 325° for 18 minutes.
Makes about 6 dozen.

- 2 **cups (4 sticks) butter or margarine**
- 2 **cups all-purpose flour**
- 1 **cup 10X (confectioners' powdered) sugar**
- 1 **cup cornstarch**
- 3 **egg whites, slightly beaten**
  Coarse sugar
  Few drops red food coloring
  Pecan halves
  Candied red cherries, halved

1. Beat the softened butter or margarine in a large bowl with an electric mixer at high speed until light and fluffy. Gradually beat in the flour, 10X (confectioners' powdered) sugar and cornstarch until well blended.
2. Divide the dough in quarters and wrap in aluminum foil. Refrigerate overnight, or until firm.
3. Preheat the oven to slow (325°).
4. Roll the dough, 1 teaspoon at a time, into balls. Place, 2 inches apart, on ungreased cookie sheets. Flatten the dough with a floured 4-tined fork to ¼-inch thickness.
5. Brush with the beaten egg whites; sprinkle with the coarse sugar that has been tinted pink with a few drops red food coloring. Place a pecan half or halved candied red cherry in the center of each cookie.
6. Bake in the preheated slow oven (325°) for 18 minutes, or until firm. Cool on wire racks.

⑤ ⧄ ◊

Kris Kringle Cookies

Use Christmas-shaped cutters to make these thin, crispy delights.

Bake at 375° for 8 minutes.
Makes 4 dozen.

½ cup vegetable shortening
1 cup granulated sugar
2 eggs
2 tablespoons milk or cream
1 tablespoon vanilla
3½ cups all-purpose flour
2 teaspoons baking powder
½ teaspoon salt
    10X (confectioners' powdered) sugar
    Egg white, slightly beaten
    Multicolored coarse sugar (optional)
    Assorted frostings and decorations

1. Beat the shortening and the sugar in a large bowl with an electric mixer at high speed until light and fluffy. Beat in the eggs, one at a time, then the milk or cream and the vanilla until well blended.
2. Sift together the flour, baking powder and salt onto wax paper; stir into the creamed mixture. Shape into a ball, wrap in plastic wrap and refrigerate overnight.
3. Preheat the oven to moderate (375°).
4. Roll out the dough, a quarter at a time, to ¼-inch thickness on a board or cloth dusted with the 10X (confectioners' powdered) sugar. Cut out with 2½- to 3-inch Christmas-shaped cutters that have been dipped in the 10X (confectioners' powdered) sugar. Place the dough, 2 inches apart, on greased cookie sheets.
5. Brush the dough with the beaten egg white; sprinkle with the multicolored coarse sugar before baking, if you wish.
6. Bake in the preheated moderate oven (375°) for 8 minutes, or until firm. Remove from the cookie sheets and cool on wire racks. Decorate as shown in photo (*page 111*).

⧄ ◊

Fruitcake Fingers

Cookies rich with fruit and nuts.

Bake at 250° for 3½ hours.
Makes about 6½ dozen.

1 package (15 ounces) raisins
1 package (12 ounces) Calimyrna figs, halved
1 package (12 ounces) black mission figs, halved
1 package (12 ounces) mixed dried fruit, cut up
2 cups chopped pitted dates
2 cups red glacé cherries
1 cup diced glacé orange peel
1 cup brandy
1½ cups (3 sticks) butter or margarine
2 cups firmly packed brown sugar
8 eggs
3 cups all-purpose flour
1 tablespoon pumpkin pie spice
2 teaspoons salt
2 cups coarsely chopped walnuts
1 cup toasted whole blanched almonds
    Fluffy Filling and Frosting (recipe follows)
    Cinnamon red hots

1. Combine the raisins, figs, mixed dried fruit and chopped dates in a very large bowl. Add the cherries and the orange peel.
2. Pour ½ cup of the brandy over the fruit and toss lightly. Cover with plastic wrap and let stand overnight.
3. Preheat the oven to very slow (250°).
4. Beat the butter or margarine in a large bowl with an electric mixer at high speed until light and fluffy. Gradually beat in the sugar until thoroughly blended.
5. Beat in the eggs, one at a time, beating well after each addition.
6. Sift together the flour, pumpkin pie spice and salt onto wax paper. Fold into the creamed mixture, part at a time. Stir in the marinated fruits and their liquid, the chopped walnuts and whole almonds.
7. Grease three 9 x 5 x 3-inch loaf pans. Line with brown paper; grease again. Fill the pans ¾ full with the batter.
8. Bake in the preheated very slow oven (250°) for 3½ hours, or until firm and golden brown.

Cool in the pans on wire racks for 10 minutes. Loosen the cakes around the edges of the pans and invert onto the wire racks. Drizzle with the remaining brandy. Wrap in aluminum foil and store in a large metal tin with a tight-fitting lid.

9. To serve, cut each loaf into 9 thick slices and cut each slice into 3 fingers. Fit a pastry bag with a medium-size star tip; fill with the Fluffy Filling and Frosting and pipe across each bar. Top with the cinnamon red hots.

Fluffy Filling and Frosting: Beat ½ cup (1 stick) softened butter or margarine and 1 package (3 ounces) softened cream cheese in a large bowl with an electric mixer at high speed until fluffy. Gradually beat in 1 pound sifted 10X (confectioners' powdered) sugar alternately with ¼ cup orange juice, until soft and very creamy. Stir in 4 teaspoons grated orange rind, a dash of salt and 1 teaspoon vanilla until well blended.

HOW TO STORE COOKIES

All cookies can be made up to one month ahead. The FRUIT AND NUT LEBKUCHEN *must be made at least two weeks ahead.*

• Store MOLASSES JACKS, BUTTERY CRISPS, glazed FRUIT AND NUT LEBKUCHEN, KRIS KRINGLE COOKIES and CHOCOLATE THUMBPRINTS in a metal tin with a tight-fitting lid.
• Store NUTTY BROWNIE COOKIES, JELLY DIAGONALS and FRUITCAKE FINGERS between layers of wax paper in a metal tin with a tight-fitting lid.
• Store ALMOND CRESCENTS, PECAN BOURBON BALLS and FRENCH JELLY HEARTS between layers of wax paper in a plastic container with a loose-fitting lid.

💲 🔪 🔖

Jelly Diagonals

We filled these cookies with apricot jam and mint jelly. Use your favorite flavor.

Bake at 350° for 15 minutes.
Makes about 3 dozen.

- ¾ **cup (1½ sticks) butter or margarine**
- ⅔ **cup sugar**
- 1 **egg**
- 2 **teaspoons vanilla**
- 2 **cups all-purpose flour**
- ½ **teaspoon ground nutmeg**
- ¼ **teaspoon baking powder**
- ¼ **teaspoon salt**
- ⅓ **to ½ cup apricot jam OR: mint jelly**

1. Preheat the oven to moderate (350°).
2. Beat the butter or margarine in a large bowl with an electric mixer at high speed until light and fluffy. Beat in the sugar, egg and vanilla until well blended.
3. Sift together the flour, nutmeg, baking powder and salt onto wax paper. Stir into the creamed mixture just until thoroughly combined, using a wooden spoon.
4. Divide the dough in quarters. Shape each into a roll, 12 inches long and ¾ inch wide. Place two rolls, 4 inches apart, on each of two greased cookie sheets, making sure the rolls are at least 2 inches from the edge of the cookie sheets.
5. Make a depression about ⅓ inch deep down the center of each roll. Fill the cavities with the jam or jelly.
6. Bake in the preheated moderate oven (350°) for 15 minutes, or until the cookies are firm and golden. Cut into diagonal slices, about 10 to a roll, while still warm, using a sharp knife dipped in water between every few slices.

Fruit and Nut Lebkuchen

These bar cookies must be made at least 2 weeks before serving for the flavors to mellow.

Bake at 400° for 25 minutes.
Makes about 3 dozen.

1½ **cups honey**
¾ **cup sugar**
   Grated rind of 1 orange
   Grated rind of 1 lemon
1 **cup dark rum**
3 **eggs**
1 **can (4 ounces) slivered almonds**
1 **container (3½ ounces) chopped candied citron**
½ **cup golden raisins**
5 **cups all-purpose flour**
2 **teaspoons baking powder**
½ **teaspoon baking soda**
¼ **teaspoon salt**
1 **teaspoon pumpkin pie spice**
   Snowy Glaze (recipe follows)
   Chopped candied fruit (optional)

1. Preheat the oven to hot (400°).
2. Heat the honey and the sugar just to boiling in a small saucepan over medium heat. Pour into a large bowl. With an electric mixer, beat in the orange and lemon rinds at low speed; cool slightly. Beat in the rum, then the eggs, almonds, chopped citron and raisins.
3. Sift together the flour, baking powder, baking soda, salt and pumpkin pie spice onto wax paper. Beat into the honey mixture, a little at a time.
4. Grease and flour two 9 x 13-inch baking pans. Divide and spread the dough between the pans, using moistened fingers. (The dough is *very* sticky.)
5. Bake in the preheated hot oven (400°) for 15 minutes. Switch the position of the pans in the oven. Continue baking for 10 minutes longer, or until the tops are golden. Cool in the pans on wire racks. Invert onto aluminum foil and wrap tightly. Wrap in large plastic bags or store in an airtight tin. Allow to mellow and soften for at least 2 weeks.
6. Cut each block crosswise into 6 strips and cut each strip into diamonds or squares. Drizzle each with the Snowy Glaze, then with chopped candied fruit, if you wish.

Snowy Glaze: Combine 3 cups sifted 10X (confectioners' powdered) sugar with ⅓ cup milk in a small bowl until well blended. Add additional 10X (confectioners' powdered) sugar or milk, if needed, to form a glaze that will still drizzle when dropped from a spoon. *Makes about 1 cup.*

Almond Crescents

Popular at Christmastime in Austria.

Bake at 350° for 20 minutes.
Makes about 2 dozen.

1 **cup (2 sticks) butter or margarine**
¾ **cup sugar**
1½ **teaspoons vanilla**
2½ **cups all-purpose flour**
1 **can (4 ounces) blanched slivered almonds, ground (1 cup)**
   10X (confectioners' powdered) sugar
   Candied rose and/or violet petals

1. Beat the butter or margarine until light and fluffy in a large bowl with an electric mixer at high speed. Beat in the sugar until fluffy, then beat in the vanilla.
2. Lower the mixer speed to slow. Gradually beat in the flour and the almonds, beating only until blended. Wrap the dough in plastic wrap. Refrigerate until firm.
3. Preheat the oven to moderate (350°).
4. Form tablespoonfuls of the dough into 1½-inch cylinders; taper the ends and curve to form crescents. Place, 1 inch apart, on ungreased cookie sheets.
5. Bake in the preheated moderate oven (350°) for 20 minutes, or until golden brown. Cool for 1 minute on the cookie sheets. Remove with a spatula and roll in the 10X (confectioners' powdered) sugar on wax paper. Cool completely on wire racks. Reroll in the 10X (confectioners' powdered) sugar. Decorate with the candied petals, just before serving.

Pecan Bourbon Balls

Lemon rind flavors these brown sugar shortbreads.

Bake at 350° for 20 minutes.
Makes about 3 dozen.

1   **cup (2 sticks) butter or margarine**
¾   **cup firmly packed brown sugar**
    Grated rind of 1 lemon
2   **tablespoons bourbon whiskey**
½   **teaspoon vanilla**
3   **cups all-purpose flour**
    10X (confectioners' powdered) sugar
    Colored sugar
    Pecan halves

1. Beat the butter or margarine until light and fluffy in a large bowl with an electric mixer at high speed. Gradually beat in the sugar until fluffy; beat in the lemon rind, bourbon and vanilla.
2. Lower the mixer speed to slow. Gradually beat in the flour, beating only until blended. Wrap the dough in plastic wrap or wax paper. Refrigerate until firm.
3. Preheat the oven to moderate (350°).
4. Form tablespoonfuls of the dough into balls between the palms of your hands. Place, 1 inch apart, on ungreased cookie sheets. Dip a 4-tined fork in additional flour; crisscross each cookie.
5. Bake in the preheated moderate oven (350°) for 20 minutes, or until firm. Cool for 1 minute and remove with a spatula. Roll in the 10X (confectioners' powdered) sugar on wax paper and cool completely on wire racks. Reroll in the 10X (confectioners' powdered) sugar. Decorate with the colored sugar and the pecan halves just before serving.

French Jelly Hearts

Sandwich rich butter cookies with your favorite preserves. Or use melted chocolate as a filling.

Bake at 375° for 10 minutes.
Makes about 4 dozen.

1   **cup (2 sticks) butter or margarine**
¾   **cup sugar**
1   **egg**
3   **cups all-purpose flour**
½   **teaspoon salt**
2   **egg whites, slightly beaten**
    Whole and sliced natural almonds
    Strained preserves or jelly OR: Melted semisweet chocolate

1. Beat the butter or margarine and the sugar until fluffy in a large bowl with an electric mixer at high speed. Beat in the egg until blended. Lower the mixer speed; beat in the flour and the salt just until blended. Wrap the dough in plastic wrap and refrigerate for at least 1 hour, or until firm.
2. Preheat the oven to moderate (375°).
3. Roll out a quarter of the dough at a time to ⅛-inch thickness on a lightly floured pastry cloth. Cut out 2-inch heart shapes; place, 1 inch apart, on ungreased cookie sheets.
4. Cut out circles, hearts and other shapes with miniature cutters or a thimble on half of the hearts. Brush some with the egg whites and sprinkle with sugar. On others, brush with the egg whites, decorate with the whole or sliced almonds, drizzle with additional egg white and sprinkle with sugar.
5. Bake in the preheated moderate oven (375°) for 10 minutes, or until golden brown. Cool for 1 minute on the cookie sheets. Remove to wire racks with a spatula and cool completely.
6. Spread the bottoms of the uncut cookies with about ¼ teaspoon of the preserves, jelly or melted chocolate. Top each with a decorated cut-out cookie and squeeze gently to join the cookies.

Nutty Brownie Cookies

Easy to make, these slice-and-bake cookies start with a mix.

Bake at 375° for 5 minutes.
Makes 4 dozen.

1 **package (15 or 21½ ounces) fudge brownie mix**
½ **cup chopped peanuts or chopped almonds**
3 **tablespoons smooth peanut butter**
1 **egg**

1. Preheat the oven to moderate (375°).
2. Combine the brownie mix with the chopped peanuts or almonds, the peanut butter and egg in a medium-size bowl, mixing well with your hands; add a few drops water, if the mixture is very dry.
3. Press the mixture firmly into a log about 2 inches in diameter. Using a sharp knife, slice the dough to a ⅛-inch thickness. Place the slices, 1 inch apart, on ungreased cookie sheets.
4. Bake in the preheated moderate oven (375°) for 5 minutes. Cool in the pans on wire racks for 10 minutes. Remove the cookies with a spatula and cool on the wire racks.

Pecan Wafers

Delicious, and only 38 calories per cookie!

Bake at 350° for 12 to 15 minutes.
Makes 5 dozen.

3 **egg whites**
⅛ **teaspoon salt**
1¼ **cups firmly packed light brown sugar**
3 **tablespoons melted butter**
1 **teaspoon vanilla**
2 **tablespoons unsifted all-purpose flour**
1 **cup finely chopped pecans**
   Corn syrup, red and green sugar for garnish (optional)

1. Cover 2 large cookie sheets with aluminum foil; grease with vegetable shortening. Preheat the oven to moderate (350°).
2. Beat the egg whites with the salt in a medium-size bowl with an electric mixer until stiff.
3. Combine the sugar, butter, vanilla and flour in a medium-size bowl. Fold the mixture into the egg whites just until uniformly combined. Fold in the nuts.
4. Drop by slightly rounded teaspoonfuls, 3 inches apart, on the prepared cookie sheets.
5. Bake in the preheated moderate oven (350°) for 12 to 15 minutes or until the centers and edges are evenly colored. Cool on the foil. If the cookies are not crisp when cooled, return them to the oven for 2 to 3 minutes. Store in an airtight container.
6. If you wish, brush two parallel lines of the syrup in each direction on the cookies while they are warm. Sprinkle red sugar over one line in each direction, and green sugar over the other lines.

Tis the season . . .
. . . for family. Anecdotes
told and memories
shared create a link to
yesteryear.

Instead of dinner, serve this dessert buffet: Continental Party Loaf; Austrian Hussar's Buns; Florentines; Rigó Jancsi Torte; Raspberry Crisps; Star-Shaped Sugar Cookies; Sugar Cookie Sandwiches; Creamy Cocoa Punch; Fruitcake.

Cent-Sational Christmas

Part of the magic of Christmas belongs to the fantastic sights and sounds of the season, the remarkable decorations, the exchange of gifts. But this is also a time that can create a strain on your budget. Our solution: Cent-sational ideas for a beautiful and unique celebration that emphasizes creativity over cost. There's a delicate origami tree which the whole family can help make; delectable gourmet gifts from the chef in your family; even cost-conscious ideas for entertaining. You'll love these affordable goodies—gifts and treats that help to make the season bright.

Cent-sational Decorations

Try these creative—not costly—ornaments for a truly unique Christmas tree.

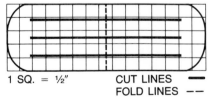

ORIGAMI & OTHER PAPER ORNAMENTS

Easy: Achievable by anyone.

General Directions: For half-patterns (the overlay patterns are full size), fold a piece of tracing paper in half, place the folded edge flush with the centerline of the overlay and trace. Cut out through both thicknesses of paper. Unfold for the full pattern.

Note: *The key to producing origami is careful, sharp creasing and perfectly matched edges and corners.*

WOVEN HEART BASKET

Materials: Solid-color glazed wrapping paper; heavy paper for tracing pattern; scissors or Exacto knife; Pritt glue stick.

Directions:
1. Cutting: Enlarge the pattern in FIG. IV, 1A on heavy paper, following the directions on page 271, and cut out. Cut 2 of these pattern sections from contrasting colors.
2. Folding: Fold the sections crosswise at the middle and slit them on the three lines indicated down the center. Weave them together as shown in FIG. IV, 1B.
3. Handle: Using contrasting colored paper, cut a strip of paper 5″ x ½″ and glue it in place inside the basket *(see photo).*

SHINING STAR

Materials: Thin gold and silver foil-covered cardboard; tracing paper; thin plain cardboard for pattern; Exacto knife or single-edge razor blade; thread for hanger; needle.

Directions:
1. Enlarge the patterns in FIG. IV, 1C *(see General Directions at left)* on thin, plain cardboard, following the directions on page 271, and cut out. On the wrong side of the foil-covered cardboard, trace the patterns; cut them out with an Exacto knife or single-edge razor blade.
2. Folding: To achieve a 3-dimensional effect, fold the star twice *(see FIG. IV, 1C)*, first from the center to each star point *(dotted lines)* and second, a reverse fold between points *(solid lines)*, by pushing the points together.
3. Hanger: See Santa's Sled *(page 124)*, Step 4, pushing the needle through one point of the star.

FIG. IV, 1A   WOVEN HEART BASKET

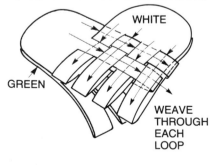

1 SQ. = ½″   CUT LINES ——
                    FOLD LINES – –

FIG. IV, 1B   HEART BASKET-WEAVING

WHITE

GREEN

WEAVE THROUGH EACH LOOP

FIG. IV, 1C   SHINING STAR   1 SQ. = 1″

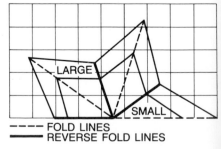

LARGE

SMALL

- - - - FOLD LINES
—— REVERSE FOLD LINES

Origami Tree

YULE TREE

Materials: See Materials for Heart *(at right)*; paper hole-punch; adhesive dots *(optional)*.

Directions:
1. See Heart, Steps 1 to 4 and General Directions, page 120, using the tree half-pattern overlay.
2. When the tree is completed, use a paper hole-punch to create holes to resemble ornaments. For contrasting colored ornaments, use adhesive dots or the dots that have been made from the hole-punch. Glue them onto the tree ornament.

YULE TREE
ACTUAL SIZE
HALF-PATTERN

SNAZZY SANTA

Materials: Red, white and blue medium-weight glazed wrapping paper; tracing paper; heavy paper for pattern; thread; Exacto knife; scissors; Pritt glue stick; paper hole-punch or adhesive dots.

Directions:
1. *From white paper,* cut 2 isosceles triangles with a 3½″ base and 3″ sides for the beard, two 3½″ x ¾″ hat trims, two 3½″ x 1⅛″ faces (the ¾″-diameter circles cut from the faces will be used for pompons). *From red paper,* cut 2 isosceles triangles the same size as the beard triangles *(see photo, page 121)* for the hat. *From blue paper,* cut four ½″-diameter circles for the eyes.
2. Cut a 14″ length of thread. Place 1 piece each of the beard, face and hat wrong side up about ¼″ apart. With a single strand of thread, glue the thread along the center of the pieces, connecting the beard, face and hat so the pieces will move like a mobile. At the top of the hat, make a loop 3½″ long and glue the end inside the hat as a hanger.
3. Place 1 blue circle wrong side up. Glue a single strand of ¾″-long thread to the center with the tail extending. Glue another blue circle over this. Repeat for the other eye. Glue the thread for each eye so that the blue circle is centered in a hole in the face piece *(see photo, page 121).*
4. Glue the second pieces to their corresponding shapes. Glue the pompon to the top of the hat, being sure that the loop is centered through the top. Glue the hat trim bottom edges flush with the bottom of the hat.
5. With a paper hole-punch, make 2 red noses from paper and glue them to the face.

BEAUTIFUL BALL

Materials: See Materials for Heart.

Directions:
See Heart, Steps 1 to 4, using 8 different colors of 3½″-diameter paper. (We also used 4½″-diameter ball ornaments.)

HEART

Materials *(for Yule Tree and Beautiful Ball also):* Solid-color glazed wrapping paper; Pritt glue stick; thread; scissors; tracing paper; heavy paper or lightweight cardboard for patterns.

HEART
ACTUAL SIZE
HALF-PATTERN

Directions:
1. Trace the heart half-pattern on heavy paper *(see General Directions, page 120)* and cut out. Cut 4 hearts in different colors.
2. Fold 2 hearts in half, their right sides together. Leave the first and fourth hearts flat.
3. Use a glue stick on the wrong side of the first flat heart. Glue ½ of one

FIG. IV, 1D FLYING BIRD, STEPS A TO O

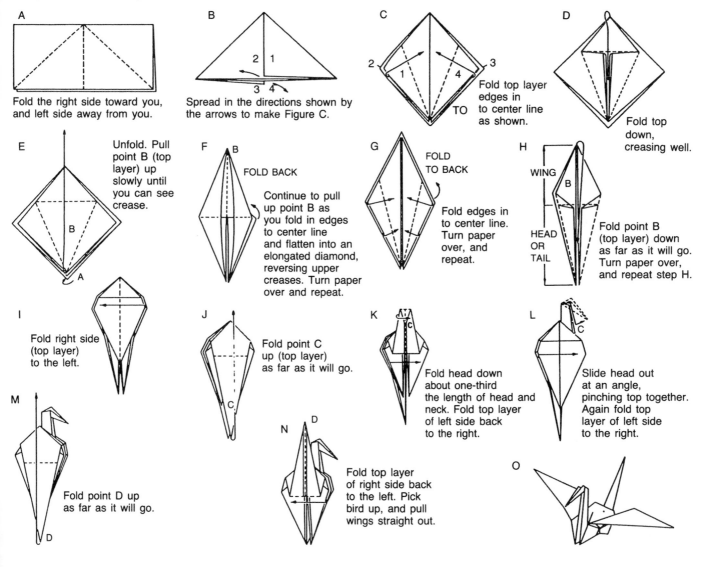

A Fold the right side toward you, and left side away from you.

B Spread in the directions shown by the arrows to make Figure C.

C Fold top layer edges in to center line as shown.

D Fold top down, creasing well.

E Unfold. Pull point B (top layer) up slowly until you can see crease.

F FOLD BACK Continue to pull up point B as you fold in edges to center line and flatten into an elongated diamond, reversing upper creases. Turn paper over and repeat.

G FOLD TO BACK Fold edges in to center line. Turn paper over, and repeat.

H WING HEAD OR TAIL Fold point B (top layer) down as far as it will go. Turn paper over, and repeat step H.

I Fold right side (top layer) to the left.

J Fold point C up (top layer) as far as it will go.

K Fold head down about one-third the length of head and neck. Fold top layer of left side back to the right.

L Slide head out at an angle, pinching top together. Again fold top layer of left side to the right.

M Fold point D up as far as it will go.

N Fold top layer of right side back to the left. Pick bird up, and pull wings straight out.

O

---

folded heart to the left side of the flat heart and ½ of the other folded heart to the right side of the flat heart.

4. Before gluing the upstanding hearts together (their other halves will stand up in the middle), place a loop of thread down the center for a hanger. Flatten the folded hearts and glue the fourth flat heart over them.

FLYING BIRD

Materials: 8″ square solid-color glazed wrapping paper; thread for hanger; needle.

Directions:
1. For each bird, fold an 8″-square piece of glazed paper in half to form a rectangle. Fold it in half again to form a square, unfold and continue folding as directed (*see* FIG. IV, 1D, *Steps A to O*). When the bird is completed, inflate it by blowing into the small hole in the stomach.

2. Hanger: See Santa's Sled, Step 4, pushing the needle into the top of the tail.

**THINK BEYOND CHRISTMAS
TO DISPLAY ORNAMENTS YEAR-ROUND**

Ornaments aren't for the tree alone. In fact, they don't need to be packed away after the Christmas season; many can be enjoyed year-round. Check out these ideas for decorative ways to use ornaments throughout the year.

- Display ornaments in a printer's box, shadow box or on bookshelves and mantel. Many ornaments now are made for this purpose.
- Trim gift packages for birthdays, anniversaries or special occasions with miniature ornaments as an added present.
- Hang flat ornaments as miniature pictures in groupings on the wall.
- Place your favorite photos in specially designed ornaments and display them on table tops.
- Hang crystal ornaments in the window to create a prism effect when the sunlight shines through.
- Decorate a kitchen wreath using a collection of themed ornaments or a series of ornaments.
- For a dinner party, place ornaments along with name cards on or near the napkins to mark the place settings. Let each guest know the ornament is a gift to take home after the party.
- When sending flowers to family or friends, include an ornament in the arrangement.
- Fill a basket or crystal bowl with ornaments and display it on your coffee table.
- Decorate a centerpiece of cut greenery, boughs or flowers using small ornaments.
- Think of special ornaments for gift-giving. They make excellent gifts at the office or for teachers at school.

FIG. IV, 1E SANTA'S SLED

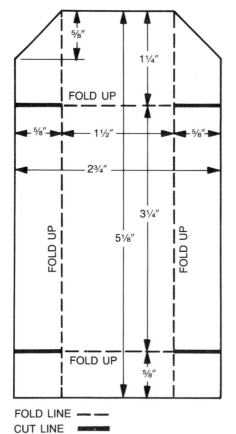

FOLD LINE — —
CUT LINE ▬▬▬

SANTA'S SLED

Materials: Solid-color glazed (on both sides) medium-weight paper; heavy paper for tracing pattern; scissors; Pritt glue stick; thread for hanger; needle.

Directions:
1. Patterns: Draw the sled diagram in FIG. IV, 1E, on heavy paper, and cut out the shape. Trace the actual-size overlay of the runners and braces. On glazed paper, cut out 2 sleds, 2 runners and 4 braces.
2. Sled Body: Glue 2 sled pieces together, right sides out. Cut the diagonal corner lines *(see* FIG.IV, 1E*)* for the backrest. Slit the edges ⅝". Fold up the long side edges and fold up the back. With a glue stick, glue the short ends inside the long edges. Repeat at the other end for the foot of the sled. Glue all ends.
3. Runners: With the glue stick, attach 2 braces ½" from each end of the sled flush with the top edge. Attach a runner to the bottom of each pair of braces, back edges even with the back of the sled.
4. Hanger: Thread a needle with a single strand of sewing thread and push it through the center top at the sled back *(see photo, page 121).*

SLED RUNNER AND BRACE
ACTUAL SIZE

SCRAP MAGIC ORNAMENTS

💲 🔪

FLYING ANGEL
(2½″ x 4″)

Easy: Achievable by anyone.
Materials: 1¾″-long wood dowel ¾″ in diameter or 1¾″-long head-end of clothespin, for torso; ¾″ wood bead for head; 12″ x 2½″ red or green calico print for skirt; 1″ square pink felt; 3″ x 1½″ white felt for sleeves; 3″ piece 2″-wide pre-ruf-fled white eyelet for petticoat; 2″ piece ⅞″-wide pre-ruffled white eye-let for wings; 3″ piece ½″-wide wov-en braid; red or yellow crochet thread for hair; two No. 2 knitting needles; black, red felt-tip perma-nent markers; 1 silver wedding ring cake decoration; glue; 2″ piece ⅛″-wide red ribbon.

Directions:
1. For the hair, wrap the crochet thread as tightly as possible around the knitting needles. Dip them in wa-ter, place them on a cookie sheet and set them in a 225° F. oven until dry (about 20 minutes). The thread will pull off the needles in a continu-ous ringlet.
2. Fold the pink felt for the hands, curving one end for "fingers." For the petticoat, wrap the gathered edge of the 2″-wide eyelet around one dowel end, letting the eyelet extend outward ¾″, and glue. Wrap and glue the edge of the white felt sleeve around the other (shoulder) dowel end, with the fold at the bottom, raw edges at the top.
3. With right sides together, seam the short ends of the skirt calico to make a tube. Stitch a ⅜″ hem at one raw edge and gather the other. Insert the dowel with the petticoat extend-

Flying Angel; Tinsel-Town Wreath

ing slightly beyond the skirt hem. Draw the gathers to fit around the dowel, abutting the sleeve and skirt edges. Glue the gathers in place and cover the skirt/sleeve edges with braid, lapping the ends.
4. Glue the "head" bead to the braid at the shoulder. Tuck the bottom fold of the sleeves up inside to form two layers; insert the folded hands (glued) and glue the top of the sleeve edges together.
5. Using permanent markers, draw the eyes and mouth. Glue the ring-lets in circles around the head to form a hairdo. Attach a wedding ring "halo" with a dot of glue. Glue an ⅛″-wide red ribbon bow under the chin. Fold the 3″ piece of "wing" eyelet in half and glue the gathered edge to the top of the skirt with the fold adjoining the head. Attach a hanger loop.

💲 🌲 🔪

TINSEL-TOWN WREATH
(3″ in diameter)

Easy: Achievable by anyone.
Materials: 3″ wooden drapery ring; metal eye screw; 1½ yds gold tinsel garland; Christmas greenery with velvet bow; 10″ piece ¼″-wide green satin ribbon; glue.

Directions:
Screw the metal eye into the ring. Wind the ring with the garland. In-sert 10″ of the ribbon in the screw eye and tie it for a hanger loop. Add the Christmas greenery with the bow.

Mushroom Mouse; Stocking Mouse

$ 🏷

STOCKING MOUSE
(5" x 3")

Easy: Achievable by anyone.
Materials: *For Stocking:* Two 6" squares pre-quilted red gingham; 6" piece ⅞"-wide pre-ruffled white eyelet; silver jingle bell; 1" square ¼"-thick Styrofoam® covered in silver paper for package; 1 candy cane cake decoration; stuffing; glue. *For Mouse:* See Materials for Mushroom Mouse.

Directions:
1. Cut 2 stocking pieces 3½" deep and 4" wide from the gingham. Cut away a section 1" wide and 1½" deep from the upper left corner. Curve the bottom corners. Right sides together, seam to form the stocking and turn. Turn the top edge to the wrong side and stitch. Glue the gathered edge of the eyelet flush with the stocking top. Stuff lightly. Sew the bell to the toe.
2. To make the Mouse, see Mushroom Mouse, Step 3 *(right)*.
3. Insert and glue the mouse, package and candy cane in the stocking. Add a hanger loop.

$ 🏷

MUSHROOM MOUSE
(3" high)

Easy: Achievable by anyone.
Materials: *For Mushroom:* Scraps of print fabric; 14" piece ⅛"-wide green ribbon; polyester fiberfill. *For Mouse:* Two beige pompons for body; scrap pink felt and beige felt for ears; silk cord for tail; 3 black seed beads; 3" piece ⅛"-wide red ribbon; calico and eyelet scraps for hat; glue.

Directions (¼" seams):
1. Cut a 3½"-diameter circle for the mushroom top and a strip 11½" x 2" for the undercap. Cut two 2" squares for the stem.
2. **Mushroom:** Seam the short ends of the undercap to form a loop. With right sides facing, sew the loop around the cap. Sew a gathering row along the raw edge and pull up the thread to gather fullness. Turn and stuff. Tie the thread ends to enclose the stuffing. Seam three sides of the squares for the stem, turn and stuff. Sew the top edge of the stem to the undercap, enclosing the raw edges. Tie a green bow around the stem.
3. **Mouse:** Glue the pompons for the head/body; add bead eyes and nose. Cut two ½" half circles in pink felt and two ¾" half circles in beige. Layer two sets of pink/beige. Pinch the straight edges to form ears and glue them to the head. Tie a knot at the end of the silk cord and glue the other end to the mouse. Tie a red ribbon bow on the tail.
4. **Cap:** Gather the edges of a 1½"-diameter calico circle and stuff. Gather a 3" piece of 1"-wide eyelet, overlapping and gluing the ends, and glue to the stuffed circle. Glue the cap to the mouse head.

DAHLIA BALL

Average: For those with some experience in embroidery.

Materials: 2½"-diameter Styrofoam® ball; fleecy cotton (like the sterile cotton found in medical emergency kits); 500 yds white sewing thread (from 2 big 300-yd spools); 2 skeins each red and pink, and 1 skein each dark and medium green 6-strand embroidery floss; 1 skein each gold and green metallic thread; straight pins.

Directions:

Read the Directions first, with the photo as reference, and try to visualize the steps as you go along.

1. Mold a thin, even layer of cotton around the ball. Keeping the ball perfectly round, completely cover it with white thread, layering the strands in every direction. Finish with a slip knot. You will sew into the threads to embroider the ball.

2. Measure the girth of the ball with a tape and insert pins at the halfway mark to establish the center top and bottom.

3. Wrap a piece of colored thread around the ball halfway between the pins to mark the center of the ball.

4. At the top mark of the ball, 1" from (and around) the center pin, insert 12 pins an equal distance from each other.

5. From the colored center thread, measure up and down ½" and insert 12 more pins, aligned with the first pins.

6. Work the embroidery one side at a time. Thread two needles with 6-strand pink floss. Starting from the pins at the top of the ball, secure the stitches by sewing into the white covering thread each time, as follows:

7. Working counter-clockwise with only one needle, stitch the pink floss from a pin at the top and lay over the ball to the pin at the center, then back up to the top, skipping every other pin to create the "V" shape.

Dahlia Ball

When you have gone all the way around, pick up the second needle and go around the pins skipped.

8. Repeat Step 7 three times with pink floss, expanding the points downward as you work, with all stitches flat and side-by-side on the ball.

9. Change the needles to red thread and repeat the same process. When you finish, the points will be about ¼" from the colored center line. You have automatically created three layers of petal points *(see photo)* which you should now outline with gold thread.

10. Repeat Steps 2 to 9 on the other half of the ball.

11. In the remaining white spaces around the center of the ball, use 2 shades of green floss and make a spoke design. Wrap the space between the points of the dahlias (around the center of the ball) with dark green floss. Make a loop at the center to hang on the tree. Use metallic green or gold thread and overlay a diamond design on the green around the center. Use French knots *(see Stitch Guide, page 270)* at each center mark, top and bottom.

ORIGAMI CRÈCHE
(7" x 13" x 23")

Average: For those with some experience in paper folding.

Materials: Glossy-coated wrapping paper in various colors *(see photo)*; metallic paper for star; illustration board; spray-on rubber cement; utility knife; single-edge razor blades or scissors; masking tape; glue; steel-edged ruler.

Directions:
1. Each figure is cut from two pieces of paper glued back to back *(see* FIG. IV, 2).
2. The stable and background are made of illustration board covered with glossy paper. Score the folded parts to achieve bends. Use the utility knife for illustration board cutting, a razor blade or scissors for paper.
Note: *When spraying rubber cement, be sure to use a mask and have lots of ventilation.*

Origami Crèche

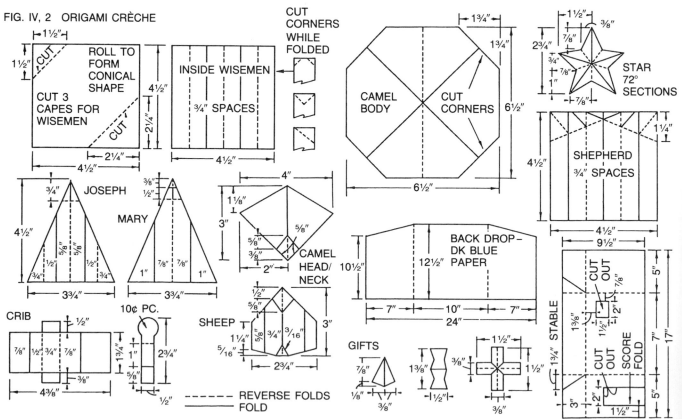

FIG. IV, 2 ORIGAMI CRÈCHE

TABLETOP TANNENBAUM

Easy: Achievable by anyone.
Materials: ¼"-wide plywood; acrylic paints; saw.

Directions:

1. Enlarge the No. 5 pattern for the tree in FIG. IV, 3, following the directions on page 271.

2. Cut the tree from the plywood. At the center of the brown trunk, cut a slot (to fit the thickness of the plywood) from the bottom upward for about 4". Cut a crosspiece 4" deep and the same shape as the base.

3. Paint the pieces. When they are dry, push the crosspiece into the slot to make a 4-footed base.

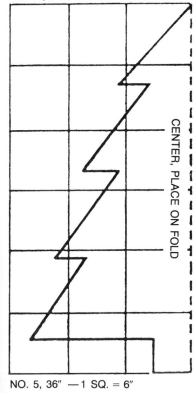

FIG. IV, 3 TANNENBAUM TREE

CENTER, PLACE ON FOLD

NO. 5, 36" — 1 SQ. = 6"

Tabletop Tannenbaum

SANTA GARLAND & CURTAIN TIEBACKS

Easy: Achievable by anyone.
Materials: ¼"-wide foam core or corrugated cardboard; acrylic paints; 1"-wide red ribbon; stapler or tape.

Directions:

1. Enlarge the No. 1 and No. 2 patterns for the Santa in FIG. IV, 4, following the directions on page 271.
2. Cut the 1"-wide ribbon long enough to drape across the window, and tie it to the curtain rod at each end.
3. From foam core or corrugated cardboard, cut three No. 2 Santas and six No. 1 Santas. Paint the Santas. Tape or staple a No. 2 Santa to the center of the ribbon, and 3 No. 1 Santas at each side *(see photo)*.
4. For the tiebacks, cut two ribbon lengths, each about 1¼ yds. Tie the ribbon around the curtains and staple the No. 2 Santas in place.

FIG. IV,4 SANTA GARLAND & CURTAIN TIEBACKS

NO. 1, 3" — 1 SQ. = ½"
NO. 2, 4½" — 1 SQ. = ¾"

Santa Garland & Curtain Tiebacks

- Search thrift stores for chandelier crystals.
- Hang jewelry, such as dangling earrings and long necklaces.
- Combine buttons and ribbons in colorful ways.
- Tie cinnamon sticks in bundles with ribbons; hang on the tree.
- Tie red or plaid ribbon around your houseplants for instant holiday trees; a few glass balls and tinsel add more festive flair!
- Make ornaments from old material, especially fabric such as lace, eyelet, velvet and satin.
- Make Salt Dough (see recipe below) and form into ornaments using cookie cutters. After baking and cooling, decorate with watercolor, acrylic or poster paints.
- Basic Salt Dough: Combine 2 cups all-purpose flour and 1 cup iodized salt in a large, flat-bottomed bowl; mix well with a spoon. Add 1 cup water, a little at a time, mixing as you pour to form the dough into a ball. (Additional water may be needed, depending on the humidity. Be careful not to add too much, or the dough will become sticky.) Knead for 7 to 10 minutes until the dough is smooth, yet firm. Place the dough in a plastic bag until ready to use, to prevent drying. The dough may be kept in a tightly sealed plastic bag in the refrigerator for up to 5 days.

DECORATIONS THAT DON'T COST A BUNDLE

The possibilities are limitless — a little imagination is all it takes!

Note: Do not use self-rising flour as it causes the sculptures to expand out of shape.

- Make a heart-shaped Eucalyptus Wreath (shown here): Bend heavy wire or a clothes hanger into a heart shape, bending the ends together at the lower tip. With floral wire, fasten sprays of eucalyptus to the heart, tucking in sprays of baby's breath. Tie a big bow and wire it to one side of the heart.
- Don't forget such favorites as popcorn garlands and colored-paper chains.
- Use paint, self-adhesive vinyl paper, ribbons, felt, yarn and wrapping paper to transform empty thread spools into miniature drums, top hats and mini-gift packages. Or, hold it sideways, wrap it in colorful paper and add bows at either end for a make-believe party "popper."
- Another use for leftover thread spools: Decorate and intersperse them with large beads, pasta shapes or ribbon bows for an unusual garland.
- Remember cutting snowflakes out of paper? Make an assortment and hang them on your tree or in your windows. Paper cut-out dolls make lovely, old-fashioned garlands, too.
- Children's toys — trains, miniature houses, shops, etc. can make a delightful village when set beneath your Christmas tree or on a mantle.
- For a lovely and unusual look to your tree, make streamers from curling gift tie ribbons: Cut 1½ yards of ribbon. Holding the strands together, make a small bow at the middle. Curl the ribbons to the desired look and attach an ornament hanger (or a bent paper clip) through the knot in the bow. Be creative with your use of color: all white ribbons for an icicle effect, white and gold for Victoriana, red and green for traditional Christmas or a colorful mixture for a country look.

Cent-Sational Gifts

Handcrafted gifts from the heart are the best way to say "Merry Christmas."

EYELET & ORGANDY

💲

EYELET PILLOW

Average: For those with some experience in sewing.
Materials: ½ yd each 44"-wide eyelet and cotton-blend lining; 2 yds 2¾"-wide ruffled eyelet; 1 yd each ½"- and ⅝"-wide red satin ribbon; 1⅔ yds ⅞"-wide green satin ribbon (*see Materials Shopping Guide, page 272*); polyester fiberfill; threads to match.

Directions:
1. Cut four 15" squares, two from the eyelet, two from the lining. Using the photo as a guide, pin the ribbons to the eyelet pillow front. Pin the eyelet front to the lining. Edgestitch the ribbons to the pillow front, then stitch around the edges of the front.
2. Also stitch the eyelet pillow back to its own lining. With right sides together, pin the eyelet ruffle to the pillow front, easing in an extra pleat of ruffle at each side of each corner, and baste. Seam the edges of the eyelet ruffle. With right sides together, pin the pillow back to the front, ruffle between. Stitch, using the basting as a stitch guide and leaving an opening at the bottom for turning. Trim the corners, turn right side out and press. Stuff with polyester fiberfill and slipstitch the opening closed.

💲

ORGANDY PILLOW

Average: For those with some experience in sewing.
Materials: ½ yd 44"-wide white cotton-blend lining; 1 yd 44"-wide cotton organdy; 1 yd each ⅞"- and ⅝"-wide green satin ribbon; 2 yds ⅝"-wide red satin ribbon; 3¾ yds ½"-wide red feather-edge satin ribbon (*see Materials Shopping Guide, page 272*); polyester fiberfill; threads to match.

Directions:
1. Cut four 15" x 17" pieces, two from the organdy, two from the lining. Cut three 4" x 44" strips of organdy for a ruffle.
2. Pin each organdy piece to a lining piece.
3. Pin the ribbons to the organdy front; edgestitch (*see photo at right*).
4. Stitch the three ruffle strips together to form a loop. Fold one edge ½" to the front and press. Edgestitch the feather-edge red ribbon over the folded raw edge of the ruffle.
5. Run two rows of gathering stitches on the unfinished edge of the ruffle. Pull up the gathers in the ruffle to fit the pillow front, easing in extra fullness at the corners. With right sides together, baste the ruffle to the pillow front. With right sides together, pin the pillow back to the pillow front (ruffle between). Stitch, using the basting as a stitch guide and leaving an opening at the bottom for turning. Trim the corners, turn the pillow right side out and press. Stuff with polyester fiberfill and slipstitch the opening closed.

💲

ORGANDY APRON

Average: For those with some experience in sewing.
Materials: ½ yd 44"-wide organdy *or* cotton voile; 3 yds 1½"-wide red satin ribbon; 1½ yds ¾"-wide green feather-edge satin ribbon; 2½ yds ⅝"-wide red satin ribbon; 2 yds ½"-wide red satin ribbon; ½ yd each red and green ⅜"-wide satin ribbon; ½ yd ½"-wide green satin ribbon; 1½ yds ⅝"-wide green satin ribbon (*see Materials Shopping Guide, page 272*); threads to match.

Directions:
1. Press the fabric. Pin the ribbons, beginning 10" in from each side edge for the verticals and 2¾" up from the bottom for the horizontals (*see photo at right*); edgestitch.
2. Fold under a ½" hem on the sides, press and stitch. Fold ½" to the front of the apron along the bottom edge and press. Fold under the ends of the green feather-edge ribbon and edgestitch it over the apron's folded raw edge.
3. Run two rows of gathering stitches at the top edge of the apron.
4. Cut off a 13" strip of 1½"-wide red ribbon and press the ends under. Mark the center of the apron and of the short and remaining long piece of ribbon.
5. Pin center of the long 1½"-wide red ribbon to the center *front* (right side) of apron. Pin the short piece of ribbon to center *back* (wrong side) pressed ends facing inward, with seam allowance raw fabric edge between the layers of ribbon. Pull up

Eyelet & Organdy set: pillows, apron, tablecloth, placemat and napkin

the gathers to fit inside the short ribbon, distributing the fullness evenly. Pin the ribbons, encasing the apron top edge and the gathering rows. Topstitch around the "waistband" portion of the apron and press.

ORGANDY TABLECLOTH

Average: For those with some experience in sewing.
Materials: 1¼ yds 44"-wide white organdy; 5 yds each ⅝"- and ⅞"-wide green satin ribbon, ½"-wide red satin ribbon and ½"-wide red feather-edge satin ribbon *(see Materials Shopping Guide, page 272)*; threads to match.

Directions:
Cut a 44" square of organdy. Using the photo as a guide *(see page 133)*, pin the ribbons to the cloth 3", 4½" and 6¼" from the tablecloth edges; edgestitch. Press the tablecoth edges ½" to the front all around. Edgestitch the red feather-edge ribbon over the folded raw edges, mitering the ribbon at the corners.

EYELET PLACE MAT

Average: For those with some experience in sewing.
Materials: ½ yd each 44"-wide eyelet and cotton lining (will make two place mats); ½ yd each ⅜"-wide green and ⅝"-wide red satin ribbon; 1 yd ½"-wide red satin ribbon; 2 yds ¾"-wide green feather-edge satin ribbon *(see Materials Shopping Guide, page 272)*; threads to match.

Directions:
1. Cut one 13"x19" block each of eyelet and lining. Using FIG. IV, 5 as a guide, edgestitch the ribbon lines to the front of the eyelet.
2. With right sides together, pin the eyelet to the lining and seam (½"), leaving an opening at the bottom for turning. Trim the corners and turn the place mat right side out. Press and slipstitch the opening closed.
3. Edgestitch the green feather-edge satin ribbon to the outside edges of the place mat, mitering the corners.

BERIBBONED NAPKIN

Easy: Achievable by anyone.
Materials: 17" square white cotton-blend (½ yd fabric will make 2 napkins); 2 yds each ¼"-wide red satin ribbon and ½"-wide green feather-edge satin ribbon.

Directions:
Pin the red satin ribbon 1½" from the napkin edges and edgestitch. Press the napkin edges ½" to the front. Edgestitch the green feather-edge ribbon over the folded raw edges, mitering the ribbon at the corners. Press.

FIG. IV, 5 RIBBON PATTERN FOR PLACE MAT

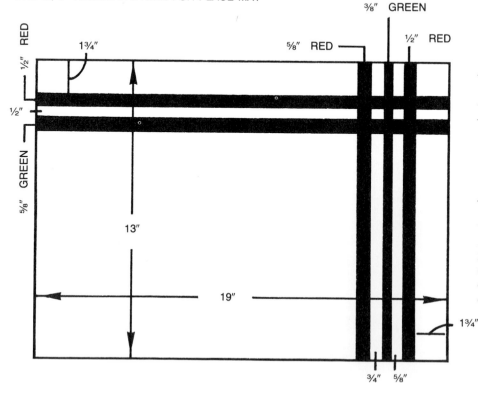

HOSTESS APRON & TEA TOWEL

Average: For those with some experience in sewing.

Materials: One pair standard-size pillow cases with 5″ eyelet hem edging; 5 yds ⅞″-wide red plaid ribbon; 3 yds ⅛″-wide red ribbon; thread to match cases.

Directions:

1. Open the seams of both pillow cases. Cut two rectangles, one 32″-wide by the length of the case, and one 12″ x 13″ *so that the attached hem or trim of the case remains on the 32″ and 12″ edges.* These pieces form the skirt and bib of the apron. You will have to cut each piece from a separate pillow case.

2. Turn under ½″ at each side of the skirt and bib pieces; stitch. Gather the top edge of the apron skirt to measure 16″ wide. Stitch the bib to the center of the gathered skirt.

3. Cut two 6-foot pieces of ⅞″-wide plaid ribbon. Starting at the waistline, stitch the ribbon along the side edges of the bib, leaving the long ends of the ribbon extending from the top corners of the bib to form long sashes.

4. Cut a 17″ piece of the plaid ribbon, lay it over the waist seam and stitch it in place. Turn the raw ends of the ribbon under and stitch.

5. Fold a 2½″ piece of the plaid ribbon lengthwise and stitch it to the rear edge of the waistline to form a belt loop. Repeat at the other edge of the waistline.

6. Thread ⅛″-wide ribbon through the eyelet, if possible. The apron is worn with the sashes criss-crossed in back, threaded through the loops and tied in the back.

7. Take the remaining pillowcase fabric, *with eyelet hem edging attached,* and make it into tea towels by cutting rectangles out of it and hemming the side edges.

Hostess Apron & Tea Towel

Plate Pizzazz

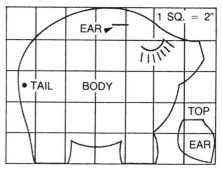

PATCHWORK PIG PILLOW

Average: For those with some experience in sewing.

Materials: 12″ square from old quilt (or patch and quilt a new square); 12″ square fabric for pillow backing; 3″ square cotton print to coordinate with quilt colors; 1″ x 7″ bias strip of coordinating fabric; one chenille stem; sewing thread; black 6-strand embroidery thread; polyester fiberfill; paper for pattern.

Directions:

1. Enlarge the body and ear patterns in Fig. IV, 6, following the directions on page 271. Cut out the pattern pieces.

2. Place the pieces on the right side of the quilted square and pin in place. Cut out the quilted fabric. Place the body piece, right side down, on the right side of the backing piece. Pin together. Cut out the backing. Repeat with the ear piece on the 3″ square of cotton. Unpin all the pieces.

FIG. IV, 6 PATCHWORK PIG

```
                              1 SQ. = 2″
         EAR ➤
                              ))))
                             ))))
  • TAIL   BODY
                              TOP

                              EAR
```

3. Mark the eyelid and lashes on the right side of the body fabric. Embroider with 3 strands of black embroidery thread.

4. Place the ear pieces with right sides together and pin. Make a ¼″ seam, leaving the straight edge open. Cut off the excess fabric and slash the curved edges to ease the seams. Turn the ear to the right side. Turn

PLATE PIZZAZZ

Easy: Achievable by anyone.
Materials: Wooden plates; spray paints; ½″-wide masking tape; fern fronds or leaves; brown paper; rubber cement; clear spray varnish.
Note: *These plates are not for dining.*

Directions:

1. Spray-paint the plates on the back first. Then spray 2 coats (drying between) on the front. Allow the paint to dry.

2. Fasten masking tape "stripes" to the plate fronts, or rubber-cement leaves or fern fronds to the fronts, to block out some of the original color. Lightly spray a contrasting color on the plate fronts. When the paint is dry, peel off the tape, or the leaf and rubber cement residue.

3. Spray the plates with clear varnish.

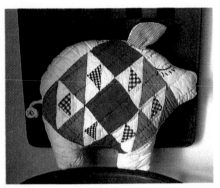

Patchwork Pig Pillow

in the raw edges and pin this edge to the body at the line indicated on the pattern. Stitch through all layers to close the opening and attach the ear to the body.

5. Fold the bias strip in half lengthwise. Fold each long raw edge in to the first fold. Press. Overcast the long edges together. Insert the chenille stem into the resulting tube. Pin one end of the wired tube at the dot marked on the body pattern with the wired tube extending across the right side of the body. Stitch at the marked point, catching the chenille stem. Cut off any excess stem. Fold the cut end of the stem under to prevent a sharp point. Turn in the raw end of the wired tube and sew it to close.

6. To finish the pillow, place the body front and backing fabric pieces right sides together. Pin. Beginning at the tail, sew the pieces together leaving a 3″ opening under the tail. Trim the seam, slash the curves and corners. Turn the fabric to the right side. Stuff with polyester fiberfill. Turn the raw edges of the opening to the inside and stitch closed.

"PICTURE THIS" FRAMES

Easy: Achievable by anyone.
Materials: Foam board; scissors; Exacto knife or single-edge razor blade; metal-edged ruler; 1 roll self-stick paper; white glue; tape; cardboard; paper; pencil.

Directions:
1. Large frame: From foam board, cut two 9⅜″ x 11″ rectangles. On one (the front frame), mark 1″ from each edge and draw the picture opening; cut it out with an Exacto knife or single-edge razor blade against the ruler. Cover the front frame with self-stick paper, clipping to the inside corners. Cover the back frame as well. Glue them together, leaving one side open to insert a picture.

2. Cut a 3″ x 9″ easel. Place it diagonally across the back frame. At the standing end, cut 2 corners parallel with the frame edges. Cover the easel with self-stick paper. Tape the top end to the frame.
3. Tape a double-faced paper "stop" (about 2″ x 3″) between the frame back and the inside surface of the easel, about 2″ from the "hinge."
4. Small frame: From cardboard, cut 2 matching rectangles (ours are 6″ x 8″ and 6¾″ x 8¼″). On one (the front frame), draw a centered rectangle to fit your picture; cut out the rectangle with the Exacto knife or single-edge razor blade against the ruler. Cover the front and back frames with self-stick paper (clipping to the inside corners) and glue them together, leaving one side open.
5. Cut and cover an easel. Tape it to the back frame and add a paper "stop" *(see Large Frame, above).*

"Picture This" Frames

Gourmet Gifts To Make

Food gifts are reasonable to prepare, but can be a little touch of luxury to the recipient, especially when artfully wrapped.

30-Minute Vegetable Pickles

Vegetables remain crisp in this fresh, zesty mixture. Be sure to keep refrigerated since these pickles are not processed. In the recipe, we give you approximate weights for the combination of vegetables we used, but feel free to use your own amounts.

Makes 12 half-pint jars.

 2 **bunches thin green onions (about 8 ounces)**
 2 **sweet red peppers (about 12 ounces)**
 2 **large zucchini (about 1¾ pounds)**
 6 **long carrots (about 12 ounces)**
 2 **cucumbers (about 1 pound)**
2½ **cups water**
 2 **cups distilled white vinegar**
 ½ **cup sugar**
 5 **slices (⅛ inch thick) pared fresh gingerroot**
 ¼ **teaspoon crushed red pepper flakes**

1. Trim and clean the green onions, sweet red peppers, zucchini, carrots and cucumbers. Cut all the vegetables into 3 x ½ x ½-inch strips, or the appropriate size to fit the jars you select.
2. Tightly pack a colorful variety of the vegetables, vertically, into 12 sterilized half-pint jars with screw-top lids.
3. Combine the water, vinegar, sugar, gingerroot and red pepper flakes in a medium-size saucepan. Bring to boiling over medium heat; boil for 3 minutes.
4. Strain the hot vinegar mixture over the vegetables in the jars, making sure the vegetables are covered in each jar. Cool slightly, for about 10 minutes. Screw on the tops tightly. Refrigerate for at least 1 day for flavors to develop. The pickles can be stored for up to 3 weeks in the refrigerator.

Dutch Cheese Twists

Bake at 400° for 10 to 12 minutes.
Makes 4½ dozen.

 1 **cup unsifted all-purpose flour**
 ¼ **teaspoon salt**
 ¼ **teaspoon cayenne pepper**
 5 **tablespoons butter, well chilled**
 4 **ounces Gouda or Edam cheese, shredded (about 1 cup)**
 1 **teaspoon caraway seeds, crushed (optional)**
 2 **tablespoons ice water**
 1 **teaspoon lemon juice**

1. Preheat the oven to hot (400°).
2. Sift together the flour, salt and cayenne pepper into a large bowl. Cut in the butter with a pastry blender or two knives until coarse crumbs are formed. Add the Gouda or Edam cheese and the caraway seeds, if you wish. Toss to combine.
3. Combine the ice water and the lemon juice in a small bowl. Add to the flour mixture, stirring with a fork until the mixture forms a dough and comes together. Add another 1 teaspoon of ice water, if necessary.
4. Divide the dough in half. Keep one half covered. Roll out the other half on a lightly floured surface into a 10 x 7-inch rectangle. Cut the dough in half to form two 7 x 5-inch rectangles. Cut each into fourteen 5 x ½-inch strips. Twist each strip 3 or 4 times. Place on an ungreased baking sheet.
5. Bake in the preheated hot oven (400°) for 10 to 12 minutes, or until golden brown. Cool on a wire rack. Repeat with the remaining dough.
6. The twists can be stored in an airtight container at room temperature for up to 1 week.

30-Minute Vegetable Pickles; Dutch Cheese Twists; Candied Nuts; Coriander Gingerbread;
Lemon Ginger Curd; No-Yeast Stollen

Candied Nuts

A pleasant blend of spices and nuts that's a perfect accompaniment to cocktails.

Makes 4 cups.

½   **cup sugar**
½   **cup water**
½   **teaspoon ground cinnamon**
¼   **teaspoon ground allspice**
1   **cup blanched almonds (5 ounces)**
1   **cup unsalted roasted cashews (5 ounces)**
1½ **cups pecans (5 ounces)**

1. Combine the sugar, water, cinnamon and allspice in a large, heavy-bottomed saucepan. Bring to boiling over medium heat; continue boiling until reduced to ⅓ cup.
2. Add the nuts all at once; stir quickly to coat all the nuts. (You have to work fast.) Spread the candy on a baking sheet or aluminum foil, breaking up the large clumps of nuts with a spoon.
3. After the candy cools, break it apart into individual nuts. Store in an airtight tin at room temperature for up to 1 month.

Coriander Gingerbread

This gift travels well, so it's perfect to mail to friends or relatives. The loaf gets better as it ages.

Bake at 300° for 45 to 55 minutes.
Makes 4 small loaves (8 slices each).

¾   **cup (1½ sticks) butter or margarine, softened**
¾   **cup sugar**
½   **cup light molasses**
3   **eggs**
2½ **cups unsifted all-purpose flour**
2   **teaspoons ground ginger**
2   **teaspoons ground coriander**
1½ **teaspoons baking powder**
¼   **teaspoon baking soda**
¼   **teaspoon salt**
½   **cup low-fat buttermilk**

1. Preheat the oven to slow (300°). Grease four 5¾ x 3½ x 2-inch disposable aluminum baby-loaf pans.
2. Beat together the butter or margarine and the sugar in a large bowl until light and fluffy, for about 2 minutes. Beat in the molasses until well blended. Add the eggs, one at a time, beating after each addition.
3. Sift together the flour, ginger, coriander, baking powder, baking soda and salt into a medium-size bowl. Add half the flour mixture to the egg-butter mixture. Beat at low speed just until incorporated. Mix in the buttermilk on low speed. Add the remaining flour mixture and mix just until incorporated; do not overbeat. Pour into the prepared pans.
4. Bake in the preheated slow oven (300°) for 45 to 55 minutes, or until a wooden pick inserted in the centers comes out clean. Cool in the pans on a wire rack. The gingerbread can be stored, tightly wrapped in the pans with plastic wrap, for up to 1 week.

Lemon Ginger Curd

Serve with toast in the A.M., scones in the P.M. Use as a quick filling for precooked tart shells or as a center filling for cake.

Makes 2½ cups.

9   **egg yolks**
1   **cup sugar**
2   **tablespoons grated lemon rind (1 lemon)**
¾   **cup lemon juice (6 lemons)**
½   **cup (1 stick) butter, cut into 8 pieces**
1½ **teaspoons grated, pared fresh gingerroot**

1. Combine the egg yolks and the sugar in the top of a double boiler over simmering water. Whisk until smooth. Add the lemon rind and juice, butter and gingerroot. Cook, stirring constantly with a rubber spatula, until thickened, for about 15 to 20 minutes. Do not let boil. Pour into sterilized jars with screw-top lids. Cover with wax paper. Chill in the refrigerator.
2. Cap the jars after the curd has completely chilled. The curd can be refrigerated for up to 3 weeks.

No-Yeast Stollen

This bread tastes better after it ages a few days, so it's an ideal gift to mail to relatives or friends.

Bake at 350° for 40 to 50 minutes.
Makes 1 large loaf (about 20 slices).

2½ **cups unsifted all-purpose flour**
¾ **cup sugar**
3 **teaspoons baking powder**
½ **teaspoon ground cardamom**
½ **teaspoon salt**
½ **cup (1 stick) butter, well chilled**
1 **cup creamy cottage cheese**
1 **egg**
1 **tablespoon vanilla**
½ **cup raisins**
3 **tablespoons butter, melted**
10X (confectioners' powdered) sugar (optional)

1. Preheat the oven to moderate (350°). Grease a baking sheet.
2. Sift together the flour, sugar, baking powder, cardamom and salt into a large bowl.
3. Cut the butter into the flour mixture with a pastry blender or two knives until coarse crumbs form.
4. Mix together the cottage cheese, egg and vanilla in a medium-size bowl. Add to the flour mixture along with the raisins. Stir until dough forms. Turn out onto a lightly floured board. Knead about 10 turns, adding more flour, if necessary, to prevent sticking. The dough should be soft, not stiff.
5. Roll the dough into a 10-inch circle. Brush with 1 tablespoon of the melted butter. Fold the dough in half just off center. Place on the greased baking sheet.
6. Bake in the preheated moderate oven (350°) for 40 to 50 minutes, or until golden brown. Brush with the remaining 2 tablespoons of melted butter while hot. Cool on a wire rack.
7. Wrap in aluminum foil or plastic wrap when completely cooled. Store at room temperature 2 days before serving. Sprinkle with the 10X (confectioners' powdered) sugar just before serving, if you wish. The stollen will keep for up to 1 week.

FOOD TO GO — SENDING FOOD BY MAIL

Be sure to choose the right cakes, breads and cookies for mailing. Foods to be mailed must be sturdy and should keep well. Soft drop, bar and fruit cookies are good travelers, as are fruitcakes and pound cakes, and all kinds of breads. Give your crisper cookies and tender pies to neighbors and family nearby.

Cylindrical containers in quart and half-gallon sizes are good choices for packing nuts, candies and cookies. Many come printed with holiday designs.

For Cookies: Use empty metal coffee or shortening tins for packing. Wrap two drop cookies back to back but wrap bar cookies individually with aluminum foil, and seal using cellophane tape.

For Breads and Cakes: These should be sent in strong cardboard boxes after you've wrapped your delicacies first in plastic wrap or strong plastic bags, and then again in aluminum foil.

To Pack:

• Line your containers with waterproof plastic wrap, wax paper or aluminum foil. As filler, use crumpled aluminum foil, tissue paper or wax paper. Do *not* pack unsalted popcorn this way; it can become moldy, especially if the package is sent overseas.

• Pack cookies close together in order to leave as little empty space as possible. Shifting will cause them to break. If you're sending a variety of cookies, place the heaviest ones on the bottom. Place wrapped cakes and breads in a filler-lined box.

• Add more filler to the container, packing it down to minimize shifting and breakage. The box should be so full that you have to use pressure to tape it shut.

• If you can, wrap your package in corrugated cardboard, then a double layer of brown paper.

• Label only the top with the address of your friend or family member. Write "Fragile— Handle with Care" and "Perishable—Keep from Heat" on the top and on the sides of your package.

• Send overseas packages by air whenever possible to avoid spoilage.

⑤ ⦀ ⬛ ⬛

Peanut Butter Kisses

These are addictive! Since they are so easy to prepare, kids can enjoy making them too.

Bake at 300° for 20 minutes.
Makes about 4 dozen.

1   **cup smooth peanut butter**
¾   **cup firmly packed light brown sugar**
1   **egg**
1   **teaspoon vanilla**
¼   **cup semisweet chocolate pieces**

1. Preheat the oven to slow (300°).
2. Combine the peanut butter, brown sugar, egg and vanilla in a large bowl; stir until smooth. Roll the dough into small balls, about ¾ inch in diameter. Place on an ungreased cookie sheet, about 1 inch apart. Flatten slightly. Press 1 chocolate piece in the center of each cookie.
3. Bake in the preheated slow oven (300°) for 20 minutes, or until light brown. The kisses can be stored in airtight containers for several days.

To keep brown sugar soft, always reclose the plastic wrapper very tightly. Then refrigerate the sugar.

⑤ ⦀ ⬛ ⬛

Italian Biscotti

In Italy, this crisp little cookie is often served after coffee with Vin Santo, a dessert wine.

Bake at 350° for 30 to 35 minutes, crisp at 350° for 12 to 15 minutes.
Makes 10 dozen.

3   **cups unsifted all-purpose flour**
1   **cup sugar**
1   **tablespoon baking powder**
½   **teaspoon salt**
1   **teaspoon anise seeds, crushed with mortar and pestle or in blender**
3   **whole eggs**
3   **egg yolks**
2   **teaspoons vanilla**
2   **cups unblanched almonds, coarsely chopped and toasted**

1. Preheat the oven to moderate (350°). Grease and flour 2 baking sheets.
2. Sift together the flour, sugar, baking powder and salt into a large bowl. Stir in the crushed anise seeds.
3. Beat together the whole eggs, yolks and vanilla in a medium-size bowl. Pour into the flour mixture; stir with a fork to form a stiff dough. Knead the chopped toasted almonds into the dough in the bowl. Do not overwork the dough.
4. Divide the dough into 4 equal pieces. Roll out each quarter with floured hands on a lightly floured surface into a roll, about 15 inches long and 1 inch in diameter. Place 2 rolls on each prepared baking sheet.
5. Bake in the preheated moderate oven (350°) for 30 to 35 minutes, or until lightly browned. Leave the oven on. (If baking one baking sheet at a time, refrigerate the second sheet.)
6. Slice the rolls diagonally into ½-inch-thick cookies; place in one layer, cut side up, on the baking sheets.
7. Bake in the preheated moderate oven (350°) for 12 to 15 minutes, or until crisp. Cool on a wire rack. The biscotti can be stored for up to 3 weeks in an airtight tin at room temperature. Let them "age" at least one day before serving.

⦀ ⬛ ⬛

Chocolate Truffles

Makes about 5 dozen.

½   **cup heavy cream**
½   **cup sugar**
¼   **cup raspberry-flavored liqueur OR: orange-flavored liqueur**
6   **squares (1 ounce each) semisweet chocolate**
2   **squares (1 ounce each) unsweetened chocolate**
¾   **cup (1½ sticks) butter, cut into small pieces**

Coating:
½   **cup unsweetened cocoa powder**
¼   **cup 10X (confectioners' powdered) sugar**
   Finely ground blanched almonds (optional)

1. Combine the cream, sugar and raspberry- or orange-flavored liqueur in a large, heavy-bottomed saucepan. Bring to boiling; boil for

1 minute, stirring to dissolve the sugar. Remove from the heat. Add both chocolates; stir until completely melted and smooth. Let stand for 10 minutes, or until just warm to the touch. Add the butter and stir until melted. Pour into a non-aluminum shallow baking dish, about 9 x 9 x 2 inches. Cover and refrigerate until completely chilled.

2. Scoop out balls about 1 inch in diameter with a melon baller. Roll quickly between your palms to form smooth balls. The heat of your hands will melt the truffles, so work quickly. If the mixture melts too much, chill for 5 minutes in the refrigerator.

3. To coat, sift together the cocoa powder and the 10X (confectioners' powdered) sugar onto wax paper. Place the ground almonds, if you wish to use them, on a second sheet of wax paper. Roll the truffles in the cocoa mixture, or the ground almonds, to coat. Place in individual candy wrappers. The truffles can be stored in the refrigerator for up to 3 weeks.

$

Swedish Rosettes

These crispy, star-shaped cookies are made on a special rosette iron — give the iron with the cookies for a wonderful gift.

Makes about 3 dozen.

1	*cup sifted all-purpose flour*
2	*tablespoons sugar*
1/2	*teaspoon salt*
2	*eggs*
1	*cup milk*
2	*tablespoons vegetable oil*
1	*teaspoon vanilla*
	Oil for frying
	10X (confectioners' powdered) sugar

1. Sift together the flour, sugar and salt into a medium-size bowl.

2. Beat together the eggs, milk, the 2 tablespoons oil and the vanilla in a small bowl until blended. Stir into the flour mixture until the batter is smooth.

3. Pour enough oil into a medium-size saucepan to fill half full; heat to 400° on a deep-fat frying thermometer.

4. Heat the rosette iron in the hot oil for 30 seconds; remove and shake off the excess oil. Dip the hot iron into the batter just up to the rim and immerse in the hot oil. Leave the iron

immersed in the oil until the rosette begins to brown, so it will hold its shape. Shake the rosette off the iron, turn over and brown on the other side. Lift out the rosette with a slotted spoon, drain on paper toweling and cool. Repeat with the remaining batter. The rosettes may be stored in a tightly covered container for up to 2 weeks. Sprinkle with the 10X (confectioners' powdered) sugar just before giving.

Homemade Fudge Sauce

Serve with ice cream or pound cake.

Makes 3 cups.

1¼	*cups sugar*
1	*cup Dutch-processed unsweetened cocoa powder*
1/2	*teaspoon ground cinnamon*
1	*cup heavy cream*
1/2	*cup milk*
1/4	*cup hazelnut liqueur OR: other nut-flavored liqueur*
1/2	*cup (1 stick) unsalted butter, cut into 8 pieces*
2	*teaspoons vanilla*

1. Mix together the sugar, cocoa powder and cinnamon in a large, heavy-bottomed saucepan until no lumps remain. Add the cream, milk and hazelnut or other nut-flavored liqueur, stirring until smooth.

2. Bring to boiling over medium heat; boil for 2 minutes, stirring constantly. Remove from the heat. Cool for 15 minutes. Stir in the butter until melted. (Do not place the saucepan back on the heat.) Stir in the vanilla. Cool to room temperature. Store, covered, in the refrigerator for up to 1 month. Stir just before using.

Note: *Always use Dutch-processed cocoa when it is called for in a recipe. It has been treated with alkali and reacts differently than regular cocoa.*

Microwave Directions *(for a 650-watt variable power microwave oven):* Mix together the sugar, cocoa powder and cinnamon in a 3-quart microwave-safe casserole until no lumps remain. Stir in the cream, milk and liqueur until smooth. Microwave, uncovered, at full power for 4½ to 5½ minutes, or until the mixture comes to a full boil, stirring once halfway through. Stir in the butter and the vanilla until the butter melts. Proceed as above.

Cent-sational Entertaining

Provençal Cocktail Party

(for 16)

Terrine de Campagne*
Melba Toast*
Aubergine Provençal*
Crudités with Aioli*
Salade Mélangée aux Noix*
Anchovy-Stuffed Eggs*
Mushroom Leek Tartlettes*
Mussels Provençal*

*Recipes follow

Terrine de Campagne with Melba Toast; Aubergine Provençal; Salade Mélangée aux Noix

Work Plan

Up to Several Days Ahead:
• Make Terrine de Campagne; chill.
• Make Melba Toast for Terrine de Campagne; keep in tightly covered containers.
• Make tartlette shells for Mushroom Leek Tartlettes.

The Day Before:
• Make Aubergine Provençal.
• Make Aioli.
• Prepare walnuts for Salade Mélangée aux Noix.
• Make filling for Mushroom Leek Tartlettes; chill.
• Hard-cook eggs for Anchovy-Stuffed Eggs. (If desired, eggs may also be halved and filling made; refrigerate filling and egg white halves separately.)

Early in the Day:
• Cut up raw vegetables for Aioli; refrigerate in plastic bags.
• Prepare endive, watercress and dressing for Salade Mélangée aux Noix.
• Make filling for Anchovy-Stuffed Eggs, if not prepared the day before; refrigerate filling and egg white halves seperately.
• Unmold Terrine de Campagne; refrigerate.

2 Hours Before:
• Assemble Anchovy-Stuffed Eggs.
• Make Mussels Provençal.

At Serving Time:
• Fill eggplant shell with Aubergine Provençal mixture.
• Prepare Salade Mélangée aux Noix.
• Fill tartlette shells and bake Mushroom Leek Tartlettes until heated.
• Reheat Mussels Provençal.

Terrine de Campagne (Layered Pâté Loaf)

Every great cook has at least one very special recipe for pâté. This one is best when made ahead and allowed to mellow in the refrigerator.

Bake at 350° for 2 hours.
Makes 12 servings.

1 **pound chicken fillets or cutlets**
½ **pound thinly sliced veal or pork**
3 **thin slices boiled ham**
1 **large onion, chopped (1 cup)**
2 **cloves garlic, minced**
1 **cup dry white wine**
1 **teaspoon salt**
1 **teaspoon leaf thyme, crumbled**
¼ **teaspoon freshly ground pepper**
1 **bay leaf**
½ **pound chicken livers**
1 **tablespoon olive or vegetable oil**
  Salt and pepper
1 **pound ground pork or veal**
3 **eggs, beaten**
2 **tablespoons dry sherry**
1 **teaspoon salt**
½ **teaspoon leaf thyme, crumbled**
½ **pound sliced bacon**
1 **jar (4 ounces) pimiento for garnish**
  Fresh dill for garnish
  Melba Toast (recipe follows)

1. Cut the chicken into very fine pieces. Cut the veal or pork and ham slices into thin strips. Arrange the meats in 3 piles in a glass utility dish.
2. Combine the onion, garlic, white wine, the 1 teaspoon salt, the 1 teaspoon thyme, the ¼ teaspoon pepper and the bay leaf in a small bowl. Spoon over the meats. Cover and chill overnight.
3. Sauté the chicken livers in the olive or vegetable oil in a small skillet, just until golden. Season with salt and pepper and chop coarsely.
4. Combine the ground pork or veal, chopped chicken, eggs, sherry, the 1 teaspoon salt and the ½ teaspoon thyme in a large bowl until well blended.
5. Preheat the oven to moderate (350°).
6. Line a 6-cup terrine or loaf pan with the bacon slices. Layer half of the ground meat mixture over the bacon slices, packing down well with

the back of a wooden spoon. Top with all of the ham strips, then all of the chicken livers and half of the marinade, then all of the veal or pork slices and the remaining ground meat mixture. Top with the bay leaf and pour the remaining marinade over. Arrange the remaining bacon strips over and cover the pan tightly with a double thickness of heavy-duty aluminum foil.

7. Place the loaf pan in a baking pan on the middle shelf of the oven and pour boiling water to a depth of 1 inch in the baking pan.

8. Bake in the preheated moderate oven (350°) for 2 hours, or until firm. Remove the loaf pan to a wire rack. Cut a piece of heavy cardboard to exactly the size of the top of the pâté and cover with aluminum foil. Place on the pâté and place 2 large cans on top, to weigh down the pâté. Refrigerate until cold. Remove the cans and chill until party time.

9. To serve, remove the pâté from the loaf pan and peel off the bacon slices. Place on a serving platter and garnish with diamonds of the pimiento and sprigs of the fresh dill. Serve with Melba Toast.

Melba Toast: Trim the crusts from 1 loaf (1 pound) thinly sliced white bread. Using a sharp knife, cut each slice in half, crosswise. Arrange the slices in single layers on large cookie sheets or jelly-roll pans. Bake in a very slow oven (275°) for 30 minutes, or until golden and crisp. Cool on a wire rack. Store in a metal tin with a tight-fitting lid.

Aubergine Provençal (Eggplant Dip)

Eggplant purée makes a piquant dip, and a raw eggplant makes the perfect container.

Bake at 350° for 45 minutes.
Makes 12 servings.

2   **large eggplants**
2   **cloves garlic, minced**
¼   **cup olive or vegetable oil**
1   **medium-size onion, quartered**
2   **tablespoons lemon juice**
1   **teaspoon salt**
¼   **teaspoon freshly ground pepper**
     Pimiento strips for garnish
     Cucumber sticks
     Cherry tomatoes

1. Preheat the oven to 350°.

2. Cut 1 eggplant in half, lengthwise, in a zigzag pattern with a sharp paring knife. Hollow out one half of the eggplant, reserving the cut-up pieces. Wrap the shell in a plastic bag and seal; refrigerate until serving time.

3. Halve the second eggplant, lengthwise, with a sharp French knife. Arrange the 3 eggplant halves, cut-sides down, in a jelly-roll pan and add the cut-up pieces of eggplant.

4. Bake in the preheated moderate oven (350°) for 45 minutes, or until the eggplant is very soft. Let stand in the pan on a wire rack until cool enough to handle.

5. Scoop out half the eggplant into an electric food processor or blender. Add half of the garlic, oil, onion and lemon juice to the processor. Cover and process on high for 1 minute, or until the mixture is very smooth. Repeat with second half.

6. Pour into a large glass or ceramic bowl and blend in the salt and pepper. Taste and add more seasoning, if necessary. Cover with plastic wrap and refrigerate.

7. At serving time, spoon the dip into the reserved shell and garnish with the pimiento strips. Serve with the cucumber sticks and the cherry tomatoes.

Aioli

There is no other dish that declares more brazenly the Provençal love affair with garlic and olive oil. It is rather like a garlic mayonnaise and makes a fine dip for chilled raw or blanched vegetables.

Makes 2½ cups.

16   **medium-size cloves garlic, peeled**
6   **large egg yolks, at room temperature**
¼   **teaspoon salt**
½   **teaspoon Dijon-style mustard**
2⅔   **cups olive oil, at room temperature**
3   **tablespoons fresh lemon juice**
     Your choice of accompanying vegetables: cauliflower or broccoli florets; cooked quartered beets; scallions; cherry tomatoes; carrot, celery, fennel or zucchini sticks

1. With the food processor running, drop the garlic cloves through the feed tube, one at a time. Process until the garlic forms a paste. (You

may also use a mortar and pestle, or pass the cloves through a garlic press.) Add the egg yolks, salt and mustard and process until well blended.
2. Slowly pour in the oil, a few drops at a time, until you have incorporated about half the oil.
3. Pour in the lemon juice, one teaspoon at a time. Continue adding the olive oil in a slow and steady stream, taking 2 or 3 breaks of a minute or so while you continue to beat, until the mixture is thick and creamy. Transfer to a serving bowl and refrigerate, covered, until ready to serve.

Note: It is essential to use firm, unblemished garlic cloves, or the Aioli may taste bitter. Should the mixture curdle while you are beating it (because you added the oil too quickly), put an additional yolk plus a teaspoon of lemon juice into a bowl and slowly beat in the curdled mixture.

Salade Mélangée aux Noix (Endive Walnut Salad)

Toasted walnuts are tossed with Belgian endive and watercress in this very special salad.

Bake at 300° for 15 minutes.
Makes 16 servings.

1	cup walnuts
6	Belgian endives OR: 1 large head curly endive
2	tablespoons lemon juice
2	bunches watercress
1/4	cup red wine vinegar
1	tablespoon Dijon-style mustard
1	teaspoon salt
1/4	teaspoon freshly ground pepper
2/3	cup olive or vegetable oil

1. Preheat the oven to slow (300°).
2. Cover the walnuts with water in a small saucepan and bring to boiling. Lower the heat and simmer for 5 minutes; drain. Arrange the walnuts in a single layer in a jelly-roll pan.
3. Bake in the preheated slow oven (300°) for 15 minutes, or until toasted. Cool in the pan on a wire rack. Spoon into a jar with a screw-top lid and store.
4. Early in the morning, cut the Belgian endive into thin slices, crosswise, with a sharp knife and cover with cold water in a large bowl. Add the

lemon juice, cover with plastic wrap and refrigerate. OR: Wash the curly endive, drain well and break into bite-size pieces. Pack in a plastic bag and refrigerate. Wash and pick over the watercress. Trim the stems, pack into a plastic bag and refrigerate.
5. Combine the vinegar, mustard, salt and pepper in a jar with a screw-top lid. Add the olive or vegetable oil and cover the jar; shake. Let stand at room temperature.
6. At party time, drain the Belgian endive and pour into a salad bowl, or pour the curly endive into a salad bowl. Add the watercress and toss to blend. Spoon the toasted walnuts into the center of the bowl. Toss with the dressing just before serving.

Anchovy-Stuffed Eggs

Eggs that are not too fresh shell more easily than those that are freshly laid. In this dish, the subtle hint of anchovy lends considerable dimension to the savory stuffing.

Makes 16 servings.

8	large eggs, at room temperature
7	fillets of anchovies packed in oil, drained
1/4	cup tuna packed in water, drained
1/2	teaspoon (about 22) green peppercorns (freshly ground pepper to taste may be substituted)
3	tablespoons olive oil
1	teaspoon fresh lemon juice
1/2	teaspoon cognac Parsley or watercress for garnish (optional)

1. Place the eggs in a saucepan and cover with cold water. Slowly bring to boiling and cook over medium heat for 9 minutes. Drain the eggs, then run cold water over them, cracking each gently and allowing water to seep between the shell and egg. (This will make peeling them easier.) Peel and halve the eggs; remove and reserve the yolks. Set the whites on a serving platter and cover them with plastic wrap. Refrigerate until needed.
2. Place the anchovies, tuna and green peppercorns in a mortar and pound them together with a pestle *(see Note)*. Add the egg yolks; pound into a paste. Transfer to a medium-size bowl.

3. Using an electric mixer, slowly beat in the olive oil, then the lemon juice and the cognac. Refrigerate in a tightly sealed container until needed.

4. To serve, press the stuffing through a pastry tube in decorative swirls to fill the egg whites. Garnish the platter with the parsley or watercress, if you wish.

Note: *If you do not own a mortar large enough to accomplish Step 2, you may combine the ingredients in a food processor, but take care not to overprocess the mixture, as it should have a bit of texture.*

$$ $ $$ 𝍌

Mushroom Leek Tartlettes

If you do not own tartlette tins, you may prepare the same pastry and filling for two 9-inch pies, but the serving pieces will not be as elegant since the mushroom-leek mixture will not hold together well when you divide the pie into slices.

Bake at 425° for 10 to 12 minutes, then at 350° for 10 minutes.
Makes 16 servings.

Pastry:
- **1 cup (2 sticks) unsalted butter, chilled and cut into bits, plus additional butter for greasing tartlette tins**
- **¼ cup lard or solid vegetable shortening, chilled**
- **3 cups unbleached all-purpose flour, plus additional flour for dusting tins**
- **1 teaspoon salt**
- **6 to 8 tablespoons ice water**

Filling:
- **8 medium-size leeks, white part only (save the greens for Mussels Provençal)**
- **½ cup (1 stick) unsalted butter**
- **1½ teaspoons dried thyme**
- **8 cups small mushrooms (about 1¼ pounds), thinly sliced**
  Salt and freshly ground black pepper to taste
- **32 small black olives, preferably Niçoise**

1. Place the butter and the lard in a bowl and sift together the flour and the salt on top. Cut the flour into the fat with a pastry blender or two knives until you form crumbs the size of small peas. Sprinkle in two tablespoons of the ice water and work in with the pastry blender or knives. Add additional ice water as needed until the dough forms into large lumps. Divide the dough into 16 parts and wrap each piece in wax paper, pressing through the wax paper first to make a round ball and then a flattened disc. Refrigerate the dough for one hour.

2. Preheat the oven to hot (425°). Thoroughly butter and lightly dust with flour sixteen 3½ x ¼-inch tartlette tins. Roll each disc of dough between two pieces of wax paper into rounds approximately 4¼ inches in diameter and a scant ⅛ inch thick. Remove the top piece of wax paper and center the dough over each tartlette tin, peeling off the bottom piece of wax paper. Press the dough into the tin, lapping it over the edges slightly to discourage shrinkage. Trim off the excess dough; prick the bottom well with a fork. Repeat to make 16 tartlette shells.

3. Place the tartlettes on a cookie sheet. Bake in the preheated hot oven (425°) until lightly browned, for about 10 to 12 minutes. (Check the tartlettes after 5 minutes of baking and pierce with a fork any air bubbles that may have formed.)

4. Gently pry out each tartlette shell with a pointed knife and cool on a wire rack. Carefully remove the cooled shells to a cookie sheet with a spatula. Store in a cool place, covered, until needed.

5. Wash the leeks very carefully to remove all sand, discarding the outer layers if they seem tough. Slice the leeks, mince them (the pieces should be smaller than the mushroom slices) and rinse again. Dry thoroughly in paper toweling.

6. Heat the butter in a large skillet. While it is melting, rub the thyme between your palms into the skillet and stir. When the butter begins to sizzle, add the chopped leeks. Cook over medium heat until tender, for 7 to 10 minutes.

7. Add the mushrooms and cook over high heat, stirring constantly, just until tender but still firm. Season well with the salt and pepper. (The filling can be prepared one day ahead. Cover and refrigerate.)

8. To serve, preheat the oven to moderate (350°). Reheat the filling and fill each baked tartlette shell with the mixture, pressing in about 2 olives, evenly distributed. Bake the tartlettes, still on the cookie sheet, in the preheated moderate oven (350°) just until heated through, for about 10 minutes. Use a spatula to serve the tartlettes, as the shells may easily be broken.

$ ◀◀◀

Mussels Provençal

Serve this in soup bowls, so everyone can enjoy the flavorful broth.

Makes 16 servings.

6	**pounds mussels**
6	**to 8 leek greens (reserved from Mushroom Leek Tartlettes, page 149), well washed and chopped**
1	**large onion, chopped (about 2 cups)**
1	**cup chopped parsley (stems included)**
6	**small cloves garlic, peeled and crushed**
1	**bay leaf**
2	**stalks celery, cut into 6 pieces**
10	**peppercorns**
4	**cups dry white wine**
4	**cups boiling water**
4	**cups (or slightly more) clam juice or fish stock**
6	**tablespoons unsalted butter**
¼	**teaspoon ground saffron (optional)**
2	**cups heavy cream**
	Salt and freshly ground pepper

1. With a wire brush, scrub the mussels under cold running water and pull off the beards. (Discard any mussels whose 2 shells may be interlocked, as these will be full of mud; also discard any mussels whose shells are open.) Soak the mussels in plenty of cold, heavily salted water to cover for 30 minutes.
2. Place the leek greens, onion, parsley, garlic, bay leaf, celery, peppercorns and wine in a very large pot. Drain the mussels and set them on top, discarding any which are wide open after soaking.
3. Cover the pot and steam the mussels over very high heat, shaking the pot vigorously a few times, just until the mussels open widely, for about 5 minutes. (Do not overcook the mussels or they will be rubbery.) Remove the mussels to a colander with a plate underneath to catch the drippings. Discard any mussels that have not opened. Let cool; cover with plastic wrap.
4. Add the boiling water to the broth and vegetables in the pot and simmer, uncovered, for 10 minutes. Remove the vegetables with a slotted spoon and strain the broth through multi-layered cheesecloth to eliminate any sand. Place the broth in a clean, heavy-bottomed soup pot, adding the broth that has dripped from the mussels. (You should have about 10 cups of broth. Add additional clam juice or fish stock, if necessary, to make 10 cups.)
5. Stir in the 4 cups clam juice or fish stock, the butter and the saffron, if you wish, and heat over medium heat, stirring, until the butter melts. Taking care that the broth is below boiling point, stir in the heavy cream; season with salt and freshly ground pepper to taste. At this point, the liquid mixture and the mussels may be left at room temperature for 1 to 2 hours.
6. Just before you are ready to serve, reheat (but do not boil) the soup; at the last minute, add the mussels. To serve, place a scant 1 cup of broth in each small bowl and garnish with the mussels.

LITTLE EXTRAS THAT DON'T COST MUCH

- Serve fancy desserts on small doilies.
- Form butter or margarine into curls or balls, or use a butter mold.
- Use candles.
- Fold napkins in unusual shapes, or tie them with pretty ribbons.
- Add color to punch bowls and tall drinks with decorative ice molds and cubes. For cubes, add lemon, lime or orange rind, mint leaves or halved strawberries.
- Garnish food to give it a festive, finished look.
- If you can't afford flowers, use a healthy houseplant or bowl of perfect fruit for a centerpiece.
- Chill beer glasses and salad plates; warm plates for hot foods.
- Serve rolls, bread and muffins warm, for just-baked flavor.
- Add sliced lemon to ice water; serve in your best goblets.
- Use placecards for a touch of elegance.
- Decant less expensive wines into pitchers or decanters.

Old Vienna Dessert Buffet

(for 16)

Rigó Jancsi Torte*
Continental Party Loaf*
Fruitcake (see Chapter I, pages 41-45)
Spritz Cookies*
Raspberry Crisps*
Austrian Hussar's Buns*
Florentines*
Star-Shaped Sugar Cookies
**Sugar Cookie Sandwiches (fill
with buttercream)**
**Marzipan, Fresh Strawberries (see
Note, below)**
Creamy Cocoa Punch*
Espresso Eggnog*
Austrian Riesling Wine
Tea   Coffee

*Recipes follow

*Note: Although fresh strawberries are a luxury at this time of year, they are still
less expensive than serving a full meal. Even 2 per person would lend an extravagant air to the menu.*

Work Plan

In Advance:
• Make fruitcake up to 1 year ahead; freeze. Or prepare up to 6 weeks ahead; store in a cool place in a tightly covered container; occasionally baste with brandy.

Up to 1 Month Ahead:
• Make and freeze layers for Rigó Jancsi Torte. Or bake up to 2 days ahead; cover with plastic wrap.
• Make Raspberry Crisps, Star-Shaped Sugar Cookies, Sugar Cookie Sandwiches, Austrian Hussar's Buns, Spritz Cookies; freeze. Or prepare 1 week ahead; store at room temperature in covered containers.

Several Days Before:
• Make Florentines; chill.
• Make cake for Continental Party Loaf.
• Prepare Shaved Chocolate for Espresso Eggnog; freeze.

Two Days Before:
• Assemble cake layers with almond filling for Continental Party Loaf; refrigerate.
• Make your favorite buttercream frosting and decorate Star-Shaped Sugar Cookies and Sugar Cookie Sandwiches.

The Day Before:
• Make Mocha Cream Filling and Royal Chocolate Frosting for Rigó Jancsi Torte; assemble cake and refrigerate.
• Make Brandy Frosting for Continental Party Loaf; frost cake and refrigerate.
• Crush candy canes for Cocoa Punch.
• Make Espresso Eggnog base; refrigerate base and egg whites separately.

1 Hour Before:
• Whip cream for Creamy Cocoa Punch, Rigó Jancsi Torte.
• Fill Austrian Hussar's Buns with jam.
• Rinse and hull strawberries.

At Serving Time:
• Top Rigó Jancsi Torte with cream.
• Make Creamy Cocoa Punch.
• Finish Espresso Eggnog.

Rigó Jancsi Torte

Since the days of the Austro-Hungarian Empire, the delectable desserts of Hungary have found an honored place on Viennese party tables.

Bake at 350° for 15 minutes.
Makes one 8-inch torte.

3 **squares (1 ounce each) unsweetened chocolate**
4 **eggs, separated**
½ **cup superfine sugar**
¾ **cup (1½ sticks) butter or margarine**
¾ **cup all-purpose flour**
½ **teaspoon salt**
1 **teaspoon vanilla**
   Mocha Cream Filling (recipe follows)
   Royal Chocolate Frosting (recipe follows)
   Whipped cream

1. Preheat the oven to moderate (350°).
2. Melt the chocolate in a 1-cup measure over simmering water; cool to lukewarm.
3. Beat the egg whites until foamy-white and double in volume in a medium-size bowl with an electric mixer at high speed. Beat in ¼ cup of the sugar, 1 tablespoon at a time, until the mixture forms soft peaks.
4. Beat the butter or margarine until fluffy in a large bowl with the electric mixer at high speed. Gradually beat in the remaining ¼ cup sugar, then beat in the egg yolks until creamy smooth. Beat in the chocolate, only until blended.
5. Sift in the flour and the salt and stir, just until blended; stir in the vanilla. Fold in the beaten egg whites with a wire whisk until blended.
6. Grease two 8-inch layer-cake pans, line with wax paper and grease the paper. Divide the batter between the pans and spread to an even layer.
7. Bake in the preheated moderate oven (350°) for 15 minutes, or until the tops spring back when lightly touched with a fingertip. ***Note:** The layers will be thin.* Cool in the pans on wire racks for 15 minutes. Loosen the layers around the edges of the pans, invert onto the wire racks, peel off the paper and cool completely.
8. To assemble, place one layer on a cookie sheet, spread the Mocha Cream Filling to make a thick layer, place the second cake layer on top and refrigerate.

9. Prepare the Royal Chocolate Frosting and spread over the top layer. Refrigerate until serving time. Garnish with the whipped cream just before serving. Cut into thin wedges with a sharp French knife.

Note: *The cake layers can be made weeks ahead. Wrap in heavy-duty aluminum foil, label, date and freeze. Thaw for 2 hours.*

Mocha Cream Filling: Cut 10 squares (1 ounce each) semisweet chocolate into small pieces. (A food processor does this job quickly.) Combine the chocolate and 2 cups heavy cream in a heavy, medium-size saucepan. Heat slowly, stirring often, until the chocolate melts. Remove from the heat and stir in 2 tablespoons Kahlua or coffee-flavored liqueur. Place in a pan of ice and water; stir often until the mixture chills. Beat the mixture until thick with an electric mixer at high speed. Spread over the cake layer immediately. *Makes enough to fill one 8-inch torte.*

Royal Chocolate Frosting: Combine 1 cup superfine sugar and ½ cup hot coffee in a medium-size saucepan; heat slowly until the sugar dissolves. Add 6 squares (1 ounce each) semisweet chocolate and 2 tablespoons light corn syrup to the saucepan. Bring to boiling, stirring constantly; lower the heat and simmer, stirring constantly, for 5 minutes. Remove from the heat and add 2 tablespoons Kahlua or coffee-flavored liqueur. Place in a pan of ice and water and beat until thick and creamy. Spread on the top layer of the torte immediately. *Makes enough to frost one 8-inch layer.*

Continental Party Loaf

Toasted almonds, sour cream and two kinds of jam are layered between a delicate pastry.

Bake at 350° for 20 minutes.
Makes 1 large loaf.

2¼ cups all-purpose flour
 ¼ teaspoon salt
 1 cup (2 sticks) butter or margarine
 1 cup sugar
 3 eggs
 1 teaspoon vanilla
 1 cup toasted slivered almonds
 1 container (8 ounces) dairy sour cream
 1 jar (12 ounces) red raspberry jam
 1 jar (12 ounces) apricot jam
   Brandy Frosting (recipe follows)
   Silver dragées for garnish

1. Preheat the oven to moderate (350°).
2. Sift together the flour and the salt onto wax paper.
3. Beat the butter or margarine until fluffy in a large bowl with an electric mixer at medium speed. Gradually add the sugar, beating until fluffy. Beat in the eggs, one at a time, until fluffy; beat in the vanilla.
4. Add the sifted dry ingredients, a third at a time, stirring with a spoon or beating with the mixer at low speed just until blended.
5. Line two 15 x 10 x 1-inch jelly-roll pans with heavy-duty aluminum foil. Grease and flour the foil.
6. Spread half the batter on each prepared pan, to make a thin layer.
7. Bake in the preheated moderate oven (350°) for 20 minutes, or just until golden around the edges. Carefully loosen the layers with a spatula and remove to a wooden board. While the layers are still warm, cut into thirds, crosswise, with a French knife, to make six 10 x 5-inch pieces.
8. Chop the almonds in an electric blender or food processor; stir into the dairy sour cream in a small bowl.
9. To put the cake together, place one layer on a cutting board or cookie sheet. Spread with ¼ cup of the raspberry jam, then with ¼ cup of the sour cream mixture. Place a second layer on top. Spread with ¼ cup of the apricot jam and ¼ cup of the sour cream mixture. Repeat with 3

more layers, alternating the jam fillings each time. Cover with the remaining cake layer. Place a wooden board on top of the layers to weigh them down and refrigerate overnight.

10. Make the Brandy Frosting. Trim the edges of the chilled cake with a sharp knife and spread the top with the Brandy Frosting. Swirl to make a pretty pattern and garnish with the silver dragées. Refrigerate until serving time.

Brandy Frosting: Combine 1½ cups 10X (confectioners' powdered) sugar, dash salt, 3 tablespoons butter or margarine, 2 tablespoons brandy and 1 teaspoon vanilla in a medium-size bowl. Add a few drops of red food coloring. Beat until creamy smooth with an electric mixer at high speed. *Makes about ½ cup.*

Variation: For Bourbon Frosting, substitute 2 tablespoons bourbon, 1 teaspoon vanilla and dash ground nutmeg for the brandy in this recipe.

🅂 🎜 ❧

Spritz Cookies

Shape a batch of these buttery cookies in just minutes.

Bake at 375° for 8 minutes.
Makes 3 dozen.

1   **cup all-purpose flour**
½   **teaspoon salt**
¾   **cup (1½ sticks) butter or margarine, softened**
½   **cup sugar**
1   **egg yolk**
½   **teaspoon almond extract**
    Chopped walnuts

1. Preheat the oven to moderate (375°).
2. Sift together the flour and the salt onto wax paper.
3. Beat together the butter or margarine, sugar, egg yolk and almond extract until fluffy in a large bowl of an electric mixer at low speed; beat in the flour until blended.
4. Fit a cookie press with a Christmas tree plate. Fill the press with the dough. Press the cookies onto chilled cookie sheets. Decorate with the chopped walnuts.
5. Bake in the preheated moderate oven (375°) for 8 minutes, or until golden.
6. Remove to wire racks with a spatula and cool completely. Store in a metal tin with a tight-fitting lid.

🅂 🎜

Raspberry Crisps

Delicate sugar cookies are sandwiched together with raspberry jam.

Bake at 350° for 15 minutes.
Makes 3 dozen.

3   **cups all-purpose flour**
1   **teaspoon baking powder**
1   **teaspoon salt**
¾   **cup (1½ sticks) butter or margarine**
1   **cup sugar**
2   **eggs**
1   **teaspoon vanilla**
    Raspberry jam
    Silver dragées

1. Sift together the flour, baking powder and salt onto wax paper.
2. Beat together the butter or margarine and the sugar in a large bowl with an electric mixer at high speed until light and fluffy. Beat in 1 whole egg and 1 egg yolk until light; reserve the egg white. Beat in the vanilla.
3. Stir in the dry ingredients to make a stiff dough. Wrap in plastic wrap and chill for 1 hour, or until firm.
4. Preheat the oven to moderate (350°).
5. Roll out the dough, half at a time, on a lightly floured surface. Cut with a 3-inch round cutter. Cut a hole in the center of half the rounds with a 1-inch round cutter.
6. Spread a thin layer of the raspberry jam on the whole rounds on cookie sheets and top with the cut-out rounds. Brush the cookies with the reserved egg white and sprinkle with additional sugar.
7. Bake in the preheated moderate oven (350°) for 15 minutes, or until the cookies are golden. Transfer the cookies to wire racks with a spatula. Decorate the centers with the silver dragées and cool completely.
8. Store between layers of wax paper in a metal tin with a tight-fitting lid.

Variations: Use dough from Raspberry Crisps to make Star-Shaped Sugar Cookies and Sugar Cookie Sandwiches. Decorate the Star-Shaped Cookies with buttercream frosting and multicolored sprinkles. Use remaining buttercream to fill Sugar Cookie Sandwiches; decorate with additional frosting and walnut pieces.

Austrian Hussar's Buns

Dainty, jam-filled cookies add a Viennese touch to a party table.

Bake at 350° for 10 minutes.
Makes 1½ dozen.

*½ cup (1 stick) butter or margarine,
    softened*
¼ cup sugar
1 egg, separated
1 cup all-purpose flour
¼ teaspoon salt
1½ cups flaked coconut
    10X (confectioners' powdered) sugar
    Strawberry preserves
    Apricot preserves

1. Beat together the butter or margarine and the sugar until light and fluffy in a large bowl with an electric mixer at high speed; beat in the egg yolk. Lower the mixer speed and blend in the flour and the salt. Wrap the dough in wax paper and chill for 30 minutes.
2. Preheat the oven to moderate (350°).
3. Form the dough into 18 balls. Dip in the slightly beaten egg white in a pie plate, roll in the coconut on a sheet of wax paper and place on a cookie sheet. Make a depression with a wooden spoon handle or index finger in the center of each ball; chill until firm.
4. Bake in the preheated moderate oven (350°) for 10 minutes, or until very lightly browned. Cool on wire racks. Dust with the 10X (confectioners' powdered) sugar. Store in a metal tin with a tight-fitting cover.
5. Fill the depressions with the strawberry or apricot preserves just before serving.

Note: The buns may be baked without their egg and coconut coating, or they may be rolled first in the beaten egg white and then in chopped nuts.

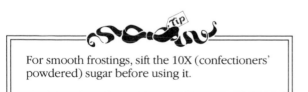

For smooth frostings, sift the 10X (confectioners' powdered) sugar before using it.

For quick chopped and ground nuts, use a food processor. First process the nuts until chopped; remove what you need. Then chop the remainder until ground. Always pulse the motor on-and-off, to avoid releasing the nut oil.

Florentines

These delicate lace cookies take time, but they're well worth it.

Bake at 350° for 8 minutes.
Makes 2 dozen.

¼ cup heavy cream
3 tablespoons butter or margarine
2 tablespoons brandy
3 tablespoons sugar
½ cup ground hazelnuts or almonds
*¼ cup chopped hazelnuts or slivered
    almonds*
¼ cup chopped dried apricots
3 tablespoons all-purpose flour
*3 squares (1 ounce each) semisweet
    chocolate, melted*

1. Preheat the oven to moderate (350°).
2. Stir together the cream, butter or margarine, brandy and sugar in a medium-size saucepan. Cook over medium heat, stirring occasionally, until the butter melts. Bring the mixture to boiling; remove from the heat and stir in the ground hazelnuts or almonds.
3. Stir together the chopped hazelnuts or slivered almonds, the chopped apricots and the flour in a small bowl; add to the saucepan and mix well.
4. Drop the batter by heaping teaspoonfuls, a few at a time, onto well-greased and floured large cookie sheets.
5. Bake in the preheated moderate oven (350°) for 8 minutes, or until golden brown at the edges. Let cool on the cookie sheets for 1 minute. Loosen with a spatula and transfer to wire racks; cool completely.
6. Turn the cookies upside down on wax paper. Brush the undersides with the melted chocolate and refrigerate until the chocolate firms up. Store between layers of wax paper in a tightly covered metal tin. Refrigerate until party time.

Creamy Cocoa Punch

Hot cocoa with a touch of liqueur makes a special welcoming cup on cold days.

Makes 16 servings.

- 8 **cups milk**
- 4 **cups light cream**
- 4 **cups water**
- 1 **container (20 ounces) hot cocoa mix**
- ¾ **cup white crème de menthe**
- 16 **small candy canes for garnish**
- 1 **cup heavy cream for garnish**

1. Stir together the milk, light cream and water in a large kettle; bring to boiling over low heat.
2. Stir in the hot cocoa mix until smooth. Remove from the heat and stir in the crème de menthe.
3. Crush 2 of the candy canes. Whip the heavy cream until stiff in a small bowl. Fold in the crushed candy canes. Transfer the cocoa to a large punch bowl. Garnish with the whipped cream and remaining whole candy canes.

IF YOU WANT TO THROW A PARTY . . .

Make it the easy-does-it kind. These three practically give themselves.

DESSERT PARTY
Instead of serving a four-course dinner, bake one cake (from a mix), brew one pot of coffee and invite a small group for a fireside get-together or a VCR showing of a holiday flick.

HOLIDAY FUN PARTY
This could be a caroling, ice-skating or gift-wrapping get-together. Afterward treat everyone to hot cocoa and warm cider, along with chestnuts roasted over the fire, freshly made popcorn or soft pretzels kept toasty on a warming tray.

MAKE-YOUR-OWN-SANDWICH PARTY
You provide the fixings, plus holiday paper plates, and your guests take it from there.

Espresso Eggnog

Espresso coffee is a great addition to the punch bowl.

Makes 16 servings.

- 4 **eggs, separated**
- 1 **cup sugar**
- 3 **cups light cream**
- 3 **cups espresso coffee, cooled**
- 1 **cup brandy**
- 1 **cup coffee-flavored liqueur**
- 1 **pint coffee ice cream**
  Shaved Chocolate for garnish (recipe follows)
- 1 **teaspoon cinnamon for garnish**

1. Beat the egg whites until stiff, but not dry, in a large bowl with an electric mixer at high speed.
2. Beat the egg yolks until lemon-colored in a second large bowl with the electric mixer at high speed. Gradually add the sugar, beating until the mixture becomes light in color. Add the light cream, then the cold espresso coffee, the brandy and coffee-flavored liqueur.
3. Fold the beaten egg whites into the espresso mixture with a wire whisk.
4. Serve in a punch bowl with scoops of coffee ice cream. Garnish with the Shaved Chocolate and a dust of cinnamon.

Note: *To prepare the Espresso Eggnog in advance, keep the unbeaten egg whites in a covered bowl in the refrigerator until 30 minutes before serving time. Mix the egg yolks with the sugar, cream, coffee, brandy and liqueur, following Step 2; cover and refrigerate. Thirty minutes before serving time, remove the egg whites from the refrigerator and let stand for 30 minutes. Beat until stiff, not dry, and fold into the egg yolk mixture.*

Shaved Chocolate: Hold one 4-ounce bar of sweet chocolate in your hand until it's slightly soft. Using long strokes with a vegetable parer, shave the chocolate into long curls and drop onto wax paper. Freeze until ready to use. *Makes enough to garnish 16 servings.*

Ways To Entertain Without Going Broke

Just because you're counting pennies doesn't mean you have to scrimp at party time. Here are some tips for painless cost-cutting.

- Serve omelets for brunch or an after-theater supper. Let guests choose from an assortment of sweet and savory fillings—such as chicken in sherry-cream sauce with toasted almonds and peas; strawberry jam and sour cream; and shredded Cheddar with sliced cooked sausage and sautéed apples. Serve with hot homemade biscuits, softly whipped butter and one or two vegetable or fruit salads.
- Buy meat for stews and casseroles in large, uncut pieces, rather than buying cubed stew meat; whole chickens cost less than parts.
- Give a sausage and mustard tasting party. Choose from sweet and hot Italian sausage, Polish kielbasa, German brockwurst or knackwurst and All-American frankfurters. Serve complementary mustards, a hearty baked bean casserole and a variety of ciders and beers.
- Divide the cost—and labor—of entertaining by hosting an "everybody bring a dish" party.
- Invite guests for a dessert smörgasbord. Balance one or two elaborate cakes—such as Sacher Torte, Black Forest Cake, Gâteau St. Honoré— with tiny butter cookies and a bowl of chilled fresh fruit sprinkled with wine and 10X (confectioners' powdered) sugar.
- Choose from the calendar's bounty, when produce is most plentiful and least expensive. Strawberries in January, asparagus in October are bound to be pricey.
- Don't eliminate luxury items—just make the most of them. A quarter pound of smoked salmon serves 4 if you add it to a dill-flavored cream sauce for pasta. One pound of crisp asparagus adds elegance to a spring crudité selection.
- Use up what you've got. Waste is a wicked budget eater. If you've bought 5 chickens, make pâté from the livers. A sauce prepared with egg yolks leaves you egg whites for making meringues.
- Serve bowls of chili with all the trimmings— chopped onion, chopped tomato and green pepper, crushed taco chips and cubed Monterey Jack cheese. Mexican beer, orange and avocado salad and flan with cinnamon butter cookies complete the meal.
- Give a beer-tasting party. Include 6 to 10 domestic and imported varieties. Freeze wet glasses or mugs to keep the beer chilled. Pass around hearty nibbles such as cheese-sausage kabobs, onion quiche squares and miniature caraway-buttermilk biscuits sandwiched with paper-thin slices of corned beef.
- Serve poultry. Many elegant recipes use chicken, turkey, duck or Cornish hens. Your guests will enjoy Chicken Marsala as much as Beef Wellington.
- Give a breakfast party—even if it's noon. Traditional early morning fare, such as pancakes, eggs and muffins, is good anytime.
- Soufflés and quiches are always impressive, yet they are neither difficult nor expensive to prepare.
- Replace veal with chicken or turkey in recipes.
- Borrow additional chairs, serving pieces and appliances for big parties, instead of buying or renting them.
- Choose local flowers instead of exotic varieties; they're just as festive. Arrange them yourself and save even more.
- Buy good, inexpensive wines for cooking and drinking at party time; cooking wines cost more per ounce.
- Prepare your own cold cut and cheese platters. Buy a total of ¼ pound per person. Bulk purchases are great if you've got a slicing machine; otherwise buy items already sliced. Arrange meats and cheeses on platters, tuck in garnishes, cover with plastic wrap and chill.
- If you're serving turkey, baste it yourself instead of buying more costly self-basting birds.
- Plan a pasta buffet: Serve 2 to 3 kinds of pasta, a meat sauce (such as sausage and cubed pepper in spicy tomato sauce), a cream sauce (ham and cheese with caraway) and a vegetable sauce (zucchini and onion in herbed garlic butter). Pass around grated cheese, chopped green onion and toasted bread crumbs for toppings.
- Tenderize chuck steak and use it instead of sirloin; tenderized shoulder lamb chops replace loin chops.

CHAPTER 5

T is the season...
...for anticipation. Little ones struggle to stay awake, but soon are dreaming of sugarplums and fairies.

Create a roomful of magic with A Gingerbread Christmas.

Christmas Through A Child's Eyes

In the eyes of a child, Christmas is an enchanted time when nutcrackers dance, reindeer fly and Santa Claus is watching. One way to make this season magical is with A Gingerbread Christmas. Calico prints and rickrack "icing" are used to make the figures. Or, send your little pardners smiling into the sunset with A Rootin' Tootin' Christmas. Our Wild West theme features cowboy boot ornaments, stockings and lariat rope wreaths to delight every cowboy and girl. There are tips to make your children's parties easy and enjoyable, and suggestions for the best toys to buy according to age. And because Christmas time is also present time, there are wonderful gifts to make for your kids—and gifts they can make themselves for family and friends. Try looking at Christmas through a child's eyes—and capture the wonder of the season.

A Gingerbread Christmas

Create a world of sugar 'n spice and everything nice!

GINGERBREAD DOLLS & ORNAMENTS

Easy: Achievable by anyone.
Materials: Rust pindot fabric and scraps of calico; rickrack; ribbon; synthetic stuffing; white glue; soutache braid; eyelet trim; corrugated cardboard; white buttons; scraps of white felt. **Note:** *Amounts vary, depending on the project.*

FIG. V, 1A GINGERBREAD DOLLS AND ORNAMENTS   1 SQ. = 1"

LARGE DOLL

SMALL DOLL AND SKIRT

ORNAMENT

CUT FOR GIRL

CUT FOR BOY

PLACE ON FOLD

EYES
x — LARGE-SMALL
● — MEDIUM

Directions:
1. Enlarge the patterns in FIGS. V, 1A, B and D, following the directions on page 271.
2. Doll: For each doll, cut a pindot front and back. Cut the appliqués from calico and pin them to the front (over the eyelet straps on the girl). Stitch (¼") the trim, then zigzag stitch. Glue the mouth (felt on the large dolls, soutache on the others). Sew the button eyes. Sew rickrack around the doll front ⅜" from the edge.
3. Seam (¼") the front to the back (right sides together), leaving an opening for turning. Turn, stuff and sew the opening. Sew on a vest button for the boy.
4. Ornament: From corrugated cardboard, cut a doll. Make a front, as for the doll, and glue it to the cardboard, turning the fabric edges toward the back. Glue a fabric back to the cardboard and trim the edges flush. Glue a 7" length of ribbon, in a loop, to the center top.

Cookies and Toys Party (see tip box, page 163)

FIG. V, 1B GINGERBREAD DOLLS
AND ORNAMENTS

1 SQ. = 1"

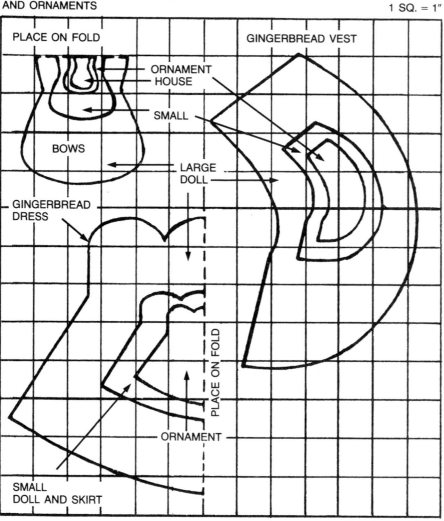

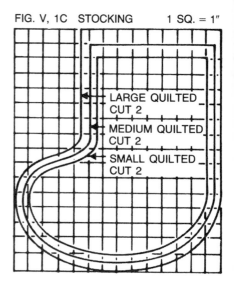

STOCKINGS
(15", 13½", 12")

Average: For those with some experience in sewing.
Materials *(for three):* ⅞ yds 45"-wide quilted print fabric; scraps of calico; jumbo rickrack; eyelet ruffling and ribbon.

FIG. V, 1C STOCKING   1 SQ. = 1"

Directions:
1. Cut a quilted front and back *(see* FIG. V, 1C*).* Cut two calico pocket squares and stitch, right sides together, leaving an opening for turning. Turn and press. Lap the top edge of the pocket over the eyelet ruffling and stitch. Stitch the pocket to the stocking front.
2. Turn under the top edges of the stockings, lap them over the ruffling and stitch. Stitch the hearts *(see* FIG. V, 1D*)* and rickrack to the stocking front. For the hanger, pin a folded 7" length of ribbon to the right side of the top corner, edges matching, and stitch in place.
3. Pin the back to the front, right sides together. Seam (½") the raw edges. Clip and turn right side out.

TREE SKIRT
(about 43" in diameter)

Easy: Achievable by anyone.
Materials: See Materials for Gingerbread Dolls and Ornaments *(page 160)*; 1¼ yds 45"-wide quilted fabric; 2¼ yds calico for back and ruffle.

Directions:
1. Cut a 44"-diameter circle from both the quilted and the calico fabrics. Draw, then cut, a 6"-diameter circle at each center. Cut an opening slit, on the straight grain, from the inner to the outer edge.

2. Cut three calico hearts and make four sets of doll fronts *(see* FIGS. V, 1A *and* D*)*; appliqué them to the quilted skirt *(see photo, page 158)*.
3. Cut 5"-wide ruffle strips to measure 8½ yds (pieced as needed). Stitch a ¼" hem along one long and two short edges. Stitch two gathering rows ¼" and ½" from the other long edge. Pin to the skirt front, right sides together, pulling up the gathers to fit. Stitch (½"). Pin a 14"-long ribbon tie to each corner of the inner circle. With right sides together, ruffles and ties toward the center, pin the skirt back to the skirt front. Stitch all edges, leaving one end open for turning. Turn and sew closed.

GINGERBREAD HOUSE ORNAMENTS
(4" x 4½" x 3")

Easy: Achievable by anyone.
Materials: See Materials for Gingerbread Dolls and Ornaments *(page 160).*

Directions:
1. From cardboard, cut two 3" x 4½" ends, two 4" x 2½" sides, one 3" x 4" base, one 6" x 4" roof.
2. Glue the sides to the base, glue the ends to the base and sides. Cut a peak at the top of each end.
3. Fold the 6" x 4" roof piece in half to form the tip of the roof. Fit the roof piece to overlap the sides. Glue in place.
4. Cover the house with fabric. Glue on the appliqués *(see Fig. V, 1D)* and baby rickrack. Near the top center, poke small holes and insert a ribbon hanger.

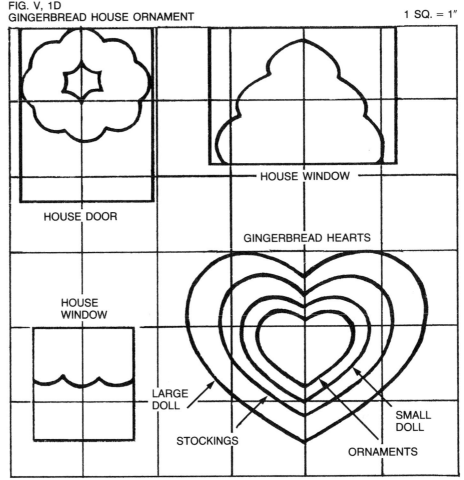

FIG. V, 1D
GINGERBREAD HOUSE ORNAMENT

1 SQ. = 1"

HOUSE DOOR

HOUSE WINDOW

GINGERBREAD HEARTS

HOUSE WINDOW

LARGE DOLL

SMALL DOLL

STOCKINGS

ORNAMENTS

COOKIES AND TOYS PARTY

What better combination for a child's party than cookies and toys!

- Begin by baking your favorite sugar cookies, using a variety of animal cookie cutters (available in cookware specialty shops). The recipes for Holiday Sugar Cookies *(page 200-201)* and Christmas Cutouts *(page 198)* are both good choices. Or, use the sugar cookie dough that comes ready-made in rolls in your supermarket's refrigerator case.
- Decorate the cookies with Cookie Glaze: Sift 3½ cups 10X (confectioners' powdered) sugar onto wax paper. Beat 2 egg whites until stiff but not dry in a large bowl with an electric mixer on high speed. Gradually add the sugar and enough lemon juice to give the frosting a smooth, spreadable consistency. Divide the frosting among small bowls and tint desired colors. Always keep the frosting

covered with damp paper toweling, then plastic wrap, to avoid hardening before being used.
- Serve the cookies with an assortment of punches, fruit juices, cocoa and, of course, milk—plain and strawberry-flavored.
- To create a centerpiece, place a 2-foot tree in a small red wagon and pile in the presents. (The candy-cane wreaths on the tree come with attached gift tags; write in each guest's name and give the wreaths out as after-dinner treats.) Be sure to invite your bear family to share the festivities with everyone else. Set the table with colorful plaid napkins and plaid place mats, your own holiday china—and don't forget to provide plates for all the children's stuffed animals!

THE SPICE IS RIGHT

For children of all ages, it just wouldn't be Christmas without the spicy-sweet aroma of gingerbread wafting through the home!

• Bake gingerbread cookies (make them from scratch or add just enough water to a packaged gingerbread mix to make a cookie-like dough that you can roll out) and let the kids decorate them. Use them throughout the house: Perch a group on the mantel; stack a bundle in baskets, tied with bright red ribbon; stand them in a row on windowpanes.

• For hanging gingerbread figures, place a raw dried bean in the top of each cookie before baking. Once baked, the cookies will have a hole for ribbon or string.

• A family gingerbread house is a classic Christmas tradition. Use your own home as a model, or let your imagination take you to the fantasy house you've always wanted . . . A Swiss chalet? A thatched cottage (use halved squares of shredded wheat cereal for the thatching)? Perhaps a Medieval castle, moat and all!

• Not all gingerbread has to be spicy! Our Gingerbread Boy (recipe at right) is a moist banana cake with chocolate frosting.

• Use gingerbread to make placecards for your holiday dinner table: Bake in 3 x 4-inch rectangles along with 1 x 2-inch stands. Decorate and inscribe names onto the cookie placecards with Royal Frosting (see recipe, page 165); let dry. Use the remaining frosting to fuse the placecards to the stands.

• Big gingerbread hearts, brightly decorated, are a traditional German and Swiss Christmas greeting. Make a 5-inch heart stencil and use it to cut out the dough. After baking, decorate the hearts with royal frosting, candied fruit and flowers.

Gingerbread Boy

Bake at 350° for 40 minutes.
Makes one 15 x 10-inch cake.

> *Banana Cake (recipe follows) OR:*
> *2 packages (18 ounces each) cake mix, flavor of your choice*
> *6 squares (1 ounce each) unsweetened chocolate*
> *Butter Cream Frosting (recipe, page 165)*
> *Raisins for decoration*

1. Preheat the oven to moderate (350°).
2. Make the Banana Cake, or make two cake mixes following the package directions. Pour into a greased and floured 15 x 10 x 2-inch roasting pan.
3. Bake in the preheated moderate oven (350°) for 40 minutes, or until the center springs back when lightly touched with a fingertip. Cool for 10 to 15 minutes, then invert onto a platter and refrigerate.
4. Enlarge the gingerbread boy pattern in FIG. V, 1E onto brown paper, following the directions on page 271. Cut out the pattern and place it on the cake.
5. Cut out the pattern on the cake with a sharp paring knife. Trim away the excess, remove the crumbs gently and refrigerate the cake.
6. Melt the unsweetened chocolate in the top of a double boiler over hot, not boiling, water; cool to room temperature. Place 4 cups of the Butter Cream Frosting in a large bowl; stir in the cooled chocolate, blending well. Using a metal spatula, spread over the top and side of the cold cake.
7. Fit a pastry bag with a #18 open star tip or a #27 closed star tip. Fill half-full with part of the remaining white frosting. Pipe onto the frosted cake, making cuffs, neckline, buttons, face and hair, following the photo. Use raisins for the eyes.

Banana Cake

Bake at 350° for 35 minutes.
Makes one 15 x 10 x 2-inch cake.

 1 **cup (2 sticks) butter or margarine**
2⅔ **cups sugar**
 4 **eggs**
 2 **teaspoons baking soda**
 2 **cups soured milk (see Note)**
 4 **ripe bananas, mashed**
 4 **cups all-purpose flour**
 2 **teaspoons baking powder**
 2 **teaspoons salt**

1. Preheat the oven to moderate (350°).
2. Beat together the butter or margarine with the sugar in a large bowl with an electric mixer at high speed until light and fluffy. Add the eggs, one at a time, beating well after each addition.
3. Dissolve the baking soda in the soured milk. Add to the creamed mixture. Beat in the mashed bananas.
4. Sift together the flour, baking powder and salt onto wax paper. With the mixer on low speed, add the dry ingredients, beating just until blended. Pour into a greased and floured 15 x 10-inch pan.
5. Bake in the preheated moderate oven (350°) for 40 minutes, or until the cake springs back when lightly touched with a fingertip. Cool for 10 minutes, loosen the cake around the edge of the pan and invert onto a platter.

Note: *To sour milk, place 1 tablespoon vinegar in a 1-cup measure. Add milk to measure 1 cup liquid. The batter may also be baked in two 8-inch layers or one 9-inch layer plus cupcakes.*

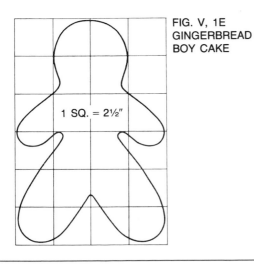

FIG. V, 1E
GINGERBREAD
BOY CAKE

1 SQ. = 2½"

Butter Cream Frosting

If the weather is hot, eliminate the milk. Add more sugar if you wish a stiffer icing.

Makes 5 cups.

 2 **boxes (1 pound each) sifted 10X (confectioners' powdered) sugar**
 2 **cups white vegetable shortening**
 1 **cup (2 sticks) butter or margarine**
 1 **teaspoon vanilla extract**
 1 **teaspoon almond extract**
 2 **tablespoons hot milk**

1. Add the sifted 10X (confectioners' powdered) sugar slowly to the shortening, butter or margarine and vanilla and almond extracts in a large bowl, using the low speed of an electric mixer. Stop the mixer and scrape the bowl several times.
2. Turn the mixer speed to medium and beat for another 5 minutes. Change to medium-low speed, add the hot milk and beat for 15 seconds.

Note: *If the frosting is too soft, add a little more 10X (confectioners' powdered) sugar. Store the frosting, covered, in a plastic container. The frosting can be stored in the refrigerator for several weeks but must be at room temperature when ready to use.*

Royal Frosting

This white frosting dries to a hard finish. It is perfect for decorating cookies, and may be tinted.

Makes 4 cups.

 4 **large egg whites, at room temperature**
 7 **cups 10X (confectioners' powdered) sugar, sifted**
 2 **to 3 teaspoons lemon juice**

1. Beat the egg whites in a large bowl with an electric mixer at high speed until foamy. Beat in the 10X (confectioners' powdered) sugar, part at a time, beating well after each addition. Add the lemon juice. Continue beating until stiff peaks form.
2. Cover with damp paper toweling and plastic wrap until ready to use. If the icing is too stiff, add a few more drops of the lemon juice.

A Rootin' Tootin' Christmas

*Round up your little buckaroos for
a happy holiday hoedown.*

WILD WEST ORNAMENT
(4½" x 6")

Easy: Achievable by anyone.
Materials: 6"-wide red and/or natural burlap ribbon; ¼"-wide red and natural suede ribbon; 5mm red cup sequins; synthetic stuffing; white glue *(see Materials Shopping Guide, page 272)*; green thread; tracing paper; dressmaker's carbon; thin wire or ornament hangers.

Directions:
1. Enlarge the pattern, including the design lines, for the boot in FIG. V, 2A on tracing paper, following the directions on page 271.
2. From the burlap ribbon, cut one front, reverse the pattern and cut one back. Using dressmaker's carbon, trace the pattern and design lines on the right sides of the boots.
3. Using green thread, stitch over all the design lines on the boots. With right sides out, edges even, stitch the lower edges of the boot pieces together between the circles. Stuff the toe and heel. Glue sequins over the lines of the star.
4. Tie two 12"-long suede ribbons together into a bow and glue them just above the design line at the back edge of the boot. For the hanger loop, cut, fold and glue together the ends of a 1¾"-long piece of suede ribbon. Glue it to the inner top edge at one side of one boot. Attach a hanger.

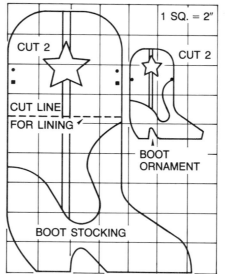

FIG. V, 2A   WILD WEST STOCKING, ORNAMENT

1 SQ. = 2"

CUT 2

CUT 2

CUT LINE
FOR LINING

BOOT ORNAMENT

BOOT STOCKING

WILD WEST STOCKING
(11½" x 17")

Easy: Achievable by anyone.
Materials: ½ yd 48"- to 50"-wide natural and/or red burlap (½ yd will make two complete stockings); ¼ yd 45"-wide red bandanna fabric for lining (enough for two stockings); ¾ yd fusible interfacing; 6"-wide natural and/or red burlap ribbon; 1⅔ yds 1⅜"-wide red bandanna ribbon; 5mm red cup sequins; glue *(see Materials Shopping Guide, page 272)*; natural and red threads; tracing paper; dressmaker's carbon.

Directions *(¼" seams allowed)*:
1. Enlarge the pattern, including the design lines and lining cut-off line, for the boot in FIG. V, 2A on tracing paper, following the directions on page 271.
2. From natural and/or red burlap, cut one each front and back boot pieces, marking the design lines; repeat for the interfacing, omitting the lines. From natural and/or red burlap ribbon, cut two stars. From bandanna fabric, cut two boot-shape lining pieces.
3. With edges even, press the interfacing to the wrong side of the burlap boot pieces. With contrasting thread, stitch on and to either side of the design lines several times. With right sides together, top and side edges even, stitch a lining to one

A Rootin' Tootin' Christmas

boot piece between the squares. Clip to the squares and around the curves. Turn right side out and press. Cut two 4″ lengths from the bandanna ribbon. Right sides out, fold one strip in half, ends even, to form a boot strap, then center and pin it ½″ over the top edge of the lining on one of the boot pieces. Repeat on the second boot piece. Between the squares, stitch ¼″ from the top edge, following the top curve of the boot, stitching down the straps at the same time.

4. With right sides together, edges even, stitch the side and lower edges together between the circles. Clip, turn, press and topstitch several rows across the bottom edges of the heel and sole. On the right side of the boot, glue a contrasting star over the stitched star and glue sequins over the edges. Cut the remaining bandanna ribbon in half lengthwise. Using both lengths, make a multi-looped bow about 5″ across. Stitch to the back edge at the heel line for "her" stocking; leave plain for "his."

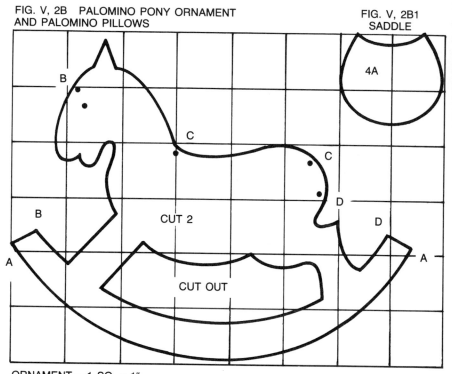

FIG. V, 2B PALOMINO PONY ORNAMENT AND PALOMINO PILLOWS

FIG. V, 2B1 SADDLE

ORNAMENT—1 SQ. = 1″
PILLOWS—SM. 1 SQ. = 2″, MED. 1 SQ. = 2½″, LG. 1 SQ. = 3¼″

LARIAT ORNAMENT
(about 4″ in diameter)

Easy: Achievable by anyone.
Materials: ¼″-diameter Manila rope; No. 30 gauge brass wire; 12″ piece ⅛″-wide red suede ribbon; white glue; scraps of natural burlap *(see Materials Shopping Guide, page 272)*; thin wire or ornament hanger.

Directions:
1. Cut the rope into a 16″ length. Form a 4″-diameter circle by looping the ends over and under each other once. Secure with wire and put a dot of glue under each overlap, leaving the rope ends free.
2. Pull about eight 12″-long strands from the cut edge of the natural burlap. Tie the suede ribbon and burlap strands together into a bow around the wired part of the lariat. Attach a wire or ornament hanger.

PALOMINO PILLOWS
(small, 15″ long; medium, 18½″ long; large, 23¾″ long; measured straight across at tips of rocker)

Average: For those with some experience in sewing.
Materials: Note: *The sides of the horse may be made with the same or contrasting color fabric.* 48″- to 50″-wide natural and/or red burlap: small ½ yd, medium ¾ yd, large 1 yd; 18″-wide fusible interfacing: small ½ yd, medium 1 yd, large 1½ yds; 2⅞″-wide bandanna ribbon for saddle: small ¼ yd, medium ½ yd, large 1 yd; 2 yds 1″-wide bandanna ribbon; ½″-wide braided piping: small 5 yds, medium 7 yds, large 9 yds; synthetic stuffing; white glue; two 4-holed black buttons: small ½″, medium ⅝″, large ¾″ *(see Materials Shopping Guide, page 272).*

Directions:
Same as Palomino Pony Ornament *(page 169)*, Steps 1 to 5, with these exceptions:
1. Enlarge the pattern in FIG. V, 2B and 2B1 in three sizes for the pillows, following the directions on page 271.
2. Mane: Measure the length from B to C. Cut a burlap rectangle 5″ wide by this length.
3. Assembly: From the burlap, cut two rectangles, each roughly 2″ larger than the shapes; assemble as for the Ornament. For each pony, trim the flat part of the braided piping to within ⅛″ from the cord. With the cut edge of the braid just over the outer stitch line, glue the braid around the edges of the pony. Repeat on the opposite side, then glue the cord edges together.
4. Saddle: Cut away the braided piping all the way to the cord; glue the cord over the edge of the saddle.
5. Eyes: See Hobby Horse, Step 6.

6. *Reins:* From the 1″-wide bandanna ribbon, cut the reins 1½ yds long by 3/16″ wide for the small and medium ponies and 1″ wide for the large pony.

PALOMINO PONY ORNAMENT
(4½″ x 6″)

Average: For those with some experience in sewing.

Materials: Note: *The sides of the horse may be made with the same or contrasting color fabric.* 18″ piece 6″-wide natural and/or red burlap ribbon; 6″ piece 1⅞″-wide red bandanna ribbon; ⅔ yds ⅛″-wide red suede ribbon; scrap of natural burlap for mane; synthetic stuffing; 5mm red cup sequins *(see Materials Shopping Guide, page 272)*; white glue; tracing paper; dressmaker's carbon; thin wire or ornament hanger.

Directions:

1. Enlarge the patterns, including the design lines, in FIGS. V, 2B and 2B1, on tracing paper, following the directions on page 271.

2. Mane: From the burlap, cut a strip 2¼″ wide x length between B and C (on the head and neck). Fold the strip, long edges even, and stitch ¼″ from the long edges to make a tube. Pull all threads from the tube to within ¼″ of the stitch line; save for the tail.

3. Assembly: From the burlap ribbon, cut two 9″ lengths. Center and trace the pony onto the right side of the ribbon. Pin the two pieces, wrong sides together. Using small machine stitches, stitch the (inner) lines of the cut-out first, then stitch only the lower edge of the rocker from A to A *(see FIG. V, 2B)*. Next stitch the front B to B, back D to D. Cut around the pony ornament ¼″ beyond the outer lines. Stuff the rocker from each end and stitch the ends. Stuff the legs and lower body.

Insert and pin the straight edges of the mane ½″ into the seam between B and C; stitch. For the tail, pin the pulled burlap threads between C and D. Stitch. Complete stuffing the head and body; stitch. Trim the edges to ⅛″.

4. Saddle and Eyes: Cut the saddle (FIG. V, 2B1) from the bandanna ribbon and glue it over the back of the horse. Outline the saddle with glued-on sequins. For the eyes, cut and glue two circles of bandanna cloth onto the head.

5. Reins: Center and pin the suede ribbon to the pony's nose *(see photo, page 167)*, wrap the ribbon under the chin, bring it up, tie it at the top of the head, twist the ends around the ribbon reins about half way down on both sides of the head and tie them into a bow at the bottom end of the mane.

6. To hang the Ornament on the tree, attach a wire loop or ornament hanger through a burlap loop at the bottom of the mane.

CHILDREN'S PARTY POINTERS

- Special invitations add to young guests' anticipation. For older children, try cutting the invitation into puzzle pieces.
- For easier cleanup, serve food on paper plates and use paper or plastic cups.
- Serve foods that can be eaten with the hands—no knives or forks.
- Have plenty of napkins on hand. Children often wind up with more food on them than in them.
- Serve fun foods, such as sandwiches or pizza. Leave grown-up food for grownups.
- Cut foods into interesting shapes using cookie cutters. Use *edible* garnishes to brighten up the dish. *Don't use toothpicks,* which can be accidentally swallowed.
- Decorate cookies or cakes with colorful frostings. Bake or buy a cake in the shape of a favorite toy or cartoon character.
- Give everyone something to take home. This way no one feels left out.
- For a bright decoration, paint a child's table and chair set Christmas red. Cover the table with an old lace cloth and

seat stuffed animals with their "gifts" as "guests" around the table.
- If the host or hostess is old enough, have him or her make something for the party. This will make the child feel special.
- Always keep kids busy! Simple games such as musical chairs and pin the tail on the donkey go over well at parties.
- When children show signs of boredom, it's time to move on to the next activity.
- Provide some sort of entertainment. Have a teenage helper dress up as a clown.
- Bright decorations put everyone in the party mood. Hang colorful balloons and crepe paper streamers.
- Hide wrapped candy for a fun scavenger hunt. Remember to hide treats where little hands can easily reach them.
- Keep the party down to a small group. A large group can be overwhelming for the children *and* for you.
- Have enough adult supervision—one adult for every four children.

HOBBY HORSE
(head, 12" x 15")

Average: For those with some experience in sewing.

Materials: ½ yd 48"- to 50"-wide natural burlap; 18" x 48" piece ½"-thick quilt batting; 1⅛ yds 18"-wide fusible interfacing; 2½ yds ⅞"-wide bandanna ribbon; heavy-duty Velcro® fasteners; two 4-holed 1" black buttons; synthetic stuffing *(see Materials Shopping Guide, page 272)*; standard mop or broom handle; tracing paper; dressmaker's carbon; 25" length twine.

Directions *(⅜" seams allowed):*
1. Enlarge the patterns in Fig. V, 2C on tracing paper, following the directions on page 271.
2. Cutting: From the burlap, cut one each right-facing and left-facing head pieces, two pairs of ears and two 6½" x 17" burlap strips for the mane. With edges even, press fusible interfacing to *both* sides of the batting. From the batting assembly, cut two horse heads, one left-facing, one right-facing. Trim 1" from the bottom edges.
3. Mane: On one mane strip, mark a ½" seam allowance on the long edges. Pull all the long threads from the center of the strip up to the ½" marks. Repeat on the second strip. With the long edges even, place one strip over the other, fold them over lengthwise, keep the long edges even and stitch the edges together just below the "mane" area.
4. Head: With the top and side edges even, pin the batting over the wrong side of one burlap head piece. Turn the bottom edge of the burlap up 1" over the edge of the batting. Machine baste around the top and side edges of the head

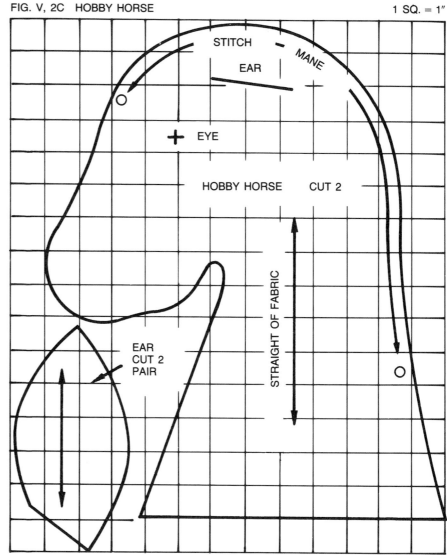

piece ¼" from the edge. Repeat on the second head piece. With cut edges even, stitch the bottom edge of the mane, between the circles, on the right side of one head piece. Pin the two heads, right sides together, edges even and stitch a ⅜" seam. Clip the curves and turn right side out.
5. Stitch two ear pieces, right sides together, around the curved side edges. Clip, turn, stuff and stitch the bottom opening. Handstitch the bottom straight edge of the ears to position them on the horse's head.
6. Stuff the nose and head (not the neck). Sew the buttons to the eye

positions from one side of the head to the other and pull tight to contour the face and hold the stuffing in place.
7. Reins: Leaving 18" flat at each end of the ribbon, fold the center of the ribbon in half lengthwise, right side out, long edges even, and press. See Palomino Pony Ornament *(page 169)*, Step 5, to attach the reins.
8. Glue one piece of Velcro® to the inside back seam and the other piece 6" down from the top of the broom handle. Insert the handle into the neck and join the Velcro® pieces. Tie a piece of twine tightly around the neck, below the mane.

LARIAT WREATH
(bandanna, 18" in diameter; rope, 14" in diameter)

Easy: Achievable by anyone.

Materials: *For Bandanna Wreath:* 15 yds 1⅞"-wide bandanna ribbon; 3¼ yds ¼"-thick Manila rope *(see Materials Shopping Guide, page 272)*; 18"-diameter Styrofoam® wreath form; fern pins; 6 artificial fir sprigs. *For Rope Wreath:* 50 ft ¼"-thick Manila rope; 5 yds 1⅞"-wide bandanna ribbon *(see Materials Shopping Guide, page 272)*; Fern pins; 6 artificial fir sprigs; 14"-diameter wire frame; No. 30 gauge brass wire *(available from craft and floral supply shops)*.

Directions:

1. Bandanna Wreath: Wind and overlap the ribbon around the wreath form, securing it at the back of the wreath with fern pins. Pin the greenery to the right side of the wreath. Cut the rope into two equal lengths and tie them together into a bow. Center and pin the bow over the greenery. Coil three rope ends separately and secure them with wire to form loops *(see photo)*.

2. Rope Wreath: If the wire frame seems too wide, snip off the two outer wires with wire cutters. Cut off 45" from the rope for a bow. Coil the remaining rope around the frame and secure it to the frame at intervals with brass wire. Wrap about 1¼ yds of the ribbon around the wreath and tie the ends securely. Pin the greenery over the ends of the ribbon. With the remaining 45" of rope, center and pin a 45" rope bow over the greenery. From 1¾ yds of the ribbon, make a multi-loop bow about 8" across. With right sides up, place the rope wreath in the center of the ribbon wreath, with the greenery and bow at the top *(see photo)*. Tie them together tightly at the center top with a 40" length of ribbon tied into another bow at the center front. Hang with wire attached at the center top.

Note: *Use the wreaths separately, if you wish, or together as we have.*

Lariat Wreath

Gifts For Children

PUPPY LOVE
(about 12" high)

Challenging: Requires more experience in sewing.
Materials: 12" x 62" fur fabric for each dog; scraps of black felt and tan felt for eyes; shanked buttons for noses; tapestry needle and thick black yarn for mouth; scraps of cotton fabric for inner ears and bows; Velcro® tape to clasp paws; synthetic stuffing; ⅛ yd tweed fabric and black bias binding for hat.

Directions *(¼" seams allowed):*
Sew all seams with right sides facing unless otherwise indicated.
1. Enlarge the patterns in Fig. V, 3 *(page 174)*, following the directions on page 271. Trace the pattern pieces to the wrong side of the fur fabric with the nap running downward in the direction of the arrows. To cut a pair, trace once with the pattern right side up and once with the pattern wrong side up. Cut through the backing fabric only, with small sharp scissors. *Do not cut the pile.* Trim the pile from all seam allowances. Use scissors to push fur away from the seams as you sew.
2. For each dog, from the fur cut one pair each of the back body, front body, back arm, front arm, tail, inner leg, ear, upper foot and side face pieces. Cut one back head gusset,

front face gusset and base. From the printed cotton, cut one pair of ears and two 12" x ⅝" strips for the bows (girl). From the felt, cut two black eyes and two tan eyelids. From the tweed fabric, cut four each of the crown, ear flap and brim pieces.
3. Sew the front arms and inner legs to the side fronts, matching the dots. Sew the back arms to the back body pieces. Sew the side fronts to the side backs from the neck around the arm and body to A. Clip the seam allowance at A on the back and continue sewing the curve of the leg. Sew the straight edge of the foot B across the leg.
4. Sew the front body pieces together from the neck to the crotch. Sew the tail pieces, turn to the right side, fill softly and sew across the opening. With raw edges together, sew the tail to one side of the back body. Sew the back seam from the base to the dot. Attach the body to the base. (Clip the seam allowance of the body, if necessary, and sew with the body side up.)
5. Join the head gusset pieces at C. Sew the fabric ears to the fur ears and turn them to the right side. Press the seam between your fingers. Make a pleat in the fabric side of the ears at the top and sew them to the side head pieces. Sew the gusset to the side head from neck to back on both sides. Turn the head right side out.

6. Insert the head inside the body and match a neck D with the D on one side body. Hand stitch securely around the neck, easing the head to fit. **Note:** *Mark D on the reverse side head and body for the second dog to make a pair.*
7. Insert small pieces of stuffing to define the shape of the feet, legs and head. Fill the arms and body softly. Handstitch the back opening, concealing the stitches. Cut ⅝" of Velcro® tape, trim the matching section of fur from the back of one paw and front of the other. Handstitch the tape securely to each paw. Glue one eyelid to each eye. Trim the fur on the face and glue on the eyes. Sew on the button nose. Using a tapestry needle and black yarn, sew two loops from under the nose to each side of the mouth; couch the yarn in place with black sewing cotton.
8. Hat: Sew the crown pieces together down the longest sides to make two halves. Press the seam open with your fingers and topstitch near each side of the seam. Sew the two halves together and topstitch in the same way. Fold a 16" strip of black bias tape in half lengthwise and sew the folded edges together. Cut the strip in half and sew one strip to the right side of each ear flap at E, with raw edges together. Sew the facings to the ear flaps and brims and turn right side out. Press the

Puppy Love

FIG. V, 3 PUPPY LOVE

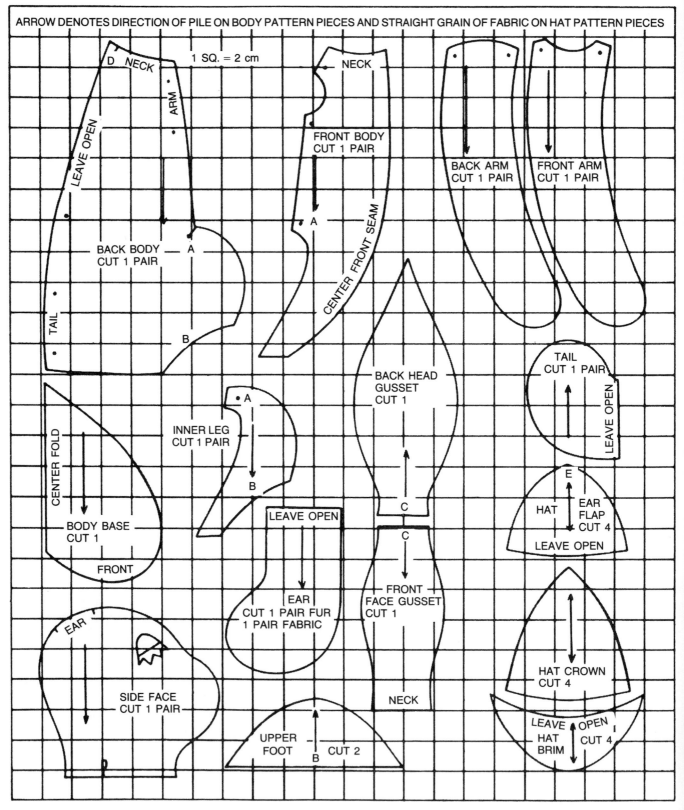

ARROW DENOTES DIRECTION OF PILE ON BODY PATTERN PIECES AND STRAIGHT GRAIN OF FABRIC ON HAT PATTERN PIECES

1 SQ. = 2 cm

D NECK

ARM

LEAVE OPEN

NECK

FRONT BODY
CUT 1 PAIR

BACK ARM
CUT 1 PAIR

FRONT ARM
CUT 1 PAIR

A

BACK BODY
CUT 1 PAIR

A

CENTER FRONT SEAM

TAIL

B

TAIL
CUT 1 PAIR

LEAVE OPEN

BACK HEAD
GUSSET
CUT 1

A

INNER LEG
CUT 1 PAIR

CENTER FOLD

B

E

HAT

EAR
FLAP
CUT 4

LEAVE OPEN

LEAVE OPEN

C

BODY BASE
CUT 1

C

FRONT

EAR
CUT 1 PAIR FUR
1 PAIR FABRIC

FRONT
FACE GUSSET
CUT 1

HAT CROWN
CUT 4

EAR

SIDE FACE
CUT 1 PAIR

NECK

UPPER
FOOT CUT 2

B

LEAVE OPEN
HAT
BRIM CUT 4

seams flat and edgestitch all pieces. Repeat. Sew the flaps and brims, matching the centers, to the opposite seams, on the right side of the crown with raw edges together. Cut bias tape to fit, slightly stretched, around the hat at the base of the crown. Open the fold on one side and sew the tape so that it encloses all raw edges when folded up inside. Press the tape and seam up inside the hat and slipstitch lightly to the crown. Tie the ear flaps at the top of the hat. Tie the bows around the ears of the girl dog.

KANGAROO, AND BABY TOO!
(about 10″ tall)

Average: For those with some experience in crocheting.

Materials: 4-ply worsted weight yarn: 3½ oz Blue, 1 oz Cream and scraps of Black for facial features; size G crochet hook, OR ANY SIZE HOOK TO OBTAIN STITCH GAUGE BELOW; polyester fiberfill; one pair each ⅜″ and ⅛″ plastic animal eyes; tapestry needle.

Gauge: 4 sc = 1″; 4 rows = 1″.

Note: *When working in rows, always ch 1 and turn. Skip the chain at beginning of next row.*

Directions:

1. Body: Starting at bottom of mother's body with Blue, ch 2. ***Rnd 1:*** Work 6 sc in 2nd ch from hook. ***Note:*** *Do not join rounds but use marker to indicate end of rounds.* ***Rnd 2:*** Work 2 sc in each sc around. ***Rnd 3:*** *Sc in 1 sc, 2 sc in next sc; rep from * around. ***Rnd 4:*** Repeat Rnd 3—27 sts. ***Rnd 5:*** * Sc in each of next 2 sc, work 2 sc in next sc; rep from * to end of rnd—36 sts. ***Rnds 6 and 7:*** Sc in each sc. ***Rnd 8:*** Repeat Rnd 5—48 sts. ***Rnds 9 and 10:*** Sc in each sc. ***Rnd 11:*** * Sc in each of next 5 sc, work 2 sc in next sc; rep from * to end of rnd—56 sts.

Kangaroo, And Baby Too!

2. Gusset—Row 1: Change to Cream color for body gusset and sc in back loops *only* for first 20 sc. Ch 1, turn. **Rows 2-7:** Sc in each sc working in back loops *only*. Continue to work in back loops only for remainder of gusset. **Row 8:** * Sc in each of next 3 sc, work 2 sc tog; rep from * to end of row—16 sts. **Rows 9-15:** Sc in each sc. **Row 16:** * Sc in each of next 2 sc, work 2 sc tog; rep from * to end—12 sts. **Rows 17-22:** Sc in each sc. **Row 23:** * Sc in 1 sc, work 2 sc tog; rep from * to end—8 sts. **Rows 24-28:** Sc in each sc. **Row 29:** Work 2 tog across—4 sts. **Row 30:** Sc in each sc. Fasten off.

3. Remainder of Body—Rows 1-8: Join Blue at joining of bottom circle and gusset (Rnd 11), and work 8 rows of sc in each sc on the 36 sts remaining on circle. **Row 9:** * Sc in each of next 2 sc, work 2 sc tog; rep from * to end—27 sts. **Rows 10-16:** Sc in each sc. **Row 17:** * Sc in each of next 7 sc, work 2 sc tog; rep from * to end—24 sts. **Rows 18-22:** Sc in each sc. **Row 23:** Repeat Row 9—18 sts. **Rows 24-28:** Work 5 rows of sc in each sc. **Row 29:** Work 2 tog across—9 sts. Fasten off. Sew the gusset to the body with overcast st, using tapestry needle. Stuff body.

4. Head: With Blue, work same as body from Rnds 1-4—27 sts. **Rnd 5:** * Sc in each of next 8 sc, 2 sc in next sc; rep from * around—30 sts. **Rnds 6-10:** Sc in each sc. **Rnd 11:** * Sc in each of next 8 sc, work 2 sc tog; rep from * to end—27 sts. **Rnd 12:** Sc in each sc. **Rnd 13:** * Sc in 1 sc, work 2 sc tog; rep from * to end—18 sts. **Rnds 14-17:** Sc in each sc. **Rnd 18:** Work 2 tog around. **Rnd 19:** Sc in each sc. Stuff head; run yarn end through stitches, pull up and fasten off. Sew head to body at a slight angle.

5. Ears (make 4 pieces): Starting at bottom of ear, ch 4. **Row 1:** Sc in 2nd ch from hook and in each ch to end. **Row 2:** Sc in each sc. **Row 3:** Inc 1 sc in center of row. **Rows 4-6:** Sc in each sc. **Row 7:** Dec 1 sc in center of row. **Rows 8 and 9:** Sc in each sc. **Row 10:** Work 3 sts tog. Fasten off. Sew 2 pieces together for each ear, around outer edges. Sew to top of head, 1½" apart.

6. Haunch (make 2): Work same as body from Rnds 1-3—18 sts. **Rnd 4:** * Sc in each of next 2 sc, work 2 sc in next sc; rep from * to end—24 sts. **Rnds 5 and 6:** Sc in each sc. **Rnd 7:** * Sc in 1 sc, 2 sc in next sc; rep from * to end—36 sts. **Rnds 8 and 9:** Sc in each sc. Fasten off. Stuff and sew to sides of body.

7. Feet (make 2): Ch 10. Join with sl st to form ring. **Rnds 1-9:** Sc in each sc. **Rnd 10:** Work 2 tog around. Run yarn through sts, pull up and fasten off. Stuff and sew opening shut. Sew to bottom of body.

8. Pocket: With Cream, ch 16. **Row 1:** Sc in 2nd ch from hook and in each ch to end. **Rows 2-15:** Sc in each sc. **Row 16:** Inc 1 st each side. **Row 17:** Sc in each sc. Fasten off. Sew to front of body, starting with Row 1 of gusset, joining bottom and side seams *(see photo)*. **Note:** *Pocket should gap open at the top.*

9. Arms (make 2): With Blue, ch 7. Join with sl st to form ring. **Rnds 1-8:** Sc in each sc. *Now* work in rows for hand as follows: **Next Row:** Sc in first 4 sc. Ch 1, turn. **Next 2 Rows:** Sc in each of next 4 sc. Ch 1, turn. **Last Row:** Work 2 sc tog across. Fasten off. Stuff arms and sew to sides of body.

10. Tail: With Blue, ch 16. Join with sl st to form ring. **Rnds 1-6:** Sc in each sc. **Rnd 7:** * Sc in each of next 2 sc, work 2 sc tog; rep from * to end—12 sts. **Rnds 8-28:** Sc in each sc. **Rnd 29:** * Sc in 1 sc, work 2 sc tog; rep from * to end—8 sts. **Rnds 30-39:** Sc in each sc. Run yarn through stitches, pull up and fasten off. *Do not* stuff. Sew closed, tacking to rear of body.

11. Baby—Body: With Blue, ch 16. **Row 1:** Sc in 2nd ch from hook and in each ch to end. Ch 1, turn. **Rows 2-5:** Sc in each sc. Fasten off. Fold in half so short ends meet; sew short ends and side seams. **Note:** *Short end is the bottom of baby's body.*

12. Arms (make 2): With Blue, ch 3. **Row 1:** Sc in 2nd ch from hook and in each ch to end. Sew to body.

13. Feet (make 2): With Blue, ch 5. Work the same as the arms. Sew to either side of short end.

14. Ears (make 2): With Blue, ch 4, and work same as arms.

15. Tail: With Blue, ch 6. **Row 1:** Sc in 2nd ch from hook and in each ch to end. **Rows 2-4:** Sc in each sc. **Row 5:** Dec 1 st each side. **Rows 6-10:** Sc in each sc. **Row 11:** Work 3 sc tog across. Fasten off. *Do not* stuff. Sew to short end of body.

16. Head: With Blue, ch 2. Join with sl st to form ring. **Rnd 1:** Work 6 sc in 2nd ch from hook. **Rnd 2:** * Sc in 1 sc, 2 sc in next sc; rep from * to end—9 sts. **Rnds 3 and 4:** Sc in each sc. **Rnd 5:** * Sc in 1 sc, work 2 sc tog; rep from * to end—6 sts. **Rnd 6:** Sc in each sc. Stuff and sew up opening. Sew to top of body.

17. Finishing—Facial Features: Mother and Baby's eyes are glued in. If they are made for a small child, use Black French knots for eyes. Work straight stitches for the mouth and nose. Place the Baby in the pocket.

Colonial Doll House

COLONIAL DOLL HOUSE

(about 2 feet high and 34 inches wide)

Challenging: Requires more experience in crafts and woodworking.
Materials: One sheet ½"x4'x8' and one piece ¼"x2"x3' AA INT grade plywood or particle board; 15 ft ½"-wide cove molding, 13 ft ¾"-wide corner guard molding; 7 ft ½"-wide lattice, 6 ft 1"-wide lattice; 1/16"x½", 1/8"x1/8" and 1/8"x½" balsa wood strips; ½" and 1" wire nails; glue; 1 front door and roof shingles *(see Materials Shopping Guide, page 272)*; paint.

Cutting Directions:

Code	Pieces	Size
A	1	½"x15"x33½" 1st floor
B	2	½"x10"x15" 1st floor inside walls
C	1	½"x15"x33½" 2nd floor
D	2	½"x10"x15" 2nd floor inside walls
E	2	½"x15"x21" Sides
F	1	½"x21"x34½" Front
G	1	½"x16¼"x35½" 3rd floor
H	2	½"x11¼"x16" Attic sides
J	1	¼"x11½"x36" Roof front
K	1	¼"x3"x36" Roof back

Directions:

1. Lay out the parts on the plywood or particle board for the most economical use of the wood. Cut the parts to size. Cut the window and door openings with a sabre saw. Sand the parts smooth.
2. Assembling: Glue/nail (1") the first floor (A) to the first floor inside walls (B). Nail through the underside of A into B. Repeat for the second floor CD *(see* Fig. V, 4 *for measurements and placement)*. Carefully toenail and glue CD to AB, aligning the first and second floor inside walls D and B *(see* Fig. V, 4*)*.

FIG. V, 4 COLONIAL DOLL HOUSE

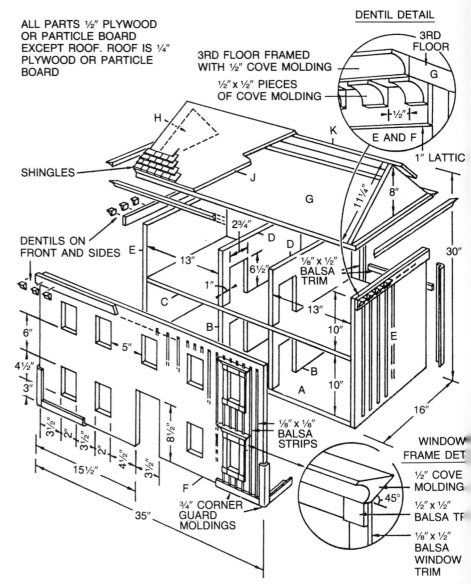

ALL PARTS ½" PLYWOOD OR PARTICLE BOARD EXCEPT ROOF. ROOF IS ¼" PLYWOOD OR PARTICLE BOARD

DENTIL DETAIL

3RD FLOOR

3RD FLOOR FRAMED WITH ½" COVE MOLDING

½" x ½" PIECES OF COVE MOLDING

SHINGLES

DENTILS ON FRONT AND SIDES

E AND F

1" LATTIC

1/8" x ½" BALSA TRIM

1/8" x 1/8" BALSA STRIPS

¾" CORNER GUARD MOLDINGS

WINDOW FRAME DET

½" COVE MOLDING

½" x ½" BALSA TR

1/8" x ½" BALSA WINDOW TRIM

Doll House interior

3. Glue/nail the sides (E) to the first and second floors A and C. Glue/nail the front (F) to the floors, walls and attic.

4. Glue/nail the attic sides (H) to the third floor (G), through G into H, ½″ in from each end *(see* FIG. V, 4*)*. Glue/nail the third floor to the doll house assembly, flush at the back and overlapping the sides ½″ and the front ¾″. Glue/nail the roof front (J) and back (K) to the attic sides. This completes the basic doll house.

5. Paint the outside of the house blue. Paint the ½″ cove and ¾″ corner guard moldings and the 1″ lattice yellow gold.

6. Miter and glue/nail (½″) the molding trim to the front and sides of the house *(see* FIG. V, 4 *details)*. The dentils are ½″ cove molding, ½″ wide with ½″ spacing.

7. The ¾″ corner guard molding is glue/nailed to the four outside corners and around the bottom edges of the house.

8. The ⅛″ x ½″ strips of balsa are cut and glued around the windows to form casings. The ½″ cove molding is cut at a 45° angle and glued across the top of each window.

9. See FIG. V, 4 for the window and batten details. Paint the battens blue after gluing to the house.

10. Affix the front door and roof shingles, as shown.

11. Decorate the interior with wallpaper and carpet remnants. *(See photo for inspiration.)* Fill with miniature furniture available in hobby stores or by mail *(see Materials Shopping Guide, page 272)*.

Teddy Bear Planter; Bulletin Board; Bear's Gotcha Framed!

💲 🏷️

TEDDY BEAR PLANTER

Average: For those with some experience in woodworking.
Materials: ½″ x 10″ x 30½″ pine; glue; nails; paints *(see photo, or to your liking)*.

Directions:
1. Enlarge the pattern in FIG. V, 5A, following the directions on page 271. Cut the planter bottom and 2 sides *(see diagram for measurements)*. Cut out the 2 bears with a jig or sabre saw.
2. Glue/nail the planter sides to the planter bottom *(see diagram)*. Glue the bears to the open-ends of the planter box. Paint the overalls, front and back, and the bear's features *(see photo)*.

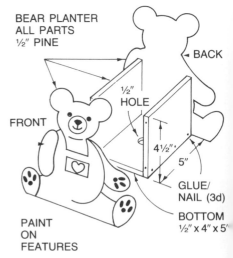

BEAR PLANTER
ALL PARTS
½″ PINE

BACK

½″
HOLE

FRONT

4½″

5″

GLUE/
NAIL (3d)

PAINT
ON
FEATURES

BOTTOM
½″ x 4″ x 5′

FIG. V, 5A   TEDDY BEAR PLANTER
1 SQ. = 1"

FIG. V, 5B   BULLETIN BOARD
1 SQ. = 1½"

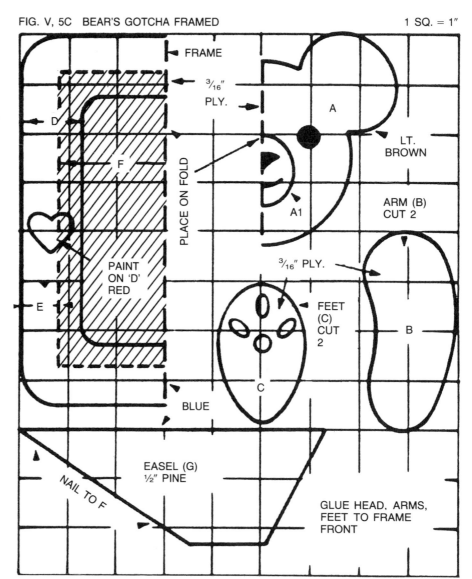

ARM SEPARATE FOR CORK BOARD ONLY GLUE TO CORK

ENTIRE BEAR ¼" PLYWOOD

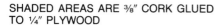

SHADED AREAS ARE ⅜" CORK GLUED TO ¼" PLYWOOD

💲 🏷️

BULLETIN BOARD

Average: For those with some experience in woodworking.
Materials: ¼" x 15" x 16½" plywood; ⅜" x 9" x 15" cork; glue; nails; paints *(see photo, or to your liking)*.

Directions:

1. Enlarge the pattern in FIG. V, 5B, following the directions on page 271. Cut out the parts with a jig or sabre saw.
2. The bear's right arm is separate from the body. Glue the cork (shaded areas) to the ¼" plywood. Glue the arm to the cork. Paint the bear's features *(see photo)*.

💲 🏷️

BEAR'S GOTCHA FRAMED!

Challenging: For those with more experience in woodworking.
Materials: 3/16" x 16" x 18" plywood; ½" x 3" x 7" pine; sandpaper; glue; nails; paints *(see photo, or to your liking)*.

Directions:

1. Enlarge patterns in FIG. V, 5C, following directions on page 271, placing on folds as indicated. Cut out head, face piece (A1), frame, frame back, 2 feet and 2 arms from 3/16" plywood. Cut easel from ½" pine.

2. Sand pieces to slightly round edges. Paint frame and bear pieces. When frame is dry, glue bear pieces to frame using photo as guide. Glue backing to frame, leaving one side open to insert picture. Glue and nail easel to frame back.

FIG. V, 5C   BEAR'S GOTCHA FRAMED   1 SQ. = 1"

FRAME

3/16" PLY.

D

PLACE ON FOLD

F

PAINT ON 'D' RED

E

A

LT. BROWN

A1

ARM (B) CUT 2

3/16" PLY.

FEET (C) CUT 2

B

C

BLUE

GLUE HEAD, ARMS, FEET TO FRAME FRONT

NAIL TO F

EASEL (G) ½" PINE

Baby Bunting

BABY BUNTING

Average: For those with some experience in knitting.
Directions are given for Toddler Size 1. Changes for Toddler Size 2, Size 3 and Size 4 are given in parentheses.
Materials: Any 4-ply worsted weight yarn: 11 (12, 14, 16) ounces Red and 7 (7, 9, 10½) ounces White; 1 pair each No. 6 and No. 8 knitting needles, OR ANY SIZE NEEDLES TO OBTAIN STITCH GAUGE BELOW; size H crochet hook; five ⅝″ buttons; 1 yd ⅛″-wide elastic; yarn needle.
Gauge: With No. 8 needles: 4 sts = 1″; 6 rows = 1″. With No. 6 needles: 5 sts = 1″; 7 rows = 1″.

Toddler Size:
Body:

(1)	(2)	(3)	(4)

Chest Size:

20″	21″	22″	23″

Directions:
1. Cardigan — Back: Starting at lower edge with Red and No. 6 needles, cast on 44 (46, 48, 50) sts. Work in k 1, p 1 ribbing for 1½ (1½, 2, 2)″. Change to No. 8 needles and work in stockinette stitch (k 1 row, p 1 row) until total length is 5½ (6, 6½, 7)″, end with a p row.
2. Armhole Shaping — Rows 1-2: Bind off first 4 (4, 5, 5) sts, work across. Continue in stockinette stitch over the 36 (38, 38, 40) sts until length from first row of armhole shaping is 4¾ (5, 5¼, 5½)″, end with a p row.
3. Shoulder Shaping — Rows 1-2: Bind off first 10 (10, 10, 11) sts, work across. Bind off.
4. Left Front: Starting at lower edge with Red and No. 6 needles, cast on 18 (20, 20, 22) sts. Work in k 1, p 1 ribbing for 1½ (1½, 2, 2)″, inc 1 (0, 1, 0) st on last row—19 (20, 21, 22) sts. Change to No. 8 needles and work in stockinette stitch until total length is 5½ (6, 6, 6½, 7)″, end with a p row.
5. Armhole Shaping — Row 1: Bind off first 4 (4, 5, 5) sts, k across. Continue in stockinette stitch over

the 15 (16, 16, 17) sts until length from first row of armhole shaping is 3¾ (4, 4¼, 4½)", end at front edge.

6. Neck and Shoulder Shaping— Row 1: Bind off first 3 (4, 4, 4) sts, p across. **Row 2:** Knit. **Row 3:** P 2 tog, p across. **Rows 4-6:** Rep Rows 2, 3 and 2. Bind off.

7. Right Front: Work as for Left Front to armhole shaping, end with a k row.

8. Armhole Shaping—Row 1: Bind off first 4 (4, 5, 5) sts, p across. Work as for Left Front until length from first row of armhole shaping is 3¾ (4, 4¼, 4½)", end at front edge.

9. Neck and Shoulder Shaping—Row 1: Bind off first 3 (4, 4, 4) sts, k across. **Row 2:** Purl. **Row 3:** K 2 tog, k across. **Rows 4-6:** Rep Rows 2, 3 and 2. Bind off.

10. Sleeves: Starting at lower edge with White and No. 6 needles, cast on 28 (30, 30, 32) sts. Work in k 1, p 1 ribbing for 1". With No. 8 needles and working in stockinette stitch, inc one st at each end on next row and every 6th (6th, 6th, 7th) row until 38 (40, 42, 44) sts are on needle. Work even until total length is 6½ (7, 7½, 8¼)". Mark each end of last row for end of sleeve seam. Work even until length from markers is 1 (1, 1¼, 1¼)". Bind off. Sew shoulder seams. Sew in sleeves. Sew side and sleeve seams.

11. Right Front Band: With right side facing, White and No. 6 needles and starting at lower front corner, pick up and k 40 (44, 48, 52) sts along front edge. Work in stockinette stitch for 1½". Bind off.

12. Left Front Band: Starting at neck corner, work as for opposite band. Fold each band in half to wrong side and sew bound-off edge of each band along line of picked-up sts. Close top and bottom edge of each band.

13. Neckband: With right side facing, White and No. 6 needles and starting at right front neckband, pick up and k 38 (41, 42, 43) sts along entire neck edge to opposite corner. Work as for Left Front Band.

14. Button Loop (make 5): Using crochet hook and Red, ch 14, fasten off. Having first loop 1¼" from lower edge and last loop 1¼" below neck edge, sew loops evenly spaced on left front band. Sew buttons in place on right front band.

15. Embroidery: Following photo on page 182, embroider duplicate stitch design on front.

16. Leggings—Front: Starting at waist with Red and No. 6 needles, cast on 42 (44, 46, 48) sts. Work in k 1, p 1 ribbing for 1½". Change to No. 8 needles and work in stockinette stitch until total length is 7½ (8, 8½, 9)", end with a p row.

17. First Leg Section—Row 1: K 19 (20, 21, 22), k 2 tog, place remaining sts on a stitch holder. **Rows 2-4:** Work in stockinette stitch over the 20 (21, 22, 23) sts. **Row 5:** K to last 2 sts, k 2 tog—19 (20, 21, 22) sts. Work in stockinette stitch until length from Row 1 of leg section is 9 (9½, 10, 10½)", end with a p row. Change to No. 6 needles and work in k 1, p 1 ribbing for 1½". Bind off in ribbing.

18. Second Leg Section: Place sts from holder onto a No. 8 needle, join Red to next st at crotch. **Row 1:** K 2 tog, k remaining sts. **Rows 2-4:** Work in stockinette stitch. **Row 5:** K 2 tog, k remaining sts—19 (20, 21, 22) sts. Complete as for other Leg Section.

19. Back: Work same as Front. Sew inner leg and crotch seam; sew side seams.

20. Tie (make 2): With crochet hook and White, make a chain 18" long. Fasten off. Draw tie through first row of each leg ribbing.

21. Pompon (make 4): Cut 2 cardboard circles each 1" in diameter. Cut a hole ½" in diameter in center of each circle. Cut 3 strands of White each 2 yards long. Place cardboard circles together and wind the 3 strands held together around the double circles, drawing yarn through center opening and over edge until center hole is filled. Cut yarn around outer edge between circles. Double a ½ yard length of White, slip be-

tween the 2 cardboard circles and tie securely around strands of pompon. Remove cardboard. Trim pompons evenly. Sew a pompon to each end of ties.

22. Cap—Ribbing: Starting at lower edge with Red and No. 6 needles, cast on 78 (80, 82, 84) sts. Work in k 1, p 1 ribbing for 1". Cut Red. Continuing with No. 6 needles and using White work in stockinette stitch until total length is 5½ (5¾, 6¼, 6½)", end with a p row.

23. Top Shaping—Row 1: K 0 (2, 4, 0), * k 2 tog, k 4. Rep from * across. **Row 2:** Purl. **Row 3:** K 0 (2, 4, 0), * k 2 tog, k 3. Rep from * across. **Row 4:** Purl. **Row 5:** K 0 (2, 0, 0), * k 2 tog, k 2. Rep from * across. **Row 6:** Purl. **Row 7:** K 0 (2, 0, 0), * k 2 tog, k 1. Rep from * across. **Row 8:** Purl. **Row 9:** * K 2 tog. Rep from * across. Leaving an 18" end, cut yarn. Draw end through remaining sts, pull up and secure. Then sew back seam.

24. Ear Flap (make 2): With Red and No. 6 needles cast on 16 sts. **Rows 1-4:** Knit. **Row 5:** K 2 tog, k to last 2 sts, k 2 tog. **Row 6:** Knit. Rep last 2 rows until 3 sts remain. Turn. P 3 sts tog. Place lp from needle onto crochet hook and make a chain 10" long. Fasten off. Sew flaps in place. Embroider duplicate stitch on cap.

25. Pompon: Follow directions above, using two 2" cardboard circles with ¾" diameter hole in center.

SNOWFLAKE SWEATER SET

Challenging: Requires more experience in knitting.

Directions are given for Child's Size 2. Changes for Sizes 4, 6 and 8 are in parentheses.

Materials: Any 2-ply sport-weight yarn (2 oz skns): 5 (5, 6, 6) skns Red, 1 skn each White and Green; No. 4 and No. 5 knitting needles, OR ANY SIZE NEEDLES TO OBTAIN STITCH GAUGE BELOW; stitch holder.

Gauge: On No. 5 needles in St st, 6 sts = 1″; 9 rows = 1″.

Finished Measurements:

Size: 2 4 6 8
Garment width around underarm:
23″ 25″ 27″ 29″

Note: Bottom edging on body and sleeves, and center front motif are worked in duplicate stitch when sweater is completed.

Directions:

1. Back: With No. 4 needles and Red, cast on 69 (75, 81, 87) sts. Work in k 1, p 1 ribbing for 1½″. Change to No. 5 needles and work in St st (k on right side, p on wrong side) until 9¼ (9½, 10, 10½)″ from beg, or desired length to underarm. **Armhole Shaping:** Bind off 5 (5, 6, 6) sts at beg of next 2 rows—59 (65, 69,75)

sts. Dec 1 st each edge every other row 2 (2, 3, 3) times—55 (61, 63, 69) sts. Work until 5 (5½, 6, 6)″ above beg of armhole shaping. **Shoulder Shaping:** Bind off 6 (7, 7, 8) sts at beg of next 4 rows—31 (33, 35, 37) sts. Sl sts to a holder for back of neck.

2. Front: Work same as back until 3″ above beg of armhole shaping. **Neck Shaping:** Work across 15 (17, 17, 20) sts, join another ball of yarn, work next 25 (27, 29, 29) sts and place on holder for front of neck, work remaining 15 (17, 17, 20) sts. Working both sides at the same time, dec 1 st every right side neck edge row 2 (3, 3, 4) times—13 (14, 14, 16) sts each side. Work until same length as back to shoulder. **Shoulder Shaping:** Bind off 6 (7, 7, 8) sts at beg of next 2 shoulder edge rows—7 (7, 7, 8) sts each side. Work 1 row even. Bind off.

3. Sleeves: With No. 4 needles and Red, cast on 35 (35, 37, 37) sts. Work in k 1, p 1 ribbing for 1½″. Change to No. 5 needles and St st, inc 0 (0, 4, 4) sts evenly spaced across first row—35 (35, 41, 41) sts. Inc 1 st each edge every 1″ 7 (8, 9, 9) times—49 (51, 59, 59) sts. Work until 10 (10, 10¼, 10¾)″ from beg, or desired length to underarm. **Cap Shaping:** Bind off 5 (5, 6, 6) sts at beg of next 2 rows—39 (41, 47, 47) sts. Dec 1 st each edge every other row 9 (10, 11, 11) times—21 (21, 25, 25) sts. Bind off.

4. Finishing: Sew one shoulder seam. **Neckband—Row 1:** Right side facing, with No. 4 needles and Red, pick up and k 14 (15, 16, 16) sts along side of front neck, pick up 25 (27, 29, 29) sts from front neck holder, 14 (15, 16, 16) sts along side of front neck, 31 (33, 35, 37) sts from back neck holder—84 (90, 96, 98) sts. **Row 2:** With Red, p and dec 0 (0, 2, 4) sts evenly spaced across—84 (90, 94, 94) sts. **Row 3:** With White, k. **Row 4:** With Green, p. **Rows 5 through 10:** With Red, work in k 1, p 1 ribbing. Bind off loosely in ribbing. Sew remaining shoulder seam and neckband.

5. Embroidery: Following Diagram A in FIG V, 6, work duplicate stitch around bottom of sweater (front and back) with bottom edge of embroidery ½″ up from top of ribbing. In the same manner, work duplicate stitch around bottom of sleeves. Following Diagram B in FIG V, 6, work duplicate stitch motif at center front of sweater. Sew sleeves in place, easing as necessary to fit. Sew underarm and side seams.

6. Cap: Beg at bottom edge, with No. 4 needles and Red, cast on 119 sts. **Row 1 (right side)** Work in k 1, p 1 ribbing. **Row 2:** With Green, p. **Row 3:** With White, k. **Row 4:** With Red, p. Continuing in Red, work in k 1, p 1 ribbing until 2¼″ from beg, end on right side. **Next Row:** Change to No. 5 needles and k.

Eddie The Elf; Snowflake Sweater Set

FIG. V, 6 SNOWFLAKE SWEATER SET

DIAGRAM A

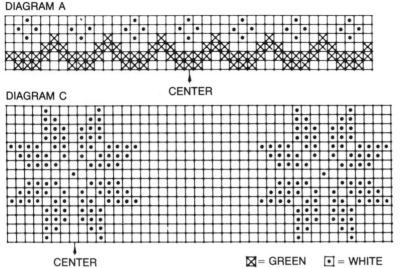

CENTER

DIAGRAM C

DIAGRAM B

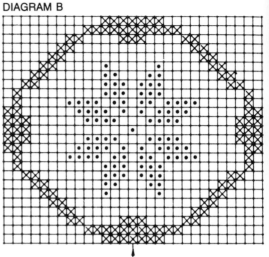

CENTER

CENTER

⊠ = GREEN   ⊡ = WHITE

Note: *With turn in hat cuff, this k row is now the right side.* **Next row:** Purl. Continue in st st (k on right side, p on wrong side) until 5″ from beg of cuff, end on wrong side. Mark center st on last row and leave marker in place for duplicate stitch to be worked later. Continue in St st for 18 rows more, dec 1 st at beg of last row—118 sts. **Crown Shaping— Row 1** *(right side):* K 4, (k 2 tog, k 10) 9 times, k 2 tog, k 4—108 sts. **Row 2:** Purl. **Row 3:** K 4, (k 2 tog, k 9) 9 times, k 2 tog, k 3—98 sts. **Row 4:** Purl. **Row 5:** K 3, (k 2 tog, k 8) 9 times, k 2 tog, k 3—88 sts. **Row 6:** Purl. Continue working as established, decreasing 10 sts every right side row until 28 sts remain. **Next Row:** *K 2 tog. Repeat from * across—14 sts. **Next Row:** P 14. Cut yarn, leaving a 20″ length.

7. Cap Finishing: Draw 20″ end through remaining sts. Draw sts together tightly and secure. Use remaining yarn to sew back seam.

8. Embroidery: Following Diagram C in FIG. V, 6, and with bottom center of snowflake matched to marked stitch at center of cap, work duplicate stitch. Skip 13 sts at each side of center snowflake; work one more snowflake at each side of center motif.

Fill little red stockings (purchased at a party store or five-and-dime) with crayons and tiny toys; hang them from the lower branches of the tree and in other easy-to-reach spots.

EDDIE THE ELF

Challenging: Requires more experience in sewing.

Materials: 12″ x 3″ strong muslin for body and finger pockets; 10″ x 24″ red cotton fabric for legs; 20″ x 24″ flesh colored fabric for head, arms and lining; 18″ x 24″ red and white cotton print for blouse; 24″ x 33″ green felt for hat, pants and shoes; four 1″ red pompons; 10 yds or more brown knitting yarn; polyester fiberfill; small amount embroidery thread in red, brown, charcoal grey and white; sewing machine; heavy cardboard; fabric marking pencil; red, white and green thread; scissors; pins; needle; iron; rouge.

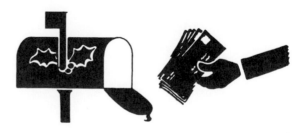

Directions:

1. Enlarge all pattern pieces in FIG. V, 7, following the directions on page 271. All seams are ¼". Pin to the fabrics and cut the number of pieces indicated. Mark and keep a pattern piece pinned to a fabric piece until it is to be used.

2. Nose and Ears: Placing right sides together, sew around both halves of the nose, leaving the straight edge open. Turn and stuff; blind stitch (see Stitch Guide, page 270) the opening closed. Make two ears using the instructions given for making the nose. Leave a 1½" opening on the long side of each ear for stuffing. Set the finished nose and ears aside.

3. Finger Pocket for Puppet's Head: Fold over the edge of 1 long side ¼" and stitch it down. Fold it in half, wrong side out, matching the C's. Stitch along the raw edges, forming the pocket. Turn and press. Set aside.

4. Hair: Use the hair card, made of heavy cardboard, for hair construction. Wind yarn around the card, one strand next to the other. Stitch back and forth through the slit to fasten the strands together. Cut the top and bottom of the yarn and remove the hair through the slit. Set aside.

5. Muslin Body: Sew the body front pieces together from A to B. Sew the body back pieces together from A to B. Put the wrong sides of the front and back together and stitch all around, leaving an opening from C to A to C. Stuff the body firmly and blind stitch it closed. Set aside.

6. Lower Body Back: Sew together the lower body back pieces from I to B. Make the darts. Turn the long straight edge down ¼" and stitch it down. Cut the darts open, press and set aside.

7. Arms: Stitch the dart in the inner arm pieces. Lay out the arm pieces, outer arm underneath, inner arm on top, right sides together. Put a muslin arm finger pocket on top, matching D's and E's. Stitch the curved edge of the finger pocket piece

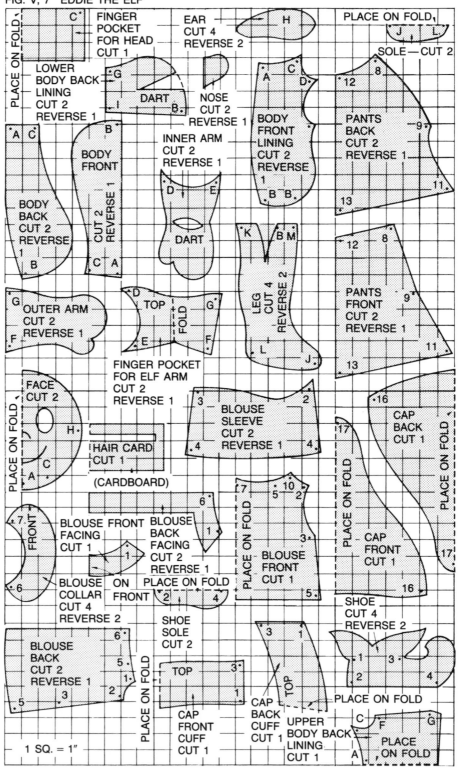

FIG. V, 7   EDDIE THE ELF

along the curved edge of the inner arm. Fold the muslin pocket on the line indicated and put F and G over D and E. Stitch the inner arm to the outer arm from E around the hand to D, catching the edges of the muslin pocket insert in the side seams. Turn and stuff the lower arm and hand with fiberfill. Push the pocket into the upper arm. Baste F and G on the muslin pocket to F and G on the outer arm piece. Repeat to make the other arm. Set aside.

8. *Flesh Colored Lining:* Place the body front lining pieces right sides together and stitch from A to B. Fold under ¼″ on the bottom edge of the upper body back lining and stitch. Stitch F and G of the outer right arm to the right side of the upper body back lining and F and G of the outer left arm to the left side of the upper body back lining. Thumbs should point upward. Stitch D and E of the inner arms to D and E of the body front lining. Stitch the muslin lower body back to the body front lining from B center back around the curve, matching G to E.

9. *Head:* On the right side of the material, lightly trace the face with a pencil on one of the face pieces. Use an outline stitch and red embroidery thread to embroider a mouth. Outline the eyes with brown. Make charcoal grey pupils, brown irises and put a sparkle in his eyes with a touch of white in the iris. Make eyebrows and eyelashes with pencil or charcoal embroidery. Tint the cheeks with rouge. Stitch the yarn hair in place along the top seam from H to H. Fasten the nose in place with blind stitches. Place the right side of the second face piece on the first, right sides together, and sew around the top of the head from C to C. Turn and stuff the head with fiberfill. Fasten the ears in place with blind stitches. Push the head finger pocket up into the head, matching C's, and sew around the bottom hem of the finger pocket to fasten it to the bottom of the face and back of the head between C's, leaving the pocket open.

Stitch C and D of the body front lining to C and F of the upper body back lining. Stitch the face on the body front lining, matching CAC, and the back of the head on the upper body back lining, also matching CAC. You should now have a stuffed head and stuffed arms with pockets inside attached to a flesh colored body lining. Insert the muslin body into the lining and tack tightly at the C's on the lining "shoulders" and front.

10. *Legs:* Sew the darts in the legs and stitch them together, matching M's and J's. Stitch the other side of the legs, matching K's and L's. Stitch the soles to the legs, matching L's and J's. Turn, stuff and shape so the darts are on the sides of the legs. Close the openings and fasten the legs securely to the body lining, matching B's on the lining.

11. *Pants:* Stitch the two fronts together, matching 8's and 9's. Stitch the two backs together, matching 8's and 9's. Stitch the front and back of the pants together, matching 11's and 9's on the inseam and 12's and 13's on the sides. Pull over the puppet's legs and handstitch the top of the pants back to the top of the muslin lower body back. Gather the bottom of the pants legs to fit the puppet's legs. Tack the pants to the legs and to the puppet torso at the waistline front and sides.

12. *Shoes:* Stitch each pair of shoe sides together, matching 1's and 2's and 3's and 4's. Stitch the sides to the shoe soles, matching 2's and 4's. Turn. Tack front flap down and put the shoes on the puppet's feet. Tack them to the feet to secure.

13. *Cap:* Stitch the front and back of the cap together, matching 1's and 2's. Stitch the front and back cuffs together, matching 1's and 3's. Stitch the cuff to the bottom of the cap, matching 1's and 3's. Turn the cuff over twice and slipstitch the cuff to the cap from inside. Fasten a pompon on the tip of the cap and stuff the cap loosely with fiberfill. Place the cap on the puppet's head and fasten it around with blind stitches.

14. *Blouse:* Gather the neckline of the blouse front from 5 to 5 to 2″. Gather the neckline of the blouse back from 5 to the edge to 1″. Stitch the blouse back facing pieces to the blouse front facing, right sides together, matching 1's. Stitch the blouse front to the blouse back pieces, matching 1's and 2's. Stitch two collar pieces, right sides together, leaving the shorter inside curve open. Turn and press. Repeat with the other two pieces. Baste them to the right side of the blouse neckline, matching 6's and 7's. Pin the right sides of the facings to the blouse back and to the neckline over the collar, matching 6's and 7's. Stitch through all thicknesses. Turn and press. Make a ¼″ hem in the sleeves from 4 to 4. Stitch the sleeves to the blouse, matching 3's. Stitch the blouse together on the sides and down the underside of the sleeves, matching 5's, 3's and 4's. Sew three pompons down the center front. Dress the puppet and stitch the back seam together by hand. Tack the clothes securely to the puppet.

Decorate a pint-sized tree and place it in your child's room for an "I'm someone special" feeling. *Bonus:* Your child can fall asleep to the lights of the Christmas tree!

SUGAR PLUM PAJAMAS

Average: For those with some experience in sewing.

Materials: 9″ square fabric scrap of each color: red, white, green, brown, yellow, striped red and white; thread to match each fabric scrap; ⅓ yd fusible webbing; ready-made "foot" pajamas; sewing machine; iron.

Directions:
1. Enlarge the pattern pieces in Fig. V, 8, following the directions on

page 271. Use the patterns to cut out: 2 red lollipops, 3 green lollipops, 3 brown gingerbread boys, 1 yellow horn, 1 striped candy cane, 1 stocking (red foot and white cuff) and a fusible webbing piece to match each appliqué.

2. Pin the stocking to the bottom of the left pajama leg. Pin goodies along the left front of the pajamas *(see photo)*. Pin a gingerbread boy and lollipop to the right front. Fuse, following fusible webbing instructions. Using a ruler, draw a 2½" "stick" on each lollipop with a fabric pencil.

3. Set your machine on a medium-width satin stitch and, with thread to match each appliqué, sew around the horn, stocking, gingerbread boys, candy cane, red lollipops, green lollipops and along each fabric pencil line with thread to match its lollipop.

FIG. V, 8 SUGAR PLUM PAJAMAS

Sugar Plum Pajamas

189

Reindeer Appliqué; Monkey Shines Appliqué

REINDEER APPLIQUÉ

Average: For those with some experience in sewing.

Materials: Two shades brown velour scraps 9″ square; ⅓ yd fusible webbing; thread to match fabric scraps; glue-on wiggle eyes; fabric glue; 3 red pompons; one ⅝″ heart-shaped button for nose; ready-made sweatshirt; sewing machine; iron.

Directions:
1. Enlarge the patterns in FIG. V, 9A, following the directions on page 271. Cut out the reindeer head and antlers from the fabric scraps. Cut out the fusible webbing, using the entire appliqué as a pattern.
2. Position the reindeer head and antlers on the sweatshirt as desired, with the fusible webbing shape under the appliqué. The reindeer head should slightly overlap the antlers. Fuse, according to the manufacturer's instructions.

3. Transfer the markings for the eyes, nose and inside detail lines. Set your machine on a medium-width satin stitch and, with thread to match the antlers, sew around the outer edge of the antlers. Change the thread to match the reindeer head and sew around the outer edge of it, including the detail lines.
4. Cut out the leaves, and sew with a regular stitch right down the middle of each leaf as indicated.
5. Glue the eyes to the face with fabric glue. Handstitch the nose and pompons as shown.

FIG. V, 9A REINDEER APPLIQUÉ

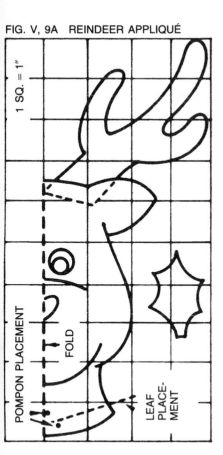

1 SQ. = 1"

POMPON PLACEMENT

FOLD

LEAF PLACE-MENT

MONKEY SHINES APPLIQUÉ

Average: For those with some experience in sewing.

Materials: Two shades brown velour fabric scraps; yellow fabric scrap; fabric paints or embroidery floss; two ½" sew-on wiggle eyes; thread to match fabric scraps; ¼ yd fusible webbing; ready-made sweatshirt; sewing machine; iron.

Directions:

1. Enlarge the patterns in FIG. V, 9B, following the directions on page 271. Cut out the monkey face, body, tail and the banana from the fabric scraps and fusible webbing.

2. Transfer the detail lines. Either paint or embroider the face onto the monkey.

3. Position the monkey body on the shirt as desired. Fuse, following the manufacturer's instructions. Clip the tail on the dotted lines. Slip the banana through the tail as shown, with the end of the tail curling *over* the banana. Position as desired on the garment. Fuse.

4. Set your machine on a medium-width satin stitch and, with thread to match the banana, sew around the outer edge and detail lines. Change the thread to match the monkey body and sew around the tail. Sew around the monkey body and detail lines. With thread to match, sew around the monkey face.

5. Handstitch the wiggle eyes to the face where indicated.

FIG. V, 9B MONKEY SHINES APPLIQUÉ

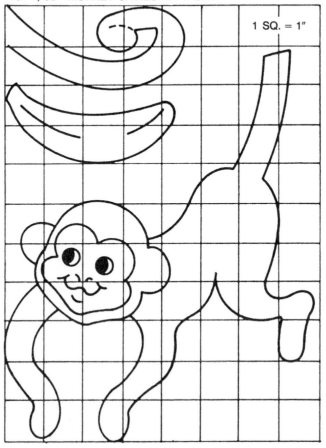

1 SQ. = 1"

The Right Toy At The Right Time

The key to selecting a child's gift is knowing his or her interests, abilities and limitations. Avoid buying toys to please yourself, ones that don't involve the child or that may be too sophisticated.

BABIES UNDER 18 MONTHS:

Today, experts agree that even infants need toys. Babies learn about size, shape, sound, texture and how things work from their playthings. Well-selected toys give babies opportunities to explore their environment in various ways.

Choose playthings that are:
- too large to swallow
- lightweight for handling and grasping
- rounded, with no sharp points or edges
- brightly colored
- non-toxic for exploring mouths

Brightly colored, lightweight toys of various textures stimulate the baby's sense of sight and touch. A colorful crib mobile will enable a baby to "play" with his or her eyes. When an infant can hold things, it's time for a rattle, squeaky rubber toy or crib exerciser for grasping.

Soft dolls or stuffed animals made of non-toxic material are fun to feel. Make sure these have strong seams that cannot be easily torn or bitten. Facial features (especially eyes and noses) should be strongly secured so they cannot be pulled off. Floating tub toys are also a good choice.

A baby that sits up is ready for blocks with rattles in them or pictures on them, nesting cups or boxes, stacking toys and rings. He or she will enjoy simple picture books that show familiar objects. (These books should be made of material that cannot be easily torn.) Push-pull toys, musical and chime toys, a small wagon or doll carriage provide stimulation and enjoyment when a baby can creep or walk, as do take-apart-and-put-together toys.

TODDLERS—18 MONTHS TO 3 YEARS:

A busy toddler needs toys for active physical play—things to ride and climb on: a first, low tricycle; a bigger wagon to ride in and other ride-on toys. Outdoor toys such as balls, inflatable toys, a wading pool and a sandbox with digging toys are all good choices. To imitate the adult world around them, toddlers can use child-size furniture, play appliances and utensils, simple dress-up clothes and costumes, dolls and stuffed animals. More skillful hands are now ready for more complicated take-apart toys, blocks of varying sizes and shapes and simple puzzles and games. Children of this age also enjoy playing with simple musical instruments such as tambourines, toy pianos, horns and drums, as well as listening to records.

Note: A child's interest in a toy will usually carry through more than one age group.

PRE-SCHOOL CHILDREN—3 TO 6 YEARS:

Children of this age group are masters of make-believe. They like to act out grown-up roles and create imaginary situations. Costumes and playthings that help them create their pretend worlds are important at this age. Included are puppets, a play store, play money, pretend food, a cash register and a telephone; also villages, forts, circuses, farms, gas stations and doll furniture. Transportation fascinates young children. Trucks, cars, planes, trains, boats, tractors and other construction toys are all fun at this age and in later years. Larger outdoor toys, including gym equipment, wheeled vehicles and a first two-wheel bike with training wheels are in order now. Introduction of simpler electronic toys and games that are geared specifically to this age group are also appropriate. Construction sets, books and records are all good for indoor fun; coloring sets, paints, crayons, puzzles, stuffed toys and dolls continue to be favorites.

CHILDREN—6 TO 9 YEARS:

Board games, table-top sports games and old favorites like marbles and kites help in learning social behavior. In experimenting with different kinds of work worlds, fashion and career dolls and all kinds of action figures appeal to girls and boys. Printing sets, science and craft kits, electric trains, racing cars, construction sets and hobby equipment are important to children in examining and experimenting with the world around them. A larger bicycle, ice and roller skates, a pogo stick, scooter, sled and other sports equipment are good choices for active physical play. Even though group play is important, children at this age also play well by themselves. They can read books written especially for them and play electronic games with others or by themselves. Paints, crayons and clay are good selections, as are costumes, doll houses, play villages, miniature figures and vehicles. These all help children develop their imaginative and imitative worlds.

OLDER CHILDREN—9 TO 12 YEARS:
Children begin developing specific skills now, and may give considerable attention to hobbies and crafts, model kits, magic sets, advanced construction and handicraft kits, chemistry and science sets, jigsaw and other puzzles. Peer acceptance is very important to girls and boys of this age group. Active physical play now finds its expression in team sports. Social skills are developed through board, card and electronic games, particularly those requiring strategy decisions and knowledge acquired in school. Table tennis, video and sports games are also popular. Dramatic play holds great appeal. Youngsters like

to plan complete productions with props, costumes, printed programs, and will frequently use puppets and marionettes. Painting, sculpting, ceramics and other art forms continue to be of interest as well as musical instruments, records and books.

TEENS:
After age 12, a child's interest in playthings begins to merge with those of adults. This is increasingly apparent in the growing market for sophisticated, electronic and video computer-based toys and games which are often considered family items. They will also be interested in adventure games and board games including those with business themes. Collectors of such items as dolls, model cars, trains, miniatures and stuffed animals often begin their hobbies in their teenage years.

A FINAL NOTE:
Select toys with care. Get involved and encourage your youngster to be creative through play. Set good examples for proper use and maintenance of toys. Youngsters tend to easily remember lessons they learn while having fun. Remember that playing with toys is a child's work and those who are creative at play as children are more creative and secure as adults.

Gifts Children Can Make

Under Mom's or Dad's watchful eye, kids can make some super holiday gifts.
(Older kids won't need any help!)

QUILTED PLACE MAT, NAPKIN

Easy: Achievable by older children; younger children may need adult supervision.

Materials: Quilted white place mats; white napkins; 6-strand cotton in 6 colors; embroidery needle.

Directions: With 6 strands in needle, sew long running stitches over quilting stitches (through top fabric only) in the place mats. Sew rows of running stitches around the napkins.

PAPER BEAD JEWELRY

Materials: Illustrated magazine pages; toothpicks; white glue; beads; jute; 1/8″ ribbon; heavy string; thin cord or fishing line; 10″ piece of 1/16″ round elastic for bracelet; earring hardware.

Directions:
1. To Cut Beads: Starting at the lower right corner, mark off each inch at the bottom edge of a magazine page. Starting at the top right corner, measure ½″ inward, then mark off each inch. Place the ruler from the bottom right corner to the first dot at the top and draw a slanted line. Place the ruler from the first top dot to the first lower dot and draw a line to finish a full thin triangle. Continue across the page—a 9″ x 11″ page will make 17 triangles. Cut the triangles out.
2. To Make Beads: Starting at the wide end, roll a triangle around a toothpick, securing the end with a little white glue. When the glue is dry, remove the toothpick.
3. Necklaces: String paper beads alternately with purchased beads to the desired length (24″ is average), leaving 6″ or 7″ of string at each end to tie. Tie a bead to the end of each string so the beads don't come unstrung. To make a *"spiked"* necklace

Quilted Place Mat, Napkin

(see photo), start with a yard of ⅛″ ribbon and work from the center out to each side. For the center spike, thread 1 paper, 1 plastic, 1 paper and 1 plastic bead; bring the thread back through the plastic bead and the previous 3 beads again. Continue on each side, threading a few beads before the next spike.

4. Earrings: Tie the center of a 10″ long strong plastic thread securely around the top loop of the earring. Thread both threads through plastic, paper and plastic beads. Then thread each thread separately through paper, plastic, paper, plastic and paper (to make the loop). Thread ends back up through each bead to the top again and tie securely.

5. Bracelet: Thread 10″-long round elastic through 7 paper beads alternating with 7 glass beads. Tie the elastic in a square knot; trim off excess, threading the tails back through the beads.

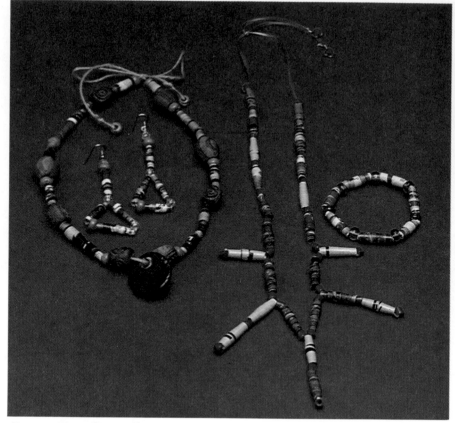

Paper Bead Jewelry

QUILTED GREETINGS

Easy: Achievable by older children; younger children may need adult supervision.

Materials: Tracing paper; quilted fabric scraps (from real quilts, or use fabric printed with a quilt motif); construction paper; scissors; white glue; felt-tipped markers for writing greetings.

Directions:

1. Choose geometric designs to be cut out from the quilt or fabric scraps; draw the designs on tracing paper. Cut out the tracing paper figures to make patterns.

2. Cut out designs from the quilt or fabric scraps, using the tracing paper patterns.

3. Fold the construction paper into cards. Glue the designs cut from the fabric scraps onto the front of the cards. Let the glue dry completely.

4. Write your Christmas greetings inside the cards with the felt-tipped markers.

Quilted Greetings

Christmas Cards

CHRISTMAS CARDS

Easy: Achievable by older children; younger children may need adult supervision.

Materials: Tracing paper; fabric scraps; string, ribbon, cotton and other trimmings; construction paper or other heavy-weight paper; white glue; scissors.

Directions:

1. Choose designs to be cut out from the fabric; draw on tracing paper. Cut out the tracing paper figures to make patterns.

2. Cut out the designs from the fabric scraps.

3. Fold the construction paper into cards. Glue the designs cut from the fabric scraps onto the paper. Let the glue dry completely.

4. Decorate the cards with string, ribbon, cotton and other trimmings.

Edible Gifts From Young Chefs

Older kids will delight in making these treats themselves; younger kids will need Mom's or Dad's supervision.

Christmas Cutouts

A honey of a holiday cookie.

Bake at 350° for 10 minutes.
Makes 2½ dozen.

- ¾ **cup honey**
- ¼ **cup (½ stick) butter or margarine**
- 4½ **cups unsifted all-purpose flour**
- 1 **teaspoon baking soda**
- ½ **teaspoon salt**
- ½ **teaspoon ground nutmeg**
- 2 **eggs**
- ¾ **cup sugar**
- ½ **cup ground almonds**
- ⅓ **cup finely chopped candied citron**

1. Heat the honey and the butter or margarine in a small saucepan just until the mixture comes to a boil; cool.
2. Sift together the flour, baking soda, salt and nutmeg onto wax paper.
3. Beat the eggs until fluffy in a large bowl with an electric mixer at high speed. Gradually beat in the sugar and continue to beat until very light. Stir in the honey mixture. Stir in the ground almonds and the chopped citron. Gradually stir in the flour mixture to make a very stiff dough. Wrap in wax paper and refrigerate overnight.
4. Preheat the oven to moderate (350°).
5. Roll out the dough, a quarter at a time, to ¼-inch thickness on a lightly floured pastry cloth or board. Cut into your favorite Christmas shapes, using a 3-inch cookie cutter. Place, 1 inch apart, on greased cookie sheets.
6. Bake in the preheated moderate oven (350°) for 10 minutes, or until light brown. Cool on wire racks and decorate as desired.

Butterscotch Nut Bells

Brown sugar and almonds give a special flavor to holiday roll-out cookies.

Bake at 400° for 10 minutes.
Makes 4 dozen.

- 3¼ **cups unsifted all-purpose flour**
- 1 **teaspoon salt**
- ½ **teaspoon baking soda**
- ¾ **cup (1½ sticks) butter or margarine**
- 2 **cups firmly packed light brown sugar**
- 2 **eggs**
- 1 **cup ground almonds**
- 1 **teaspoon vanilla**
  Pink frosting from a 4-ounce tube

1. Sift together the flour, salt and baking soda onto wax paper.
2. Beat together the butter or margarine and the brown sugar until fluffy in a large bowl with an electric mixer at high speed. Beat in the eggs, one at a time, then the ground almonds and the vanilla.
3. Stir in the flour mixture to make a stiff dough. Wrap in wax paper and refrigerate for 3 hours, or overnight.
4. Preheat the oven to hot (400°).
5. Roll out the dough, a quarter at a time, to ¼-inch thickness on a lightly floured pastry cloth or board. Cut into bells, using a 3-inch cookie cutter. Place, 1 inch apart, on cookie sheets.
6. Bake in the preheated hot oven (400°) for 10 minutes, or until the cookies are golden. Remove to wire racks with a spatula and cool completely before decorating.
7. Place a star tip on the frosting tube and pipe lines to decorate the bells, if you wish. Let dry before packing.

Baking With Young Chefs

Best Chocolate Cookies

Even at holiday time, true chocolate lovers want their favorite flavor in cookies.

Bake at 350° for 10 minutes.
Makes 4 dozen.

3¼	**cups unsifted all-purpose flour**
½	**cup cocoa powder (not a mix)**
½	**teaspoon salt**
½	**teaspoon baking soda**
1	**cup (2 sticks) butter or margarine**
1½	**cups sugar**
2	**eggs**
1	**teaspoon vanilla**
½	**teaspoon bottled aromatic bitters**
	Assorted frostings and decorations

BAKING WITH KIDS

*Kids love to work in the kitchen and Christmas is a great time for them to learn many cooking techniques that will be helpful in years to come. But they must learn that **safety is always first when baking.***

- **AN ADULT MUST BE PRESENT.** Never allow young children to start cooking without an adult to give undivided attention for the time needed to complete the baking project.
- **CLEAN HANDS AND APRONS** are a must before starting to work.
- **ONLY AN ADULT LIGHTS THE OVEN.** Caution must be practiced around a hot oven to prevent burns. Never allow a child to open the oven unless an adult is standing there.
- **USE THICK MITTS OR POT HOLDERS** when taking cookie sheets out of the oven and always place them on wire racks, never the countertop. Use mitts also while removing baked cookies from hot sheets.
- **KEEP SHARP KNIVES AWAY FROM YOUNG CHILDREN** and allow older children to use them only with the supervision of an adult.
- **STORE ALL COOKIES IN METAL OR PLASTIC CONTAINERS** with tight-fitting covers to keep cookies fresh and insects out.
- **WASH UP ALL WORK SURFACES** with hot sudsy water after baking, so the kitchen is in perfect order after the baking session.

1. Sift together the flour, cocoa, salt and baking soda onto wax paper.
2. Beat together the butter or margarine and the sugar until fluffy in a large bowl with an electric mixer at high speed. Beat in the eggs, one at a time, then the vanilla and the bitters until well blended.
3. Stir in the flour mixture to make a stiff dough. Wrap in wax paper and refrigerate for 3 hours, or overnight.
4. Preheat the oven to moderate (350°).
5. Roll out the dough, a quarter at a time, to ¼-inch thickness on a lightly floured pastry cloth or board. Cut into assorted shapes, using your favorite 3-inch cookie cutters. Place on cookie sheets.
6. Bake in the preheated moderate oven (350°) for 10 minutes, or until the cookies are firm. Remove to wire racks with a metal spatula and cool. Store in an airtight metal tin.
7. If you wish, decorate the cookies with canned frosting or icing in a tube; place cinnamon red hots or colored sprinkles on top.

Holiday Sugar Cookies

A crisp roll-out cookie flavored with a hint of lemon.

Bake at 375° for 10 minutes.
Makes 5 dozen.

5	**cups unsifted all-purpose flour**
1	**teaspoon baking powder**
1	**teaspoon salt**
1	**cup (2 sticks) butter or margarine**
2¼	**cups sugar**
2	**eggs**
2	**teaspoons vanilla**
1	**teaspoon lemon extract**
	Assorted frostings and decorations

1. Sift together the flour, baking powder and salt onto wax paper.
2. Beat together the butter or margarine and the sugar until fluffy in a large bowl with an electric mixer at high speed. Beat in the eggs, one at a time, beating well after each addition. Add the vanilla and the lemon extract until blended.
3. Stir in the flour mixture to make a stiff dough.

Wrap in wax paper and refrigerate for 3 hours, or overnight.

4. Preheat the oven to moderate (375°).
5. Roll out the dough, a quarter at a time, to ¼-inch thickness on a lightly floured pastry cloth or board. Cut into assorted shapes, using your favorite 3-inch cookie cutters. Place on lightly greased cookie sheets, 2 inches apart.
6. Bake in the preheated moderate oven (375°) for 10 minutes, or until lightly brown. Remove with a metal spatula to wire racks and cool. Store in a metal tin.
7. If you wish, decorate the cookies with canned frosting or icing in a tube; place cinnamon red hots or colored sprinkles on top.

$ 🍪 🔥

Orange Wreaths

Add a California touch to Christmas cookie baking.

Bake at 350° for about 10 minutes.
Makes 2 dozen.

2¼ **cups unsifted all-purpose flour**
1   **tablespoon baking powder**
½   **teaspoon salt**
½   **cup (1 stick) butter or margarine**
1⅓ **cups sugar**
1   **egg**
1   **tablespoon heavy cream**
1½ **teaspoons orange extract**
1   **egg yolk**
1   **tablespoon water**
¼   **cup finely chopped pistachio nuts**
¼   **cup chopped candied red cherries**
1½ **teaspoons grated orange rind**

1. Sift together the flour, baking powder and salt onto wax paper.
2. Beat together the butter or margarine and 1 cup of the sugar until fluffy in a large bowl with an electric mixer at high speed. Beat in the egg, cream and orange extract.
3. Stir in the flour mixture, a third at a time, blending well to make a soft dough. Refrigerate for several hours, or until firm enough to roll.
4. Preheat the oven to moderate (350°).
5. Roll out the dough, a quarter at a time, to ¼-inch thickness on a lightly floured pastry cloth or board. Cut into wreaths, using a 3-inch cookie cutter. Place on greased large cookie sheets.

6. Mix the egg yolk with the water in a cup. Mix the remaining ⅓ cup of sugar, the chopped pistachio nuts and red cherries and the grated orange rind in a second cup. Brush the cookies with the egg yolk mixture, then sprinkle with the orange mixture.
7. Bake in the preheated moderate oven (350°) for 10 minutes, or until firm but not brown. Remove carefully from the cookie sheets to wire racks with a spatula and cool completely. Store in an airtight metal tin.

$ 🍪 🔥

Spicy Molasses Cookies

Tasty cookies to leave out for Santa.

Bake at 350° for 10 minutes.
Makes 5 dozen.

4½ **cups unsifted all-purpose flour**
2   **teaspoons baking soda**
2   **teaspoons pumpkin pie spice**
½   **teaspoon salt**
⅓   **cup milk**
½   **cup vegetable shortening**
¼   **cup (½ stick) butter or margarine**
1½ **cups light molasses**
     Assorted frostings and decorations

1. Sift together the flour, baking soda, pumpkin pie spice and salt onto wax paper.
2. Combine the milk, shortening and butter or margarine in a medium-size saucepan. Heat just until melted; pour into a bowl. Stir in the molasses.
3. Add the flour mixture, a third at a time, blending well to make a stiff dough. Cover the bowl with plastic wrap and refrigerate for several hours, or until firm enough to roll.
4. Preheat the oven to moderate (350°).
5. Roll out the dough, a quarter at a time, to ¼-inch thickness on a lightly floured pastry cloth or board. Cut out assorted shapes, using your favorite 3-inch cookie cutters. Place, 1 inch apart, on lightly greased cookie sheets. Reroll and cut out the trimmings.
6. Bake in the preheated moderate oven (350°) for 10 minutes, or until firm. Remove from the cookie sheets with a spatula and cool completely on wire racks. Decorate with an assortment of colored frostings and cookie decorations, if you wish.

Sugar Angels

They're buttery, old-fashioned roll-out cookies with a sugary glaze.

Bake at 350° for 10 minutes.
Makes 3 dozen.

- **3 cups unsifted all-purpose flour**
- **1 teaspoon baking powder**
- **½ teaspoon salt**
- **¾ cup (1½ sticks) butter or margarine**
- **1 cup sugar**
- **2 eggs**
- **1 teaspoon vanilla**
- **Coarse sugar**

1. Measure the flour, baking powder and salt into a sifter.
2. Beat together the butter or margarine and the sugar until fluffy in a large bowl with an electric mixer at high speed; beat in 1 of the eggs. Separate the remaining egg and beat in the yolk, then the vanilla. Reserve the egg white.
3. Sift in the dry ingredients, a quarter at a time, blending well to make a stiff dough. Refrigerate for 1 hour, or until firm enough to roll.
4. Preheat the oven to moderate (350°).
5. Roll out the dough, a quarter at a time, to ¼-inch thickness on a lightly floured pastry cloth or board. Cut into angels, using a 3-inch cookie cutter.
6. Place, 2 inches apart, on cookie sheets. Brush with the reserved egg white, slightly beaten, and sprinkle with the coarse sugar.
7. Bake in the preheated moderate oven (350°) for 10 minutes, or until firm. Separate and remove from the cookie sheets with a spatula. Cool on wire racks.

Chocolate Covered Pretzels

Makes 5 dozen.

- **1 package (6 ounces) semisweet chocolate pieces**
- **1 tablespoon vegetable shortening**
- **60 small pretzels**

1. Melt the chocolate with the shortening in a small bowl over simmering water. Remove from the heat, but keep over the water.
2. Drop the pretzels, one at a time, into the chocolate. Lift out with a fork, lightly tapping the fork against the side of the bowl to let the excess chocolate drip back into the bowl.
3. Place the pretzels on a wire rack over wax paper. Allow to dry.

Peanut Butter Munchies

No cooking and only one mixing bowl!

Makes about 3 dozen.

- **1¼ cups graham cracker crumbs**
- **1 cup unsifted 10X (confectioners' powdered) sugar**
- **1 cup creamy peanut butter**
- **¼ cup (½ stick) butter or margarine, softened**
- **½ cup chopped walnuts**
- **½ cup flaked coconut**

1. Mix the graham cracker crumbs, 10X (confectioners' powdered) sugar, peanut butter and butter or margarine in a medium-size bowl, using a wooden spoon.
2. Roll between your palms to shape into small balls. Roll half in the chopped walnuts and half in the flaked coconut. Refrigerate.

Pizza Popcorn

Makes 12 cups.

- **½ cup (1 stick) butter or margarine**
- **½ teaspoon leaf oregano, crumbled**
- **½ teaspoon garlic salt**
- **½ teaspoon leaf basil, crumbled**
- **⅛ teaspoon red pepper flakes**
- **12 cups freshly popped corn**
- **2 tablespoons grated Parmesan cheese**

1. Melt the butter or margarine in a small saucepan over low heat. Stir in the oregano, garlic salt, basil and pepper flakes. Heat for 1 minute.
2. Pour over the popcorn in a large bowl. Sprinkle with the Parmesan cheese and toss lightly until coated.

Chocolate Fudge Sauce

Smooth and delicious!

Makes 2 cups.

1 **package (6 ounces) semisweet chocolate pieces**
1 **can (14 ounces) sweetened condensed milk (not evaporated milk)**
1 **teaspoon vanilla**
 Pinch salt
1/3 **cup hot water**

1. Melt the chocolate pieces in the top of a double boiler over simmering water. Add the sweetened condensed milk, vanilla and salt, stirring constantly until the mixture is slightly thickened. Then stir in the hot water.
2. Let cool, cover and refrigerate. The sauce can be thinned more by adding hot water, 1 tablespoon at a time, before serving.

Rocky Road Fudge

Fudge is everyone's favorite candy. Try this for your friends or children.

Makes 24 squares.

1 **package (10½ ounces) miniature marshmallows**
2 **cups dry roasted peanuts**
1 **package (12 ounces) chocolate-flavored wafers (available at candy making supply stores)**
1 **can (14 ounces) sweetened condensed milk (not evaporated milk)**

1. Line a 9 x 13-inch pan with wax paper (allow the paper to extend over the edge for easy lifting of the candy).
2. Combine the marshmallows and the peanuts in a large bowl. Set aside.
3. Melt the chocolate wafers with the sweetened condensed milk in a medium-size saucepan over medium heat, stirring constantly, until well blended.
4. Pour the chocolate mixture over the marshmallows and peanuts; mix well. Spread into the prepared pan.
5. Refrigerate; cut into squares.

Granola Snack

Let the kids make this nutritious nibble to give to family and friends.

Bake at 300° for 1 hour.
Makes 8 cups.

4 **cups bran flakes with raisins**
1½ **cups coarsely chopped walnuts**
1 **can (3½ ounces) flaked coconut**
½ **cup wheat germ**
2 **tablespoons sesame seeds**
1 **teaspoon ground cinnamon**
1 **teaspoon salt**
1 **can (14 ounces) sweetened condensed milk (not evaporated milk)**
¼ **cup vegetable oil**
1 **cup banana chips**

1. Preheat the oven to slow (300°).
2. Combine the bran flakes with the chopped walnuts, the coconut, wheat germ, sesame seeds, cinnamon and salt in a large bowl. Stir in the sweetened condensed milk and the oil with a wooden spoon until well combined.
3. Line a 15 x 10 x 1-inch jelly-roll pan with aluminum foil. Spoon the mixture into the prepared pan, spreading evenly.
4. Bake in the preheated slow oven (300°) for 1 hour, stirring occasionally.
5. Remove from the oven. Stir in the banana chips. Cool in the pan on a wire rack. When cold, pack into small plastic bags and tie with decorative ribbon.

Note: *This mixture is a nutritious snack you can prepare and store in metal tins all year long.*

Cookie Glaze *(see tip box, page 163)* may be used to decorate animal crackers for miniature cookies.

CHAPTER 6

'Tis the season . . .
. . . steeped in history.
Stories told and retold of
a child born into this
world, the Savior and
light of a people.

Caught in the Christmas time crunch? Try our Here Comes Santa Claus!
Quilt-Block Decorations!

Christmas In A Flash

"But Thanksgiving was only yesterday!" It always seems that December speeds by, and families on-the-go find themselves with everything to do and no time to do it. If you're time-short but spirit-willing, this chapter can help you create an overnight sensation for Christmas. There are 11th-hour decorations, one-stop shopping gift ideas and a tantalizing array of Hors d'Oeuvres in a Hurry, Quick-Fix Desserts and Last-Minute Food Gifts. These ideas will help you put time on your side to create a warm, wonderful and very merry Christmas!

Presto!
Yuletide Magic

Fast and fabulous ways to fill your home with Christmas cheer.

THE GOLD RUSH

Easy: Achievable by anyone.
Materials: Whole walnuts; thin gold cord; scissors; quick bonding craft glue; gold spray paint; newspaper.

Directions:
Spread the walnuts out on the newspaper and spray them with the gold paint, following the manufacturer's directions. When they are dry, turn them over and spray their other side. Cut a 9″ length of gold cord and knot the ends together. Glue the knot to the broad end of the walnuts, creating a loop to hang on the tree.

HERE COMES SANTA CLAUS! QUILT-BLOCK DECORATIONS

Easy: Achievable by anyone.

General Directions:
This patchwork is not seamed. It is fused in place and stitched. Cut fusible webbing into strips and slide the strips under the edges of the patch against the foundation felt. Following the manufacturer's directions, iron to fuse the layers together. Then edgestitch in a thread color to match the patch. If your machine can do a zigzag stitch, use that for edgestitching, set at a medium width.

STOCKING

Materials: 25″ square each red, green and black felt; 9″ x 12″ piece each pink and white felt; 1⅛ yd of 1½″-wide black polka dot ribbon; fusible webbing; pinking shears *(optional)*.

Directions:
1. Enlarge the stocking in FIG. VI, 1A, following the directions on page 271. Cut a whole red stocking (with pinking shears if you have them). Cut green toe and heel patches and a 2″ x 9″ green band.
2. Pin the 2 green patches to the black felt. Cut matching patches from the black felt that are flush with the outside edges, but extend ¼″ beyond the green on the inside edges of the patches. Fuse and stitch the patches to the stocking.
3. Stitch a green band to the stocking 1″ from the top edge, trimming the ends flush. Stitch the black polka dot ribbon centered between the green edges.

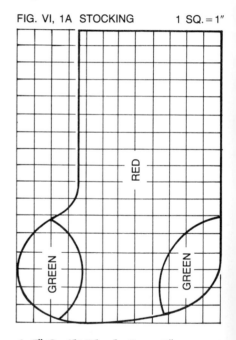

FIG. VI, 1A STOCKING   1 SQ. = 1″

RED
GREEN
GREEN

4. 5″ Quilt Block: Cut a 5″ green, a 3½″ red, a 1½″ white and a 1¼″ pink square. Also cut a ¼″ x 8″ black strip. Cut the pink square in half diagonally. Cut out the shaded area of the larger red square *(see* FIG. VI, 1B*)* but change its dimensions as follows: 5½″ = 3½″, 2½″ = 1½″, 2″ = 1¼″ and 1″ = ¾″.
5. Make a 5″-square quilt block *(see general instructions for Wall Hang-*

The Gold Rush

FIG. VI, 1B RED SQUARE

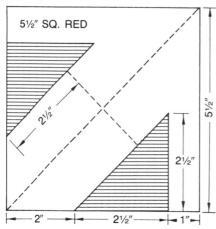

Here Comes Santa Claus! Wall Hanging

ing, Step 2). Stitch it centered over a 6" black square. Stitch the block diagonally to the stocking *(see photo).*
6. Pin the stocking to the black felt. With pinking shears, cut the black felt ¼" outside the red all around. Topstitch the red stocking to the black except at the top edge.
7. Tie a ribbon bow about 6" wide. Fold a 7" length of ribbon in half to make a hanger loop. Stitch the raw ends to the top back corner of the black stocking. Sew the bow on top at the corner of the red stocking.

QUILT-BLOCK WALL HANGING

Materials: 1⅓ yds black, ½ yd green, ¼ yd red and ⅛ yd white 72"-wide felt; 9" x 12" pink felt; 1 yd fusible webbing; 1 skein black 6-strand embroidery floss; 2 curtain rings.

Directions:
1. Cutting: For each 8"-square quilt block, cut the following squares: an 8" green, a 5½" red, a ¾" red and a 2½" white. Also cut a 1¾" pink square and cut it in half diagonally, saving the extra triangle for another block. Then cut a ⅜" x 12" black strip. From the larger red square, cut away a right triangle (shaded area) at two adjoining edges *(see FIG. VI, 1B).*
2. 8" Quilt Block: Center the black strip on the two broken lines *(see*

FIG. VI, 1B) of the red piece. Stitch the red piece at one corner of the 8" green square. Stitch the 2½" white square at the opposite corner. Stitch the ¾" red square at the opposite corner of the white from the larger red square and stitch the pink triangle below it, equidistant from the 2 white edges *(see photo).* Work 2 black French knot eyes *(see Stitch Guide, page 270).* Make 8.
3. Cutting: Cut two 47" x 35" black felt rectangles. Cut two 5½" and three 8" green felt squares. Cut five 1" white squares. Cut all of these squares in half diagonally to make 4 small and 6 large green triangles and 10 white triangles. Also cut 7 more 1" white squares, but leave them whole.
4. On one of the black pieces, measure 5" from each edge and chalk the borders of a 37" x 25" design area.
5. Patchwork Frame: Pin a small green triangle at each chalked cor-

ner *(see photo).* Center and pin the longest edge of a large green triangle along each short edge of the design area. Pin 2 large triangles at each longer chalked edge, leaving equal space (about 1⅜") between the triangles. Pin the long edge of a white triangle at each space on the chalked outlines *(see photo).* Fuse and stitch all the edges.
6. Patchwork Center: Pin the 8 quilt blocks within the fused "frame," leaving 1"-wide black spaces between them *(see photo).* Pin 7 white squares at the black intersections *(see photo).* Fuse and stitch.
7. Assembly: Pin the black rectangles right sides together and seam (½") around 3 sides and 4 corners. Clip the corners. Turn right side out and press. Turn in the open edges and slipstitch *(see Stitch Guide, page 270).* Sew a curtain ring behind each top corner.

QUILT-BLOCK TABLECLOTH

Materials: 1⅔ yds red, ⅔ yd green, ¼ yd black and ⅛ yd white 72"-wide felt; 9" x 12" pink felt; four 5" quilt blocks *(see Stocking, Step 4)*; fusible webbing.

Directions:

1. Cut a 60" red square. Fold each edge over ½" and press, trimming the corners to lie flat.

2. Corners: At each corner of the cloth, hemmed edge up, fuse a 1" white square between two 1" x 5" black strips. Fuse a 5" quilt block against them *(see photo)*. Add 3 more white squares and 2 more black strips around each quilt block. Fuse and stitch the edges.

3. Edges: Cut eight 1" x 48" black and four 5" x 48" green felt strips and stitch them between the corners to make a green border edged with black *(see photo)*. Also cut 8 more 1" white squares and 4 more 1" x 5" black strips. Stitch these across the center of each border *(see photo)*.

QUILT-BLOCK PILLOWS

Materials: One 8" and two 15" squares green felt; 10" square black felt; four 1" squares white felt; 3" x 72" red felt; materials for one 8" quilt block *(see Wall Hanging, Step 1)*; fusible webbing; synthetic stuffing; 2 yds filler cord.

Directions:

1. Pillow Top: Make an 8" quilt block *(see Wall Hanging, Step 2)*. Center it over the 10" black square and fuse. Fuse a 1" white square in each corner. Fuse the black square diagonally on a 15" green square. Zigzag over all edges.

2. Piping: Fold the red strip over the cord and, with a zipper foot,

The Holly & The Ivy

stitch against the cord. Trim the seam allowance to ½". Pin the piping to the pillow top, right sides together and raw edges even. Clip the seam allowance at each corner. Stitch along the previous stitching.

3. Assembly: Place the remaining 15" green square over the pillow front, right sides together, and stitch around 3 sides and 4 corners. Turn right side out and stuff. Turn in the open edge and slipstitch *(see Stitch Guide, page 270)*.

THE HOLLY & THE IVY

Easy: Achievable by anyone.
Materials: Light, medium, dark and darkest green felt; white glue; red berries; green floral tape; wire clippers; tie wire; heavy spool wire and Nos. 18 and 21 wire; grapevine wreath; firm cardboard or heavy paper.

Directions:

1. Patterns: Trace the actual-size holly and ivy leaves from FIG. VI, 2. From cardboard or heavy paper, cut 3 sizes for each leaf.

2. Cutting: Cut through 2 layers of felt for each leaf. Use light green for the small ivy, medium green for the medium-size ivy and dark green for the large ivy leaves. Use medium, dark and darkest green for all the holly.

3. Holly Leaf: Cut heavy spool wire at least 3″ longer than each leaf. Separate a pair of leaves. Spread glue on one leaf and place the piece of wire on top for the central "vein." Press the second leaf over that. Wrap floral tape around the extending wire "stem."

4. Ivy: For the "vine", cut No. 21 wire about 20″ long and wrap it with floral tape. Beginning with the smallest leaves, attach the ivy leaves with tie wire onto the vine wire an inch or so apart. Let the leaves stand up about an inch. Cover the tie wire with floral tape.

5. Holly Swags: Cut No. 18 wire stems 4″, 8″ or 10″ long and wrap them with floral tape. Wrap about 2 dozen berries together with tie wire. Attach holly leaves with tie wire to the stem, about ½″ apart, adding a cluster of berries close to the stem after 5 or 6 leaves. Repeat for the longer stems. Shape the leaves as you like.

6. Holly and Ivy Wreath: Twist the ivy vines into a grapevine wreath and top the wreath with holly.

FIG: VI, 2 THE HOLLY AND THE IVY

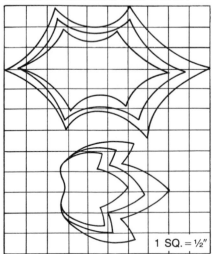

1 SQ. = ½″

CHRISTMAS CHEER TABLE SET

FELT TABLECLOTH

Easy: Achievable by anyone.
Materials: 2¼ yds green and 1⅜ yds red 72″-wide felt; white glue or fusible webbing.

Directions:
1. Enlarge the pattern in Fig. VI, 3, following the directions on page 271.
2. Cut a 72″ green and a 48″ red square. Also cut 4 green 8″ trees and 4 red hearts. Cut four 1¾″ x 20″ red strips for bow tails. Then cut a 2½″ x 15″ green and a 1¾″ x 15″ red strip, and a 1″ x 4″ green "knot" for the bow itself; repeat for 3 more bows.
3. Bow: Glue a 15″ red strip across the center of a green one. Lap one short end over the other to make a loop about 7″ long. Handstitch across the center and draw up the thread to gather it slightly. Wrap a 1″ x 4″ green strip over the center. Lap and sew the ends in back. Gather across the center of a 20″ red strip and sew to the back of the "knot". Cut each end at an angle. Make 4 bows. Pin a bow to the center of each edge of the 48″-square red tablecloth.
4. Tree: Cut 4 large green trees and 4 hearts (see Fig. VI, 3). Glue the hearts to the trees. Then glue a tree to each corner of the red tablecloth (see photo).
5. Spread the green cloth over a table. Put the red tablecloth on top, with a bow at each corner of the table.

FIG. VI, 3 CHRISTMAS CHEER MOTIF

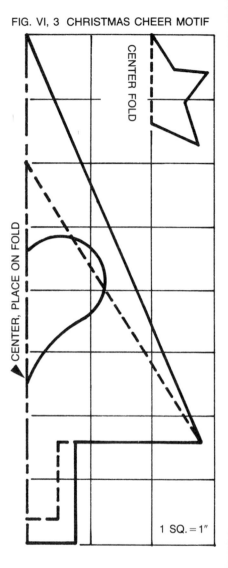

CENTER FOLD

CENTER, PLACE ON FOLD

1 SQ. = 1″

Remember, gifts don't have to be difficult or time-consuming to be special. A basket of ornaments (from here or from other chapters), a wreath or Christmas stockings all make wonderful— and much appreciated— presents.

FOLDING CHAIR SLIPCOVER

Average: For those with some experience in sewing.

Materials *(for 1):* About ½ yd 72″-wide red felt; ½ yd 36″-wide green felt; poly/cotton batting; white glue.

Directions:

1. Patterns: Trace the chair seat to paper and add ¾″ all around. Trace the chair back; extend its lower edge to 10″ deep and add ¾″ around the top and side edges.

2. Cutting: *From red,* cut 1 chair seat, 2 chair backs, four 1½″ x 20″ red ties and 3 red stars *(see* FIG. VI, 3). *From green,* cut 1 chair seat, two 1½″ x 20″ green edgings and 3 small trees *(see broken lines,* FIG. VI, 3).

3. Reversible Chair Cushion: Spread 2 or 3 layers of batting over each chair seat. Pin and machine-baste ⅝″ from the edges. Against the stitching, trim away the batting from the seam allowance. Pin the squares together along the basting, batting sides facing. Topstitch along the basting lines. Trim the green edge narrower than the red edge, if you like.

4. Cushion Ties: Fold each tie in half lengthwise and edgestitch. Fold a tie in half crosswise. Pin this fold under the side edge (just inside the stitching) to match the position of a chair leg. Repeat for the second chair leg *(see photo).* Repeat at the other side. Topstitch across the folds.

5. Chair Back: Glue a green edging to each chair back, extending ¼″ from the lower edge. Seam the 2 chair backs, right sides together, at the side and top edges. Turn right side out and press. Glue the trees to the chair back *(see photo).* Glue a star to each tree.

Christmas Cheer Table Set

211

Deck The Hall!

ONE-STOP SHOPPING

One quick trip is all you need to put together super last-minute gifts from store-bought items. To inspire you, we've made up a store-by-store list of gifts. You'll probably think of lots more.

STATIONERY/ART SUPPLY

- **Home office organizer:** File box, paper box, budget record and inexpensive calculator.
- **Date book:** Look for one reflecting the person's special interest.
- **Writing kit:** Pretty stationery, pens and a folder to keep it all together.
- **Watercolor set:** Paints, brushes and paper.

DRUGSTORE

- **Traveler's bonus:** Plastic case with sample sizes of soaps, creams, spot remover, etc.
- **Bath kit:** Plastic bath tray filled with soaps, bubble baths, sponges, sachets.

FIVE-AND-DIME

- **New cook kit:** Baking dishes, measuring cup and a recipe.
- **Holiday entertaining set:** Christmasy towels and potholders.
- **For a tea lover:** A selection of gourmet teas and a cute mug.

SPORTING GOODS

- **Beginner's luck tennis pack:** Wristband, tennis balls, racquet and tote.
- **Athlete's feet:** Colored tube socks — six to a pack — and jazzy laces.

SUPERMARKET

- Put together a breakfast basket filled with a gourmet pancake mix, maple syrup, preserves, tea or coffee and napkins.

OTHER ONE-STOPS

- There's also the **Bookstore,** the local **Nursery** and the **Hardware Store** — just to name a few.

DECK THE HALL!

Easy: Achievable by anyone.
Materials: Boxwood spray; evergreen wreath; ribbon; red candles; floral wire.

Directions:
Gather a large spray of boxwood with a generous bow; wire the spray to the banister. For the table, loop a wreath of greens with ribbon matching the bow and fill in the center with bright red candles of various heights.

• **Make a Bells 'n Ribbons Ball** (shown here; how to's, page 215).

• **For a luminous coffeetable centerpiece,** place a large terracotta saucer, with a platter underneath it, on your table. Fill it to the top with water; add sprigs of fresh pine and float small star-shaped candles between the top branches.

• **If you didn't get around to buying a tree,** or are using an artificial one, use pine-scented candles, incense and sprays to evoke that wonderful woodsy smell.

• **For instant table "vases,"** fill cored apples and green peppers with water-soaked floral foam; make holes in the foam with a toothpick. Insert galax or rose leaves to cover the edges. Then arrange combinations of your favorite small flowers.

• **In-A-Flash Trees.** Use these instant decorations for your tree:
— Bundles of baby's breath, tied with pre-tied red ribbon.
— Cookie cutters hung from red ribbon.
— Christmas cards, perforated at the top with a hole puncher, hung from ribbon pulled through the hole.
— Purchased bows with lights (blue lights with silver bows or silver lights with blue bows would be very dramatic).
— Jewelry, especially single earrings, tied with bright ribbons. Bracelets and necklaces are also attractive, but keep them

NIGHT-BEFORE-CHRISTMAS DECORATIONS

out of the reach of jewelry-yanking toddlers and pets!
— Doilies, used in many ways:
• Hang them just the way they are. • Fold them in half, to make Victorian fans. • Affix Christmas decals and/or pre-made bows to them. • Cut out photos (your own or from a magazine) and glue in the center of the doilies.
— Glass balls with adhesive metallic stars affixed to them.
— Adhesive metallic stars, glued back to back with a looped ribbon between them for hanging.
— Sachets and little stuffed toys.

• **Put together a theme tree:**
— **Baby Tree:** (A great idea for an expectant family!) Decorate a small tree with booties, baby's breath, silver spoons and drinking cups, little plastic toys. Wrap the bottom of the tree in a baby blanket and intersperse pastel ribbon bows all over.
— **Kitchen Tree:** Use spoons, cookie cutters and other pretty, small kitchen utensils, tied to the tree with kitchen twine.
— **Fruit And Nut Tree:** Use quick-bonding glue to affix ribbon loops to nuts in the shell. Hang from the tree along with tiny red apples and fresh kumquats tied with bright bows.

• **Gather bundles of yarn in twig baskets,** the more varieties the better. Place the baskets under the tree, on the mantel or stair landing.

• **Use candles all over the house.** Keep them out of the reach of kids and pets and always place them on fireproof surfaces.

• **Buy wooden beads, painted red,** in Christmas supply stores. They're a quick alternative to stringing cranberries.

• **Other garland ideas:** Long beaded necklaces; chains of self-sticking gold ribbon tied in loops; ribbon candy (especially sweet with wrapped candy canes on the tree).

BEST TIMES TO SHOP AND OTHER SECRETS

The managers of the world's largest department store—Macy's Herald Square in New York City—suggested the first four of these five shopping tips.

AVOID THE CROWDS. In big cities, shop very early or very late, never at lunchtime or just after work. In the suburbs, you'll do better between the hours of 10 A.M. and noon, and 2 to 5 P.M.

SKIP THE BUSIEST DEPARTMENTS: Accessories (belts, scarves, jewelry), men's shirts and sweaters, women's departments, toys and tree trimmings. If you can think up some imaginative gifts to buy in stationery or sporting goods, you'll save a lot of time.

CONSIDER PREBOXED, WRAPPED GIFTS. Departments that frequently display these time-savers are: housewares, cosmetics, china and glassware.

PICK A PERSONAL SHOPPER—FOR FREE! At many department stores, you can have someone else do all your shopping for you—at no extra charge! You make out your Christmas list, indicating the amount you want to spend on each gift. A shopper selects the items and even has them gift-wrapped. Check stores in your area to see if these services are available.

OR TRY THESE IDEAS FOR ARMCHAIR SHOPPING: Magazine subscriptions; tickets for the theater, ballet or circus; gift certificates from department stores, bookstore chains, salons, supermarkets, restaurants. And for faraway loved ones, give a long-distance call certificate.

Kitchen Spruce-Up; Cookie Cutter Potholders; Basket of "Berries"

KITCHEN SPRUCE-UP

Easy: Achievable by anyone.
Materials: Metal cheese grater; blue spruce branches; assorted small "fruit" on wires; 1 yd 1½"-wide tartan craft ribbon; 1 yd ⅞"-wide red satin ribbon.

Directions:
Turn the grater wide-end up. Add the spruce branches. Make about 12 clusters of 4 fruits each, twisted together, and wrap them around the branches. With the tartan ribbon, make an 8-loop bow. Make a smaller 6-loop bow with the satin ribbon. Tie both bows to the handle with a fruit cluster.

COOKIE CUTTER POTHOLDERS

Easy: Achievable by anyone.
Materials (for one): Three cotton fabrics in Christmas prints: ¼ yd main print, 6" square second print and a scrap for center design; 8" square ½"-thick batting; red, green and white threads; cookie cutters for designs.

Directions:
1. Cut two 8" squares of the main print. With right sides together and the batting on top, machine-stitch around three sides and three corners. Turn right side out and press.

2. To make a hanger, cut a 3″ x 1″ piece of the main print, fold several times, press and sew. Tuck the raw edges of the pot holder to the inside, press and pin. Fold the hanger in half, tuck it into the open corner and pin. Topstitch the seam. Using a contrasting thread, topstitch all four sides.

3. Center the 6″ square of the second color on top, turn the edges under and topstitch all around. Using a cookie cutter as a pattern, trace and cut the third print. Center and zigzag stitch in place around the edges with contrasting thread.

BASKET OF "BERRIES"

Easy: Achievable by anyone.
Materials: 5″-square basket; ¼ yd 54″-wide green moire taffeta; 3″ x 3″ x 2½″-deep Styrofoam®; about 2 dozen small red balls; glue gun or extra-thick white glue; 1 yd 1½″-wide craft ribbon.

Directions:

1. Cut the fabric about 5″ deeper than the basket height.

2. Press ½″ pleats, starting with a fold, pressing and pleating until you have enough to go around the basket. Overlap the first and last pleats on the basket and glue the edges. Turn and glue 2½″ at the top into the basket. Fold and glue the excess under at the bottom.

3. Cut a square of fabric slightly smaller than the pattern and glue it over the pleated raw edges. Insert the Styrofoam®. Remove the hangers from the balls. Place them top side down. Cover the foam with the balls and glue them in place.

4. Measure and cut the ribbon, fold it in half and press. Glue it around the edge of the basket. Add a separate bow *(see photo).*

Holiday Lights

HOLIDAY LIGHTS

Easy: Achievable by anyone.
Materials: Clay flowerpots and saucers; votive candles; pine boughs; small silk flowers; wire-backed ribbons.

Directions:

Turn the clay flowerpots upside down. Top each with a saucer and one votive candle. Add boughs of pine, small silk flowers (they're wilt-free!) and loops of wire-backed ribbon.

BELLS 'N RIBBONS BALL

Easy: Achievable by anyone.
Materials: Glass ball ornament; ⅞″-wide ribbon; jingle bells; craft glue.

Directions:

Place four dots of craft glue in a row, top to bottom, on a glass ball ornament. Cut a 12″ length of ⅞″-wide ribbon and, starting with a 1½″ loop at the top, affix at the glue dots, leaving excess ribbon between dots to create a "loop"*(see photo, page 213).* Allow the ends to trail. Repeat three times, making the four rows equidistant. Add a 4″ loop and jingle bells at the top and 4 more bells at the neckline loops.

Lollipop Ornaments

QUICK-FIX GIFT WRAPS

• **BROWN BAG IT.** You know all those brown paper grocery bags you have stashed under the sink to use for the trash? Turn them over to your resident artists (the kids) to decorate with holiday drawings. Then drop a gift in each bag and tie with pretty ribbon or yarn. Or punch a couple of holes at the top on each side and knot ribbons through for handles.

• **BANDANNA IT.** They're colorful, inexpensive and make a jiffy wrap for smaller gifts. Knot the bandanna ends and you've got two gifts in one. For larger presents, make a "Santa Sack" using pieces of fabric in red, green or a seasonal print. Pull up the edges, tie with yarn and trim with pinking shears.

• **BASKET IT.** Buy them at the five-and-dime for a dollar, fill and tie with a bow. Basketable items include breakfast treats (jams, teas, muffins), party snacks (cheeses, pâté, crackers, cocktail napkins), fresh fruit, bath accessories, pinecones for sweet-smelling kindling.

• **BOTTLE IT.** Many grocery and cosmetic products come in attractive bottles. Instead of tossing them, wash them in hot, sudsy water and refill with Christmas gifts —potpourri, bath salts, Christmas candy, spices, coffee beans, your own homemade spaghetti sauce. A bow at the neck and it's wrapped!

Gift-Box Ornament

LOLLIPOP ORNAMENTS

Easy: Achievable by anyone.
Materials: 1½" Styrofoam® ball; lollipop stick, or drinking straw cut in two; 8" piece Christmas fabric; gold thread; needle; glue; ribbon.

Directions:
1. Push the stick or straw into the ball of Styrofoam® and glue it in place. When it's dry, center the piece of fabric and cut it into a circle over the ball. Tie it with ribbon and make a bow.
2. Thread a needle with gold thread and sew a loop to the top of the lollipop for hanging.

GIFT-BOX ORNAMENT

Easy: Achievable by anyone.
Materials: 1"-thick sheet Styrofoam®; ribbon; cord; wrapping paper; yarn; paper clips or ornament hooks.

Directions:
Cut a large piece of 1"-thick Styrofoam® into smaller square and rectangular shapes no longer than 4". Cover the Styrofoam® "gift boxes" with wrapping paper, gluing or using straight pins to keep the paper in place. Decorate the ornaments to look like gift packages with scrap yarns, ribbons, cords. Attach an open paper clip or tree ornament hook to one end of each ornament to hang.

LAST-MINUTE FOOD GIFTS

- **Apricot Almond Truffles:** Soak 1 cup minced dried apricots with 2 tablespoons rum for 30 minutes, stirring occasionally. Add ½ cup chopped blanched almonds, ½ cup ground blanched almonds and 1 roll (7 ounces) marzipan. Work together with your hands until well blended, adding additional ground almonds, if needed, to make a moist, but not wet, mixture. Roll into balls with the palms of your hands, dusted with 10X (confectioners' powdered) sugar. Drizzle with melted chocolate, if you wish. Pack into tiny paper cases. *Makes 25 to 30.*

- **Smoked Salmon and Cream Cheese Loaf:** Warm a knife under hot water and slice a chilled 8-ounce piece of cream cheese into 3 equal horizontal slices. Finely chop 2 ounces smoked salmon with 1 tablespoon chopped fresh dill and 1½ teaspoons minced onion. Sandwich the cream cheese layers with the salmon, leaving the top layer plain. Cover with plastic wrap and refrigerate until firm. Decorate with a smoked salmon rosette and whole dill sprigs. Keep refrigerated and plan to give within a day or two. *Makes 1 loaf.*

- **Lemon Lime Mustard:** Combine 4 cups prepared Dijon-style mustard, 1 cup dairy sour cream, grated rind and juice of 1 lemon, grated rind and juice of 2 limes and ⅓ cup honey in a medium-size bowl until well blended. Spoon into decorative jars. Refrigerate for up to 3 weeks. *Makes about 5 cups.*

- **Rum Raisin Fudge Sauce:** Soak 2 tablespoons golden raisins in 1 tablespoon rum in a small bowl for at least 2 hours, stirring often. Stir into 1 jar good-quality fudge sauce. Spoon into a decorative jar.

- **Marinated Artichoke Hearts:** Combine 2 cups olive oil, ¾ cup wine vinegar, 4 mashed garlic cloves, 1 teaspoon dried basil, 1 teaspoon dried thyme and 3 chopped sun-dried tomatoes in a glass jar. Add 2 packages frozen artichoke hearts, cooked and drained, covering them with the oil. Refrigerate. Transfer to decorative jars for giving. *Makes 4 cups.*

- **Chocolate Amaretti Sandwiches:** Melt ½ pound semisweet chocolate and ¼ cup orange-flavored liqueur over simmering water, stirring often. Remove from the heat. Sandwich the prepared amaretti biscuits, flat sides together, with the melted chocolate. Let dry on wire racks. Dust with a mixture of 2 tablespoons 10X (confectioners' powdered) sugar and 2 tablespoons unsweetened cocoa powder. Wrap these delicate confections in colored tissue paper. *Makes about 16.*

- **Oriental Chicken Liver Spread:** Rinse, pat dry and trim 1 pound chicken livers. In a large skillet over medium heat, sauté 2 cloves garlic, minced, and 2 slices fresh gingerroot, peeled and minced, in ½ cup (1 stick) butter for 1 minute. Add the chicken livers. Sauté for 2 to 3 minutes longer, or until the livers are golden but still pink on the inside. Pour in ¼ cup sake or dry sherry and 2 tablespoons soy sauce; sprinkle with 2 green onions, trimmed and chopped. Cook for 1 minute longer. Transfer the mixture to a food processor. Purée. Spoon the mixture into a 2-cup crock. Cover with plastic wrap and refrigerate. Decorate with a scallion fan before giving. *Makes about 2 cups.*

- **Blue Cheese Spread:** Combine 1 pound blue cheese, at room temperature, and ½ cup (1 stick) unsalted butter, softened, in a food processor. Process until smooth. Slowly pour in 2 to 4 tablespoons Port wine through the feed tube, adding only enough to make a soft spread. Season with white pepper and transfer to three 8-ounce crocks or custard cups. Cover the surfaces with plastic wrap. Refrigerate. Plan to give within a couple of days. *Makes about 1½ pounds.*

- **Spicy Petit Fours:** Buy packaged gingerbread, or prepare gingerbread from a mix. Cut the gingerbread into 1-inch cubes, using a sharp knife. Place the cubes, 1 inch apart, on a wire rack over an aluminum foil-lined cookie sheet. Make a glaze of 2½ cups 10X (confectioners' powdered) sugar, sifted, 2 tablespoons lemon juice and enough water to make a smooth, pourable consistency. Pour the glaze over the cubes. Let stand for 20 minutes. Top each cube with chopped candied ginger and glacé cherries. Let stand for at least 3 hours longer, or until the glaze dries completely. Pack each petit four into a tiny paper case. *Makes about 80.*

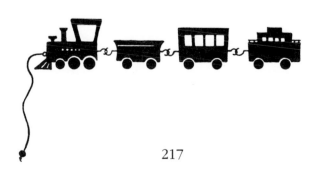

Time Smart & Tempting Finger Foods

(Serves 16 if all prepared together)

Lobster Mousse*
Chinese Chicken Wings*
Sausage en Croute*
Harlequin Dip*
Pimiento Cheese*
Curry Surprises*
Party Pizzas*
Pistachio Cheese Ball*
Tapenade*

*Recipes follow

These hors d'oeuvres can be served together; or choose your favorites for small gatherings.

(clockwise from top) **Chinese Chicken Wings; Curry Surprises; Sausage en Croute; Lobster Mousse; Pimiento Cheese; Harlequin Dip**

�△◁ ◣

Lobster Mousse

Fresh lobster may be substituted in this spread.

Makes 8 to 10 servings.

- 1   **envelope unflavored gelatin**
- 1   **can (10¾ ounces) tomato soup, heated**
- 2   **packages (3 ounces each) cream cheese with pimiento, softened**
- ¼   **cup finely chopped celery**
- 1   **tablespoon instant minced onion**
      Salt and pepper to taste
      Worcestershire sauce to taste
- 1   **cup mayonnaise**
- 2   **cans (6½ ounces each) lobster**
      Vegetable oil
      Cooked lobster tails and lettuce leaves for garnish (optional)

1. Dissolve the gelatin in heated tomato soup in a large bowl with an electric mixer. Add the cream cheese and beat until the mixture is smooth. Add the celery, minced onion, salt, pepper and Worcestershire sauce. Fold in the mayonnaise until no streaks of white remain. Break the lobster into pieces and add to the mixture.
2. Rub a 4-cup mold with vegetable oil. Spoon the lobster mixture into the prepared mold. Refrigerate for 8 hours, or overnight.
3. To unmold, loosen the mold around the edges with a sharp knife. Dip the mold into a pan of hot water for 30 seconds, turn to one side to loosen and invert onto a serving platter sprinkled with cold water. Refrigerate until serving time. Garnish with lobster tails and lettuce, if you wish.

💲 ◁ ◣

Pimiento Cheese

Makes 4 cups.

- 5   **cups grated sharp Cheddar cheese (1¼ pounds)**
- 2   **jars (4 ounces each) diced pimientos, drained**
- 1   **jar (8 ounces) taco sauce**
      Freshly ground black pepper
- 3   **tablespoons mayonnaise**
      Sweet red peppers (optional)
      Sweet green pepper strips for garnish

1. Combine the grated cheese, diced pimientos and taco sauce in a large bowl until smooth. Add the pepper to taste. Add the mayonnaise, blending well. Store in the refrigerator until serving time.
2. Serve in hollowed out sweet red peppers garnished with sweet green pepper strips, if you wish.

💲 ◁

Sausage en Croute

Pastry-wrapped bundles everyone will love.

Bake at 325° for 25 minutes.
Makes 80.

- 1   **package (8 ounces) cream cheese, softened**
- 1   **cup (2 sticks) butter or margarine**
- 2¼ **cups unsifted all-purpose flour**
- 1   **teaspoon salt**
- 1   **large onion, chopped (1 cup)**
- 1   **cup chopped celery**
- ½   **cup (1 stick) butter or margarine**
- 2   **cups cooked, crumbled pork sausage**
- 1   **cup minced parsley**
      Salt and pepper to taste
- 2   **eggs, beaten**
- 1   **egg white**
- 1   **egg, beaten**
- 1   **tablespoon water**

1. Beat together the cream cheese and the 1 cup butter or margarine in a medium-size bowl with an electric mixer at high speed until smooth and creamy. Add the flour and the 1 teaspoon salt. Knead until the dough clings together. Wrap in wax paper and refrigerate for 2 to 3 hours, or overnight. When ready to assemble, remove the dough from the refrigerator and let stand at room temperature for 30 minutes.
2. Brown the onion and the celery in the ½ cup butter or margarine in a large skillet. Add the cooked sausage, parsley, salt and pepper. Sauté lightly. Drain the oil, add the 2 beaten eggs and remove the pan from the heat. Cool.
3. Roll out the dough, a quarter at a time, on a lightly floured surface to a 20 x 4-inch rectangle. Spoon 1 cup of the cooled filling down the center of each rectangle. Fold the dough in half lengthwise, using the egg white to moisten and seal the edges. Place in a 15 x 10 x 1-inch jelly-roll pan, seam side down. Refrigerate for 1 hour.

4. Preheat the oven to slow (325°).
5. Slice the rolls into 1-inch pieces, leaving in place in the jelly-roll pan. Brush with the remaining egg beaten with the water.
6. Bake in the preheated slow oven (325°) for 25 minutes, or until lightly browned. Serve hot.

Note: To make ahead, proceed through step 3. Wrap the pan tightly with heavy-duty aluminum foil and freeze. Just before heating, brush the frozen rolls with an egg beaten with 1 tablespoon water. Do not thaw, but increase the baking time to 30 minutes.

Time Savers: • To soften cream cheese in a hurry, briefly immerse the unopened foil package in a bowl of hot water. Or, open the package and heat for 20 seconds on a piece of wax paper in the microwave. • If you're really short on time, use prepared pastry dough.

Chinese Chicken Wings

We highly recommend these spicy appetizers!

Bake at 375° for 50 minutes.
Makes 30.

3 **pounds chicken wings, tips removed**
    Salt and pepper
2 **tablespoons vegetable oil**
1 **cup honey**
½ **cup soy sauce**
¼ **cup orange juice**
2 **tablespoons ketchup**
1 **clove garlic, mashed**
1 **teaspoon ground ginger**
    Italian parsley sprigs and cherry
    tomatoes for garnish (optional)

1. Preheat the oven to moderate (375°).
2. Halve the chicken wings. Place in a 9 x 12-inch shallow baking pan. Sprinkle with the salt, pepper and oil.
3. Combine the honey, soy sauce, orange juice, ketchup, garlic and ginger in a 2-cup measure, blending well. Pour over the chicken, coating evenly.
4. Bake in the preheated moderate oven (375°) for 50 minutes, or until bubbly. Garnish with Italian parsley sprigs and cherry tomatoes, if you wish.

Note: To make ahead, wrap in heavy-duty aluminum foil; refrigerate. Increase the baking time by 20 minutes.

Curry Surprises

Unique and elegant appetizers.

Makes 24.

1 **cup chopped cooked chicken**
2 **tablespoons chopped apple**
2 **tablespoons chopped green onion**
1 **cup finely chopped peanuts**
½ **cup mayonnaise**
½ **teaspoon curry powder**
    Dash hot sauce
1 **bag (7 ounces) shredded coconut**

1. Combine the chicken with the chopped apple, green onion and peanuts, the mayonnaise, curry powder and hot sauce in a large bowl, blending well. Cover with plastic wrap and refrigerate for 4 hours, or until well chilled.
2. Shape the chilled chicken mixture into 1-inch balls (about 1 tablespoon each). Roll in the shredded coconut on wax paper. Refrigerate until serving time.

Harlequin Dip

An unusual recipe with southwestern flair.

Makes 3 cups.

2 **cans (4 ounces each) whole green**
    chilies, seeded and chopped
2 **cans (4½ ounces each) chopped black**
    olives
3 **tomatoes, chopped**
4 **green onions, chopped**
2 **tablespoons lemon juice**
1 **tablespoon vegetable or olive oil**
    Garlic salt and pepper to taste
1 **sweet red pepper (optional)**

1. Combine the chopped green chilies with the chopped olives, tomatoes and green onions, the lemon juice, oil, garlic salt and pepper in a medium-size bowl, blending well. Serve immediately, or refrigerate overnight to heighten the flavors.
2. Hollow out a sweet red pepper, if you wish, and fill with the dip.

Pistachio Cheese Ball; Tapenade; Party Pizzas

Party Pizzas

We topped these pizzas with salami, ripe olives and rolled anchovies with capers, but you can vary the toppings as you wish.

Bake at 350° for 25 minutes.
Makes 12 servings.

  1 **package (12³/₈ ounces) deluxe French bread pizza**
 12 **thin slices salami**
      Sliced green onion (green part only)
  6 **pitted ripe olives, halved**
  1 **can (2 ounces) rolled anchovies with capers**

1. Preheat the oven to moderate (350°). Remove the plastic wrap from the pizzas.
2. Bake the pizzas in the preheated moderate oven (350°) for 25 minutes.
3. Roll the salami slices into cones; stuff each with some sliced green onion. Arrange the stuffed salami cones along one side of each of the pizzas. Alternate the halved olives and the rolled anchovies with capers on the other side. Cut into slices on the diagonal. Serve hot or at room temperature.

Pistachio Cheese Ball

Makes one 8-inch ball.

 1½ **pounds sharp Cheddar cheese, shredded (6 cups)**
  2 **packages (8 ounces each) cream cheese, softened**
  2 **to 4 tablespoons dry sherry**
  2 **teaspoons Dijon-style mustard**
  6 **drops liquid red-pepper seasoning**
 ½ **cup chopped pistachio nuts**
  2 **sweet red pepper strips for garnish**
      Assorted sliced fresh vegetables and crackers

1. Combine the Cheddar cheese, cream cheese, sherry, mustard and liquid red-pepper seasoning in a large bowl. Beat with an electric mixer until thoroughly blended.
2. Cover with plastic wrap and chill for 45 minutes, or until the mixture is firm.
3. Shape the chilled mixture into a ball; roll in the chopped pistachio nuts on wax paper. Wrap and refrigerate at least overnight. Garnish with the sweet red pepper strips. Serve with an assortment of sliced fresh vegetables and crackers.

Tapenade

The French Provençal version of caviar.

Makes 1 cup.

1 **can (6 ounces) pitted ripe olives, drained**
1 **can (2 ounces) flat anchovies, rinsed and dried**
2 **tablespoons drained capers**
¼ **cup olive or vegetable oil**
1½ **teaspoons leaf thyme**
½ **teaspoon dry mustard**
1 **tablespoon cognac (optional)**
1 **large beefsteak tomato**
   Sliced pitted ripe olives and celery leaves for garnish
   Toast squares or triangles

1. Place the olives, anchovies, capers, olive or vegetable oil, thyme, dry mustard and the cognac, if you wish, in the container of a food processor or electric blender. Cover; process until the mixture is a thick paste. Spoon the mixture into a small dish and cover with plastic wrap. Refrigerate for up to two days.
2. Thirty minutes before serving, remove the mixture from the refrigerator.
3. Cut a thin slice off the top of the beefsteak tomato. Hollow out, leaving a ¼-inch shell. Spoon the mixture into the shell. Garnish with the sliced olives and the celery leaves. Serve with toast squares or triangles.

Variation: Spoon a teaspoon of Tapenade into each of 24 scooped-out cherry tomatoes.

MORE SPEEDY HORS D'OEUVRES

- *Dry-Sautéed Cashews:* Drop raw cashews into a wok (no oil) over medium heat. Stir-fry until the nuts turn golden, watching for burning. Sprinkle with coarse salt and sugar. Sauté for 30 seconds longer.
- *Nutty Goat Cheese Logs:* Roll 2 goat cheese logs (about 8 ounces each) in a mixture of 1½ cups minced toasted hazelnuts or almonds, ¼ teaspoon cayenne pepper and ¼ teaspoon salt. Refrigerate until firm. Serve the logs whole on a cheese tray, or cut into ¼-inch slices and serve on crackers.
- *Apricot Mustard Chicken Wings:* Combine ½ cup prepared Dijon-style mustard, 1 small jar apricot baby food, 3 tablespoons soy sauce and 3 tablespoons vegetable oil in a large bowl. Add 12 chicken wings, split. If possible, marinate at room temperature for 2 hours, or cover and refrigerate overnight. Bake the wings in a preheated hot oven (400°), brushing with the marinade, for about 25 minutes, or until golden. *Makes 6 servings.*
- *Roast Beef Canapés:* Spread melba toast rounds or cocktail rye bread slices with a mixture of ½ cup (1 stick) butter, 3 tablespoons prepared Dijon-style mustard and 1 tablespoon dry red wine. Top with pieces of delicatessen roast beef. Decorate with gherkin pickle slices and pimiento cubes.
- *Ham Roll-Ups:* Spread boiled ham slices with chive or pimiento cream cheese, softened with a little milk or cream. Roll up, jelly-roll style. Refrigerate until serving time. Slice and serve on crackers or small bread slices. Decorate with parsley sprigs.
- *Curry Dip:* Combine ½ cup dairy sour cream or yogurt, ½ cup mayonnaise, 1 to 2 tablespoons curry powder and 1 to 2 tablespoons chopped mango chutney. Serve with vegetables.
- *Cocktail Meatballs:* Combine 1 pound ground beef, 1 tablespoon prepared Dijon-style mustard, 1 tablespoon minced onion, 1 small clove garlic, finely minced, and 2 tablespoons heavy cream just until blended. Form into small balls. Sauté in butter until done as you like meatballs. Serve with mustard. *Makes about 20.*
- *Caviar Silver Dollars:* Use pancake mix to prepare tiny pancakes. Top with dollops of sour cream mixed with freeze-dried chives, then a spoonful of red caviar.
- *Deviled Ham Canapés:* Spread party rye bread slices with prepared deviled ham. Top with gherkin pickle slices.
- *Mushroom Spread:* Combine 1 package (8 ounces) cream cheese with 2 tablespoons freeze-dried chives and 2 teaspoons dry sherry. Stir in 1 cup chopped raw mushrooms. Spread on toast points. Top with shreds of red onion.
- *Stuffed Peppers Hors d'Oeuvre Style:* Stuff whole canned jalapeño peppers with cold pack cheese food mixed with crushed corn chips. Slice in half, crosswise.

Quick-Fix Desserts

*Scrumptious cookies, candies and pies,
all with a minimum of fuss!*

Lemon-Glazed Persimmon Bars

You can substitute canned peaches for persimmon.

Bake at 350° for 25 minutes.
Makes about 40.

1 **cup fresh or frozen persimmon pulp, thawed if frozen**
1 **teaspoon baking soda**
1 **egg**
1 **cup sugar**
½ **cup vegetable oil**
1 **box (8 ounces) pitted dates, finely snipped**
1¾ **cups all-purpose flour**
1 **teaspoon salt**
1 **teaspoon ground nutmeg**
1 **teaspoon ground cinnamon**
¼ **teaspoon ground cloves**
1 **cup chopped walnuts or pecans**
1 **cup 10X (confectioners' powdered) sugar**
1 **tablespoon lemon juice**
Candied red cherries, halved
Green frosting from a tube

1. Preheat the oven to moderate (350°).
2. Mix together the pulp with the baking soda in a small bowl; set aside. Lightly beat the egg in a large bowl. Stir in the sugar, oil and dates.
3. Combine the flour with the salt, nutmeg, cinnamon and cloves. Add to the date mixture alternately with the pulp, mixing just until well blended. Stir in the chopped walnuts or pecans. Pour into a greased and floured 15 x 10 x 1-inch pan.
4. Bake in the preheated moderate oven (350°) for 25 minutes. Cool in the pan for 5 minutes.

5. Combine the 10X (confectioners' powdered) sugar and the lemon juice in a cup and spread over the warm cookies. Cool completely; cut into bars or diamonds. Decorate with the halved candied red cherries and the green frosting from a tube.

Just about any drop cookie recipe (such as chocolate chip) can be converted to a bar cookie. Press the mixture into a greased 9 x 13-inch or 10 x 15-inch pan. Bake until golden.

NO-BAKE FROZEN PIES

Cool, creamy make-aheads for a perfect finish.

Special Strawberry Pie

Makes 6 servings.

1 **package (8 ounces) cream cheese, softened**
½ **cup sugar**
1 **cup dairy sour cream**
2 **packages (10 ounces each) quick-thaw strawberries, thawed and drained**
1 **packaged ready-to-use (no-bake) 8-inch crumb pie crust**

Lemon-Glazed Persimmon Bars

1. Beat together the cream cheese and the sugar in a medium-size bowl until light and fluffy. Gently fold in the sour cream and the strawberries. Pour the mixture into the piecrust. Place in the freezer until hardened, for at least 8 hours or overnight.
2. Remove the pie from the freezer 1 hour before serving.

Clever Chocolate Pie

Chocolate and chocolate chip ice creams layered with a rich chocolate sauce.

Makes 6 servings.

½ **cup heavy cream**
1 **package (6 ounces) semisweet chocolate pieces**
1 **teaspoon vanilla**
1 **pint chocolate ice cream, slightly softened**
1 **packaged ready-to-use (no-bake) 8-inch crumb pie crust**
1 **pint chocolate chip ice cream, slightly softened**

1. Heat the cream in a small saucepan until bubbles appear around the edge. Remove from the heat. Add the chocolate pieces; stir until melted and smooth. Stir in the vanilla. Set aside in the refrigerator to cool and thicken, for about 15 to 20 minutes.
2. Spoon the chocolate ice cream evenly into the piecrust. Place in the freezer for about 20 minutes to harden. Spoon about two-thirds of the chocolate sauce over the top. Place in the freezer for about 20 minutes to harden.
3. Spoon the chocolate chip ice cream on top of the sauce. Place in the freezer for about 20 minutes to harden. Drizzle the remaining chocolate sauce over the top of the pie. Freeze until hardened, for at least 8 hours or overnight.
4. Remove from the freezer 30 minutes before serving.

Mixed Fruit and Yogurt Pie

Makes 6 servings.

1 **can (11 ounces) mandarin oranges, drained**
1 **can (16 ounces) pitted tart red cherries, drained**
1 **ripe banana, peeled and diced**
¼ **cup flaked coconut**
1 **large container (16 ounces) vanilla yogurt**
1 **packaged ready-to-use (no-bake) 8-inch crumb pie crust**

1. Gently fold together the oranges, cherries, banana, coconut and yogurt in a large bowl. Pour into the piecrust. Place in the freezer until hardened, for at least 8 hours or overnight.
2. Remove from the freezer 1 hour before serving.

Heavenly Pineapple Pie

Makes 6 servings.

1 **cup heavy cream**
1 **can (20 ounces) crushed pineapple in heavy syrup**
1 **package (8 ounces) cream cheese, softened**
1 **package (3¾ ounces or 4-serving size) instant vanilla pudding and pie filling**
1 **packaged ready-to-use (no-bake) 8-inch crumb pie crust**

1. Whip the cream in a small bowl. Refrigerate.
2. Drain the pineapple, reserving the juice.
3. Beat together the cream cheese, reserved pineapple juice and instant vanilla pudding in a medium-size bowl until smooth.
4. Gently fold the crushed pineapple and the whipped cream into the pudding mixture. Spoon into the piecrust. Place in the freezer until hardened, for at least 8 hours or overnight.
5. Remove from the freezer 1 hour before serving.

Mint Mist Pie

Mint Mist Pie

Makes 6 servings.

1 **package (8 ounces) cream cheese, softened**
1 **can (14 ounces) sweetened condensed milk**
1 **teaspoon mint extract**
   Few drops green food coloring (optional)
1 **container (8 ounces) nondairy whipped topping**
²⁄₃ **cup miniature chocolate pieces**
1 **packaged ready-to-use (no-bake) 8-inch crumb pie crust**
   Fresh mint leaves for garnish (optional)

1. Beat the cream cheese in a medium-size bowl until light and fluffy. Gradually add the sweetened condensed milk, mint extract and the food coloring, if you wish. Beat the mixture until smooth.
2. Gently fold in the whipped topping with a rubber spatula. Fold in the chocolate pieces. Spoon into the piecrust. Place in the freezer until hardened, for at least 8 hours or overnight.
3. Remove from the freezer 5 minutes before serving. Garnish with additional chocolate pieces and fresh mint leaves, if you wish.

Luscious Lemon Pie

Makes 6 servings.

1   **package (3 ounces) lemon-flavored
       gelatin**
¼   **cup sugar**
½   **cup boiling water**
4   **tablespoons fresh lemon juice**
1   **cup evaporated milk**
1   **tablespoon grated lemon rind**
1   **packaged ready-to-use (no-bake)
       8-inch crumb pie crust**

1. Add the gelatin and the sugar to the boiling
   water in a small bowl. Stir until completely
   dissolved. Add 2 tablespoons of the lemon juice.
   Set aside in the refrigerator to chill and thicken
   to the consistency of unbeaten egg whites, for
   about 45 to 60 minutes.
2. Meanwhile, pour the evaporated milk into a
   shallow dish. Place in the freezer until soft ice
   crystals form around the edge, for about 20 to 30
   minutes. Transfer to a medium-size bowl and
   beat with an electric mixer until soft peaks form.
   Add the remaining 2 tablespoons lemon juice
   and beat until stiff peaks form.
3. Gently fold the gelatin mixture and the lemon
   rind into the whipped evaporated milk mixture.
   Spoon into the piecrust. Place in the freezer
   until hardened, for at least 8 hours or overnight.
4. Remove the pie from the freezer 1 hour before
   serving.

Mocha Pie

Makes 6 servings.

1   **package (3¼ ounces) butterscotch
       pudding and pie filling**
¼   **cup sugar**
1   **teaspoon instant coffee granules**
1½   **cups (13-ounce can) evaporated milk**
2   **tablespoons orange juice**
1   **packaged ready-to-use (no-bake)
       8-inch crumb pie crust**

1. Mix together the pudding, sugar and coffee in a
   small saucepan. Add ½ cup of the evaporated
   milk. Bring to boiling over medium heat,

stirring constantly. Cook for 1 minute. Pour into
a medium-size bowl. Cover the surface of the
pudding with wax paper or plastic wrap to
prevent a skin from forming. Set aside in the
refrigerator to cool, for about 30 minutes.
2. Meanwhile, pour the remaining 1 cup
   evaporated milk into a shallow dish. Place in the
   freezer until soft ice crystals form around the
   edge, for about 20 to 30 minutes. Transfer to a
   small bowl and beat until soft peaks form. Add
   the orange juice. Beat until stiff peaks form.
3. Gently fold about 1 cup of the whipped
   evaporated milk mixture into the pudding; fold
   in the remaining whipped evaporated milk
   mixture. Spoon into the piecrust. Place in the
   freezer until hardened, for at least 8 hours or
   overnight.
4. Remove from the freezer about 5 minutes
   before serving.

NO-BAKE TREATS

**By eliminating baking, you can pare down
preparation time and still produce
scrumptious holiday goodies.**

Layered Mint Melts

**Kids will love to cut and spread this recipe for easy
candy.**

Makes about 60 candies.

1½   **cups (12 ounces) chocolate-flavored
       wafers (available in stores selling
       candy-making supplies)**
1½   **cups (12 ounces) vanilla-flavored
       wafers (available in stores selling
       candy-making supplies)**
½   **teaspoon peppermint extract**
2   **drops red or green food coloring**
1   **or 2 tablespoons heavy cream or
       evaporated milk**

1. Melt the chocolate wafers, following the package
   directions.
2. Place wax paper on a cookie sheet and, using a
   ruler as a guide, draw a rectangle to measure
   11 x 7 inches (or trace around a pan this size).
3. Spread half the melted chocolate wafers evenly

over the rectangle. Refrigerate the chocolate rectangle until set.

4. Melt the vanilla wafers, following the package directions. Stir in the peppermint extract and the food coloring; the mixture will become stiff. Stir in the cream or evaporated milk until the mixture is creamy and spreadable.

5. Spread the mint mixture over the chocolate layer. Spread the remaining chocolate over the mint layer; refrigerate.

6. Bring the candy to room temperature before cutting. Cut into small pieces using a thin, sharp knife.

Krispies Treat

Breakfast cereal is the main ingredient of this quick-to-mix chewy snack.

Makes 24 squares.

- ¼ **cup (½ stick) butter or margarine**
- 1 **bag (10 ounces) marshmallows**
- ⅓ **cup smooth peanut butter**
- ½ **cup raisins**
- 5 **cups oven-toasted rice cereal**

1. Melt the butter or margarine in a large saucepan. Stir in the marshmallows and the peanut butter. Cook over low heat for 3 minutes, or until melted and well combined.

2. Remove from the heat. Add the raisins and the cereal, stirring until well coated.

3. Turn the mixture out into a greased 13 x 9 x 2-inch pan. Using a wad of folded wax paper, quickly press the mixture evenly into the pan. Cool completely, then cut into 2-inch squares with a sharp knife. Pack into decorative boxes to give as gifts.

Lemon Wafers

You can also make mint wafers by substituting ½ teaspoon peppermint extract.

Makes about 2½ dozen.

- 1 **package (12 ounces) chocolate-flavored wafers (available in stores selling candy-making supplies)**
- ½ **teaspoon lemon extract**
- 1 **box vanilla wafer cookies**

1. Melt the chocolate wafers, following the package directions.

2. Stir the lemon extract into the melted chocolate.

3. Using your fingers, dip the vanilla wafer cookies into the lemon mixture. You may also use a fork or dipping spoon instead of your fingers.

4. Tap the wafers gently on the side of the pan to remove excess lemon mixture. Cool on wax paper in the refrigerator.

Note: The lemon extract can be eliminated and mint extract used instead. Or, use the melted chocolate wafers alone and dip pretzels, graham crackers or large nuts. Try this also on potato chips for a treat that will be the talk of your next party or holiday gathering.

Double Chocolate Chunks

This snack was developed with chocoholics in mind!

Makes 36 squares.

- 1 **package (6 ounces) semisweet chocolate pieces**
- ½ **cup crunchy peanut butter**
- 3 **cups ready-sweetened chocolate-flavored rice cereal**
  Chopped peanuts (optional)
  Chocolate drink mix (optional)

1. Melt the chocolate pieces and the peanut butter in a large saucepan, stirring constantly, until smooth. Remove from the heat.

2. Stir in the cereal until well coated. Press the mixture evenly into a 9-inch square pan. Scatter the top with chopped peanuts and a few tablespoons dry chocolate drink mix, if you wish.

3. Refrigerate for 2 hours, or until firm. Let stand at room temperature for 10 minutes before cutting into 1½-inch squares with a sharp knife. Pack into decorative boxes to give as gifts.

Muffins & Quick Breads

Easy to mix, quick to bake!

💲 《《 ⚡
Honey Wheat Muffins

Good nutrition and tastes delicious, too.

Bake at 400° for 15 minutes.
Makes 12 large muffins.

1½ **cups all-purpose flour**
1 **teaspoon baking soda**
1 **teaspoon baking powder**
½ **teaspoon ground mace**
½ **teaspoon salt**
1 **cup whole wheat flour**
1 **egg**
1 **cup buttermilk**
½ **cup molasses**
¼ **cup vegetable oil**
½ **cup raisins**

1. Preheat the oven to hot (400°).
2. Sift together the flour, baking soda, baking powder, mace and salt into a medium-size bowl. Stir in the whole wheat flour until well blended.
3. Beat the egg in a 2-cup glass measure with a fork. Beat in the buttermilk, molasses and oil; pour over the dry ingredients. Stir just to blend and add the raisins. Grease 12 large muffin pan cups and spoon in the batter, dividing evenly.
4. Bake in the preheated hot oven (400°) for 15 minutes, or until golden brown. Cool in the pan on a wire rack for 5 minutes. Loosen the muffins around the cups with a sharp knife. Pile into a serving basket and serve hot, or freeze for future use.

💲 《《 ⚡
Carrot Pecan Muffins

Grated winter squash or zucchini can be substituted for the carrot.

Bake at 400° for 20 minutes.
Makes 12 large muffins.

2 **cups all-purpose flour**
1 **tablespoon baking powder**
1 **teaspoon pumpkin pie spice**
½ **teaspoon salt**
¾ **cup grated carrot**
⅓ **cup firmly packed light brown sugar**
1 **egg**
¾ **cup milk**
¼ **cup vegetable oil**
½ **cup chopped pecans**
Strawberry jelly

1. Preheat the oven to hot (400°).
2. Sift together the flour, baking powder, pumpkin pie spice and salt into a medium-size bowl. Stir in the carrot and the brown sugar until well blended.
3. Beat the egg in a 2-cup glass measure with a fork; add the milk and the oil. Pour over the dry ingredients and stir just to blend. Stir in the chopped pecans. Grease 12 large muffin pan cups. Spoon in the batter, dividing evenly. Spoon the jelly into the center of each muffin.
4. Bake in the preheated hot oven (400°) for 20 minutes, or until golden brown and starting to shrink from the sides of the cups. Cool in the pan on a wire rack for 5 minutes. Serve immediately, or freeze.

Honey Wheat Muffins; Carrot Pecan Muffins; Spicy Blueberry Muffins; Country Nut Bread

🈂️ 《 ⇵

Spicy Blueberry Muffins

Bake them in standard muffin cups for breakfast or mini-muffin tins to serve at tea time.

Bake at 400° for 20 minutes.
Makes 12 large muffins.

1	**cup all-purpose flour**
2	**teaspoons baking powder**
½	**teaspoon ground nutmeg**
½	**teaspoon salt**
¾	**cup quick cooking oatmeal**
½	**cup firmly packed light brown sugar**
1	**egg**
1	**cup milk**
¼	**cup vegetable oil**
1	**cup frozen blueberries, thawed**

1. Preheat the oven to hot (400°).
2. Sift together the flour, baking powder, nutmeg and salt into a medium-size bowl. Stir in the oatmeal and the brown sugar until well blended.
3. Beat the egg in a 2-cup measure with a fork; add and beat in the milk and the oil. Pour over the dry ingredients and stir just until blended. Fold in the blueberries. Grease 12 large muffin pan cups and spoon in the batter, dividing evenly.
4. Bake in the preheated hot oven (400°) for 20 minutes, or until golden brown. Cool in the pan on a wire rack for 5 minutes. Serve immediately, or freeze.

Note: The muffin batter can also be spooned into tiny loaf pans. Bake at 375° for 25 minutes.

Use quick bread and muffin mixes as the foundation for your own holiday creations. Add chopped fruits and nuts, spices and different liquids such as cider, sherry or orange juice, following package directions.

🈂️ 《 ⇵

Country Nut Bread

Make a day or two before serving, since this loaf gets better as it ages.

Bake at 350° for 30 to 55 minutes.
Makes one large loaf, or four to six smaller loaves.

2	**cups chopped dates**
1	**cup sweet sherry**
2	**cups all-purpose flour**
1	**teaspoon baking powder**
1	**teaspoon baking soda**
¼	**teaspoon salt**
¼	**cup butter-flavored vegetable shortening**
1	**cup firmly packed light brown sugar**
1	**egg**
½	**cup chopped candied red cherries**
½	**cup chopped walnuts**

1. Combine the chopped dates and the sherry in a medium-size saucepan; heat slowly to bubbling. Remove the saucepan from the heat and let stand for 30 minutes.
2. Preheat the oven to moderate (350°).
3. Sift together the flour, baking powder, baking soda and salt onto wax paper.
4. Beat together the shortening and the brown sugar in a medium-size bowl with an electric mixer at high speed; beat in the egg until creamy.
5. Add the sifted dry ingredients alternately with the sherry-date mixture, stirring with a wooden spoon, just until blended. Stir in the chopped red cherries and the chopped walnuts.
6. Grease one 9 x 5 x 3-inch loaf pan, or four 5½ x 3 x 2-inch loaf pans, or six 5 x 2½ x 1½-inch loaf pans. Add the batter and smooth the top.
7. Bake in the preheated moderate oven (350°) for 30 minutes for the small loaves, 40 minutes for the medium loaves and 55 minutes for the large loaf, or until a wooden skewer inserted in the center comes out clean. Cool in the pan on a wire rack for 10 minutes. Loosen the loaf around the edges of the pan and invert onto the wire rack. Cool completely. Wrap in plastic and let stand at room temperature for two days before slicing.

Note: For quick cutting of sticky dried and candied fruit, oil your knife or scissors after each few snips.

Pumpkin Bread

Bake at 350° for 65 minutes.
Makes 8 servings.

- 2 **cups sifted all-purpose flour**
- ½ **teaspoon each ground cinnamon, ground ginger, ground nutmeg, salt**
- 1 **teaspoon baking soda**
- 1 **tablespoon wheat germ (optional)**
- 1½ **cups sugar**
- 1 **cup canned pumpkin**
- ½ **cup vegetable oil**
- 2 **eggs**
- 3 **tablespoons molasses**
- ½ **cup water**
- ½ **cup raisins**
- ½ **cup chopped nuts (optional)**

1. Grease a 9 x 5 x 3-inch loaf pan. Preheat the oven to moderate (350°).
2. Sift together the flour, cinnamon, ginger, nutmeg, salt, baking soda and the wheat germ, if you wish, into a medium-size bowl.
3. Beat together the sugar, pumpkin, oil, eggs and molasses in a second medium-size bowl until well blended. Stir in the dry ingredients until well mixed. Stir in the water. Fold in the raisins and the chopped nuts, if you wish; mix well. Turn into the prepared pan.
4. Bake in the preheated moderate oven (350°) for 65 minutes, or until the center springs back when lightly pressed with a fingertip.
5. Cool in the pan on a wire rack for 10 minutes; remove from the pan onto the wire rack. Cool to room temperature.

Note: *This loaf slices best if it is stored overnight after baking. Cool the loaf completely and wrap it in plastic wrap. Use a knife with a serrated edge to slice the loaf.*

Apple Oatmeal Bread

A moist, lightly spiced loaf that is delicious spread with softened butter.

Bake at 350° for 1 hour and 5 minutes.
Makes 1 loaf (8 servings).

- 1½ **cups sifted all-purpose flour**
- 1 **teaspoon baking powder**
- 1 **teaspoon baking soda**
- 1 **teaspoon salt**
- 1 **teaspoon ground cinnamon**
- ½ **teaspoon ground nutmeg**
- ⅔ **cup firmly packed light brown sugar**
- 1 **cup quick oats, uncooked**
- 1 **cup coarsely chopped walnuts**
- 2 **eggs**
- ¼ **cup milk**
- ¼ **cup butter or margarine, melted and cooled**
- 2 **medium-size apples (¾ pound), halved, cored and coarsely shredded (1½ cups)**

1. Preheat the oven to moderate (350°). Lightly grease and flour an 8½ x 4½ x 2¾-inch loaf pan. *(See Note.)*
2. Sift together the flour, baking powder, baking soda, salt, cinnamon and nutmeg into a large bowl. Stir in the brown sugar, oats and chopped walnuts.
3. Mix the eggs, milk and butter or margarine in a small bowl; add all at once to the oatmeal mixture. Add the apples. Stir lightly with a fork just until the liquid is absorbed and the mixture is thoroughly moistened (do not overmix). Spoon into the prepared baking pan.
4. Bake in the preheated moderate oven (350°) for 1 hour and 5 minutes, or until a wooden pick inserted in the center comes out clean. Cool in the pan on a wire rack for 10 minutes. Loosen the edges with a knife and turn out onto the rack. Cool completely. Wrap and store overnight.

Note: *The bread can be baked in a 9 x 5 x 3-inch loaf pan. Bake in the preheated moderate oven (350°) for 55 minutes, or until a wooden pick inserted in the center comes out clean.*

CHAPTER 7

Tis the season...
...to begin anew. The best wishes, the brightest hopes for a New Year filled with love.

For New Year's Eve: Pineapple Cheese Ball with Crackers; Spiced Walnuts; Mexican Deviled Eggs; Piquant Stuffed Cucumber Cups; Salmon Ribbon Sandwiches; Gorgonzola-Stuffed Endive; Salmon Onion Roll-Ups; Sausage Balls à l'Orange; Curried Artichoke Bites; Fried Rice Patties; Marinated Sun-Dried Tomato Appetizers; Phyllo Egg Rolls; New Orleans Butterflied Shrimp.

Ring In The New!

Three . . . two . . . . one . . . . Happy New Year! Whether you celebrate the New Year with a big group or just an intimate gathering, this chapter will help make the occasion festive. You'll find unusual party ideas, fabulous food, pointers on making the perfect toast, and even smart advice on being a good host as well as a good guest. If you're a fan of New Year's Eve, we have elegant edibles that are ideal for a Dress-to-the-Nines bash. Or if you prefer to celebrate on New Year's Day, welcome friends and family with a wonderful Open House Buffet. However you choose to celebrate this special day, we at Family Circle wish you and yours a very happy—and healthy—New Year.

New Year's Sparkle!

Welcome 1989 with a little pizzazz!

§ ↘

GLIMMERING GOLD CENTERPIECE

Easy: Achievable by anyone.
Materials: Six wicker bells, 8″ to 10″ high *(see Materials Shopping Guide, page 272)*; gold spray paint; 12 gold tree balls: 6 of the largest that will fit inside bells and 6 to 8 smaller ones for the top of the centerpiece; fine floral wire; 2 to 2½ ft square 1″-thick Styrofoam®; knife; mixed greenery; tall yellow candles; votive candleholders; candle wax or floral clay.

Directions:
1. Spray the wicker bells with the gold paint and let them dry. Place the large gold tree balls inside the bells, attaching a piece of fine floral wire to the loop of each ball and inserting it through the small end of the bell. Push the wire back through the wicker a second time and twist it in place, leaving several inches extending.
2. Cut a circle of Styrofoam to the desired dimension for the centerpiece (20″- to 24″-diameter). Insert snips of mixed greenery to cover the foam. Make a circle of the painted bells, twisting the extended wires together at the center, and place the circle on top of the greenery. Push the twisted wires into (but not through) the Styrofoam to anchor them. Place the candles in the votive candleholders, securing them with candle wax or floral clay, and arrange them in the center of the bells. Cover the wires with additional greenery and place the remaining smaller gold balls on the circle.

Note: *This centerpiece can be used throughout the holiday season.*

Glimmering Gold Centerpiece

Midas Touch Centerpiece

💲 ↘
MIDAS TOUCH CENTERPIECE

Easy: Achievable by anyone.
Materials: Container (bowl, terra cotta pot, basket); heavy gold foil; lemon leaves; pine cones; tinsel; gold bow; gold spray paint.

Directions:
1. Cover the container with the heavy gold foil.
2. Spray the lemon leaves and pine cones gold and let them dry. Fill the container with the leaves.
3. Add the tinsel, bow and gold-sprayed pine cones.

💲
GLEAMING ELEGANCE

Easy: Achievable by anyone.
Materials: Glass or crystal vase; fresh or silk lilies; gold platter; variety of tree balls; candleholders; mini-bud vases; small fresh or silk flowers; tablecloth with metallic gold threads; linen napkins; gold-mesh ribbons.

Directions:
1. For the centerpiece, place a vase of fresh or silk lilies on a platter and surround it with tree balls. Use clear accessories, such as star-shaped glass candleholders *(see photo),* to catch the light.
2. Place small fresh or silk flowers in mini-bud vases in front of each table-setting. (We chose freesia and iris.)
3. Underneath it all, place a white tablecloth with metallic gold thread for even more sparkle. Tie the napkins with wide gold-mesh ribbons.

PARTY PERFECT!

It takes two to make a successful party — be sure to do your part!

BE A GOOD HOST

- Invite early.
- Make the group eclectic and include a few colorful characters as well as talkers and listeners, single and married, young and old, people with different backgrounds, foreign friends, etc.
- To make people comfortable, give an indication of what to wear or make it clear that anything goes and encourage unusual attire.
- Because a relaxed host makes for the best kind of party, make it easy on yourself:

  Hire as much help as you can afford.

  Have one unusual, exotic, elaborate food item and make the rest simple.

  Use paper plates and napkins, plastic glasses and plastic eating utensils with a spectacular centerpiece.

  Don't knock yourself out "tidying up" before guests arrive. *After* the party is the time for heavy cleaning.

  Have fun at your own party. Whether spur of the moment or planned, keep in mind that a New Year's Eve party is for the purpose of celebrating and enjoying friends. The next day, guests will remember if you stole the show on the dance floor or the decorations were a knock-out. They won't remember if the mirror in the second floor bathroom got cleaned nor whether you made the canapés yourself or picked them up at your favorite deli.

- Be creative with your party themes:

  Have a "Dress to the Nines" party (men in suits or tuxes; women in party dresses). It will still be cost-effective because you'll be celebrating at home rather than in a restaurant or club.

  For a Black and White party, ask guests to come dressed in black and white. Decorate in these colors and serve some black and white food, too. Of course, a color theme party can be fun in any shade of the rainbow!

  For close friends who like informality, host a games party. Play Charades, trivia games or games dealing with morals or scruples.

  For a family-oriented get-together, keep the children in mind, too. If they're happy, the adults will have a better time at your party. Have a Children's Hour from 7-9, then gather the children in a separate room. If you can afford a babysitter, all the better. Young children can be expected to go to sleep. For the older ones, provide a TV with a VCR if possible (rent one if you don't have one). Pass around popcorn, cocoa and mulled cider.

  Host an old movies or old music night. Old movies (and VCRs) can be rented from your local video store. Good choices are "A Christmas Carol," "Miracle on 34th Street," "It's A Wonderful Life" and "Holiday Inn."

  Hire local talent to provide singing, caricatures, piano playing — even tarot card readings for the new year!

  Gather people together for a midnight picnic with candlelight. More atmosphere can be provided with mini lights strung across the room. Serve food on blankets in front of the fire.

- Help your guests avoid overdrinking:

  Keep passing snacks.

  Have a bartender to make sure drinks are properly mixed.

  Provide plenty of non-alcoholic drinks and mixers. Wine spritzers, for example, are far less powerful than straight glasses of wine.

  Stop serving liquor ½ to 1 hour after midnight. Provide attractive alternatives such as coffee, cocoa and mulled cider.

KEEP THE PARTY GOING

- Take party pictures *(see Chapter II, page 69)*. Depending upon the group, hire a photographer or ask one of your guests to do the honors.
- Make a video to play at the end of the evening, or at next year's party if the group tends to celebrate New Year's Eve together each year.
- Hold impromptu contests — most charming couple, most creative outfit, best dancers, best joke teller. (You may choose to decide yourself and make a big production out of awarding the prizes.)
- Introduce as many people as possible and point out what they might have in common.
- Make New Year's predictions to be sealed and opened the following New Year's Eve or Day.

ATMOSPHERE IS EVERYTHING

- Pick a theme, color, mood, etc. and play it to the hilt using paper products — the quick, inexpensive way to transform your living quarters into a party place.
- If possible, mail invitations that set the mood. For example, a blank inside card with a sparkling champagne bottle on the front might be a perfect choice for your creative message. Or choose party theme invitations that are designed to go with decorations and partyware.
- Take a cue from stage designers and pay particular attention to lighting — not too bright for New Year's Eve. Choose soft, pink lighting that does not cast unflattering shadows.

- Let the music deliver a message by setting the mood. Change the music during the evening to build to a climactic bout of dancing just before midnight, for example. Or play a fanfare just before the countdown to midnight.
- Let guests know when the party's over:

  Turn the music down.
  Turn the lights up.
  Serve coffee.
  Tell people how much you enjoyed having them.
  Ask if anyone needs transportation. Suggest cabs for anyone who might have overimbibed. (Many cities offer special free transportation services on New Year's Eve.)

BE A GOOD GUEST

- Always R.S.V.P: Let your hosts know that you will — or won't — be there.
- Ask what you can bring and insist on bringing something:

  Wrap a few bottles of wine in mailing tubes; tie with ribbon *(see photo at left)*.
  Bring a bouquet of helium balloons tied with silver or gold ribbon; have guests attach their New Year's wishes and/or resolutions to the balloons and let them off into the sky at midnight.
  Bring a bouquet of candles tied with ribbon.
  Make up a breakfast basket for your hosts' New Year's Day: Bake muffins or quick breads and place them in a napkin- or doily-lined container. Add freshly squeezed juice, one or two varieties of jam and some freshly ground coffee appropriate for your hosts' coffee machine.
- Offer to help with the festivities:

  Bring extra chairs and tables so your hosts don't have to rent them.
  Bring a camera or movie camera to record the festivities. A Polaroid is especially welcome because guests enjoy seeing how they look right at that moment.
  Put together some cassette tapes for both dancing and "atmosphere."
- Offer to share your babysitter and have your hosts' children over to your house for the evening.
- Offer — and really mean it! — to help clean up after the party, either right after or the next day.
- Adhere to the rules of the party.
- When the party's over, leave!
- Send a thank you note the very next day after the party.

Puttin' On The Glitz!

New Year's Eve Cocktail Party

(for 24)

Pineapple Cheese Ball with Crackers*
Spiced Walnuts*
Mexican Deviled Eggs*
Piquant Stuffed Cucumber Cups*
Salmon Ribbon Sandwiches*
Gorgonzola-Stuffed Endive*
Salmon Onion Roll-Ups*
Sausage Balls à l'Orange*
Curried Artichoke Bites*
Fried Rice Patties*
Marinated Sun-Dried Tomato Appetizers*
Phyllo Egg Rolls*
New Orleans Butterflied Shrimp*
Pink Champagne Punch*

*Recipes follow

Gorgonzola-Stuffed Endive; New Orleans Butterflied Shrimp; Curried Artichoke Bites; Marinated Sun-Dried Tomato Appetizers; Sausage Balls à l'Orange

Work Plan

Up to 1 Week Ahead:
• Make ice!

Up to 2 Days Ahead:
• Make Spiced Walnuts.
• Make cheese mixture for Pineapple Cheese Ball; refrigerate.

The Day Before:
• Hard-cook eggs for Mexican Deviled Eggs. (If desired, filling may be made the day before; refrigerate egg white halves and filling separately.)
• Prepare and cook sausage balls for Sausage Balls à l'Orange.
• Shape Pineapple Cheese Ball; refrigerate.
• Prepare gorgonzola stuffing for Gorgonzola-Stuffed Endive; refrigerate, but bring back to room temperature before using.
• Layer loaves for Salmon Ribbon Sandwiches; chill.
• Prepare Phyllo Egg Rolls; refrigerate.
• Prepare batter for Fried Rice Patties; refrigerate.

Early in the Day:
• Prepare Salmon Onion Roll-Ups; refrigerate.
• Assemble Curried Artichoke Bites; refrigerate.
• Assemble Marinated Sun-Dried Tomato Appetizers; cover and refrigerate.
• Make Mexican Deviled Eggs; cover and refrigerate.
• Make orange sauce for Sausage Balls à l'Orange; add sausage balls and let stand.

• Make base for Pink Champagne Punch.
• Make filling for New Orleans Butterflied Shrimp; refrigerate.
• Prepare filling for Piquant Stuffed Cucumber Cups; refrigerate.

2 to 4 Hours Before:
• Garnish Gorgonzola-Stuffed Endive.
• Prepare cucumbers and stuff Piquant Stuffed Cucumber Cups.
• Slice Salmon Ribbon Sandwiches; cover and refrigerate.
• Decorate Pineapple Cheese Ball; let stand at room temperature.
• Prepare and stuff shrimp for New Orleans Butterflied Shrimp, but do not bake.

1 Hour Before:
• Assemble Mexican Deviled Eggs, Salmon Ribbon Sandwiches, Salmon Onion Roll-Ups and Gorgonzola-Stuffed Endive on platters.

½ Hour Before:
• Bake Phyllo Egg Rolls.
• Prepare Fried Rice Patties; keep warm.

At Serving Time:
• Prepare Pink Champagne Punch.
• Broil Marinated Sun-Dried Tomato Appetizers.
• Bake Curried Artichoke Bites.
• Bake New Orleans Butterflied Shrimp.
• Heat Sausage Balls à l'Orange.
• Garnish Fried Rice Patties.

Salmon Ribbon Sandwiches

This mosaic sandwich lends itself to endless variations. For example, try ham and peas instead of the salmon and capers.

Bake at 425° for 10 minutes.
Makes 32.

32 small mushrooms
2 packages (9 ounces each) frozen
     asparagus spears
½ pound sliced smoked salmon
8 slices whole wheat bread
     Dill Butter (recipe follows)
4 tablespoons drained capers

1. Clean the mushrooms with a damp cloth. Remove and save the stems for another use. Place the caps, hollow side up, on an ungreased cookie sheet.
2. Bake in the preheated hot oven (425°) for 10 minutes, or until the juices run. Remove from the oven. When the mushrooms are cool enough to handle, pour off the liquid.
3. Cook the asparagus, following the package directions, and drain. Cut the salmon into julienne slices.
4. Trim the crusts from the bread. Spread both sides of the slices with 2 tablespoons Dill Butter.
5. Working with half the bread and fillings at a time, place one slice of bread on a sheet of wax paper. Arrange four mushroom caps on the bread, pressing down slightly. Top with a second slice of bread. Arrange four rows of sliced salmon on the bread. Place the drained capers in between the rows of salmon.
6. Top with a slice of bread, pressing down slightly. Arrange the asparagus over, alternating directions so the spears will fit. Trim the ends.
7. Place another slice of bread on the asparagus. Spread Dill Butter in a thin layer around the sides of the loaf. Repeat for the second loaf.
8. Chill the loaves, uncovered, for 1 hour, or until firm.
9. To serve, cut in ½-inch slices; halve each slice on the diagonal, if you wish.

Dill Butter: Beat 2 cups (4 sticks) softened butter with an electric mixer until creamy. Stir in ¼ cup finely chopped dill until blended. *Makes 2 cups.*

Mexican Deviled Eggs

Stuffed eggs are always popular. This spicy filling is sure to please.

Makes 12.

6 hard-cooked eggs, shelled
¼ cup shredded Cheddar cheese
¼ cup bottled taco sauce
¼ teaspoon chili powder
     Sliced pimiento-stuffed olives for
       garnish
     Sliced pitted ripe olives for garnish

1. Cut the eggs in half lengthwise. Remove the yolks and set aside the whites.
2. Press the yolks through a sieve into a bowl. Blend in the cheese, taco sauce and chili powder until well combined.
3. Refill the egg whites, using about 1 tablespoon of the yolk mixture for each egg half. Garnish with the olive slices.

Piquant Stuffed Cucumber Cups

The creamy mixture can also be stuffed into celery, then cut diagonally into bite-size pieces.

Makes 16.

2 cucumbers
   Salt
1 package (8 ounces) cream cheese,
     softened
⅓ cup mayonnaise
2 tablespoons prepared horseradish
1 teaspoon seasoned salt
1 teaspoon Worcestershire sauce
¼ teaspoon freshly ground black pepper
1 tart apple
1 cup diced cooked ham
½ cup chopped pecans

1. Mix the cream cheese, mayonnaise, horseradish seasoned salt, Worcestershire sauce and pepper until smooth.
2. Core the apple; do not peel. Chop finely and add to the cheese mixture. Stir in the ham and the chopped pecans; mix well. Cover and refrigerate for 1 hour.

3. Score the cucumbers lengthwise. Cut horizontally into 1-inch pieces. Using a melon baller, scoop out the cucumber to within ¼ inch of the side and bottom. Sprinkle with the salt and invert onto paper toweling to drain.
4. Stuff the cucumbers with the cream cheese mixture. Refrigerate, covered, until serving time.

Curried Artichoke Bites

Spicy morsels sure to disappear fast.

Bake at 450° for 1 minute.
Makes 24.

- 1 **can (14 ounces) artichoke hearts, drained**
- ¼ **cup (½ stick) butter**
- 1 **teaspoon curry powder**
- ¼ **teaspoon ground cumin**
- 6 **slices firm-textured bread**
- 1¼ **cups shredded Jarlsberg cheese**
  Paprika

1. Cut the artichoke hearts into quarters and drain on paper toweling.
2. Melt the butter in a medium-size skillet over low heat. Stir in the curry powder and the cumin until blended. Add the drained artichokes and toss gently to coat evenly.
3. Slightly toast the bread. Remove the crusts and cut the bread into 1-inch squares. Arrange in a single layer on a cookie sheet. Place an artichoke piece on each; drizzle any excess butter over. Top each with about 1 tablespoon of the shredded cheese. (The recipe may be prepared ahead up to this point. Refrigerate.)
4. Preheat the oven to very hot (450°).
5. Bake the hors d'oeuvres in the preheated very hot oven (450°) for 1 minute, or until the cheese is melted. Sprinkle with the paprika. Serve hot or warm.

To keep canapés with bread bases moist and appetizing, place them on platters lined with dampened paper toweling. Cover with plastic wrap and refrigerate for up to 8 hours.

New Orleans Butterflied Shrimp

Andre Ledoux, executive chef at the Fairmont Hotel in New Orleans, shares this recipe.

Bake at 350° for 5 minutes.
Makes 12 servings.

- ¼ **cup finely chopped celery**
- ¼ **cup finely chopped shallots**
- 1 **tablespoon butter**
- 1 **tablespoon all-purpose flour**
- ¼ **cup light cream**
- 2 **tablespoons dry white wine**
- ¼ **pound crabmeat**
- 12 **jumbo shrimp**

1. Sauté the celery and the shallots in the butter in a medium-size skillet for 3 minutes, or until the celery softens.
2. Add the flour and cook for 1 minute. Add the cream and the wine. Bring to boiling; cook for 1 to 2 minutes, or until thickened.
3. Stir in the crabmeat. Cook for 1 minute. Remove from the heat and cool slightly.
4. Peel the shrimp, leaving the tail on. Blanch in boiling water for 30 seconds.
5. Preheat the oven to moderate (350°).
6. Cut a thin sliver from the outer curve so that the shrimp will stand upright. Working on the inner curve, make a slit almost all the way through. Using your fingers, open up to partially butterfly. Fill the shrimp with the crab mixture.
7. Bake in the preheated moderate oven (350°) for 5 minutes, or until heated through.

Note: The shrimp may be filled and refrigerated. Bake just before serving.

Gorgonzola-Stuffed Endive

This creamy cheese mixture is equally delicious when piped into mushroom caps or spread on celery.

Makes about 36.

- ½ **pound Gorgonzola cheese**
- ½ **cup (1 stick) butter, softened**
- 2 **tablespoons finely chopped fresh parsley**
- ½ **cup chopped pistachio nuts**
- 36 **leaves fresh endive**
  Shelled natural pistachio nuts for garnish

1. Beat together the cheese and the butter with an electric mixer until creamy and smooth. Add the chopped parsley and the chopped pistachio nuts until blended.
2. Mound or pipe out the mixture on the endive. Cover lightly with plastic wrap and chill.
3. At serving time, garnish with the shelled pistachio nuts.

Marinated Sun-Dried Tomato Appetizers

This hors d'oeuvre is a marriage of many cuisines.

Broil for 3 minutes.
Makes about 30.

- 1 **baguette (about 16 inches long)**
- 1 **container (6 ounces) frozen guacamole dip, thawed**
- 1 **cup shredded Jarlsberg cheese or mozzarella**
- 1 **jar (6 ounces) marinated sun-dried tomatoes**

1. Preheat the broiler to medium.
2. Cut the bread into ½-inch slices on the diagonal. Spread with a thin layer of the guacamole. Sprinkle with the cheese.
3. Halve the tomatoes lengthwise. Arrange the strips over the cheese. Drizzle with the marinade. Place on an ungreased cookie sheet.
4. Broil for 3 minutes, or until the cheese is bubbly. Serve hot.

Note: *If prepared marinated sun-dried tomatoes*

are not available, you may substitute a homemade product: Let sun-dried tomatoes stand in boiling water for 2 minutes to soften; drain. Place in top-quality olive oil to cover.

Sausage Balls à l'Orange

Meatballs with a hint of citrus.

Bake at 350° for 30 minutes.
Makes about 20.

- 1 **pound bulk sausage**
- ½ **cup dry bread crumbs**
- 1 **small onion, chopped (¼ cup)**
- 1 **egg, slightly beaten**
- ¼ **teaspoon dry mustard**
- 3 **tablespoons firmly packed brown sugar**
- 1 **tablespoon cornstarch**
- ⅛ **teaspoon ground cloves**
- 1 **cup orange juice**
- 1 **fresh orange, sliced and cut into bitesize pieces, for garnish (optional)**

1. Preheat the oven to moderate (350°).
2. Mix the sausage, bread crumbs and onion until blended.
3. Combine the egg and the dry mustard. Add to the sausage mixture and mix well.
4. Shape into 1½-inch balls and place on a rack in a shallow baking dish.
5. Bake in the preheated moderate oven (350°) for 30 minutes.
6. Combine the brown sugar, cornstarch, cloves and orange juice in a small saucepan. Cook over medium heat, stirring constantly, until thickened.
7. Lower the heat, add the sausage balls and simmer for 10 minutes, or until heated.
8. Serve on wooden picks, garnished with fresh orange pieces, if you wish.

Did You Know . . .

The Dutch in their New Amsterdam settlement originated New Year's celebrating in the mid-seventeenth century. In some areas groups of bachelors called on groups of young women in one of their homes.

⧀ Salmon Onion Roll-Ups

An easy softening trick transforms Norwegian crispbread into rolled slices. Here they encase a savory filling.

Makes 12.

> 4   **ounces cream cheese, softened**
> 2   **teaspoons lemon juice**
> ½   **teaspoon prepared horseradish**
> 1   **tablespoon chopped parsley**
> 10 **slices thin-style Norwegian crispbread**
> 2   **ounces thinly sliced smoked salmon**
> 4   **to 5 green onions, cut in 2-inch lengths**

1. Combine the cream cheese, lemon juice, horseradish and parsley, blending well.
2. Fill a deep bowl with warm water. Dip the crispbread slices, one at a time, quickly in and out of the water. Pat dry on a clean cloth towel. (The bread should be moist and just pliable but not wet.) Cover the slices and let rest for 45 minutes.
3. Spread each slice with the cream cheese mixture and halve crosswise. Top each piece with a small slice of the salmon.
4. Split the onions lengthwise. Place a few onion slivers along one side of each crispbread. Roll up, letting ½ inch onion stick out of the end of each roll.

$ ⧀ Fried Rice Patties

Makes 18.

> 1   **cup short-grain rice, cooked in chicken broth, cooled**
> 2   **tablespoons all-purpose flour**
> 2   **eggs**
> ¼   **cup heavy cream**
> 3   **tablespoons snipped fresh chives**
> ¼   **teaspoon black pepper**
> ¼   **cup vegetable oil**
> ¼   **cup dairy sour cream**
> 2   **ounces red salmon caviar**

1. Mix the rice and the flour in a bowl. Stir in the eggs, one at a time. Add the cream, chives and pepper. Mix well and refrigerate overnight.
2. Spoon 2 teaspoons of the batter into the heated oil in a skillet. Cook over medium heat for 1 minute per side. Drain the patties on paper toweling.
3. Place a dollop of the sour cream on each patty. Top with the caviar. Serve hot.

⧀ Phyllo Egg Rolls

Phyllo dough replaces the traditional egg roll skins. This version is baked, not deep-fried.

Bake at 350° for 25 minutes.
Makes 24.

> ⅓   **cup peanut or vegetable oil**
> 1   **cup finely chopped celery**
> 1½ **cups shredded Chinese cabbage**
> 1   **cup chopped mushrooms**
> ⅓   **cup finely chopped green onions**
> ½   **pound shrimp, shelled and deveined**
> 1   **cup diced cooked pork**
> 1   **cup finely chopped water chestnuts**
> 1   **cup bean sprouts**
> 2   **cloves garlic, minced**
> 1   **teaspoon sugar**
> ¼   **cup soy sauce**
> 1   **pound phyllo dough, thawed**
> 1   **cup (2 slices) butter, melted**
>   **Chinese mustard or duck sauce (optional)**

1. Heat the peanut or vegetable oil in a wok or large skillet. Add the celery, cabbage, mushrooms and green onions. Stir-fry just until wilted.
2. Dice the shrimp and add to the wok with the pork. Cook for 3 minutes.
3. Add the chopped water chestnuts, the bean sprouts, garlic, sugar and soy sauce. Cook for 5 minutes. Remove from the heat and cool.
4. Preheat the oven to moderate (350°).
5. Brush a sheet of phyllo with some of the butter. Fold in half, then in half again (9 x 7 inches).
6. Place ¼ cup of the cooled filling on the bottom third of the phyllo. Roll up the end to cover the filling. Fold the sides over, envelope-fashion. Gently flap over to make a roll. Brush the top lightly with the butter. Repeat with the remaining phyllo, filling and butter.
7. Bake in the preheated moderate oven (350°) for 25 minutes, or until golden brown. Serve with Chinese mustard or duck sauce, if you wish.

Pineapple Cheese Ball

Spiced Walnuts

Great for snacking any time.

Makes about 4 cups.

 1 **cup (2 sticks) butter**
 4 **cups walnut halves**
 3 **cups 10X (confectioners' powdered) sugar**
 2 **tablespoons ground cinnamon**
 2 **tablespoons ground cloves**
 2 **tablespoons ground nutmeg**

1. Melt the butter in a large, heavy skillet; stir in the walnuts. Cook over low heat, stirring frequently, for 20 minutes, or until the walnuts are lightly browned. Remove with a slotted spoon to paper toweling.
2. Sift together the 10X (confectioners' powdered) sugar, cinnamon, cloves and nutmeg into a large bowl or paper bag. Add the walnuts and toss or shake until evenly coated. Place the walnuts in a colander and shake off any excess sugar. Spread on paper toweling to dry.

Pineapple Cheese Ball

A cheese ball formed into the shape of a pineapple, the symbol of hospitality. Be sure to start the recipe the day before serving.

Makes about 50 servings.

 6 **cups grated sharp Cheddar cheese (1½ pounds)**
 2 **cups grated Swiss cheese (½ pound)**
 1 **package (8 ounces) cream cheese, softened**
 ¼ **pound blue cheese, crumbled**
 ½ **cup (1 stick) butter, softened**
 ½ **cup brandy**
 2 **tablespoons lemon juice**
 1 **tablespoon Worcestershire sauce**
    Whole cloves
    Paprika
 1 **leafy crown from a large, fresh pineapple**
    Crackers

1. Beat together the Cheddar, Swiss, cream and blue cheeses with the butter in a bowl with an electric mixer until blended.
2. Add the brandy, lemon juice and Worcestershire sauce. Continue beating, scraping down the side of the bowl, for 5 minutes, or until blended.
3. Cover and chill overnight, or until firm enough to handle.
4. Form the cheese mixture into a pineapple shape. Smooth the top flat. Cover the entire cheese ball with wax paper. Chill for 4 hours, or until very firm.
5. Before serving, mark the cheese with the top of a teaspoon, making crisscross lines that form diamond shapes. Place a whole clove in each diamond. Sprinkle the ball with paprika.
6. Lift the ball onto a serving plate, using a spatula. Place the pineapple crown on top of the ball and secure with wooden picks, if necessary. Serve with crackers.

Did You Know . . .

Some families eat blackeyed peas on New Year's Day for good luck.

Punches With Panache

*A burst of bubbles or the right spice can add sparkle
to your New Year's celebration.*

Pink Champagne Punch

*A sparkling champagne punch is our choice beverage
for New Year's Eve.*

Makes 32 four-ounce servings.

1   **can (6 ounces) frozen lemonade
concentrate, thawed**
2   **cups brandy**
¼   **cup bottled grenadine syrup**
1   **bottle (28 ounces) ginger ale, chilled**
1   **bottle (28 ounces) club soda, chilled**
2   **bottles (750 ml each) pink champagne,
chilled**
    Ice cubes

1. Combine the thawed lemonade concentrate
with the brandy and the grenadine syrup in a
large bowl until blended. (The recipe may be
prepared up to this point. Let stand.)
2. At serving time, stir in the ginger ale, club soda
and champagne. Top with the ice cubes.

FROZEN ASSETS

- Add colorful pieces of fruit to ice cube trays
and ice block molds before freezing.
- To keep fruit "suspended" in ice, fill the mold
or tray with a layer of liquid; freeze. Top with
the fruit and a shallow layer of liquid; freeze.
Fill the mold to the top; freeze.

Open House Punch

*Lemonade and limeade are combined with a spicy
syrup and quinine water.*

Makes 16 four-ounce servings.

½   **cup sugar**
1   **two-inch piece stick cinnamon**
5   **whole cloves**
5   **whole allspice**
1   **cup water**
1   **can (6 ounces) frozen lemonade
concentrate, thawed**
1   **can (6 ounces) frozen limeade
concentrate, thawed**
2   **cups vodka or gin**
1   **bottle (28 ounces) quinine water,
chilled**
1   **bottle (28 ounces) club soda, chilled
Strawberry Ice Ring (recipe, page 252)
Green grape clusters for garnish
(optional)**

1. Combine the sugar, cinnamon stick, cloves,
allspice and water in a small saucepan. Bring to
boiling over medium heat. Lower the heat and
simmer for 5 minutes. Strain into a medium-size
bowl and chill.
2. When ready to mix the punch, pour the spiced-
water mixture into a punch bowl. Stir in the
thawed lemonade and limeade concentrates
until blended. Add the vodka or gin, quinine
water and club soda.
3. Float the Strawberry Ice Ring. Surround the
bowl with clusters of green grapes, if you wish.

Pink Champagne Punch

Did You Know . . .

Throughout history, the celebration of the New Year has included such rites as the confession of sins and driving off of demons; extinguishing and rekindling of fires; masked processions and receptions for the dead; fights between opposing teams; and festivals.

Strawberry Ice Ring

Makes 1 ring.

At least one day before the ice ring is needed, pour water to a depth of ¼ inch into a ring mold that will fit into your punch bowl. Freeze for about 20 minutes, or until firm. Arrange whole strawberries on top of the frozen layer. Pour in ¾ cup very cold water and freeze for 15 minutes, or until the water is frozen. To keep the berries in place, keep adding very cold water a little at a time, freezing after each addition, until the mold is filled. Freeze overnight, or until solid. To unmold, quickly dip the mold in and out of a pan of hot water, or let stand at room temperature for about 5 minutes, or until the ring is movable in the mold. Invert onto a cookie sheet and slide carefully into the punch bowl.

Note: *Club soda or sparkling water can be used instead of the water.*

Ice Block

Makes 1 mold.

The day before the party, fill a metal bowl or ring mold that will fit into your punch bowl with water. Set in the freezer overnight, or until frozen solid. To unmold, dip the mold quickly in and out of a pan of hot water, or let stand at room temperature for about 5 minutes, or until the ice is movable in the mold. Invert onto a cookie sheet and slide carefully into the punch bowl.

Note: *Other liquids also can be frozen and used as an ice block. You can freeze leftover coffee or tea, orange juice or the juices drained from canned fruits. Just be sure the liquid's flavor is compatible with that of the punch.*

Cranberry Fizz Punch

Club soda adds sparkle to non-alcoholic punch.

Makes 30 four-ounce servings.

- 2 **bottles (32 ounces each) cranberry juice cocktail, chilled**
- 2 **bottles (28 ounces each) club soda, chilled**
  Ice Block (recipe, below left)
  Mint sprigs for garnish (optional)

1. Combine the cranberry juice cocktail and the club soda in a large punch bowl.
2. Slide in the Ice Block. Garnish with mint sprigs, if you wish.

Party Bowl

Strawberries and pineapple enliven a rum-based punch. Perfect for an open house.

Makes 20 four-ounce servings.

- 1 **bottle (750 ml) light rum**
- 2 **cups pineapple juice**
- 1 **cup lemon juice**
- ¾ **cup light corn syrup**
- 1 **pint strawberries, hulled**
- 1 **can (14 ounces) pineapple tidbits in natural juice**
  Ice Block (recipe at left)
- 2 **bottles (28 ounces each) club soda**

1. Combine the rum, the pineapple and lemon juices, the corn syrup, strawberries and pineapple and juice in a punch bowl. Cover the bowl and refrigerate the punch for at least 2 hours.
2. To serve, add the Ice Block. Then add the club soda.

Tropical Punch

If you can't get away to a South Sea island for the holidays, bring the exotic flavor of the islands to your next party.

Makes 18 four-ounce servings.

1   **bottle (750 ml) Mai-Tai mixer**
2   **cups dark rum**
1   **bottle (750 ml) ginger ale**
     Ice Block (recipe, page 252)
     Maraschino cherries for garnish
     Fresh pineapple spears for garnish

1. Combine the Mai-Tai mixer, rum and ginger ale in a small punch bowl. Refrigerate until just before party time.
2. Float the Ice Block on the punch. Ladle into punch cups and garnish with the maraschino cherries and the pineapple spears.

Hot Mulled Cider

You'll love this spicy classic on wintry nights.

Makes 16 eight-ounce servings.

1   **bottle (1 gallon) apple cider**
1   **cup firmly packed light brown sugar**
9   **whole cloves**
9   **whole allspice**
4   **three-inch pieces stick cinnamon, broken into 1-inch pieces**
2   **lemons, thinly sliced**

1. Combine the apple cider and the brown sugar in a large kettle.
2. Tie the cloves, allspice and cinnamon in cheesecloth and place in the kettle. Simmer the mixture for 5 minutes. Discard the spice bag.
3. Serve the cider in mugs and float a lemon slice in each.

THE NEW YEAR'S TOAST

The New Year's Toast is an American tradition that has spawned a plethora of boring and predictable toasts. Both guest and host should be armed with clever toasts, either original or borrowed.

Toasting Tips:

- To sound like a silver-tongued orator, memorize the toast — no stumbling, groping or breaking of rhyme or rhythm.
- If you make up your own toast, be brief — probably no more than 60 to 90 words. Make each word count. Mark Twain toasted: "Let us toast the fools; but for them the rest of us could not succeed." When George Bernard Shaw was asked to propose a toast to sex, he said, "It gives me *great* pleasure. . ." and sat down. Sometimes simple is best, such as Humphrey Bogart's famous toast from *Casablanca:* "Here's looking at you, Kid."
- Depending upon the situation, tap with a utensil on a glass, stand in an elevated place, stop the music or have guests pass the word along that a toast will be proposed. When you have everyone's attention, speak loudly and clearly.
- Match the toast to the occasion: For a New Year's toast, the coming year is the focus, of course. Consider the group: Are they new acquaintances, old friends, business associates?
- Toasting tends to go by seniority when a person is toasted. At a time like New Year's Eve the host, hostess or a guest may propose a toast.
- Unless the party is a roast, never use the occasion to put someone down.
- If the group is too large to clink glasses, simply gesture upward with your glass and others will follow. More than eight people constitutes a physically impossible clinking situation.

New Year's Day Open House

(for 12)

Party Bowl (recipe, page 252)
Open House Punch (recipe, page 250)
Sandwich Platter*
Bread and Butter Sandwiches*
Lemon Party Tarts*
Pecan Apple Tarts*
New England Raisin Cake*
Spiced Tea*   *Regular Tea*

*Recipes follow

Party Bowl; Sandwich Platter; Bread and Butter Sandwiches; Pecan Apple Tarts;
Lemon Party Tarts; New England Raisin Cake

Work Plan

Up to 1 Month Ahead:
• Bake and freeze Candied Orange Tea Bread and Date and Nut Bread for Bread and Butter Sandwiches. Bake and freeze New England Raisin Cake (or bake up to 2 days before and store at room temperature).

Up to 1 Week Before:
• Make Ice Block for Party Bowl, Strawberry Ice Ring for Open House Punch.
• Make Spiced Tea Blend, if desired.

Up to 2 Days Before:
• Bake tiny tart shells for Lemon Party Tarts and Pecan Apple Tarts.

The Day Before:
• Make fillings for Sandwich Platter; refrigerate.
• Make lemon filling for Lemon Party Tarts.

Early in the Day:
• Make Sandwich Platter; refrigerate.
• Make Bread and Butter Sandwiches.
• Make apple filling for Pecan Apple Tarts.
• Make base for Party Bowl and Open House Punch.

At Serving Time:
• Assemble Lemon Party Tarts and Pecan Apple Tarts.
• Finish Party Bowl and Open House Punch.
• Prepare Spiced Tea and regular tea.

SPICED TEA TIME

For a quick-to-make Spiced Tea blend, combine in a small bowl ¼ pound loose Orange Pekoe tea with three 3-inch pieces stick cinnamon, crumbled, and 1 tablespoon whole cloves.

For orange cardamom tea, combine in a small bowl ¼ pound loose tea with the grated rind of 2 oranges and 6 whole cardamom pods, peeled.

Bread and Butter Sandwiches

Delicious little bites of savory nut breads with just a bit of softened butter.

Makes 60 tiny sandwiches.

1 **loaf Candied Orange Tea Bread (recipe at right)**
1 **loaf Date and Nut Bread (recipe at right)**
½ **cup (1 stick) butter, softened**
Orange slices for garnish

1. Cut the Candied Orange Tea Bread and the Date and Nut Bread into very thin slices with a sharp slicing knife. (You should have at least 20 slices, plus 2 end pieces, from each loaf.)
2. Put the slices together with the softened butter. Cut each sandwich, diagonally, into 3 slices. Pile into a large metal pan lined with dampened paper toweling. Cover with plastic wrap and refrigerate until party time.
3. Arrange the sandwiches on a serving platter and garnish with the orange slices.

Note: *For easier slicing, bake the breads at least a day before cutting them.*

Sandwich Platter

Delectable tea sandwiches with pizzazz.

Makes 28 tiny sandwiches from each loaf.

1 **loaf (1 pound) each square pumpernickel, square dark rye, rye with caraway and sliced white breads**
Ham and Cucumber Spread (recipe top right)
Anchovy Egg Filling (recipe top right)
Almond Cheese Spread (recipe top right)
Watercress for garnish

1. Trim the crusts from the bread slices. (Use for croutons or bread crumbs.)
2. Spread half the bread slices with the fillings. (We used Ham and Cucumber Spread with square pumpernickel and square dark rye; Anchovy Egg Filling with the rye with caraway and Almond Cheese Spread with white bread.)

Top the fillings with the remaining bread slices and cut the sandwiches into quarters, diagonally.

3. Pile into a large metal pan lined with dampened paper toweling. Cover with plastic wrap and refrigerate until party time.
4. Garnish sandwiches with watercress; serve.

Ham and Cucumber Spread: Combine 2 cans (4½ ounces each) deviled ham, ½ cup very finely chopped cucumber, 2 tablespoons mayonnaise or salad dressing and 1 tablespoon prepared mustard in a small bowl until well blended. *Makes enough to fill 28 tiny sandwiches.*

Anchovy Egg Filling: Combine 6 shelled and chopped hard-cooked eggs, ¼ cup mayonnaise or salad dressing and 1 tablespoon anchovy paste in a small bowl until well blended. *Makes enough to fill 28 tiny sandwiches.*

Almond Cheese Spread: Soften 1 package (8 ounces) cream cheese in a small bowl. Blend in ¼ cup well drained crushed pineapple and ¼ cup toasted sliced almonds until well blended. *Makes enough to fill 28 tiny sandwiches.*

💲 《《

Candied Orange Tea Bread

First candy your own orange peel, then bake the best tea bread ever.

Bake at 325° for 1 hour, 20 minutes.
Makes 1 large loaf.

2	**large eating oranges**
½	**cup sugar**
2	**eggs**
1	**cup sugar**
¾	**cup milk**
½	**cup (1 stick) butter or margarine, melted**
3	**cups all-purpose flour**
1	**teaspoon baking soda**
1	**teaspoon baking powder**
1	**teaspoon salt**
½	**teaspoon ground ginger**
½	**cup chopped walnuts**

1. Pare the orange peel with a sharp knife and cut into slivers. Cover with cold water and bring to boiling. Pour off the hot water and cover with cold water. Bring to boiling and simmer for 5 minutes.
2. Drain off the water and add the ½ cup sugar. Cook, stirring constantly, for 5 minutes, or until thick and syrupy. Cool completely in the pan.

3. Preheat the oven to slow (325°).
4. Beat the eggs until light with a wire whisk. Beat in the 1 cup sugar until well blended. Beat in the milk. Stir in the candied orange peel, then the melted butter or margarine.
5. Sift together the flour, baking soda, baking powder, salt and ginger into a mixing bowl. Add the egg mixture. Stir with a wooden spoon, just until blended. Fold in the walnuts. Pour into a greased 9 x 5 x 3-inch loaf pan.
6. Bake in the preheated slow oven (325°) for 1 hour, 20 minutes, or until a wooden skewer inserted in the center comes out clean. Cool in the pan on a wire rack for 10 minutes. Loosen bread around the pan edges and invert onto the wire rack; cool completely. Wrap in a plastic bag and allow to mellow at room temperature for 2 days, or freeze until party time.

💲 《《 ↘

Date and Nut Bread

Bake at 350° for 1 hour, 20 minutes.
Makes 1 large loaf.

1	**package (10 ounces) pitted dates**
1¼	**cups boiling water**
1	**teaspoon baking soda**
1	**cup firmly packed brown sugar**
2	**eggs, beaten**
½	**cup chopped pecans**
1	**cup all-purpose flour**
2	**teaspoons baking powder**
1	**teaspoon salt**
1	**cup whole-wheat flour**

1. Preheat the oven to moderate (350°).
2. Cut up the dates and place them in a large bowl. Pour the boiling water over. Add the baking soda and cool for 20 minutes. Beat in the sugar until dissolved; beat in the eggs and the pecans.
3. Sift together the flour, baking powder and salt into a bowl. Add the whole-wheat flour. Add the date mixture. Stir with a wooden spoon, just until well blended. Spoon into a well greased 9 x 5 x 3-inch loaf pan.
4. Bake in the preheated moderate oven (350°) for 1 hour, 20 minutes, or until a wooden pick inserted in the center comes out clean. Cool in the pan on a wire rack for 10 minutes. Loosen the bread around the edges of the pan. Invert onto the rack and cool completely. Wrap in a plastic bag and allow to mellow at room temperature for 2 days, or freeze until used.

Lemon Party Tarts

You can make the tart shells well ahead of time, but fill them just before serving time.

Makes 12 tiny tarts.

5 egg yolks
⅔ cup sugar
1 tablespoon grated lemon rind
⅓ cup lemon juice
Tiny Tart Shells (recipe at right)
Fresh mint sprigs for garnish

1. Beat the egg yolks until frothy in the top of a double boiler with an electric mixer at high speed. Beat in the sugar, a little at a time, until the mixture is thick and light. Stir in the lemon rind and juice.
2. Cook over hot, not boiling, water, stirring constantly with a wooden spoon, until the filling is thick, for about 13 minutes. Remove from the heat. Transfer to a small bowl and cover the surface lightly with a piece of plastic wrap. Cool to room temperature, then chill.
3. At serving time, spoon the chilled lemon filling into the tart shells. You will have some left over, which can be used in another dessert. Garnish with the fresh mint sprigs.

Use leftover Christmas cake for New Year's petit fours: Cut the cake into small pieces, frost and decorate. This is an especially nice idea for an open house buffet.

Pecan Apple Tarts

Brown sugar and nuts, plus slices of apple — what could be more delicious?

Makes 12 tiny tarts.

1 can (20 ounces) pie-sliced apples
½ cup firmly packed brown sugar
1 tablespoon cornstarch
1 teaspoon pumpkin pie spice
Tiny Tart Shells (recipe at right)
Whole pecans for garnish

1. Drain the liquid from the pie-sliced apples into a medium-size saucepan. Stir in the brown sugar, cornstarch and pumpkin pie spice until smooth.
2. Cook, stirring constantly, until the mixture thickens and bubbles, for 1 minute. Remove from the heat. Add the apple slices and stir well. Cool to room temperature.
3. Just before serving, spoon the apple filling into the tart shells. Garnish with the whole pecans.

Tiny Tart Shells: Preheat the oven to hot (400°). Prepare 1 package pie crust mix, following label directions. Roll out, half at a time, to a ¼-inch thickness on a lightly floured pastry cloth or board. Using 3-inch tart pans as guides, cut out rounds 1 inch larger than the tart pans. Fit pastry into the tart pans, prick with a four-tined fork and place on a large cookie sheet. Bake in the hot oven (400°) for 12 minutes, or until golden brown. Cool in tart pans on wire racks. Loosen pastry from pans with a thin knife. Stack carefully, bolstered with plastic wrap, in a metal tin with a tight-fitting cover. *Makes 1 dozen.*

New England Raisin Cake

Two hundred years ago, the housewives of Hartford, Connecticut, baked a raisin-rich yeast bread to serve to legislators who came to the state capital. This bread-like cake has become a traditional part of New England holiday baking.

Bake at 350° for 45 minutes.
Makes one 10-inch tube.

1 cup milk
½ cup (1 stick) butter or margarine
¾ cup firmly packed light brown sugar
1 teaspoon salt
¼ teaspoon ground nutmeg
½ teaspoon ground cloves
1 container (4 ounces) candied citron
½ cup raisins
1 tablespoon sweet sherry
1 teaspoon grated lemon rind
2 envelopes active dry yeast
1 teaspoon granulated sugar
½ cup very warm water
4 eggs
5½ cups all-purpose flour
Vegetable oil
Unseasoned fine dry bread crumbs
10X (confectioners' powdered) sugar

1. Heat the milk, butter or margarine, brown sugar, salt, nutmeg and cloves, just until the butter melts, in a small saucepan over low heat. Cool to room temperature.
2. Combine the citron, raisins, sherry and lemon rind in a small bowl and allow to stand for 10 minutes, stirring several times.
3. Dissolve the yeast and the 1 teaspoon sugar in very warm water in a large bowl. ("Very warm" water should feel comfortably warm when dropped on your wrist.) Stir until well blended and allow to stand for 10 minutes, or until the mixture begins to bubble.
4. Insert the dough hook in your electric mixer, if your mixer has this feature. Beat the cooled milk mixture and the eggs into the yeast mixture until well blended.
5. Add 4 cups of the flour and beat on medium-high speed for 3 minutes, scraping down the side of the bowl several times. Or, beat by hand 300 strokes. Lower the mixer speed and gradually add the remaining flour to make a soft dough. Or, stir in the flour with a wooden spoon. Stir in the fruit and sherry mixture until evenly distributed.
6. Coat the top of the dough with the oil and cover the bowl with plastic wrap. Let rise in a warm place, away from drafts, for 2 hours, or until double in bulk.
7. Grease a 10-inch fancy tube pan well and sprinkle with the bread crumbs. Beat the dough down, spoon into the pan and cover with plastic wrap. Allow to rise in a warm place, away from drafts, for 1 hour, or until double in bulk.
8. Meanwhile, preheat the oven to moderate (350°).
9. Bake in the preheated moderate oven (350°) for 45 minutes, or until the bread is golden and hollow-sounding when tapped. Loosen the bread around the edges of the pan and invert onto a wire rack; cool completely. Wrap in heavy-duty aluminum foil, label, date and freeze. Or, wrap in a plastic bag and seal, if you plan to eat the cake within a few days. Sprinkle with the 10X (confectioners' powdered) sugar just before serving.

CHASE AWAY THE WINTER BLAHS

After the gaiety of the holiday season subsides, don't let the winter blues set in. Here are some tips for rekindling enthusiasm for the winter months ahead:

- Have a midwinter picnic and spread a red-checked tablecloth in front of the fireplace or in the den. Set the "table" with colorful paper partyware. Relive warm-weather memories by asking guests to bring home movies, slides or photos of their summer vacations.
- For a cozy and warm ambience, use bright quilts as tablecloths and herb wreaths as centerpieces. Roll up the carpet and have a country hoedown dancing to American folk music.
- Plan a fantasy winter escape with a regional or ethnic dinner as the theme. Pennsylvania Dutch, Southwest or Cajun cuisine are some of the most popular choices. Carry out the theme in accessories, decor and tableware.
- Get a jump on spring and plan a culinary trip to the islands. Decorate your house with palms and flowers and ask guests to wear a sarong or Hawaiian shirt.
- Plan a game night and invite guests to bring their favorite board games, chess, checkers, etc.
- Set up a large card table in the living room or den, and keep a 1,500-piece jigsaw puzzle in progress at all times. Family, friends or guests can enjoy adding a few pieces as they sip hot apple cider by the fire.
- Hearty winter foods taste best after a day of winter sports. Build healthy appetites by organizing skating relays, sledding competitions, cross-country skiing, winter nature walks or snowman-building contests.
- Have a "grazing" party with the entire meal made up of finger foods. Ask guests to contribute.
- Plan your spring flower or vegetable garden. You can get a head start by planting seedlings indoors.
- Consider a new spring wardrobe. Look at catalogues to decide what types of styles are available, and which will suit you best.
- Begin a family project: discover your family tree; start a new photo album (include pictures from this past Christmas!); read stories aloud to the youngsters.
- Give a room a burst of color with flowers or plants. Carnations, for example, are available year-long, last a good while, and are not too expensive.
- Get into a new exercise routine. Now's the time to whittle away the extra pounds from the holidays, before the warm weather months are here! Consider joining a class with a friend for mutual support.
- Decorate a room! Sometimes all it takes is a different tablecloth, a fresh coat of paint or a new throw rug to breathe life into a room again. Experiment with colors and fabrics to discover new looks.

Crafts Basics And Abbreviations

How To Knit

KNITTING ABBREVIATIONS AND SYMBOLS

Knitting directions are always written in standard abbreviations. They look mysterious at first, but you'll soon know them: **beg**—beginning; **bet**—between; **bl**—block; **ch**—chain; **CC**—contrasting color; **dec(s)**—decrease(s); **dp**—double-pointed;" or **in(s)**—inch(es); **incl**—inclusive; **inc(s)**—increase(s); **k**—knit; **lp(s)**—loop(s); **MC**—main color; **oz(s)**—ounces(s); **psso**—pass slipped stitch over last stitch worked; **pat(s)**—pattern(s); **p**—purl; **rem**—remaining; **rpt**—repeat; **rnd(s)**—round(s); **sc**—single crochet; **sk**—skip; **sl**—slip; **sl st**—slip stitch; **sp(s),**—space(s); **st(s)**—stitch(es); **st st**—stockinette stitch; **tog**—together, **yo**—yarn over; **pc**—popcorn stitch.

* (asterisk)—directions immediately following * are to be repeated the specified number of times indicated in addition to the first time—i.e. "repeat from * 3 times more" means 4 times in all.

( ) (parentheses)—directions should be worked as often as specified—i.e., "(k 1, k 2 tog, k 3) 5 times" means to work what is in ( ) 5 times in all.

THE BASIC STITCHES

Get out your needles and yarn, and slowly read your way through this special section. Practice the basic stitches illustrated here as you go along. Once you know them, you're ready to start knitting.

Casting On: This puts the first row of stitches on the needle. Measure off about two yards of yarn (or about an inch for each stitch you are going to cast on). Make a slip knot at this point by making a medium-size loop of yarn; then pull another small loop through it. Place the slip knot on one needle and pull one end gently to tighten (FIG. 1).

FIG. 1

• Hold the needle in your right hand. Hold both strands of yarn in the palm of your left hand securely but not rigidly. Slide your left thumb and forefinger between the two strands and spread these two fingers out so that you have formed a triangle of yarn.

Your left thumb should hold the free end of yarn, your forefinger the yarn from the ball, while the needle in your right hand holds the first stitch (FIG. 2).

FIG. 2

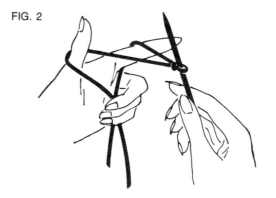

You are now in position to cast on. See ABBREVIATIONS for explanations of asterisk (*).

• Bring the needles in your right hand toward you; slip the tip of the needle under the front strand of the loop on left thumb (FIG. 3).

FIG. 3

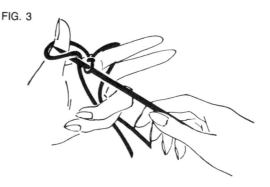

• Now, with the needle, catch the strand of yarn that is on your left forefinger. (FIG. 4).

FIG. 4

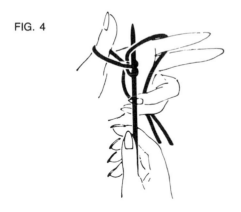

• Draw it through the thumb loop to form a stitch on the needle (FIG. 5).

FIG. 5

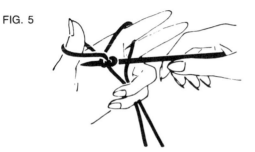

• Holding the stitch on the needle with the right index finger, slip loop off your left thumb (FIG. 6). Tighten up the stitch on the needle by pulling the freed strand back with your left thumb, bringing the yarn back into position for casting on more stitches (FIG. 2 again).

FIG. 6

• ***Do not cast on too tightly.*** Stitches should slide easily on the needle. Repeat from * until you have cast on the number of stitches specified in your instructions.

Knit Stitch (k): Hold the needle with the cast-on stitches in your left hand (FIG. 7).

FIG. 7

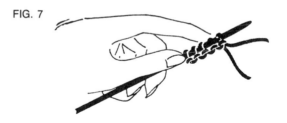

• Pick up the other needle in your right hand. With yarn from the ball in ***back*** of the work, insert the tip of the right-hand needle from ***left to right*** through the front loop of the first stitch on the left-hand needle (FIG. 8).

FIG. 8

• Holding both needles in this position with your left hand, wrap the yarn over your little finger, under your two middle fingers and over the forefingers of your right hand. Hold the yarn firmly, but loosely enough so that it will slide through your fingers as you knit. Return the right-hand needle to your right hand.
• With your right forefinger, pass the yarn under (from right to left) and then over (from left to right) the tip of the right-hand needle, forming a loop on the needle (FIG. 9).

FIG. 9

• Now draw this loop through the stitch on the left-hand needle (FIG. 10).

FIG. 10

• Slip the original stitch off the left-hand needle, leaving the new stitch on right-hand needle (FIG. 11).

FIG. 11

Keep stitches loose enough so that you can slide them along the needles, but firm enough so they do not slide when you don't want them to. Continue until you have knitted all the stitches from the left-hand needle onto the right-hand needle.

• To start the next row, pass the needle with stitches on it to the left hand, reversing it, so that it now becomes the left-hand needle.

Purl Stitch (p): Purling is the reverse of knitting. Again, keep the stitches loose enough to slide, but firm enough to work with. To purl, hold the needle with the stitches in your left hand, with the yarn in ***front*** of your work. Insert the tip of the right-hand needle from ***right to left*** through the front loop of the first stitch on the left-hand needle (FIG. 12).

FIG. 12

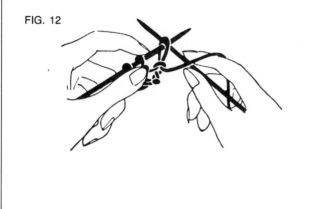

• With your right hand holding the yarn in the same manner as to knit, but in ***front*** of the needles, pass the yarn over the tip of the right-hand needle, then under it, forming a loop on the needle. (FIG. 13).

FIG. 13

• Holding the yarn firmly so that it won't slip off, draw this loop through the stitch on the left-hand needle (FIG. 14).

FIG. 14

• Slip the original stitch off the left-hand needle, leaving the new stitch on the right-hand needle. (FIG. 15).

FIG. 15

Slip Stitch (sl st): Insert the tip of the right-hand needle into the next stitch on the left-hand needle, as if to purl, unless otherwise directed. Slip this stitch off the left-hand needle onto the right, ***without working it*** (FIG. 16).

FIG. 16

Binding off: This makes a finished edge and locks the stitches securely in place. Knit (or purl) two stitches. Then, with the tip of the left-hand needle, lift the first of these two stitches over the second stitch and drop it off the tip of the right-hand needle (FIG. 17).

FIG. 17

One stitch remains on the right-hand needle, and one stitch has been bound off.

• Knit (or purl) the next stitch; lift the first stitch over the last stitch and off the tip of the needle. Again, one stitch remains on the right-hand needle, and another stitch has been bound off. Repeat from * until the required number of stitches have been bound off.

• Remember that you work two stitches to bind off one stitch. If, for example, the directions read, "k 6, bind off the next 4 sts, k 6 . . ." you must knit six stitches, then knit ***two more*** stitches before starting to bind off. Bind off four times. After the four stitches have been bound off, count the last stitch remaining on the right-hand needle as the first stitch of the next six stitches. When binding off, always knit the knitted stitches and purl the purled stitches.

• Be careful not to bind off too tightly or too loosely. The tension should be the same as the rest of the knitting.

• To end off the last stitch on the bound-off edge, if you are ending this piece of work here, cut the yarn leaving a six-inch end; pass the cut end through the remaining loop on the right-hand needle and pull snugly (FIG. 18).

FIG. 18

SHAPING TECHNIQUES

Now that you know the basics, all that's left to learn are a few techniques which will help shape whatever it is you are making.

Increasing (inc): This means adding stitches in a given area to shape your work. There are several ways to increase.

1. To increase by knitting twice into the same stitch: Knit the stitch in the usual way through the front loop (FIG. 19), but ***before*** dropping the stitch from the left-hand needle, knit ***another*** stitch on the same loop by placing the needle into the back of the stitch. (FIG. 20). Slip the original stitch off your left-hand needle. You have made two stitches from one stitch.

FIG. 19

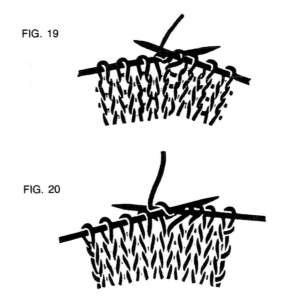

FIG. 20

2. To increase by knitting between stitches: Insert the tip of the right-hand needle under the strand of yarn ***between*** the stitch you've just worked and the following stitch; slip it onto the tip of the left-hand needle (FIG. 21).

FIG. 21

Now knit into the back of the loop (FIG. 22).

FIG. 22

3. To increase by "yarn-over" (yo): Pass the yarn over the right-hand needle after finishing one stitch and before starting the next stitch, *making an extra stitch (arrow in FIG. 23). If you are knitting,* bring the yarn under the needle to the back. *If you are purling,* wind the yarn around the needle once. On the next row, work all yarn-overs as stitches.

FIG. 23

Decreasing (dec):
This means reducing the number of stitches in a given area to shape your work. Two methods for decreasing are:
1. To decrease by knitting (FIG. 24) or purling (FIG. 25) two stitches together:

FIG. 24

FIG. 25

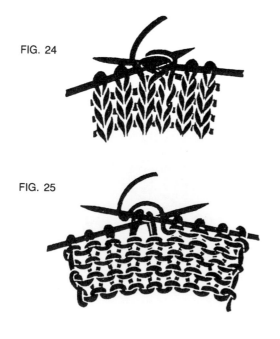

Insert the right-hand needle through the loops of two stitches on the left-hand needle at the same time, complete the stitch. This is written as "k 2 tog" or "p 2 tog."
• If you work through the *front* loops of the stitches in the usual way, your decreasing stitch will slant to the right. If you work through the *back* loops of the stitches, your decreasing stitch will slant to the left.
2. Slip 1 stitch, knit 1 and psso: Insert the right-hand needle through the stitch on the left-hand needle, but instead of working it, just slip it off onto the right-hand needle (go back to FIG. 16). Work the next stitch in the usual way. With the tip of the left-hand needle, lift the slipped stitch over the last stitch worked and off the tip of the right-hand needle (FIG. 26).

FIG. 26

Your decreasing stitch will slant to the left. This is written as "sl 1, k 1, psso."
Pass Slipped Stitch Over (psso): Slip one stitch from the left-hand needle to the right-hand needle and, being careful to keep it in position, work the next stitch. Then, with the tip of the left-hand needle, lift the slipped stitch over the last stitch and off the tip of the needle (FIG. 26).

ATTACHING THE YARN
When you end one ball of yarn or wish to change colors, begin at the start of a row and tie the new yarn with the previous yarn, making secure joining. Continue to knit or purl (FIG. 27).

FIG. 27

How To Crochet

CROCHET ABBREVIATIONS

Following is a crochet abbreviations listing, with definitions of the terms given. To help you become accustomed to abbreviations used, we have repeated them through our stitch instructions.

beg—begin, beginning; **ch**—chain; **dc**—double crochet; **dec**—decrease; **dtr**—double treble crochet; **hdc**—half double crochet; **in(s)** or ″—inch(es); **inc**—increase; **oz(s)**—ounce(s); **pat**—pattern; **pc**—picot; **rem**—remaining; **rnd**—round; **rpt**—repeat; **sc**—single crochet; **skn(s)**—skein(s); **sk**—skip; **sl st**—slip stitch; **sp**—space; **st(s)**—stitch(es); **tog**—together; **tr**—triple crochet; **work even**—continue without further increase or decrease; **yo**—yarn over; *****—repeat whatever follows * as many times as indicated; **( )**—do what is in parentheses as many times as indicated.

DIRECTIONS FOR RIGHT-HANDED AND LEFT-HANDED CROCHETERS

Most crochet stitches are started from a base of chain stitches. However, our stitches are started from a row of single crochet stitches which gives body to the sample swatches and makes practice work easier to handle. When making a specific item, follow the stitch directions as given.

Holding the crochet hook properly (see FIG. 1), start by practicing the slip knot (see FIG. 2) and base chain (see FIG. 3, page 266).

FIG. 2 THE SLIP KNOT
(BASIS FOR CHAIN STITCH)

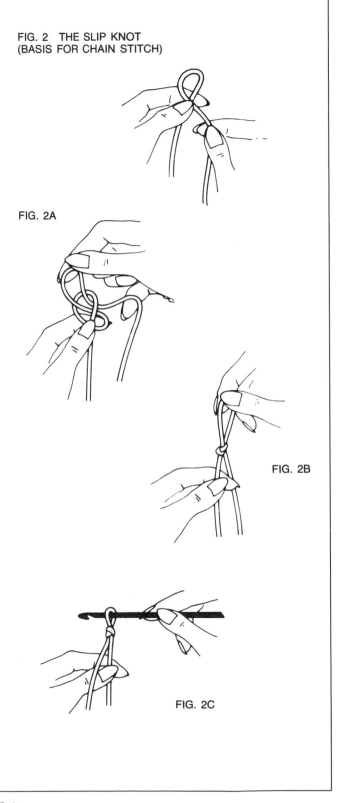

FIG. 2A

FIG. 2B

FIG. 2C

FIG. 1 HOLDING THE HOOK

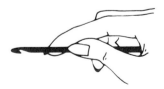

Chain Stitch (ch): Follow the steps in Fig. 3. As you make the chain stitch loops, the yarn should slide easily between your index and middle fingers. Make about 15 loops. If they are all the same size, you have maintained even tension. If uneven, rip them out by pulling on the long end of the yarn. Practice making chains and ripping out until you have a perfect chain.

For Left-handed Crocheters

Figs. 1 to 3 are for right-handed crocheters and are repeated in Figs. 1 Left to 3 Left for left-handed crocheters.

LEFT-HANDED CROCHETERS
FIGS. 1 LEFT TO 3 LEFT

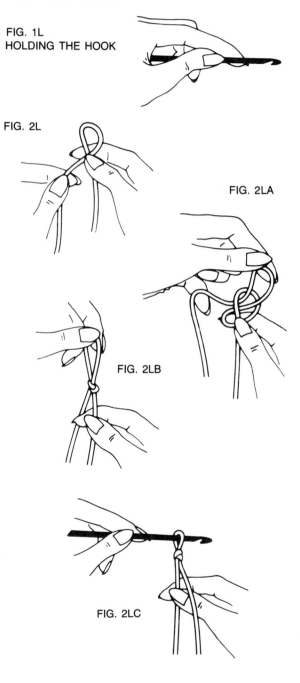

FIG. 1L
HOLDING THE HOOK

FIG. 2L

FIG. 2LA

FIG. 2LB

FIG. 2LC

FIG. 3   CHAIN STITCH (CH)

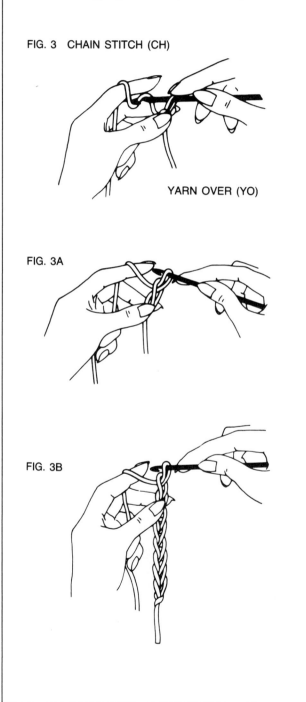

YARN OVER (YO)

FIG. 3A

FIG. 3B

CHAIN STITCH (CH)

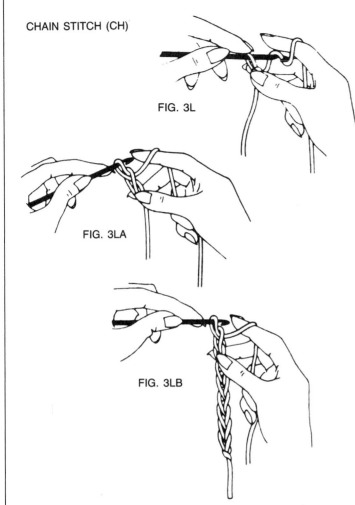

FIG. 3L

FIG. 3LA

FIG. 3LB

**FIG. 4
SINGLE CROCHET (SC)**

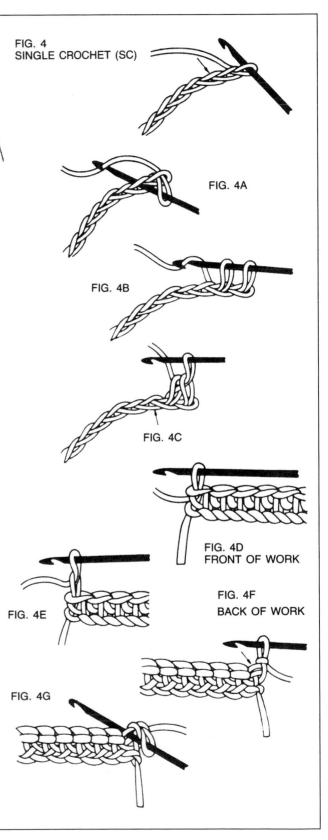

FIG. 4A

FIG. 4B

FIG. 4C

FIG. 4D
FRONT OF WORK

FIG. 4E

FIG. 4F
BACK OF WORK

FIG. 4G

From here on, we won't be showing hands—just the hook and stitches. Left-handed crocheters can use all the following right-handed illustrations by simply turning the book upside down and using a mirror (with backstand) that will reflect the left-handed version.

Single Crochet (sc): Follow the steps in FIG. 4. To practice, make a 20-loop chain (this means 20 loops in addition to the slip knot). Turn the chain, as shown, and insert the hook in the second chain from the hook (see arrow) to make the first sc stitch. Yarn over (yo); for the second stitch, see the next arrow. Repeat to the end of the chain. Because you started in the second chain from the hook, you end up with only 19 sc. To add the 20th stitch, chain one (called a turning chain) and pull the yarn through. Now turn your work around (the "back" is now facing you) and start the second row of sc in the first stitch of the previous row (at the arrow). Make sure your hook goes under both of the strands at the top of the stitch. Don't forget to make a ch 1 turning chain at the end before turning your work. Keep practicing until your rows are perfect.

Ending Off: Follow the steps in FIG. 5. To finish off your crochet, cut off all but 6″ of yarn and end off as shown. (To "break off and fasten," follow the same procedure.)

FIG. 5 ENDING OFF

FIG. 5A

FIG. 6C

FIG. 6D

FIG. 6E

FIG. 7

Double Crochet (dc): Follow the steps in FIG. 6. To practice, ch 20, then make a row of 20 sc. Now, instead of a ch 1, you will make a ch 3. Turn your work, yo and insert the hook in the second stitch of the previous row (at the arrow), going under both strands at the top of the stitch. Pull the yarn through. You now have three loops on the hook. Yo and pull through the first two, then yo and pull through the remaining two — one double crochet (dc) made. Continue across the row, making a dc in each stitch (st) across. Dc in the top of the turning chain (see arrow in FIG. 7). Ch 3. Turn work. Dc in second stitch on the previous row and continue as before.

FIG. 6
DOUBLE CROCHET (DC)

FIG. 6A

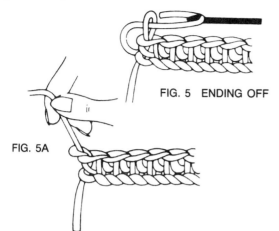

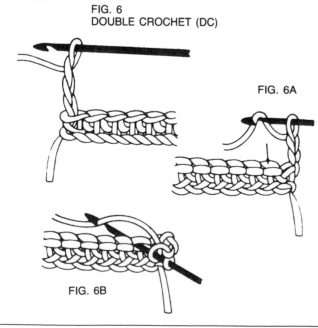

FIG. 6B

Note: You may also start a row of dc on a base chain (omitting the sc row). In this case, insert the hook in the fourth chain from the hook, instead of the second (see FIG. 8).

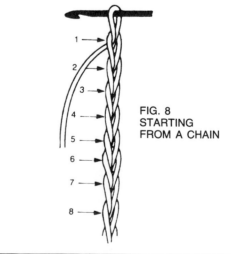

1
2
3
4
5
6
7
8

FIG. 8
STARTING
FROM A CHAIN

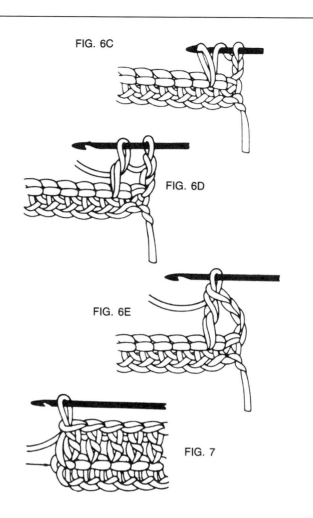

Slip Stitch (sl st): Follow the steps in FIG. 9. This is a utility stitch you will use for joining, shaping and ending off. After you chain and turn, *do not yo.* Just insert the hook into the *first* stitch of the previous row (see FIG. 9A), and pull the yarn through the stitch, then right through the loop on the hook—sl st made.

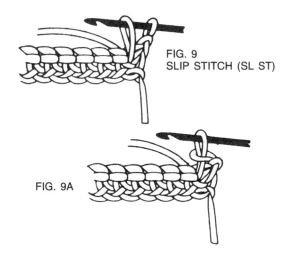

FIG. 9
SLIP STITCH (SL ST)

FIG. 9A

Half Double Crochet (hdc): Follow the steps in FIG. 10 and 10A. To practice, make a chain and a row of sc. Ch 2 and turn; yo. Insert the hook in the second stitch, as shown; yo and pull through to make three loops on the hook. Yo and pull the yarn through *all* three loops at the same time—hdc made. This stitch is used primarily as a transitional stitch from an sc to a dc. Try it and see—starting with sc's, then an hdc and then dc's.

FIG. 10
HALF DOUBLE CROCHET
(HDC)

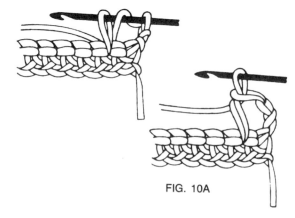

FIG. 10A

TECHNIQUES OF CROCHETING:

Now that you have practiced and made sample squares of all the basic stitches, you are ready to learn about adding and subtracting stitches to change the length of a row whenever it's called for. This is achieved by increasing (inc) and decreasing (dec).

To increase (inc): Just make two stitches in the same stitch in the previous row (see arrow in FIG. 11). The technique is the same for any kind of stitch.

FIG. 11 INCREASING (INC) FOR SINGLE CROCHET

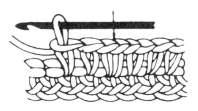

To decrease (dec) for single-crochet (sc): Yo and pull the yarn through two stitches to make three loops on the hook (see steps in FIG. 12). Pull the yarn through all the loops at once—dec made. Continue in regular stitches.

FIG. 12 DECREASING (DEC)
FOR SINGLE CROCHET

FIG. 12A

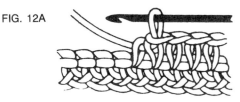

To decrease for double crochet (dc): In a dc row, make the next stitch and stop when you have two loops on the hook. Now yo and make a dc in the next stitch. At the point where you have three loops on the hook, pull yarn through all loops at the same time. Finish the row with regular dc.

Embroidery Stitch Guide

BLANKET STITCH

Work from left to right, with the point of the needle and the edge of the work toward you. The edge of the fabric can be folded under or left raw. Secure the thread and bring out below the edge. For the first and each succeeding stitch, insert the needle through the fabric from the right side and bring it out at the edge. Keeping the thread from the previous stitch *under* the point of the needle, draw the needle and thread through, forming a stitch over the edge. The stitch size and spacing can be the same or varied.

BLANKET STITCH

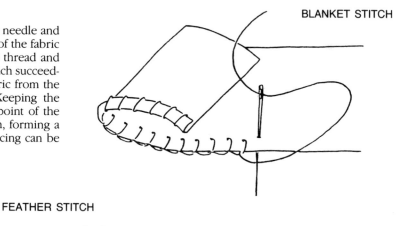

CHAIN STITCH

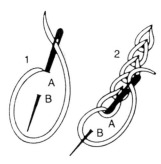

FEATHER STITCH

FLY STITCH

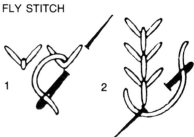

FRENCH KNOT

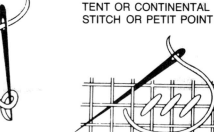

TENT OR CONTINENTAL STITCH OR PETIT POINT

CROSS STITCH

BLIND STITCH

INTERLOCKING GOBELIN STITCH

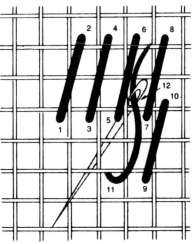

How To Enlarge Designs

If the design is not already marked off in squares, make a tracing of it. Mark the tracing off in squares: For a small design, make squares ¼″; for larger designs, use ½″ or 2″ squares, or the size indicated in the directions. Decide the size of enlargement. On another sheet of tracing paper, mark off the same number of squares that are on the design or original tracing. For example, to make your design, each new square must be 6 times larger than the original. Copy the outline from your original tracing to the new one, square by square. Use dressmaker's carbon and a tracing wheel to transfer the design onto the material you are decorating.

SLANTED GOBELIN STITCH (worked vertically)

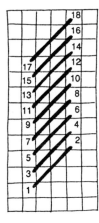

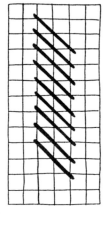

LONG AND SHORT STITCH

STRAIGHT STITCH

MOSAIC STITCH

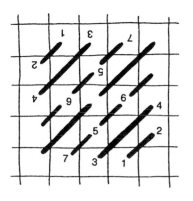

SCOTCH STITCH

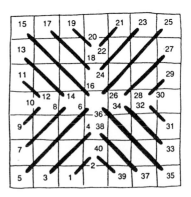

SCOTCH STITCH VARIATION

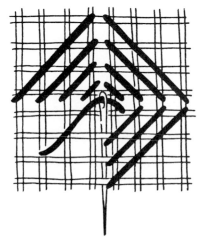

Materials Shopping Guide

Some of the projects in this volume suggest using specific manufacturers' products.
Here's a list of those products with the names and addresses of their manufacturers.

PROJECTS AND PRODUCTS

Chapter II *(page 60):* Glimmer and Picette ribbons in Ribbon Pine Cone from Lion Ribbon Co.

Chapter III *(pages 76-81):*
Plaid fabrics (pillow, tree ornaments and gift boxes), "Danflair Tartans Mylar" by Dan River, Inc.; tree and green garland by American Tree and Wreath, available at fine department stores nationwide; gold wreaths and star (used as tree top) by American Decorations, available at fine department stores nationwide; candles and gift wrap by Hallmark Cards Inc., available at Hallmark stores nationwide; metallic gift box tie decorations, "Starburst Spray" and "Stretch Loops," also metallic stretch trim on tree ornaments, "Sparkle," all by Stribbons; poinsettias furnished by Paul Ecke Poinsettia Ranch, available through your local florist or floral merchant; gold garland by F. C. Young & Co. Inc., available at variety stores; plaid ribbons by C.M. Offray & Son, Inc.; panda and monkey hand puppets from the Gingerbread House; Styrofoam® balls (for tree ornaments) from Modern-Miltex Corp.; jingle bells from LeeWards Creative Crafts Center, available at all Lee-Wards stores; adhesive used on plaid fabric-covered boxes, "Scotch" Craft Mount spray adhesive, Minnesota Mining & Mfg. Co.

Chapter III *(pages 82-84):* "Daisy" #183-4039-030 Lace in White Lace Christmas Tree Ornaments is from Wright's *Home Sewing Co.*; fabric stiffener is Aleene's Fabric Stiffener & Fabric Draping Liquid (available at fabric stores); gold-edge white ribbon #2343 comb. ⅛"-wide from C.M. Offray and Son, Inc.; thick craft glue is Aleene's Thick Designer Tacky Glue (available at fabric stores).

Chapter III *(pages 90-91):*
Gold Picot Braid #230 in Brocade Victorian Stocking and Swiss Lace #9 Color Gold in Lace/Taffeta Stocking, are both from Lion Ribbon Co.

Chapter IV *(pages 132-134):* All ribbon in Organdy and Eyelet projects from C.M. Offray and Son.

Chapter V *(page 166-169)* (all the Wild West, Palomino Pony and Lariat tree ornaments including wreath)*:*
Lariat ornaments: Burlap fabric, "Champion" (48/50" wide) in natural, from Lawrence Textiles, Inc.; white glue, Velverette, by Slomans Laboratories; suede ribbon (Style #8259 in camel, ⅛" wide) by WRF Ribbon Corp.; manila rope (¼"), by Lehigh Cordage; **Wild West ornaments:** Red and natural burlap ribbon (6" wide), by Lion Ribbon Co.; fiber fill, Poly-fil® by Fairfield Processing Corp.; white glue, Velverette, by Slomans Laboratories; red sequins (5mm), by Holiday Handicrafts, Inc.; suede ribbon (Style #8259 in camel, ⅛" wide), by WFR Ribbon Corp. **Palomino Pony ornaments:** Burlap ribbon (6" wide, red and natural) by Lion Ribbon Co.; burlap fabric, "Champion" (48/50" wide) in natural and Chinese red, by Lawrence Textiles, Inc.; fiberfill, Poly-fil®, by Fairfield Processing Corp.; sequins (5mm), by Holiday Handicrafts, Inc.; bandanna ribbon (Style #7405, 1-⅞" wide) and suede ribbon (Style #8259, ⅛" wide in red and camel), by WFR Ribbon Corp. **Palomino pillows:** Burlap fabric, "Champion" (48/50" wide) in natural and Chinese red, by Lawrence Textiles, Inc.; bandanna ribbon (1-⅞" wide), by WFR Ribbon Corp.; fusible interfacing, Dura-Bond® (Style #808, 18" wide) by Pellon Corp.; buttons (for eyes), by Streamline Industries; braided piping cord (red-128), by J.&P. Coats, white glue, Velverette, by Slomans Laboratories; fiberfill, Poly-fil®, by Fairfield Processing Corp.
Lariat wall wreath: Wire wreath frame (14" diameter), available from craft and floral supply shops; manila rope (¼), by Lehigh Cordage; bandanna ribbon (Style #7405, 1-⅞" wide), by WFR Ribbon Corp. **Bandanna wreath:** Styrofoam® wreath (18" diameter), by Custom Foam; bandanna ribbon (Style #7405, 1-⅞" wide), by WFR Ribbon Corp.; manila rope (¼" diameter), by Lehigh Cordage. **Wild West stockings:** Burlap fabric, ("Champion" 48/50" wide, in natural and Chinese red), by Lawrence Textiles, Inc.; bandanna fabric from "Heirloom Prints" line (Style #9-1110, color 182, 44/45" wide), by Ely & Walker; fusible interfacing, Dura-Bond® (Style #808, 18" wide), by Pellon Corp.; burlap ribbon (6" wide, red and natural), by Lion Ribbon Co.; bandanna ribbon (Style #7405, ⅝" wide and 1-⅞" wide), by WFR Ribbon Corp.; white glue, Velverette, by Slomans Laboratories; sequins (8mm), by Holiday Handicrafts. Inc. **Hobby Horse head:** Burlap fabric, "Champion" (48/50" wide in natural), by Lawrence Textiles, Inc.; fusible interfacing, Dura-Bond®, (Style #808, 18") by Pellon Corp.; batting, Poly-Fil® Extra-Loft®, by Fairfield Processing Corp.; bandanna ribbon (⅞" wide), by WFR Ribbon Corp.; Velcro® self-gripping fastener, by Talon American; buttons (for eyes), by Streamline Industries. **Christmas**

Tree, wrappings, etc. "Dresden Spruce" (artificial and flame retardant, Style #84-1143-651) by American Tree Co.; "Mini-lites" by NOMA-Worldwide, Inc.; glass ball ornaments, "Candy Glaze" in red by Rauch Industries; candy canes and multi-color canes, by Bobs® Candies, Inc., rainbow canes by Asher Bros.; miniature wooden baskets in red and natural by Texas Basket Co.; "Watermelon" popcorn from Jack's Corn Crib; red velvet bows, "Bow-Tyes" by Lion Ribbon Co.; wrapping paper in solid red and herringbone totes, by Sample House; brown "Kraft" paper by Dennison.

Chapter V *(page 177-179):* Door and shingles in dollhouse from Illinois Hobbycrafts, Inc.
Furniture and accessories from Federal Smallwares Corp. (send $1 for catalog); needle-point rugs from Create Your Own (send for free color catalog); floor coverings and wall coverings from Tiny Dollhouse (send $3 for catalog).

Chapter 7 *(page 7):* Wicker bells in Glimmering Gold Centerpiece from Pier I Imports.

MANUFACTURERS AND ADDRESSES

American Decorations
1107 Broadway, New York, NY 10010
American Tree and Wreath
1107 Broadway, New York, NY 10010
Asher Bros. (Div. of Beatrice Foods Co.)
1815 Gilford Ave., New Hyde Park, NY 11040
Bobs® Candies Inc.
P.O. Box 3170, Albany, GA 31708
C.M. Offray & Son, Inc.
261 Madison Ave., New York, NY 10016
or
Route 24, Chester, NJ 07930
Create Your Own
Hickory Rd., Milford, NJ 08848
Custom Foam
Ludington, MI 49431
Dan River, Inc.
111 W. 40th St., New York, NY 10018
Dennison
275 Wyman St., Waltham, MA 02154
Ely & Walker
823 E. Holmes Rd., Memphis, TN 38116
Fairfield Processing Corp.
88 Rose Hill Ave., Danbury, CT 06810
F. C. Young & Co. Inc.
322 Howell St., Bristol, PA 19007
Federal Smallwares Corp.
Dept. FC, 85 Fifth Ave., New York, NY 10003
Gingerbread House
9 Christopher St., New York, NY 10014
Hallmark Cards Inc.
Kansas City, MO 64141

Holiday Handicrafts, Inc.
P.O. Box 470, Winsted, CT 06098
Illinois Hobbycrafts, Inc.
Mail Order Div., 605 North Broadway, Aurora, IL 60505
Jack's Corn Crib
524 W. 34 St., NY, NY 10001
Lawrence Textiles, Inc.
1412 Broadway, NY, NY 10018
LeeWards Creative Crafts Center
Retail Division
1210 St. Charles Rd., Elgin, IL 60120
Lebigh Cordage
Allentown, PA 18105
Lion Ribbon Co.
100 Metro Way, Secaucus, NJ 07094
Minnesota Mining & Mfg. Co.
3M Center, St. Paul, MN 55101
Modern-Miltex Corp.
280 E. 134th St., Bronx, NY 10454
NOMA-Worldwide, Inc.
200 Fifth Ave., NY, NY 10010
Paul Ecke Poinsettia Ranch
Encinitas, CA 92024,
Pellon Corp.
119 W. 40th St., NY, NY 10018
Pier I Imports
302 Commerce St., Suite 600, Fort Worth, TX 76102
Rauch Industries
PO Box 609, U.S. Highway 321 South, Gastonia, NC 28052
Sample House
4722 Bengal, Dallas, TX 75235
Slomans Laboratories
1000 Zeckendorf Blvd., Garden City, NY 11530
Streamline Industries
234 W. 39th St., NY, NY 10018
Stribbons
99 Powerhouse Rd., Roslyn Heights, NY 11577
Talon American
Consumer Products Div., High Ridge Park, Stamford, CT 06905
Texas Basket Co.
Box 1110, Jacksonville, TX 75766
Tiny Dollhouse
231 E. 53rd St., New York, NY 10022
WFR Ribbon Corp.
115 W. 18th St., NY, NY 10011
Wright's Home Sewing Co.
South St., West Warren, MA 01092

Index

Italicized page numbers refer to photographs.

• A •

Acorn Squash Rings and Green Beans, *2-3,* 4, 6, 9
Afghan, Log Cabin, *49,* 48-50
Aioli, 144-148
almond
  Apricot, Truffles, 217
  Cheese Spread, 257
  Crescents, *111,* 115
anchovy
  Egg Filling, 257
  Stuffed Eggs, 144-149
angel
  Flying, *125*
  Sugar, 202
"Antique" Lace Dolls, 88-*89*
appetizer
  Sun-Dried Tomato, *234-235,* 242, *243,* 244, 247
  Warm Shrimp, Salad, 102, 104-105
apple
  Cream Cheese Pie, 102, 104, 109
  Mulled Cider with, Brandy, *17,* 16-18, 21
  N' Berries Centerpiece, *35*
  Oatmeal Bread, 233
  Pecan Stuffing, *24-25*
  Pecan, Tarts, 254-*255,* 256, 258
  Sugar-Dusted, Pie, 16, 18, 22-*23*
appliqué
  Freezer Paper Method of, 101
  Monkey Shines, *190*-191
  Reindeer, *190*
apricot
  Almond Truffles, 217
  Mustard Chicken Wings, 223
  Orange Chutney, 38
  Pecan Rice Stuffing, *24-25*
apron
  Hostess, & Tea Towel, *135*
  Organdy, *133,* 132-134
artichoke
  Curried, Bites, *234-235,* 242-*243,* 244, 246
  Marinated, Hearts, 217
Asparagus, Buttered, *103,* 102-104, 106-107
Aubergine Provençal, *145,* 144-147
Austrian Hussar's Buns, *118-119,* 151-152, 155
Autumn Squash Bisque, *2-3,* 4, 6, 7

• B •

Baby Bunting, *182*-183
Baked Baby Tomatoes, *103,* 102-104, 106
Banana Cake, *164*-165
Basket of "Berries," *214*-215
Beans, Green, with Lemon Vodka Butter, *17,* 16-18, 20
bear
  Bulletin Board, *180*-181
  Christmas, 85-86
  Gotcha Framed!, *180*-181
  Teddy, Planter, *180*
Beary Christmas, 85-86
beautiful
  Ball, *121*-122
  Bay Window, *58*
beef
  Regal Roast, *103,* 102-105
  Roast, Canapés, 223
Bells 'N Ribbons Ball, *213,* 215
Beribboned Napkin, *133*-134
Best Chocolate Cookies, 200
Bird, Flying, *123*
Blueberry, Spicy, Muffins, *231*-232
Blue Cheese Spread, 217
Bonnie Scotland Stocking, *80*
Brace of Roasted Capons, *17,* 16-19
brandied
  Chestnut Stuffing, 26
  Golden Fruitcakes, *40*-41
brandy
  Frosting, 154
  Glaze, 41
  Mulled Cider with Apple, *17,* 16-18, 21
bread, 232
  Apple-Oatmeal, 233
  and Butter Sandwiches, 254-*255,* 256
  Candied Orange Tea, *255,* 256-257
  Coriander Gingerbread, *139*-140
  Country Nut, *231*-232
  Cranberry, *2-3,* 4, 6, 11
  Date and Nut, 254-*255,* 256-257
  No-Yeast Stollen, *139,* 141
  Pumpkin, 233
Broth, Turkey, 28
Bulletin Board, *180*-181
butter
  Cream Frosting, 165
  Dill, 245

Green Beans with Lemon Vodka, *17,* 16-18, 20
Vanilla Pear, 38-39
buttered
  Asparagus, *103,* 102-104, 106-107
  Crumbs, 9
Butterscotch Nut Bells, 198
Buttery Crisps, *111*-112

• C •

cake, 258
  Banana, *164*-165
  Brandied Golden Fruitcakes, *40*-41
  California Fruitcake, 42
  Cherry Ring, 44
  Continental Party Loaf, *118-119,* 151-154
  Dark Fruitcake Batter, 42
  Georgia Fruitcake, 45
  Gingerbread Boy, *164*
  Hawaiian Ring, 43
  Irish Fruitcake, 45
  Lemon-Glazed Persimmon Bars, 224-*225*
  Light Fruitcake Batter, 41-42
  New England Raisin, 254-*255,* 256, 258-259
  Old World Fruitcake, 43
  Rigó Jancsi Torte, *118-119,* 151-153
  Southern Fruitcake, 43
  Sunshine Fruitcake, 44-45
  Yankee Fruitcake, 44
California Fruitcake, 42
canapés, 246
  Deviled Ham, 223
  Roast Beef, 223
candied
  Carrots, *17,* 16-18, 21
  Nuts, *139*-140
  Orange Tea Bread, *255,* 256-257
  Yams, *2-3,* 4, 6, 9-10
candy
  Apricot Almond Truffles, 217
  Chocolate Truffles, 142-143
  Double Chocolate Chunks, 229
  Krispies Treat, 229
  Layered Mint Melts, 228-229
  Peanut Butter Kisses, 142
  Peanut Butter Munchies, 202·

canning tips, 39
cards, 66
    Christmas, *197*
    Quilted Greetings, *197*
    Quiz, 70-73
carrot
    Candied, *17*, 16-18, 21
    Pecan Muffins, 230-*231*
Cashews, Dry-Sautéed, 223
Caviar Silver Dollars, 223
centerpiece
    Apples 'N Berries, *35*
    Cinnamon Stick, *31,* 30-32
    Gleaming Elegance, 238-*239*
    Glimmering Gold, 236-*237*
    Midas Touch, *238*
    Punch Bowl, *34*
Champagne, Pink, Punch, 250-*251*
cheese
    Almond, Spread, 257
    Blue, Spread, 217
    Dutch, Twists, 138-*139*
    Grilled Turkey, and Tomato
        Sandwiches, 27
    Nutty Goat, Logs, 223
    Pimiento, *219,* 218-220
    Pineapple, Ball, *234-235,* 242, 244,
        249
    Pistachio, Ball, 218, *222*
    Turkey in Cheddar, Sauce, 27
cherry
    Orange-Glazed, Pie, 16, 18, 22-*23*
    Ring, 44
chicken
    Apricot Mustard Wings, 223
    Brace of Roasted Capons, *17,* 16-19
    Chinese, Wings, 218-*219,* 221
    Oriental, Liver Spread, 217
Chinese Chicken Wings, 218-*219,* 221
chocolate
    Amaretti Sandwiches, 217
    Best, Cookies, 200
    Clever, Pie, 226
    Covered Pretzels, 202
    Double, Chunks, 229
    Fudge Sauce, 203
    Rocky Road Fudge, 203
    Royal, Frosting, 153
    Shaved, 156
    Thumbprints, 110-*111*
    Truffles, 142-143
Christmas
    Book, 97
    Card Quiz, 70-73
    Cards, *197*

Cheer Table Set, 210-*211*
    Cutouts, 198
    In-The-Country Quilt, *99*-101
    tree tips, 58
Chutney, Apricot Orange, 38
cider
    Hot Mulled, 253
    Mulled, with Apple Brandy, *17,* 16-18, 21
Cinnamon Stick Centerpiece & Place
    Cards, *31,* 30-32
Clever Chocolate Pie, 226
Cocktail Meatballs, 223
Cocoa, Creamy, Punch, *118-119,* 151-
    152, 156
Colonial Doll House, *177-179*
Continental Party Loaf, *118-119,* 151-154
cookie, 114, 224
    Almond Crescents, *111,* 115
    And Toys Party, *161,* 163
    Austrian Hussar's Buns, *118-119,*
        151-152, 155
    Best Chocolate, 200
    Butterscotch Nut Bells, 198
    Buttery Crisps, *111*-112
    Chocolate Amaretti Sandwiches, 217
    Chocolate Thumbprints, 110-*111*
    Christmas Cutouts, 198
    Florentines, *118-119,* 151-152, 155
    French Jelly Hearts, *111,* 116
    Fruit and Nut Lebkuchen, *111,* 115
    Fruitcake Fingers, *111,* 113-114
    Holiday Sugar, 200-201
    Italian Biscotti, 142
    Jelly Diagonals, *111,* 114
    Kris Kringle, *111,* 113
    Lemon Wafers, 229
    Molasses Jacks, *111*-112
    Nutty Brownie, *111,* 117
    Orange Wreaths, 201
    Pecan Bourban Balls, *111,* 116
    Pecan Wafers, 117
    Raspberry Crisps, *118-119,* 151-152,
        154
    Spicy Molasses, 201
    Spritz, *118-119,* 151-152, 154
    Sugar Angels, 202
    Swedish Rosettes, 143
Cookie Cutter Potholders, *214*-215
Coriander Gingerbread, *139*-140
Corn, Southern, Sticks, *17,* 16-18, 21
Cornbread, Cranberry, Stuffing, *24*-25
Country
    Accents, 98
    Charmers, 98
    Christmas-In-The, Quilt, *99*-101

Nut Bread, *231*-232
    Village, 94-*95*
cranberry, 11
    Bread, *2-3,* 4, 6, 11
    Cornbread Stuffing, *24*-25
    Fizz Punch, 252
    Ice, 16, 18, 22-*23*
    Orange Liqueur, 36-37
    Orange Relish, *2-3,* 4, 6, 10
    Pear Tart, 102, 104, 108
    Reduced-Calorie, Pear Tart, 102,
        104, 108-109
    Wine Mold, *103,* 102-104, 107-108
cream
    Mocha, Filling, 153
    of Turkey Soup, 29
Creamed Onions, *2-3,* 4, 6, 9
Creamy Cocoa Punch, *118-119,* 151-
    152, 156
Crèche, Origami, *128*
crochet
    Edging, *47,* 46-48
    Kangaroo, And Baby Too! *175-176*
    Log Cabin Afghan, *49,* 48-50
    Look of Lace Tablecloth, *53,* 52-55
Crocheted Edging, *47,* 46-48
Cucumber, Piquant Stuffed, Cups, *234-
    235,* 242, 244-246
curried
    Artichoke Bites, *234-235,* 242-*243,*
        244, 246
    Pumpkin Soup, *17,* 16-18
curry
    Dip, 223
    Surprises, 218-*219,* 221
    Turkey and Broccoli with, Sauce, 28
Curtain, Santa Garland &, Tiebacks, *130*

D

Dahlia Ball, *127*
Dark Fruitcake Batter, 42
Date and Nut Bread, 254-*255,* 256-257
Deck The Hall!, *212*
decorations, 66-67, 98, 186, 189, 131, 213
    Basket of "Berries", *214-215*
    Christmas Cheer Table Set, 210-*211*
    Cookie Cutter Potholders, *214*-215
    Deck The Hall!, *212*
    Here Comes Santa Claus! Quilt-Block,
        204-205
    Holiday Lights, *215*
    Kissing Ball, *98*
    Kitchen Spruce-Up, *214*
    Swans A-Swimming, 60-*61*

Deviled Ham Canapés, 223
Dill Butter, 245
dip
    Aioli, 144-148
    Aubergine Provençal, *145,* 144-147
    Curry, 223
    Harlequin, 218-*219,* 221
    Tapenade, 218, *222*-223
doll
    "Antique" Lace, 88-*89*
    Colonial, House, *177-179*
    Eddie The Elf, *185*-188
    Gingerbread, & Ornaments, *158-159,*
        160
Doorstop, Village, *95*
double
    Chocolate Chunks, 229
    Wedding Ring Pillow, *51*-52
Dove of Peace, *94*
Dressing, Russian, 4, 6, 10
Dry-Sautéed Cashews, 223
Dutch Cheese Twists, 138-*139*

E

Eddie The Elf, *185*-188
edging
    Crocheted, *47,* 46-48
    Simple Tatted Ring, 86
egg
    Anchovy Filling, 257
    Anchovy-Stuffed, 144-149
    Mexican Deviled, *234-235,* 242,
        244-245
    Phyllo, Rolls, *234-235,* 242, 244, 248
Eggnog, Espresso, 151-152, 156
endive
    Gorgonzola-Stuffed, *234-235,* 242,
        243-244, 247
    Salade Mélangée aux Noix, 144, 146,
        148
entertaining, 150, 157
    Childrens Party Pointers, 169
Espresso Eggnog, 151-152, 156
etiquette, 68, 240-241
Eucalyptus Wreath, *131*
eyelet
    Pillow, 132-*133*
    Place Mat, *133*-134

F

fan
    Lace, 82, *83-84*
    Ribbon, *62*

felt
    Folding Chair Slipcover, *211*
    Here Comes Santa Claus! Quilt-Block
        Decorations, *204-205*
    Tablecloth, 210-*211*
filling
    Fluffy, and Frosting, 114
    Mocha Cream, 153
Florentines, *118-119,* 151-152, 155
Fluffy Filling and Frosting, 114
Fluted Mushrooms, *103,* 102-104, 107
flying
    Angel, *125*
    Bird, *123*
Folding Chair Slipcover, *211*
folk art
    Frames, *96*
    Ornaments, 92-*93*
    Tree Skirt, 92-*93*
frames
    Bear's Gotcha Framed!, *180*-181
    Folk Art, *96*
    "Picture This", *137*
French Jelly Hearts, *111,* 116
Fresh Rose Wreath, 32
Fried Rice Patties, *234-235,* 242, 244, 248
frosting
    Brandy, 154
    Butter Cream, 165
    Fluffy Filling and, 114
    Royal, 165
    Royal Chocolate, 153
    Royal Rum, 45
fruit
    and Nut Lebkuchen, *111,* 115
    Mixed, and Yogurt Pie, 226
fruitcake, 43, 44
    Brandied Golden, *40*-41
    California, 42
    Cherry Ring, 44
    Dark, Batter, 42
    Fingers, *111,* 113-114
    Georgia, 45
    Hawaiian Ring, 43
    Irish, 45
    Light, Batter, 41-42
    Old World, 43
    Southern, 43
    Sunshine, 44-45
    Yankee, 44
fudge
    Chocolate, Sauce, 203
    Homemade, Sauce, 143
    Rocky Road, 203
    Rum Raisin, Sauce, 217

G

garland, 213
    Santa, & Curtain Tiebacks, *130*
Georgia Fruitcake, 45
Giblet Gravy, *2-3,* 4, 6, 8
gift, 66-67, 210, 212
    Box Ornament, *216*
    Last-Minute Food, 217
    Mailing, 64-65
    Wrapping, 62, 63, 216
gingerbread, 164
    Boy (cake), *164*
    Coriander, *139*-140
    Dolls & Ornaments, *158-159,* 160
    House Ornaments, *158-159,* 163
    Spicy Petit Fours, 217
    Stockings, *158-159,* 162
    Tree Skirt, *158-159,* 162
glaze
    Brandy, 41
    Dark Fruitcake, 42
    Honey 42
    Orange, Cherry Pie, 16, 18, 22-*23*
    Snowy, 115
Gleaming Elegance, 238-*239*
Glimmering Gold Centerpiece, 236-*237*
Gorgonzola-Stuffed Endive, *234-235,*
    242-*243,* 244, 247
Granola Snack, 203
gravy, 8
    for Roasted Capons, 18-19
    Giblet, *2-3,* 4, 6, 8
    Rich Pan, 102-105
green beans
    Acorn Squash Rings and, *2-3,* 4, 6, 9
    with Lemon Vodka Butter, *17,* 16-20
Grilled Turkey, Cheese and Tomato
    Sandwiches, 27

H

ham
    and Cucumber Spread, 257
    Deviled, Canapés, 223
    Roll-Ups, 223
Harlequin Dip, 218-*219,* 221
Hawaiian Ring, 43
heart
    ornament, *121*-122
    Shelf, 96-97
    Sweet, *85,* 84-86
Heavenly Pineapple Pie, 226
Here Comes Santa Claus! Quilt-Block
    Decorations, *204-205*

Highland Ribbon Ornament, *80*
Hobby Horse, *167,* 170
holiday Hints, 66-67
    Lights, *215*
    plant care, 67
    Sugar Cookies, 200-201
Home Sweet Home Sampler, *85,* 87
homemade
    Fudge Sauce, 143
    Pastry, 23
honey
    Glaze, 42
    Wheat Muffins, 230-*231*
Hostess Apron & Tea Towel, *135*
Hot Mulled Cider, 253
Hydrangea Wreath, 32-*33*

• I •

ice
    Block, 252
    Cranberry, 16, 18, 22-*23*
    Strawberry, Ring, 252
Icicle Magic, 58-*59*
Irish Fruitcake, 45
Italian Biscotti, 142

• J •

jelly
    Diagonals, *111,* 114
    French, Hearts, *111,* 116
Jewelry, Paper Bead, 194, *196*

• K •

Kangaroo, And Baby Too!, *175*-176
Kissing Ball, *98*
Kitchen Spruce-Up, *214*
knitting
    Baby Bunting, *182*-183
    Snowflake Sweater Set, *185,* 184-186
Kris Kringle Cookies, *111,* 113
Krispies Treat, 229

• L •

lace
    And Taffeta Stocking, *90*-91
    "Antique", Dolls, 88-*89*
    Chains, 82, *83-84*
    Fans, 82, *83-84*
    Nosegay Cones, 82, *83-84*
    Patchwork, Stocking, 84-*85*

    Rosettes, *83-84*
    White, Ornaments, 82, *83-84*
lariat
    Ornament, *167*-168
    Wreath, *171*
Layered Mint Melts, 228-229
lemon
    Ginger Curd, *139*-140
    Glazed Persimmon Bars, 224-*225*
    Green Beans with, Vodka Butter, *17,*
        16-18, 20
    Lime Mustard, 217
    Luscious, Pie, 228
    Party Tarts, 254-*255,* 256, 258
    Wafers, 229
Light Fruitcake Batter, 41-42
lights
    Beautiful Bay Window, *58*
    Holiday, *215*
    Icicle Magic, 58-*59*
Liqueur, Cranberry Orange, 36-37
Lobster Mousse, *219,* 218-220
Log Cabin Afghan, *49,* 48-50
Lollipop Ornaments, *216*
Look of Lace Tablecloth, *53,* 52-55
Luscious Lemon Pie, 228

• M •

mailing, 64-65, 141
marinated
    Artichoke Hearts, 217
    Sun-Dried Tomato Appetizers, *234-*
        235, 242-*243,* 247
    Vegetables, *2-3,* 4, 6, 10
Mashed Potato Soufflé, *17,* 16-18, 20-21
meatballs
    Cocktail, 223
    Sausage Balls à l'Orange, *234-235,*
        242-*243,* 244, 247
Melba Toast, *145,* 144-147
Mexican Deviled Eggs, *234-235,* 242,
    244-245
microwave
    Apple Pecan Stuffing, *24*-25
    Homemade Fudge Sauce, 143
    Oven Cooking Schedule for Turkey, 13
    Pumpkin Nut Muffins, 4, 6, 11
Midas Touch Centerpiece, *238*
mincemeat
    Pie, *5*-6, 14
    Pumpkin, Pie, 15
mint
    Layered, Melts, 228-229
    Mist Pie, *227*

Mixed Fruit and Yogurt Pie, 226
mocha
    Cream Filling, 153
    Pie, 228
molasses
    Jacks, *111*-112
    Spicy, Cookies, 201
Monkey Shines Appliqué, *190*-191
mouse
    Mushroom, *126*
    Stocking, *126*
Mousse, Lobster, *219,* 218-220
muffins, 232
    Carrot Pecan, 230-*231*
    Honey Wheat, 230-*231*
    Pumpkin Nut, 4, 6, 11
    Spicy Blueberry, *231*-232
Mulled Cider with Apple Brandy, *17,*
    16-18, 21
mushroom
    Fluted *103,* 102-104, 107
    Leek Tartlettes, 144-149
    Mouse, *126*
    Spread, 223
    Turkey with, And Snow Peas, 29
Mussels Provençal, 144, 146, 150
mustard
    Apricot, Chicken Wings, 223
    Lemon Lime, 217

• N •

napkin
    Beribboned, *133*-134
    Quilted Place Mat, 194-*195*
New England Raisin Cake, 254-*255,* 256,
    258-259
New Orleans Butterflied Shrimp, *234-*
    235, 242-*243,* 244, 246
No-Yeast Stollen, *139,* 141
Nosegay Cones, 82, *83-84*
nut
    Candied, *139*-140
    Country, Bread, *231*-232
    Date and, Bread, 254-*255,* 256-257
    Dry-Sautéed Cashews, 223
    Pumpkin, Muffins, 4, 6, 11
    Salade Mélangée aux Noix, 144,
        146, 148
    Spiced Walnuts, *234-235,* 242, 244,
        249
nutty
    Brownie Cookies, *111,* 117
    Goat Cheese Logs, 223

O

Old World Fruitcake, 43
onion
    Creamed, *2-3,* 4, 6, 9
    Stuffed, *17,* 16-18, 20
Open House Punch, 250
orange
    Apricot, Chutney, 38
    Candied, Tea Bread, *255,* 256-257
    Cranberry, Liqueur, *36-37*
    Cranberry, Relish, *2-3,* 4, 6, 10
    Glazed Cherry Pie, 16, 18, 22-*23*
    Wreaths, 201
organdy
    Apron, *133,* 132-134
    Pillow, 132-*133*
    Tablecloth, *133*-134
Oriental
    Barbecue Sauce, 38
    Chicken Liver Spread, 217
origami
    Crèche, *128*
    Flying Bird, *123*
    Tree, *121*
ornament, 124, 131, 186, 213
    Beautiful Ball, *121*-122
    Bells´N Ribbons Ball, *213,* 215
    Dahlia Ball, *127*
    Dove of Peace, *94*
    Flying Angel, *125*
    Flying Bird, *123*
    Folk Art, 92-*93*
    Gift Box, *216*
    Gingerbread Dolls &, *158-159,* 160
    Gingerbread House, *158-159,* 163
    Heart, *121*-122
    Highland Ribbon, *80*
    Lace Fans, 82, *83-84*
    Lace Rosettes, *83-84*
    Lariat, *167-168*
    Lollipop, *216*
    Mushroom Mouse, *126*
    Nosegay Cones, 82, *83-84*
    Palomino Pony, *167,* 169
    Ribbon Fans, *62*
    Ribbon Pine Cones, *60*
    Santa's Sled, *121,* 124
    Shining Star, 120-*121*
    Snazzy Santa, *121*-122
    Stocking Mouse, *126*
    Tartan, *74-75,* 76
    The Gold Rush, 206-*207*
    Tinsel-Town Wreath, *125*
    Woven Heart Basket, 120-*121*

    Yule Tree, *121*-122
Oyster and Rice Stuffing, *17,* 16-19

P

Pajamas, Sugar Plum, 188-*189*
Palomino
    Pillows, *167*-168
    Pony Ornament, *167,* 169
Paper Bead Jewelry, 194, *196*
party, 156, 171, 259
    Bowl, 252
    Children's, Pointers, 169
    Cookies And Toys, *161,* 163
    Perfect!, 240-241
    Pizzas, 218, *222*
pastry
    Crust Designs, 15
    Homemade, 23
    Tiny Tart Shells, 258
patchwork
    Christmas-In-The-Country Quilt, 99-101
    Double Wedding Ring Pillow, *51*-52
    Lace Stocking, 84-*85*
    Pig Pillow, 136-*137*
    Pretty 'N Pink, Throw, *51*
pâté, Terrine de Campagne, *145,* 144-147
peanut butter
    Kisses, 142
    Munchies, 202
pear
    Cranberry, Tart, 102, 104, 108
    Reduced-Calorie Cranberry, Tart, 102, 104, 108-109
    Tarragon, 39
    Vanilla, Butter 38-39
pecan
    Apple, Stuffing, *24*-25
    Apple Tarts, 254-*255,* 256, 258
    Apricot, Rice Stuffing, *24*-25
    Bourban Balls, *111,* 116
    Carrot, Muffins, 230-*231*
    Southern, Pie, *5-6,* 14
    Wafers, 117
Peppers, Stuffed, Hors d'Oeuvres Style, 223
photo tips, 66, 69
Phyllo Egg Rolls, *234-235,* 242, 244 248
Pickles, 30-Minute Vegetable, 138-*139*
"Picture This" Frames, *137*
pie
    Apple Cream Cheese, 102, 104, 109
    Clever Chocolate, 226

    Heavenly Pineapple, 226
    Luscious Lemon, 228
    Mincemeat, *5-6,* 14
    Mint Mist, *227*
    Mixed Fruit and Yogurt, 226
    Mocha, 228
    Orange-Glazed Cherry, 16, 18, 22-*23*
    Pilgrim Pumpkin, *5-6,* 14
    Pumpkin Mince, 15
    Southern Pecan, *5-6,* 14
    Special Strawberry, 224, 226
    Sugar-Dusted Apple, 16, 18, 22-*23*
Pilgrim Pumpkin Pie, *5-6,* 14
pillow
    Double Wedding Ring, *51*-52
    Eyelet, 132-*133*
    Organdy, 132-*133*
    Palomino, *167*-168
    Patchwork Pig, 136-*137*
    Plaid, *74-75,* 78
    Quilt-Block, *204-205,* 209
Pimiento Cheese, *219,* 218-220
pineapple
    Cheese Ball, *234-235,* 242, 244, *249*
    Heavenly, Pie, 226
pine cone
    & Dried Flower Wreath, *32-33*
    Ribbon, *60*
Pink Champagne Punch, 250-*251*
Piquant Stuffed Cucumber Cups, *234-235,* 242, 244-246
Pistachio Cheese Ball, 218, *222*
pizza
    Party, 218, *222*
    Popcorn, 202
Place Cards, Cinnamon Stick, Centerpiece &, *31,* 30-32
place mat
    Eyelet, *133*-134
    Quilted, Napkin, 194-*195*
Plaid Pillow, *74-75,* 78
Planter, Teddy Bear, *180*
plants, 67, 79
Plate Pizzazz, *136*
Plum Conserve, 36
poinsettia, 79
Pomanders, 30-*31*
Popcorn, Pizza, 202
Popovers, Yorkshire, *103,* 102-104, 107
Pork and Spinach Stuffing, *24,* 26
potato
    Mashed, Soufflé, *17,* 16-18, 20-21
    Roasted, *103,* 102-105
Potholders, Cookie Cutter, *214*-215
Potpourri, Sunshine, 30-*31*

Pretty´N Pink Patchwork Throw, *51*
Pretzels, Chocolate Covered, 202
Provençal
    Aubergine, *145,* 144-147
    Mussels, 144, 146, 150
pumpkin
    Bread, 233
    Curried, Soup, *17,* 16-18
    Mince Pie, 6, 15
    Nut Muffins, 4, 6, 11
    Pilgrim, Pie, *5*-6, 14
punch
    Bowl Centerpiece, *34*
    Cranberry Fizz, 252
    Creamy Cocoa, *118-119,* 151-152, 156
    Open House, 250
    Party Bowl, 252
    Pink Champagne, 250-*251*
    Tropical, 253
Puppy Love, *173,* 172-175

Q

quilt
    Christmas-In-The-Country, *99*-101
    Double Wedding Ring Pillow, *51*-52
    Pretty´N Pink Patchwork Throw, *51*
quilt-block
    Here Comes Santa Claus! Decorations,
        204-205
    Pillows, *204-205,* 209
    Stocking, *204-205,* 206
    Tablecloth, *204-205,* 209
    Wall Hanging, *204-205, 208*
quilted
    Greetings, *197*
    Place Mat, Napkin, 194-*195*

R

Raspberry Crisps, *118-119,* 151-152, 154
Reduced-Calorie Cranberry Pear Tart,
    102, 104, 108-109
Regal Roast Beef, *103,* 102-105
Reindeer Appliqué, *190*
Relish, Cranberry Orange, *2-3,* 4, 6, 10
ribbon, 62, 66
    Fans, *62*
    Highland, Ornament, *80*
    Pine Cones, *60*
    Ruffled, Wreath, 76-77
    Take a Bow! *62*
rice
    Apricot Pecan, Stuffing, *24*-25
    Fried, Patties, *234-235,* 242, 244, 248

Oyster and, Stuffing, *17,* 16-19
Rich Pan Gravy, 102-105
Rigó Jancsi Torte, *118-119,* 151-153
ring
    Cherry, 44
    Hawaiian, 43
roast
    Beef Canapés, 223
    Holiday Turkey, *2-3,* 4, 6, 7
    Regal, Beef, *103,* 102-105
Roasted Potatoes, *103,* 102-105
Rocky Road Fudge, 203
roux, 8
royal
    Chocolate Frosting, 153
    Frosting, 165
    Rum Frosting, 45
Ruffled Ribbon Wreath, 76-77
Rum Raisin Fudge Sauce, 217
Russian Dressing, 4, 6, 10

S

salad
    Salade Mélangée aux Noix, 144, 146,
        148
    Warm Shrimp Appetizer, 102, 104-105
salmon
    Onion Roll-Ups, *234-235,* 242, 244,
        248
    Ribbon Sandwiches, *234-235,* 242,
        244-245
    Smoked, and Cream Cheese Loaf, 217
Sampler, Home Sweet Home, *85,* 87
sandwich
    Bread and Butter, 254-*255,* 256
    Grilled Turkey, Cheese and Tomato, 27
    Platter, 254-*255,* 256-257
    Salmon Ribbon, *234-235,* 242, 244-245
Santa
    Garland & Curtain Tiebacks, *130*
    Here Comes, Decorations, *204-205*
    Sled, *121,* 124
    Snazzy, *121*-122
sauce
    Chocolate Fudge, 203
    Homemade Fudge, 143
    Oriental Barbecue, 38
    Rum Raisin Fudge, 217
    Turkey and Broccoli with Curry, 28
    Turkey in Cheddar Cheese, 27
Sausage Balls à l'Orange, *234-235,* 242-
    243, 244, 247
savory
    Stuffing, *2-3,* 4, 6, 8

Winter Squash, *103,* 102-104, 106
Shelf, Heart, 96-97
Shining Star, 120-*121*
shopping tips, 212, 214
shrimp
    New Orleans Butterflied, *234-235,*
        242-*243,* 244, 246
    Warm, Appetizer Salad, 102, 104-105
skirt
    Folk Art Tree, 92-*93*
    Gingerbread Tree, *158-159,* 162
    Tartan Tree, *81*
Smoked Salmon and Cream Cheese Loaf,
    217
Snazzy Santa, *121*-122
Snow Peas, Turkey with Mushrooms and,
    29
Snowflake Sweater Set, *185,* 184-186
Snowy Glaze, 115
Soufflé, Mashed Potato, *17,* 16-18, 20-21
soup
    Autumn Squash Bisque, *2-3,* 4, 6, 7
    Cream of Turkey, 29
    Curried Pumpkin, *17,* 16-18
    Turkey Broth, 28
    Turkey, with Egg Dumplings, 28-29
southern
    Corn Sticks, *17,* 16-18, 21
    Fruitcake, 43
    Pecan Pie, *5*-6, 14
Special Strawberry Pie, 224, 226
Spice Nuggets, 30-*31*
Spiced Walnuts, *234-235,* 242, 244
    249
spicy
    Blueberry Muffins, *231*-232
    Molasses Cookies, 201
    Petit Fours, 217
Spinach, Pork and, Stuffing, *24,* 26
spread
    Almond Cheese, 257
    Blue Cheese, 217
    Ham and Cucumber, 257
    Mushroom, 223
    Oriental Chicken Liver, 217
Spritz Cookies, *118-119,* 151-152, 154
squash
    Acorn, Rings and Green Beans, *2-3,*
        4, 6, 9
    Autumn, Bisque, *2-3,* 4, 6, 7
    Savory Winter, *103,* 102-104, 106
Star, Shining, 120-*121*
stocking
    Bonnie Scotland, *80*
    Gingerbread, *158-159,* 162

Lace and Taffeta, *90*-91
Mouse, *126*
Patchwork Lace, 84-*85*
Quilt-Block, *204-205,* 206
Victorian Brocade, *90-91*
Wild West, 166, 168
Stollen, No-Yeast, *139,* 141
strawberry
Ice Ring, 252
Special, Pie, 224, 226
stuffed
Onions, *17,* 16-18, 20
Peppers Hors d'Oeuvres Style, 223
stuffing, 12, 24
Apple Pecan, *24*-25
Apricot Pecan Rice, *24*-25
Brandied Chestnut, 26
Cranberry Cornbread, *24*-25
Oyster and Rice, *17,* 16-19
Pork and Spinach, *24,* 26
Savory, *2-3,* 4, 6, 8
Tex-Mex, *24*
sugar
Angels, 202
Dusted Apple Pie, 16, 18, 22-*23*
Holiday, Cookies, 200-201
Plum Pajamas, 188-*189*
Sun-Dried Tomato Appetizer, *234-235,*
242, *243,* 244, 247
sunshine
Fruitcake, 44-45
Potpourri, 30-*31*
Swans A-Swimming, 60-*61*
Sweater, Snowflake, Set, *185,* 184-186
Swedish Rosettes, 143
Sweet Hearts, *85,* 84-86

———— • T • ————

tablecloth
Christmas Cheer Felt, 210-*211*
Look of Lace, *53,* 52-55
Organdy, *133*-134
Quilt-Block, *204-205,* 209
Tabletop Tannenbaum, *129*
Take A Bow!, *62*
Tapenade, 218, *222*-223
Tarragon Pears, 39
tart
Cranberry Pear, 102, 104, 108
Lemon Party, 254-*255,* 256, 258
Pecan-Apple, 254-*255,* 256, 258
Reduced Calorie Cranberry Pear, 102,
104, 108-109
Tiny, Shells, 258

tartan
Bonnie Scotland Stocking, *80*
Ornaments, *74-75, 76*
Plaid Pillow, *74-75,* 78
Presents, *74-75,* 79
Ruffled Ribbon Wreath, 76-77
Tree Skirt, *81*
Tartlettes, Mushrooms Leek, 144-149
Teddy Bear
Bear's Gotcha Framed!, *180*-181
Beary Christmas, *85*-86
Bulletin Board, *180*-181
Planter, *180*
Terrine de Campagne, *145,* 144-147
Tex-Mex Stuffing, *24*
The Gold Rush, 206-*207*
The Holly & The Ivy, *204-205, 209*
Tinsel-Town Wreath, *125*
Toast, Melba, *145,* 144-147
tomato
Baked Baby, *103,* 102-104, 106
Grilled Turkey, Cheese and,
Sandwiches, 27
Sun-Dried, Appetizer, *234-235,* 242,
243, 244, 247
toy, 192-193
Colonial Doll House, *177-179*
Cookies And, Party, *161,* 163
Eddie The Elf, *185*-188
Hobby Horse, *167,* 170
Kangaroo, And Baby Too!, *175*-176
Puppy Love, *173,* 172-175
tree, 58, 213
Tabletop Tannenbaum, *129*
The Gold Rush, 206-*207*
Yule, *121*-122
tree skirt
Folk Art, 92-*93*
Gingerbread, *158-159,* 162
Tartan, *81*
Tropical Punch, 253
truffles
Apricot Almond, 217
Chocolate, 142-143
turkey, 7, 12-13
and Broccoli with Curry Sauce, 28
Broth, 28
in Cheddar Cheese Sauce, 27
Cream of, Soup, 29
Grilled, Cheese and Tomato
Sandwiches, 27
Microwaving, 13
with Mushrooms and Snow Peas, 29
Roast Holiday, *2-3,* 4, 6, 7
Soup with Egg Dumplings, 28-29

———— • V • ————

Vanilla Pear Butter, 38-39
vegetable
Marinated, *2-3,* 4, 6, 10
30-Minute, Pickles, 138-*139*
Victorian Brocade Stocking, *90-91*
village
Country, 94-*95*
Doorstop, *95*

———— • W • ————

Wall Hanging, Quilt-Block, *204-205, 208*
Warm Shrimp Appetizer Salad, 102, 104-
105
White Lace Ornaments, 82, *83-84*
Wild West
Ornament, 166-*167*
Stocking, 166, 168
window
Beautiful Bay, *58*
Icicle Magic, 58-*59*
Wine, Cranberry, Mold, *103,* 102-104,
107-108
Woven Heart Basket, 120-*121*
wrapping, 62, 63, 66-67, 216
wreath
Eucalyptus, *131*
Fresh Rose, 32
Hydrangea, 32-*33*
Lariat, *171*
Orange, 201
Pine Cone & Dried Flower, *32*-33
Ruffled Ribbon, 76-77
The Holly & The Ivy, *204-205, 209*
Tinsel-Town, *125*

———— • Y • ————

Yams, Candied, *2-3,* 4, 6, 9-10
Yankee Fruitcake, 44
Yogurt, Mixed Fruit and, Pie, 226
Yorkshire Popovers, *103,* 102-104, 107
Yule Tree, *121*-122